The Evolution of Women's Asylums Since 1500

STUDIES IN THE HISTORY OF SEXUALITY
Judith C. Brown and Guido Ruggiero, *General Editors*

IMMODEST ACTS
The Life of a Lesbian Nun in Renaissance Italy
JUDITH BROWN

THE EVOLUTION OF WOMEN'S ASYLUMS SINCE 1500
From Refuges for Ex-Prostitutes to Shelters for Battered Women
SHERRILL COHEN

THE BOUNDARIES OF EROS
Sex Crime and Sexuality in Renaissance Venice
GUIDO RUGGIERO

The Evolution of Women's Asylums Since 1500

From Refuges for Ex-Prostitutes to Shelters for Battered Women

SHERRILL COHEN

New York   Oxford
OXFORD UNIVERSITY PRESS
1992

Oxford University Press

Oxford New York Toronto
Delhi Bombay Calcutta Madras Karachi
Kuala Lumpur Singapore Hong Kong Tokyo
Nairobi Dar es Salaam Cape Town
Melbourne Auckland

and associated companies in
Berlin Ibadan

Copyright © 1992 by Sherrill Cohen

Published by Oxford University Press, Inc.,
200 Madison Avenue, New York, New York 10016

Oxford is a registered trademark of Oxford University Press

Library of Congress Cataloging-in-Publication Data
Cohen, Sherrill.
The evolution of women's asylums since 1500 : from refuges for ex-
prostitutes to shelters for battered women / Sherrill Cohen.
p. cm. (Studies in the history of sexuality)
Includes bibliographical references and index.
ISBN 0-19-505164-5
1. Women's shelters—Italy—History—16th century. 2. Women's
shelters—Italy—History—17th century. 3. Women—Italy—Social
conditions. I. Title. II. Series.
HV1448.I8C65 1992   362.83'85'0945—dc20   91-36251

Parts of this book originally appeared in *Women in Reformation and
Counter-Reformation Europe,* edited by Sherrin Marshall. Copyright ©
1989 by Indiana University Press. Reprinted by permission.

1 3 5 7 9 8 6 4 2

Printed in the United States of America
on acid-free paper

For my mother, Lenore Cohen,
who gave me every kind of support

ACKNOWLEDGMENTS

This book is an extension of my dissertation, and to bestow proper credit, I must acknowledge the role of people whose involvement began during that phase of the enterprise. Ronald F. E. Weissman introduced me to sources that prompted me to study early modern women's institutions. Ruth P. Liebowitz generously shared with me her pioneering scholarship and data regarding Italian *convertite*. I owe a great debt to Natalie Zemon Davis and Anthony T. Grafton for their help in guiding my dissertation and responding to a partial draft of this work. Kay B. Warren and the late David Herlihy, who also served as readers, offered suggestions and support that considerably aided me in extending my research. In addition, Brian Pullan and Gene A. Brucker provided valuable comments on the dissertation.

A number of scholars helped me in Italy during the research for my dissertation and subsequent investigations. I would like to thank Roberto Barducci, Daniela Lombardi, Gino Corti, Renato Pasta, Richard Goldthwaite, Linda Duchamp, Paola Di Cori, Maria Vasaio, Lucia Ferrante, and Anna Benvenuti Papi. I am especially grateful to Orsola Gori, at the Archivio di Stato in Florence, for her many kindnesses in arranging for me to see and photograph research materials. My thanks go as well to Sara Matthews Grieco and Allen Grieco for being gracious hosts in the Tuscan countryside.

Other individuals contributed to this work by reading various sections, providing additional references, or answering queries. I very much appreciate the assistance of Virginia Reinburg, Nadine Taub, Laurie Nussdorfer, Dale V. Kent, Samuel K. Cohn, Jr., Katherine Gill, Marjorie Swann, Mary Elizabeth Perry, Elizabeth Lunbeck, Laura Guidi, Margaret F. Rosenthal, Mary Gibson, John K. Brackett, Barbara Stein, Stanley Stein, William C. Jordan, Harold James, Michael Donnelly, John Gillis, Donna T. Andrew, Jo Ann McNamara, Joanne Meyerowitz, Lynn Weiner, Marcia Carlisle, and the staff of the Mary Magdalene Project. Madelaine Shellaby, an artist and friend, shared her insights and advice concerning the illustrations and the title.

I could not have carried out certain investigations without the aid of two key individuals at Firestone Library, Princeton University. Reference librarian Mary George constantly amazed me with respect to her ability to track down incomplete or obscure references. I also wish to thank the interlibrary loan staff, particularly Angela Cannon; I depended heavily on their services, and they were always friendly and interested in my work.

I would like to express my gratitude for funding that supported my research and writing. The American Council of Learned Societies provided two vital grants. The University Committee on Research in the Humanities and

Social Sciences at Princeton University covered the costs of the illustrations.

Publishing this book with Oxford University Press has been a felicitous experience. Series editors Judith C. Brown and Guido Ruggiero closely read my dissertation and book manuscript; their editorial suggestions greatly improved this work. Senior editor Nancy Lane and editor David Roll have been extremely helpful to me.

Finally, I wish to thank my family and friends, whose support made this project possible. My husband and fellow historian, Sheldon Garon, has done much to sustain my endeavor; his incisive suggestions and critiques were of immense value to me. While I was writing the book, my young daughters, Claire and Thea, brought merriment into my world. And, at times, their antics gave me a sense of what it must be like to live in an asylum.

CONTENTS

Illustrations follow page 80.

ABBREVIATIONS

Archivio di Stato, Florence	ASF
Archivio di Stato, Pistoia	ASP
Conventi Soppressi	CS
Conventi Soppressi: Debitori e Creditori	CS D&C
Mediceo Avanti il Principato	MAP

A Note Concerning Dates

Until 1751 the Florentines used a system of dating in which the year began on March 25. All dates from Florentine sources have been left in their original form. Likewise, all dates from Pistoian sources have also been left in their original form. However, the Pistoians used a different system of dating, with the year beginning on January 1.

The Evolution of Women's
Asylums Since 1500

INTRODUCTION

When we think of social institutions that have addressed the problems women face in modern societies, those that come to mind are women's residence halls, homes for unwed mothers, and battered women's shelters. Few recognize that these institutions have deep roots in the past. In the Western world their antecedents appeared in the Middle Ages and came to fruition in early modern Europe. Sixteenth- and seventeenth-century European Catholic societies saw a proliferation of newly founded institutions designed to shelter penitent prostitutes or vulnerable girls. The surge of institution building grew out of the Catholic reform movement and the Counter Reformation. Centered in Italy and affecting all the Catholic societies in Europe, these religious movements encouraged widespread philanthropic initiatives aimed at ameliorating the lot of society's neediest groups, including females. The result was the emergence of networks of institutions for women and girls unprecedented in number and scope of purpose. These multidimensional establishments served as the prototypes for a variety of institutions for females that emerged in later centuries. They also laid the groundwork for many of the techniques in correction and social welfare that would subsequently be applied to the populace at large.

It might seem farfetched to posit a connection between an establishment created to "convert" unholy prostitutes into godly women in a distant age and a residence hall intended to provide housing for working women in our modern, secular society. Yet the two are linked both by historical patterns of institutional evolution and by attitudes toward women embedded in the cultural gender system of Judeo-Christian societies. In terms of institutional evolution, the convent, which traditionally performed a multiplicity of functions, spawned a group of related institutions for females: reformatories, schools, and dormitories or boardinghouses for working women. In terms of attitudes, from ancient times to the present day a gender system based on male control over female sexuality and on women's socioeconomic and political subordination has shaped Western societies' perceptions of women's needs and how best to fulfill them.

To grasp the significance of the early modern institutions for women, we must examine them against the backdrop of recent scholarship concerning the nature and history of institutions. In *Asylums* (1961) the sociologist Erving Goffman coined the term "total institutions" to describe enclosed, formally administered establishments for residence and work that undermine the autonomy and sense of self of those who live there. These institutions ranged from monasteries and mental hospitals to armies. From a different disciplinary perspective, historians have debated whether institutions should be viewed as vehicles for social control or as agencies of humanitarian reform. In *Madness and Civilization* (1961) Michel Foucault characterized the spread of poor-houses (*hôpitaux généraux*), houses of correction, and madhouses in early modern Europe as an oppressive "great confinement." In *Discipline and Punish* (1975) he portrayed the power of prisons and other institutions as tools of political repression. David J. Rothman's *Discovery of the Asylum* (1971) analyzed the growth of penal institutions, almshouses, and insane asylums in Jacksonian America as an attempt to contain social disorder. On the other side of the debate is Gerald N. Grob's *Mental Institutions in America* (1973), which argued that foremost among the motives impelling the founders of mental institutions was their religiously based desire to improve the world. Grob credits the founders' sincerity despite the frequently failed outcomes of their good intentions.[1]

Whatever other issues divide them, scholars of the history of institutions concur that institutions emerge as solutions to perceived social problems. One such historian, Michael B. Katz, explains: "Characteristically, we respond to a widespread problem through the creation of an institution," with the accompanying development of a coterie of experts.[2] Among other themes, this book is concerned with what constitutes a "problem" meriting a response in different societies. As sociologist Herbert Blumer has stressed, the discovery of a social problem is more a matter of "collective definition" than an objective detection of existing "condition[s] or arrangement[s] in the texture of a society." Various categories of people—the poor, lawbreakers, and the insane—can pose "problems," and so can social circumstances such as war or ecological disasters.[3] I will argue that females as a group have been particularly problematic for Western societies.

Many of the scholars studying institutions also emphasize the interrelatedness of types of institutions. As will become apparent in this study, the interrelatedness is as characteristic of women's institutions as it is of other social institutions. Sometimes the interrelatedness arose as a result of utilitarian factors, such as the frequent reuse or transformation of old institutions for new purposes. Monasteries often became prisons. A seventeenth-century pesthouse in Milan became a twentieth-century refuge for prostitutes and other women suffering from venereal disease. The same place in Beaulieu, Normandy, served as the site for a leprosarium in the Middle Ages, a poorhouse in the eighteenth century, and a penitentiary in the nineteenth.[4] In other instances the interrelatedness was of a more conceptual nature. Rothman has demonstrated that the nineteenth-century movements to establish social institutions "proceeded apace, the supporters of one taking their place as leaders in the others."[5] The founders of new institutions were quite aware of this process. In the early nineteenth century the Boston Prison Discipline Society argued that what could be learned from the new institution of the penitentiary would benefit not only other custodial institutions like almshouses, but also "would greatly promote order, seriousness, and purity in large families, male and female boarding schools, and colleges."[6] Several studies document the importance of models in institutional evolution. The monastery, the military, the factory, and the hospital served as models for the organization of prisons, schools, and therapeutic asylums.[7]

Taking a broad look at institutional evolution in his essay "Origins of the Asylum," Christopher Lasch usefully employs the concept of differentiation or dissociation. In his analysis, penitentiaries and insane asylums replaced indiscriminate confinement only when notions of crime and madness became dissociated from those of vagabondage, pauperism, and folly in late-eighteenth-century Europe. He alludes to the process by which "the school . . . had been divorced from other institutions (like the church)."[8] Lasch speaks of differentiation both at the level of ideas and at the level of specialized institutions. This formulation further illustrates the interdependency and lineal connections among institutions. Although one must not minimize the crucial contrasts in structure and function among institutions as different as, for instance, a prison and a hospital, institutions do merit analyses that take into account the entire range of related institutions. As Michael B. Katz has written,

> An adequate interpretation must encompass not only the asylum, not only prisons, mental hospitals, and poorhouses, but also public schools, academies, the YMCA, and ultimately, the family. Striking parallels exist between the timing, theory, and shape of those developments which affect deviants, dependents, children, adolescents, and families. An understanding of any of them depends upon an exploration of their interconnection.[9]

Scholars of social institutions have identified different epochs as the periods when landmark developments took place in the creation of institutions. In *Madness and Civilization* Foucault located the emergence of institutions of confinement in seventeenth-century Europe.[10] Rothman asserts that the turning toward institutions as the preferred solution to social problems in America was an innovation of the nineteenth century. Katz too believes that "institutions are a modern invention."[11]

This book introduces a new perspective in the debates about institutional origins by arguing that the women's institutions of early modern Europe pioneered in the development of key social institutions. The major scholarly studies of institutions have either been silent about separate women's institutions or mentioned them only as variants on men's and gender-neutral institutions. But, in fact, early modern women's institutions preceded and anticipated many later developments in the creation of institutions. In *Discipline and Punish* Foucault depicts the growth of a nineteenth-century "carceral archipelago," a continuum of correctional and charitable institutions that used the techniques of supervising, training, and inculcating conformity to norms in the service of creating a disciplined society. He, and his fellow scholars writing on institutions, appear unaware of the existence of an extensive, finely graded network of institutions to correct, help, and supervise females in sixteenth-century Europe. Foucault speaks of a "panoptic regime," the extension of

Jeremy Bentham's institution for surveillance, the Panopticon, into the fibers and sinews of an entire society.[12] For women, however, Western patriarchal society has long been a "panoptic regime," with females being watched, measured, judged, and corrected when they deviate from prescriptions. The institutions established for women in early modern Europe were the training grounds for practices in the fields of correction and social welfare that were later applied to men and to the populace in general.[13]

The early emergence of institutional networks designed specifically for women can be attributed to the fact that females as a group were particularly problematic for Western societies. As we have seen, what poses a problem often generates an institutional response. The work of Michel Foucault depicts how certain segments of the population were perceived as problematic and institutions were established to segregate them: lepers, the poor, the mad, criminals, the sick, and in general the lower strata whom society characterized as the "dangerous classes." Alongside these categories encompassing both men and women, females per se have been problematic simply because of their biological sex—their unique capacity as childbearers and relatively greater physical vulnerability.

Within Western ideologies of gender roles, women are frequently seen as deviant or potentially deviant. In *Labeling Women Deviant* the sociologist Edwin M. Schur cites the classic definition that powerful "social groups create deviance by making the rules whose infraction constitutes deviance."[14] He goes on to discuss the many ways that women can be labeled deviant by explaining that "women are subject to an enormous array of . . . norms, which cover virtually all aspects of women's behavior and regular life situations . . . [and] imply corresponding 'deviances' for which women are likely to be stigmatized."[15] Schur refers to the present day, but his characterization is equally valid for the past. In early modern Western societies that placed high value on control over women's reproduction and were based on the male's control of property, men devised myriad normative prescriptions to regulate women's sexual, domestic, and economic behavior. These societies invented a range of institutional, as well as noninstitutional, means for attempting to manage deviant and potentially deviant women. The identification of problematic women has varied according to the society and the time. In sixteenth-century Catholic Europe it was the prostitute who seemed most threatening to public morality. According to one scholar of nineteenth-century England, "middle-class single women were seen as a problem during the Victorian period."[16] And in the 1970s in the United States, "battered women" figured prominently in the public consciousness as a major social problem. One of the tasks of this book is to elucidate how societies of the past and present have perceived various categories of women as problematic and have developed institutional responses. This study analyzes what the implications of those perceptions and those institutions are for the sociopolitical ordering of the societies.

Another theme of this study is the recovery of women's experience in the past. In the last twenty years historians have increasingly documented the lives of women in past ages. They have demonstrated the value of knowing women's history both for itself and for what it can tell us about a past society as a whole. One valuable terrain that has been explored is the relationship between women and institutions. Historians have investigated how female reformers of the nineteenth and twentieth centuries founded and administered institutions to help and socialize needy female members of the lower classes. Other scholars, including Martha Vicinus in her book *Independent Women,* have additionally described women's efforts to establish new institutions such as schools and colleges for themselves and their peers. Estelle B. Freedman approvingly characterizes the latter pattern as a separatist feminist strategy of "female institution building."[17] The institutions analyzed by these scholars provide fertile ground for comparison with the early modern women's institutions that are the subject of this book. Social institutions are one important determinant of the issues that concern all those studying women's history: the parameters for women's autonomy, economic independence, and behavioral options in the past and present. This study does not purport to examine women's historical experiences of living in all types of institutions. Rather, it selectively focuses on gender-specific institutions. Among those, it excludes the brothel, for the reason that, unlike the others studied here, the main purpose of the brothel was not to benefit women.

In exploring its themes, this study will pay close attention to issues of religion and philanthropy. These subjects are particularly relevant for the sixteenth and seventeenth centuries and the nineteenth century, two ages of concentrated institution building. The seventeenth century has been called the age of the "great confinement," and the nineteenth century "the age of the asylum."[18] Some of the societies that experienced the burst of institution building shared an important characteristic, intense religious ferment. The societies of sixteenth-century Europe were all affected by waves of religious activism in the shape of the Catholic reform movement, the Protestant Reformation, and the Catholic Counter Reformation. In nineteenth-century Britain and the United States, evangelism and religious revivals like the Second Great Awakening had a profound influence. All these religious movements preached "conversion," the spiritual rebirth and transformation of the individual soul. They also called on the "converted" to convert others. Conversion of the self was not only inner-directed toward spirituality but also outer-directed toward the performance of good deeds. Such philanthropy often took the form of founding or supporting institutions designed to improve the world by bettering the state of the poor. Religious conversion spilled over into social conversion of the character of members of the lower classes, to bring about increased conformity with bourgeois values. Of course the great surges of institution building in the past cannot be attributed solely to the efforts of religious movements. The social, cultural, political, and economic changes unique to specific societies also spurred the creation of institutions, as did other common variables like war and its after-math. However, religion did play a central role in many instances, as I will attempt to demonstrate.

This book focuses on Italy, the seedbed of many major socioeconomic and cultural developments that shaped the lives of men and women in Western societies. It is not surprising that Italy was the center of an important social experiment, the creation of networks of women's institutions. Italy was an amalgamation of city-states in the early modern period, and it did not emerge as a unified nation until 1860. Nonetheless, it did have surplus wealth and a highly developed sense of communal life and responsibilities. It bore a double mantle of symbolic leadership as the heir of the Roman Empire and the headquarters of the Catholic Church and papacy. In the Middle Ages Italian cities, especially Florence, gave rise to the forms of mercantile and industrial capitalism that later became widespread in the West. Medieval Italian burgers employed a portion of their wealth to commission monumental works of art intended to benefit the public as well as the patron. They also funded charita-ble organizations and hospices for pilgrims and the sick. Florence was the home of Europe's first foundling hospital, the Innocenti, established in 1410. The tradition of supporting institutions devoted to social welfare flourished early on Italian soil.[19]

The confluence of the Catholic reform movement in early-sixteenth-century Italy, a long-ingrained tradition of philanthropy, and the availability of funds resulted in new foundations of institutions for problematic women. From the time of the Council of Trent (1545–63) onward, Italy served as the center for the Counter Reformation, and churchmen concerned with revitaliz-ing the Catholic religion continued the founding of institutions for women. The English priest Gregory Martin, who visited Rome in 1576–78, com-mented favorably on that city's institution for unhappy wives, "[s]uch as are to[o] many in al[l] places, but in few places so good a remedy for the party oppressed."[20] Like Italy's artistic treasures, the social institutions of Italian cities drew many visitors from other European locales and elsewhere in the Renaissance and modern age.

At the end of the early modern era, Italy led the way in two new fields of study, penal policy and criminal anthropology. Cesare Beccaria's treatise, *Dei delitti e delle pene* (An Essay on Crimes and Punishments), published in 1764, had a major influence in reshaping systems of law and correction throughout the Western world. Implementing Beccaria's recommendation to make punish-ments more rational and humanitarian, Grand Duke Pietro Leopoldo of Tus-cany set an example by ending capital punishment in 1786 before any other European ruler did so. Cesare Lombroso's works on criminal anthropology at the end of the nineteenth century similarly drew an international audience. The fact that Lombroso came from a society with a long tradition of gathering and segregating deviant women no doubt contributed to his interest in writing his widely read study *La donna delinquente, la prostituta, e la donna normale,* translated as *The Female Offender.* At the turn of the twentieth century,

Salvatore Ottolenghi employed Lombroso's theories about female and other deviants to train officials of Italy's centralized police forces in techniques of "scientific policing."[21] With its tradition of expertise in religion, philanthropy, education, penal policy, and criminal anthropology, Italy was a great exporter of ideas and practices. In the early modern era and afterward, the influence of many ideas and institutions prominent in Italian cities penetrated beyond Italy, as I will argue happened in the case of the institutions for women as well.

This study offers an in-depth look at early modern women's institutions, but with an overarching argument that links the distant past and the present. The first chapter provides an overview of medieval and early modern gender ideology, highlighting the roles of wife, nun, and prostitute. Chapter 2 focuses on the problem of prostitution. It examines the rationale behind the operations of three early modern Tuscan refuges for "converted" prostitutes: the Monastero delle Convertite and Casa delle Malmaritate in Florence and Santa Maria Maddalena in Pistoia. Chapter 3 explains why the three Tuscan refuges housed "anomalous" women who were not former prostitutes. Chapter 4 portrays life inside the Tuscan refuges. Chapter 5 analyzes the significance of the Tuscan refuges as social institutions, in the contexts of the local community and early modern society. Chapter 6 traces the adaptation of the Catholic institutional model of the refuge for ex-prostitutes, as it spread to Protestant societies from the eighteenth century onward. Finally, chapter 7 discusses the legacies of the early modern women's institutions for the nineteenth and twentieth centuries—their influences upon the development of later social institutions for both women and the populace in general.

In addition to analyzing institutions, this study also investigates the lives of predominantly lower-class women. The past three decades have seen the rise of the "new social history." Advocates of this kind of historiography want history to cease being exclusively the chronicle of great events and great individuals. They wish instead to research the experiences of the lower classes in order to reinsert common people into our picture of the past. A variant on this theme has been articulated by Michael Ignatieff and other historians of institutions. They wisely urge their colleagues not to reduce the lower classes to "the controlled" but to try to grasp how the lower orders may have resisted institutional power or used institutions to fulfill their own desires.[22] I have noted earlier the significant scholarly attention that has been directed toward recovering women's history. The study that follows attempts to heed both these calls in its effort to reconstruct the experiences of lower-class women living in institutions.

The sentiments of early modern women usually come to us filtered through the writing of others, because of the era's low levels of literacy for the nonelite and women. We must seek women's voices in the documents compiled by male record keepers or in the formulaic writing composed for women by notaries, clergy, and others who helped them to communicate in the styles of official discourse. Sometimes the sentiments of the women themselves come through unmistakably between the lines, and sometimes their thoughts spill forth in their own scrawling hands. Although little of their writing from that distant era has survived, I have tried in this study to include, whenever possible, women's own writings.

A brief explanation of terminology is in order. "Early modern" means the sixteenth through eighteenth centuries, and "modern" means the nineteenth and twentieth centuries. "Monastery" is the generic term for a community of persons of either sex under religious vows. "Convent" refers to a monastery of nuns. The word "asylum" has a specific usage dating back to the eighteenth century, when it was employed in England to designate establishments for the mentally ill. Today, however, "asylum," as used in the scholarship on institutions, has a more general meaning, referring to establishments that may house the insane, aged, alcoholic, or other problematic groups. In the public mind "asylum" has the dual connotation of a sanctuary and a place of confinement. When describing actual events in the early modern period, I will stay close to the language of the time, using such words as "refuge" or "house."[23] At other times, I will employ "asylum," adopting this terminology in order to engage in a dialogue with the scholarship on institutions and because I value the term's dual connotations, which suit the nature of the early modern women's institutions. When making a more interpretive or theoretical point, I will use "institutions" and "asylums" interchangeably. Unless otherwise specified, in this work "institutions" and "asylums" refer to residential establishments.

This study unashamedly seeks to link the past and the present. When a historian is told that he or she has "presentist concerns," the characterization is usually derogatory. I would respond by echoing the words of Michel Foucault, who explained why he wrote the history of the prison: "Simply because I am interested in the past? No, if one means by that writing a history of the past in terms of the present. Yes, if one means writing the history of the present."[24] What this means is that we should not describe or interpret the past anachronistically. But we can and should look to the past to understand how we came to have certain social structures and experiences today. The early modern European institutions for women were important archetypes for certain specialized present-day institutions designed to serve a single sex, namely, women. In a broader sense, the history of the early modern women's institutions is also linked to the development of correctional, educational, and charitable institutions for the general populace in later centuries. For this reason, the history of women's asylums may offer valuable insights into the character of modern social institutions.

I

Women and Social Institutions

1

The Wife, the Nun, and the Prostitute: Gender Ideology in Medieval and Early Modern Europe

The statutes of the Compagnia di Santa Maria Maddalena sopra le Malmaritate, a late-sixteenth-century Florentine lay religious confraternity, open with this explanation:

> It has come to the notice of a number of propertied persons that there exists in the city of Florence a great multitude of immoral women, many of whom would turn to penitence if they had a place to which to retire. . . . There is the Monastero delle Convertite [Monastery of the Converted Prostitutes]; but it takes in women who want to be nuns, leaving many who remain in sin since they are unable to become nuns because they have husbands [or for other reasons]. . . . We want the house that we will set up for them to be called the Casa delle Malmaritate [House of the Unhappily Married Women].[1]

In the words of the confraternity's founders we recognize the predominant options available to women in the Catholic societies of early modern Europe: prostitution, monasticism, marriage, and a lay form of institutional life that the authors of the text are proposing to sponsor. All these options can be identified as "social institutions" in the early modern period. Social institutions performed both normative and logistical functions. They served as crucibles for the formation and transmission of cultural values, and they provided practical solutions to the exigencies of day-to-day living. While some social institutions like marriage were constituted as legal and economic relationships, others such as monasticism also involved a physical component—an actual built environment for residence. Three residential institutions for females in the early modern grand duchy of Tuscany form the central subject of this study. Two of the institutions, the Monastero delle Convertite and the Casa delle Malmaritate, were located in the capital of the duchy, Florence. The third, Santa Maria Maddalena, another refuge for converted prostitutes, was in Pistoia, which had been under Florentine rule since 1351.

Medieval Social Institutions and Gender

The norms governing gender ideology and the behavior of the sexes in the past were embodied in institutional form. Before we focus on the early modern period, we will do well to survey the prospects for women in the preceding era. The social institutions that shaped women's lives in the Middle Ages as a whole created a highly circumscribed environment. Male authorities, from the leaders of church and state to fathers and husbands, wielded considerable coercive power to direct how women should behave. Most women from all social strata of medieval societies were channeled into the institution of marriage, and largely women from the upper strata were alternatively channeled into the institution of monasticism.[2] Religious and lay culture dictated that the women of this era would be most valued for maintaining sexual modesty. The outlook is epitomized in the words of the fifteenth-century preacher Bernardino of Siena, "We see in Ecclesiasticus XXVI that 'The best of divine graces is the woman who is holy and chaste.' . . . I mean this not only for the young girl but also for the widow and the married woman."[3] The institutions of marriage and monasticism helped to keep a rein on female sexuality. Feminine virtue lay in the restriction of sexual activity to the marital bed or in the complete chastity required of the nun who swore monastic vows. Families strove not to let female members out of their purview and to guard the sexual mores of their women.[4] Of course numerous males in medieval societies were steered by their families toward monasticism or marriage, but if they resisted, the social environment sanctioned their desire to be on their own in a way that it did not for females.

What of women who could not or would not fit the patterns expected of them? Social institutions beckoned to deviant females as well. From late antiquity onward, convents, hospitals, and other residential institutions opened their doors to females dislodged from their accustomed niches in society: widows; orphaned girls; temporary boarders needing a safe place to stay; girls running away from families or employers; wives parted from or abandoned by their husbands; women in bigamous marriages or illicitly wed to clerics; victims of rape; and women involved in wrongdoing. Convents traditionally served as storage grounds for females in such circumstances, and hospitals and orphanages took in the overflow of plebeian untethered females. Medieval males sought refuge in and were subject to compulsory stays in institutions in the same fashion, but probably with much less frequency than women.[5]

Social institutions grew up even around women who openly desecrated the ideal of female virtue, women perceived as "whores." Formal institutions evolved in connection with female promiscuity: prostitution and brothels. The Roman law that medieval Christians inherited, and the canon law that they developed in the twelfth century, often equated promiscuous and adulterous females with the created legal category of the *meretrix,* or prostitute. Roman law generally defined the prostitute as the inmate of a brothel, an establishment for facilitating the exchange of sexual services for payment.

This classification of "prostitute" in the two bodies of law encompassed both a pejorative moral judgment and a juridical attitude toward the practice of an occupation.[6]

Ecclesiastical and lay authorities in the Middle Ages had ambivalent views toward prostitution and brothels. Christian theologians abhorred all premarital and extramarital sexual intercourse as sinful fornication. Yet theology, canon law, and medieval mores operated on a double standard that more readily allowed men than women to indulge in the sin of fornication. So that wives and nuns could live up to the Christian valuation of chastity as the highest female virtue and the guarantee of the familial and civic patrimony, another group of devalued women had to exist to absorb the unlawful sexuality. To avoid the worse evil of having all females subject to illicit fornication, religious and lay authorities—following the lead of Augustine in the fourth century—realized that they had to tolerate the lesser evil of prostitution. While some unmarried clerical experts in canon law wished at least to punish brothel keepers, lay civic officials gave priority to ensuring the virtue of their wives and daughters and therefore banned neither the brothel keeper nor the independent streetwalking prostitute. From the midfourteenth century on, in cities throughout medieval Europe they went so far as to subsidize institutionalized prostitution in municipal brothels, to deter the rape of respectable women and other ignominies. The public brothels in cities such as Venice and Lucca and in many locales in southeastern France ranged in size from an inn full of rooms to several blocks equivalent to a modern red-light district.[7]

Social institutions also grew up around ex-prostitutes. In Christian culture the sanctified image of the reformed prostitute went back to Jesus Christ, who had proclaimed that redeemed tax collectors and whores would precede the unbelieving Pharisees into heaven.[8] Although they acknowledged the unavoidable functional role of prostitution, medieval Catholics were duty-bound to try constantly to keep sin in society as limited as possible. It was through this process of doing good works and combatting sin, or even ceasing in the act of sinning, that they could obtain divine grace in their economy of salvation. Religious and lay leaders treated prostitution in the same way they treated another tolerated evil, usury. While denouncing the phenomenon, they sought to control and benefit from it and to derive moral credit from waging struggles against the so-called sin. In mercantile Florence both the usury and the prostitution that thrived in the city pricked consciences.[9]

Thus in almost every medieval milieu hospitable to prostitutes, there was also an officially encouraged impetus for prostitutes to quit their sinful ways and return to the path of "decent women." From at least the twelfth century on, public and private benefactors in France, Germany, Italy, and elsewhere in Europe set up residential institutions for former prostitutes to invite and ease this transition. They founded monasteries specifically for the spiritual conversion of ex-prostitutes. In such convents sinful women dedicated themselves to lives of secluded penance. These institutions echoed traditions of penitential confinement that had long been used to discipline religious personnel within the Church who committed infractions. In 1227 Pope Gregory IX approved the inauguration of the Order of Saint Mary Magdalen, named after the penitent prostitute whom Jesus had converted. Branches of this order and communities like it spread across the continent. Florence, too, had its share of establishments for ex-prostitutes in the High Middle Ages. In 1257 a group of women lived under the rule of Saint Benedict in Florence's Borgo Pinti, and they were known as the *convertite* (converted prostitutes) of Santa Maria Maddalena Penitente (the Penitent Saint Mary Magdalen). Many medieval cities also sheltered ex-prostitutes in lay institutions that differed in one respect from the penitential monasteries: they offered former prostitutes the chance to be rehabilitated and to merge back into the mainstream of respectable life, supporting themselves at an honest trade and even marrying. In 1198 Pope Innocent III had issued a decree lauding men who married public harlots to reform them. The lay institutions for ex-prostitutes offered disgraced women a second chance in the society that had proved dangerous to their virtue.[10]

Beyond the institutional destinies toward which social and parental authorities steered them, women themselves founded institutions meant to widen the range of choices available to them. The Middle Ages saw periodic bursts of this female creativity aimed at generating new institutional outlets and resources. Medieval women faced the challenge of trying to carve out meaningful roles in a Church that, since the days of early apostolic Christianity, had barred females from becoming priests and from preaching. Monastic life in loosely enclosed convents headed by abbesses provided some women with an existence that could be both spiritually and socioeconomically sustaining, but between the tenth and early thirteenth centuries male ecclesiastics curtailed the independence of the convents. They cut inroads into the power of the abbesses and sought to impose strict "cloister," the symbolic and physical segregation of the nuns from the world.

Yet women of all social strata were still attracted to the religious life that enabled them to transcend quotidian drudgery by acceding to higher planes of spirituality or altruism. They wished to participate in the religious passion sweeping Europe in the twelfth and thirteenth centuries, the movement to imitate the apostles of early Christianity in lives of voluntary poverty, proselytizing, and service to one's fellows. From this ambience grew the new Franciscan and Dominican orders for males, whose mendicant friars were determined to roam the map fervently preaching and begging for their food. Women in towns across the continent acted on their desires to create a nonmonastic activist path for themselves. They banded together, sometimes with encouragement from male advisors, and formed uncloistered residential communities in which they wished to lead pious lives and support themselves not by begging but by their own labor. Often gathering around a charismatic female holy figure, they were known as *beguines* in Germany, the Low Countries, and France. Italy had the *humiliate* in Milan, the Poor Clares in Umbria, and the *mantellate* in Tuscany. The wave of female enthusiasm for flexible religious activism fostered the development of the Third Orders, aggregations of laymen and laywomen affiliated with the old and new religious orders. These "tertiaries," of whom Saint Catherine of Siena was the best-known example, included many married women. Among the thousands of females who joined the new communities were aristocratic women, working women, older women, and a preponderance of young women avoiding marriage. Some male ecclesiastics praised the enclaves of pious women, while others distrusted independent unenclosed communities of women, especially those in which females governed and guided other females.[11] These initiatives on the part of women themselves to multiply their options continued and increased in the early modern period.

Early Modern Institutions for Women

In the sixteenth century, social institutions specifically designed to serve females proliferated in the societies of Catholic Europe. Henceforth, more women would spend time in institutional settings, on their own impulse or at the demand of their families and authorities of church and state. The sixteenth century was an age of religious cataclysm and social upheaval generally. The Protestant Reformation, among other effects, wrought landmark changes in gender ideology and gender roles. It was the age in which Catholic leaders, from the popes and the exemplary bishops and archbishops—Gian Matteo Giberti in Verona, Nicolò Ridolfi in Vicenza, and Carlo Borromeo in Milan— to the founders of new religious orders like Ignatius Loyola and his army of Jesuits, mounted a heroic response to the Protestant revolt. In efforts to revitalize the Church, both the Catholic reform movement predating Protestantism and also the subsequent Counter Reformation reached out in multiple directions, including toward the female sex.

One reason for the increased institutionalization of women was the revival of the medieval imperative to convert prostitutes. Two circumstances lay behind it. The prostitute had always served as a scapegoat, a first target for reformers trying to purify Christendom. In addition, syphilis had become the dreaded scourge of the late fifteenth and sixteenth centuries. A papal bull of 1520, issued by Leo X, marked the establishment of a nunnery of the Convertite in Rome. The message of the bull greatly emphasized the call for what Brian Pullan has termed "the spiritual conquest of prostitution":

> Our savior Jesus Christ, the son of God, when he took on human form, came, as he himself said, to save the sheep which had strayed. Hence, when the Pharisees and the publicans complained that he associated with sinners, he chose to recite the parable (now in the Gospel of St. Luke) of the sheep which had strayed and was afterward found, so that he might show, as the same evangelist bears witness, that there is more joy in heaven over one sinner that repents, than over ninety-nine righteous people who have no need to repent.[12]

The mission of reforming that high-profile repentant sinner, the ex-prostitute, captured the public imagination in the sixteenth and seventeenth centuries. Funded by private, municipal, and ecclesiastical sources, new monastic and lay refuges for penitent prostitutes sprang up throughout the Catholic societies of Europe.[13]

The refuges for converted prostitutes multiplied first in Italy. Confraternities of Divine Love in Genoa, Rome, Venice, and elsewhere sponsored monasteries for former prostitutes, starting with one in Genoa in about the first decade of the sixteenth century.[14] The Augustinian nunnery for *convertite* established in Rome in 1520 flourished. Its reputation spread and inspired the foundation of similar institutions. Another large nunnery for *convertite* appeared in Venice, growing from a group of penitent prostitutes living at the hospital of the Incurabili (Syphilitics) in the 1520s. This nunnery received many ex-prostitutes converted by the Jesuits after those dedicated reformers acquired a base in Venice in 1552. The institution's population ranged between 200 and 400 women over the next century. From the 1520s through the 1560s, the mainland cities of the Venetian dominion acquired their own refuges for *convertite*. Sometime in the first half of the sixteenth century, Bishop Giberti founded a community for *convertite* in Verona, starting with a core of approximately thirty women. In the same period, members of the confraternity of Divine Love and the Jesuits successively organized settlements for *convertite* at Padua. Male and female religious and laypersons set up refuges for *convertite* in Palermo (1524), Vicenza (1537), Naples (1538), Messina (1542), Treviso (1559), and Mantua (by 1575).[15] Milan had a settlement of twenty *convertite* in 1532, which eventually became a sizable establishment, Santa Valeria, housing over a hundred women at times. In the 1550s Milan gained another institution for ex-prostitutes, the Rimesse (Forgiven), which was grafted onto an existing Augustinian convent and grew to hold almost a hundred women.[16] Other Lombard cities likewise sponsored homes for former prostitutes. In 1580 Brescia's establishment for *convertite*, founded earlier in the century, sheltered sixty women. Bergamo in 1596 hosted forty-four young *convertite* living by alms in a refuge started some sixty years earlier. Pavia founded a refuge in 1601. Crema in 1608 supported about ten penitent females in a community including two women of citizen rank with supervisory responsibilities.[17]

In central Italy at this time, those medieval foundations for *convertite* that persisted experienced an influx of entrants, and for others that had died out, phoenixes rose in their place. Bologna had lost its medieval refuges, but in 1559 it acquired a new convent for former prostitutes, the Convento dei Santi Giacomo e Filippo, detto delle Convertite. Siena again had a convent for repentant prostitutes in 1570, catering to thirty-one women in its first half decade of operation. A "Monastery of the Convertite" existed in Pisa by 1622.[18] In Florence, the Monastero delle Convertite had been continuously active in the work of reform since the early fourteenth century. By the sixteenth century it, too, held over a hundred women.[19] In 1604 well-to-do

Pistoian citizens founded their smaller shelter for ex-prostitutes, which bore the name Santa Maria Maddalena (Saint Mary Magdalen).

Some refuges for *convertite* concentrated on reforming married prostitutes. In 1543 Ignatius Loyola spurred the foundation of Rome's refuge of Santa Marta, which was primarily for married women engaged in prostitution or other illicit sexual activities. This institution invoked a symbolic link with Saint Martha, the Biblical figure associated with care of the household and the active life, in contrast to the contemplative life eventually adopted by her putative sister, Mary Magdalen. It aimed to reform married prostitutes and restore them to their husbands rather than make them into lifelong penitent recluses. Two years after its founding, the institution housed almost forty women. During the decade before Loyola's death, 1546–56, his admirers founded establishments resembling Santa Marta at Modena, Trapani, Agrigento, Messina, and Palermo.[20] The Casa delle Malmaritate opened in Florence in 1579, welcoming married *convertite* and other women with marital difficulties (see illustration insert, Figure 1). The various institutions for *convertite*, whether single women or married women, differed from one another in their regimens and ultimate goals concerning the destinies of their residents. What they had in common was the desire to provide a refuge from prostitution and to rehabilitate former "whores" by inculcating proper deportment.

The sixteenth century also brought the proliferation of another set of important new institutions for women, establishments designed to *prevent* females from falling from virtue and turning to prostitution. The preventive institutions, as well as the refuges for *convertite*, were related to a broader sixteenth-century phenomenon, a heightened concern for poverty as a social problem. Catholic and Protestant societies had to respond to the successive economic travails of a harsh century. Whether it was demographic pressure, urbanization, unemployment, inflation caused by silver from the New World, war, plagues, or famines that tipped the balance in a specific locale, poverty became highly visible and acutely troubling at this time.[21]

The response came in the form of attempts by intellectuals, clerics, and lay civic officials to find ways of discriminating and determining who would get the limited poor relief available. Italian urban elites organized more confraternities to aid the *poveri vergognosi* (shameful poor), or formerly rich members of the patriciate and respectable artisans. They set up agencies like the Monte di Pietà, which were intended to replace Jewish moneylenders in providing financial assistance to unemployed workers. When street begging grew to tumultuous proportions and threatened social order, it could no longer be permitted. Even in Catholic societies the traditional legitimacy accorded the begging of the Christlike "holy poor" often gave way before the goal of preserving civic order. Instead, elites who pitied the poor took inspiration from Jesus' example of consorting with outcasts and pulling them into the fold. They devised new civic institutions to shelter and enclose the poor. They tried to uplift the needy by offering a combination of relief and moral education as a weapon against the toll that poverty could take on the soul. Catholic clerics and laypersons worked to spread confession and communion, the essential rites of orthodoxy, to the lower classes.[22] Rome, known as a showplace for charity in this period, and Milan, the model Counter-Reformation city for all of Europe, offered many examples of new institutions to emulate.[23]

The connection between poverty and prostitution was axiomatic in the sixteenth century. It appeared in Pope Pius IV's decree of 1560 establishing the Opera dei Poveri Mendicanti (Institution for Poor Beggars) in Bologna. The papal decree implied that prostitution was the inevitable outcome of vagabondage and misery.[24] This outlook led to the development of preventive or protective institutions specifically for females. Benefactors sponsored a variety of asylums for needy girls and women seen as being at risk of falling into immoral behavior. As in the case of the refuges for *convertite,* some females were pressed to enter these institutions, whereas others came of their own volition.

The common factor among the preventive institutions was the emphasis on preventive care through the placement of females with trustworthy custodians. The girls and women placed in such institutions might stay from youth to adulthood or for much shorter spans of time. Venice in 1539 implemented a policy of having houses of good reputation in each parish shelter servant girls in the process of changing employers. The servant girls could stay temporarily in these safe harbors and thus would not wind up in brothels if they failed to find a new position immediately. Ignatius Loyola and his fellow reformer Filippo Neri backed the efforts of a confraternity to sponsor a home for *vergini miserabili* (miserable virgins) in Rome in the late 1540s. Two hundred girls resided at the Roman convent of the Vergini Miserabili by the early seventeenth century, under the supervision of respectable male and female members of the confraternity.[25]

New preventive institutions cropped up in all the major regions of Italy. In the 1530s the Milanese male and female religious activists known as the Paulines and Angeliche visited the Venetian dominion at the request of Bishops Ridolfi and Giberti and the officials of various hospitals. A group of aristocratic Venetian women wanted to help the visitors institute a Conservatorio delle Zitelle Periclitanti (Conservatory for Single Females in Peril). By 1560 Venice had a community of *zitelle* planning a move to a spacious site, thanks additionally to the efforts of the Jesuit Benedetto Palmio, who had set up a refuge for *convertite* in Padua two years before. Toward the end of the century, the Venetian Zitelle grew quite large, housing 180 girls.[26] A conservatory for girls likely to be sold into prostitution opened in Naples in 1564. Two preventive or protective institutions served the female population of Milan in the late 1570s, each holding probably fewer than a hundred residents. The senior of the two was the Soccorso (House of Assistance); Archbishop Carlo Borromeo launched the second, the Deposito (Depot), in 1575.[27] From the midsixteenth century on, Bologna boasted the Conservatorio di Santa Maria del Baraccano, which sought to preserve the honor of plebeian girls and help them to acquire dowries. Three other conservatories there accepted the daughters of prostitutes and poor girls. Bishop Nicolò Sfondrati started a Soccorso in Cremona in 1575. In 1577 and 1589, respectively, Venice and Bologna each acquired a Soccorso housing under fifty women.[28] Patrons in Vicenza funded a Soccorso in 1600, and plans were afoot to set up an establishment for *zitelle* linked to the same church. By the late sixteenth or early seventeenth century, Brescia had a Soccorso and one or more houses for *zitelle*. The Conservatorio for *zitelle disperse* (Conservatory for Lost Single Females) was founded in Rome in 1595 and the Deposito in Turin in 1684.[29]

Tuscany, too, joined in the rush to organize preventive institutions. In the sixteenth and seventeenth centuries, Florence had at least five preventive institutions for abandoned and plebeian girls, Pistoia two such establishments, and Prato another.[30] By the second half of the seventeenth century, Florence's Ospedale dei Mendicanti (Beggars' Hospital) and the city's new Deposito specialized in the internment of females.[31] As we have seen, many sixteenth-century Italian locales possessed clusters of new institutions directed toward aiding both *convertite* and imperiled females: Rome, Venice, Milan, Brescia, Bologna, and the situs that will capture our attention, the Florentine dominion.

The refuges for *convertite* and the other new institutions for women often overlapped in intent, function, and populations. Taken collectively, the preventive or protective establishments can best be designated with the umbrella term of "custodial institutions." The three Tuscan refuges, the Monastero delle Convertite, the Casa delle Malmaritate, and Santa Maria Maddalena, like their analogues elsewhere in Italy, provided residential communities and shaping environments for hundreds of disestablished females. The women in the refuges for *convertite* and custodial institutions had a common variable in their pasts: all had lost or risked losing their good reputation in the eyes of their social superiors or peers.[32] For many of them, this slippage in status was connected to problems of practical need and poverty. Social authorities and the elite intervened and tried to better the lot of these women because they felt responsible for the public interest, the "honor of God and tranquillity of our city," as the founders of Santa Maria Maddalena of Pistoia expressed it.[33] By examining at close range the three Tuscan refuges for converted prostitutes and other problematic women, we can deepen our understanding of the world of early modern women and the development of European social institutions.

Women's Lives in Early Modern Tuscany

In Renaissance Florence and Pistoia the tenets of gender ideology were often articulated in the vocabulary of honor (*onore*). Anthropologists have written extensively about the dyad of social values, honor and shame, in Mediterranean cultures. They provide a definition of honor that could apply to almost every member of a society: "honor signals the respect and esteem one is accorded by society which is interiorized and then claimed as a right."[34] Analyzing the language and ideological constructs of the Florentine upper classes,

Gene A. Brucker has concluded that the elites treaded warily among four competing and often conflicting codes of values: Christian, feudal, mercantile, and communal. Honor, a concept that came largely from the feudal chivalric tradition, "permeated the whole system of patrician values," and Brucker's definition of what honor meant accords with that of the anthropologists. It connoted living in conformity with the ideals of one's social rank; acceding to the rewards of property, position, and public recognition; and being considered a person of moral probity. In societies of dense social networks such as Florence and Pistoia, everything rested on personal reputation, one's changeable status as an honorable or dishonorable individual.[35]

Male representatives of learned and patrician culture applied this value system to the women of their own social rank and to members of the lower social strata as well. The actions of such "others" were characterized by scribes in the terminology of *onore*, and their behavior was often judged by magistrates using the standards of *onore*. To "lead [a daughter] to honor" (*condurre ad honore*) signified arranging for her to marry or to enter a convent. Preachers spoke of preserving the "honor" of daughters in their vernacular sermons to educated and popular audiences.[36] Upper-strata women sometimes used this language to speak of their sons or families "[winning] honor" or to express a wish to "live in the world with honor" themselves.[37] What is less known is whether the lower classes and particularly lower-class women themselves employed this terminology in reference to their own lives. Did Florentine plebeians use *onore* to signify a meaning known in their own subculture, did they not use the term at all, or did they adopt the usage of their social superiors?[38]

Of particular interest for us is the question of whether both patrician and plebeian women internalized the value system of *onore*.[39] The producers of learned culture in the Middle Ages were men, and they traditionally had distinct ideas about what honor for females comprised. From late antiquity onward, Christian gender ideology portrayed women as having a dualistic nature: females were potentially like the holy Virgin Mary or sinful Eve. These two components of medieval gender ideology were in tension with each other. The culture of the age, in its religious and lay dimensions, valued women's reproductive capacity and yet yearned for female sexual purity in the virgin, the faithful wife, and the chaste widow. This was the essence of honor for women. Ironically, both the biological science that derived from classical sources and the myth of Eve, the temptress who committed original sin, imputed to women a greater sexual appetite than that of men. It was female sexuality, seen as voracious, that was the cause of dishonor for women. And women were the source of "all . . . dishonors," wrote Paolo da Certaldo, a paterfamilias and businessman who authored a book of domestic advice for fourteenth-century Florentines.[40] These persistent views split woman into an honorable and a dishonorable half, with each half resembling one of her two role models. The contradictory ideals of motherhood and female sexlessness kept the two halves irreconcilable.

Women had an inferior status in both Christian gender ideology and social organization. On the one hand, theologians such as Thomas Aquinas described an equality of souls among men and women, since both sexes had been created in the "image of God." On the other hand, they argued that men were intellectually, morally, and physically more like God than women were.[41] This view of the male resemblance to God excluded women from the priesthood and limited the access of women to position and power in medieval societies. In a cogent essay Lucia Ferrante has suggested that to understand notions of female honor in the Renaissance, it is useful to think of the intersection of two codes: the religious code of sin (a relationship between a person and God) and the lay code of honor (a social relation). From this stance, Renaissance determinations of an individual female's honorable or dishonorable status lay within the interplay of such variables as religious morality, economics, class ideology, and patronage.[42] In addition, it is important to remember that the maintenance of honor met with different obstacles at different stages of the female life cycle; the adolescent did not face the same choices as the widow. A pertinent question in this study is whether women interiorized the constructs of honor in early modern Tuscany. A related query is how much did reputation really matter for patrician and plebeian Tuscan women in terms of securing their economic subsistence. As preparation for understanding the relationship between the institutions for *convertite* and the value system of *onore,* let us traverse briefly the two honorable paths for females—marriage and monasticism—and the dishonorable path of prostitution.

Marriage

[W]omen were created to replenish this free city, and to live chastely in matrimony. —Fifteenth-century Florentine lawmakers[43]

The majority of Florentine and Pistoian females of all social ranks grew up anticipating that, if luck was with them, they would marry. Females in medieval and early modern Tuscany usually either married or entered convents. Very few remained single in lay society. According to the Catasto (tax survey) of 1427, 97 percent of the twenty-five-year-old women in Tuscany were already married or widowed. For Florentine patrician women, this proportion nearly declined by half in the sixteenth and seventeenth centuries, but climbed upward again in the eighteenth.[44] Marriage at all ranks of Tuscan society represented an economic, social, and political alliance not only between two spouses but also between their respective families. The fifteenth-century preacher Bernardino of Siena referred to the bond created between families: "Marriage . . . unites in-laws by reinforcing in them a mutual affection."[45] The parties who benefited from marital alliances strove to aggrandize the patrimony of the household, operating according to the prevailing rules of male succession. The property owned by females, whether unmarried or married, was subject to control by their father (or at his death, by their brothers), subsequently by their husband, and finally by their male children. To transact and bequeath, all females had to have authorization from a male guardian (*mundualdo*), often a relative or the husband of the woman in question. From 1415 on, Florentine females could no longer themselves initiate suits in civil court to protect property and other rights, but had to do so through a *mundualdo*. Property acquired by wives during their marriages was at the disposal of their husbands, unless benefactors legally specified otherwise. These basic structures governed married women's relationships to property in the Florentine dominion throughout the early modern period.[46] In many respects, however, the experiences of patrician and plebeian Tuscan women in marriage and family life were so different that we will have to consider them separately.

In the upper and middle ranks of society, Florentine and Pistoian parents arranged marriages for their sons and daughters, with the goal of accruing economic and political advantage and honor. Patrician parents often shared their homes with their unmarried adult children and the family of the eldest married son. All in the household would subsist on a common patrimony, as the parents strove to preserve and augment the family wealth for future generations. Tensions between brothers seeking individual shares of the patrimony, or the death of the father, could cause such extended families to split into smaller households. The average patrician household held between four and six persons, plus servants, in the fifteenth and sixteenth centuries.[47] The marriage market revolved around sizable dowries as the ultimate prize. Alessandra Strozzi, a merchant's widow who referred to prospective brides as "merchandise," aptly summed up the attitudes of her fifteenth-century contemporaries: "He who takes a wife wants money."[48]

In commercial Florence and Pistoia, young men of the patriciate traditionally postponed marriage until they acquired experience in business, often in foreign cities. They married comparatively late—in their early thirties—whereas upper-strata females married comparatively early, in their midteens. Only after the plague known as the "Black Death" had ravaged the population in the 1340s did Florentine men of the upper classes for a few decades marry at younger ages.[49] By the early fifteenth century they had reverted to their old patterns, and religious and lay authorities voiced alarm at the insufficient number of marriages, the sluggishness of the populace in replenishing itself. Patrician families faced a mounting crisis concerning the difficulty of marrying off their daughters. As families competed in offering higher dowries to attract reluctant suitors, dowry inflation spiraled. In the first half of the fifteenth century, patrician dowry levels increased almost twofold, so that by midcentury two thousand florins was common.[50] Members of Florentine and Pistoian confraternities exerted themselves to provide dowries for marriageable females, and by 1425 Florentine civic leaders had set up the Monte delle Doti, an investment fund to help fathers save for their daughters' dowries. None of these measures could arrest the crisis of the Florentine patrician family. The limitation of marriages had little deleterious effect on patrician males, who, unlike their sisters, did not risk loss of reputation by remaining unwed. But generations of unmarriageable females—Bernardino of Siena pityingly called them "the scum and vomit of the world"—were shunted into convents. The predicament of surplus daughters only worsened and grew more widespread in the sixteenth and seventeenth centuries, as marital ages rose. In that period Florentine patrician males often deferred marriage until their midthirties, and patrician parents delayed marrying off daughters until their late teens or early twenties.[51]

Those women of the middle and upper strata who did marry lived in a style more isolated from public life than was the case with their peers elsewhere in European cities. Both in prescription and in fact, Tuscan patrician women led restricted lives. The fourteenth-century moralist Paolo da Certaldo advised husbands to "keep females in the house" stewarding the family possessions. A century later Leon Battista Alberti in his treatise *On the Family,* either in sincerity or perhaps mocking the mores of his contemporaries, passed on the Greek historian Xenophon's recommendation that wives should remain "locked up at home."[52] And indeed, social practice limited the mobility of patrician women to excursions to church and festivities, visits to female neighbors, and appearances at the windows of their townhouses. In 1610 a French traveler noted that "in Florence women are more enclosed than in any other part of Italy; they see the world only from the small openings in their windows."[53]

The informal tutelage and occasional training in reading, writing, and arithmetic received by girls of the upper and middle strata aimed at preparing them to supervise the domestic environment. Some women helped their spouses manage rural estates or business firms, and widows like Alessandra Strozzi carried on the administration of familial properties.[54] A small number of women from this stratum practiced trades, which they may have learned from their fathers and husbands, and a tiny percentage held guild membership.[55] The few women who obtained a solid humanist education and aspired further found it difficult to persevere. The culture frowned on mixing marriage and scholarship and on admitting females to the learned professions. Erudite Alessandra Scala could not succeed her father Bartolomeo as chancellor for the Florentine state. No civic government would hire women, however learned, to be scribes, and only rarely would universities retain them as lecturers.[56] While the courtly milieu of the sixteenth- and seventeenth-century grand duchy may have brought expanded ceremonial roles to a small segment of Tuscan patrician women, it did not offer them wider opportunities to be involved in learned and artistic culture, let alone politics. The late medieval *querelle des femmes,* a debate on whether women should be permitted more freedoms, surfaced in sixteenth-century Florence only as a subject addressed by playful male literati. The *querelle* had little impact on the lives of housebound patrician women in that or the next century.[57]

For women of the lower social ranks, too, marriage was an alliance of multiple facets. Dowries changed hands also at the bottom strata of Tuscan

society, in both city and countryside. Parents, benefactors, and women themselves contributed the dowries, which were much smaller than those of the
elite. In the middle decades of the fifteenth century a servant girl might offer a
dowry of fifteen florins, a peasant woman thirty florins, and the daughter of a
skilled artisan about seventy florins, as compared to a patrician dowry at that
time of upward of six hundred florins. Among urban workers and rural sharecroppers (*mezzadri*), young people possibly had greater leeway to select their
own marital partners than did young members of the elite, since the monetary
transactions at stake were smaller.[58] At the time of the tax survey in 1427,
almost 70 percent of both the rural poor and the well-off peasantry were
married, and we can surmise that the proportion was just a bit lower among
urban laborers.[59] Laboring men and women of the city and countryside married at ages similar to those of patrician couples, with plebeian males wedding
a few years younger, in their late twenties, and lower-strata females waiting
somewhat longer than their patrician counterparts, until their late teens. The
average household size for Florentine artisans in 1427 was four people, with
larger households in the countryside among sharecroppers.[60] Plebeian women
led lives much more in the public arena than those of their patrician female
contemporaries. They were simply in the streets more, traveling to places of
employment, procuring food—by riot, if necessary—and engaging in conversations or altercations with men and women alike.[61] They migrated more
frequently so as to find jobs, to marry, or to return to native villages when
widowed.[62]

Plebeian females picked up a smattering of literacy and arithmetical skills
and sometimes put this knowledge to use in the work they did.[63] Just as female
members of the elite served as unpaid adjuncts to their husbands, so did
women in peasant and artisanal families help with agricultural work or crafts.
One of the most significant differences between the lives led by women of the
patriciate and women of the plebs was that plebeian girls and women commonly worked for pay. Single and married females of all ages from many
plebeian families found jobs as domestic servants, as laborers in manufacturing, and occasionally as vendors of goods or services.[64] Unlike the Tuscan
patriarchs of the middle and upper ranks of society who wished to keep the
materfamilias at home, many plebeian husbands could not sustain their families without the wages brought in by spouses. Working men knew that they
would "have to live from the labor of their hands and those of their wives," as
one respectable wage earner declared in 1375.[65] In Florence and Pistoia plebeian women tended especially to find employment in the textile trades. The
midseventeenth-century municipal statutes of Pistoia stipulated that husbands
were officially to have charge of looms placed in their wives' possession for
textile work. Some women took in piecework to perform in their own dwell-
ings in city or countryside, and others walked daily from their homes to labor
in textile manufacturing in shops and mills. The employment of working
women in Tuscany fell off for the two centuries following the Black Death,
and then it rose to striking proportions in late sixteenth- and seventeenth-

century Florence, where by 1663 more than three quarters of all silk workers were female.[66]

Marriage served highborn and lowborn Tuscan women as a viable strategy for economic survival, albeit not a perfect one. Experts in canon law and preachers buttressed the institution of marriage in its economic aspects. They said that fathers had an obligation to dower daughters, and husbands had an obligation to undertake financial responsibility for wives.[67] When marriages failed, wives who wished to break away from abusive spouses could hope for a financial safety valve. Civil authorities arranged for some erring husbands to send regular payments to wives who had separated from them.[68] At the death of their spouses, wives had the right to reclaim their dowries in order to support themselves honorably or remarry. This system worked well for some women at both levels of Tuscan society. Upper-strata widows were on occasion able to live comfortably on the income from rents, being concentrated in the urban centers of Tuscany and enjoying opportunities for participation in civic religious life and philanthropy.[69] Plebeian widows might have adequate resources to carry on with businesses and support their children independently, and many of them, especially in the countryside, remarried easily.[70]

But for numerous women widowhood brought complications and poverty. In the upper classes, the delayed male age of marriage produced an inordinate number of widows. In trying to remarry, these widows faced a wall of discouragement. Hemmed in more than plebeian women were by customs meant to guard them from sexual contamination, they were more vulnerable to preachers' exhortations that widowed chastity surpassed in holiness a return to carnal wedlock. Their husbands' wills sometimes stipulated that the widow had to remain unmarried and chaste in order to inherit. Patrician widows wrangled with their dead spouse's relatives (and with their own children), whose interests lay not in refunding the dowry but in keeping the patrimony intact. The patrician widow faced an array of discomfiting facts: no man would marry her if she did not have a refunded dowry; she might be able to retrieve her dowry and remarry only at the cost of relinquishing her children to her husband's family; and cultural sanctions deterred her from working to provide her own income.[71] While plebeian widows could support themselves by laboring, they often had to make do on one set of low wages where there had been two incomes before.[72] Even when a widow retrieved her dowry, as a daughter she was throughout her life subject to the *patria potestas,* the authority of her father. Fathers at times sought to gain control of refunded dowries, particularly in the case of patrician widows who had received substantial sums. Women could legally be freed from parental authority only if they were formally emancipated, a practice important mainly for patrician women and dwindling in frequency after the early fifteenth century.[73] Poor struggling widows were always legion in Florence and Pistoia at all levels of society. In 1427 one in four adult women in Florence was a widow, and one in six in the countryside.[74] Although marriage might be one route to economic survival, it left a legacy of obstacles for the woman accustomed to being cared for, who was then cut loose from that security.

Monasticism

> "A perfect life and great merit place in a higher heaven
>   a lady [Saint Clare] under whose rule," she said,
>   "in your world the veil and dress are worn. . . .
> To follow her, while a girl, I fled from the world
>   and dressed myself in her gown,
>   and pledged myself to the ways of her order."
> —PICCARDA DONATI, IN DANTE'S *Divine Comedy*[75]

Down the other honorable path strode countless Tuscan females who became the brides of Christ. Florence and Pistoia had produced numerous female monastic houses since the ninth century. Foundations of convents increased in the fourteenth and fifteenth centuries, and by 1545 Florence had forty-two of them and Pistoia, thirteen. Late-seventeenth-century Florence was graced by sixty-three convents.[76] In 1429 just over 2 percent of the female population of Florence lived in a monastery. By 1552 the figure had risen to 13 percent. This compares with only 3 to 7 percent of the female population of the towns of Lombardy and a mere 0.11 percent of the female population of England. In 1552, four times as many women as men in Florence adopted a religious habit. R. Burr Litchfield, in a study encompassing 2,427 individuals in twenty-one Florentine patrician families of the sixteenth through eighteenth centuries, found that fully 44 percent of the daughters of these families entered monasteries.[77]

Women in Tuscany entered monastic life primarily for two different reasons: genuine religious calling and the tendency of families to place surplus daughters in convents, taking advantage of the fact that conventual dowries were cheaper than marital dowries. In the fifteenth century a patrician father would have had to spend about three times the amount of a conventual dowry to enable his daughter to marry, and in the seventeenth century, five times the amount.[78] Newly admitted monks or their parents also made payments to religious houses, but these payments were neither so standardized nor so large as the dowries for novice nuns. Although girls from the upper and middle strata of Tuscan society in general married partners lower than themselves on the social scale, entry into a convent could save some women and their families from the diminished honor resulting from a marital alliance too far down the scale. Unlike the mobile monks from distant cities who filled the male religious houses, Tuscany's female religious came from local families.[79]

Certain features characterized Tuscan conventual life throughout the medieval and early modern epochs.[80] In Florence and Pistoia the local convents differed considerably from one another in wealth and prestige. They ranged from rich institutions with long histories like Florence's San Piero Maggiore and Pistoia's San Giovanni Battista to communities on the verge of extinction like Santa Maria Verzaria, tucked away at the periphery of midfifteenth-century Florence.[81] Likewise, the residents of convents differed from one another in class background, monastic status, and economic well-being. Patrician girls became choir nuns (*vocale* or *velate*), whereas plebeian females, including many from the countryside, became servant nuns (*converse*) who aided the choir nuns.[82] Convents ranged in size from a few women to two hundred residents. In the larger communities of from one hundred to two hundred residents, about six to eight new members entered annually. Most entrants were not adult women but girls, either in their teens or as young as three years of age. The memberships of convents generally included many sets of female relatives.[83]

Nuns occupied themselves with sacral activities and work. Tuscan convents often owed their beginnings to devout foundresses. Florence's convents were the settings for numerous female holy figures with extensive spiritual and temporal influence: in the High Middle Ages, Saint Giuliana Falconieri; in the sixteenth century, Suor (Sister) Domenica da Paradiso, Saint Caterina de' Ricci, and Saint Maria Maddalena de' Pazzi; and in the seventeenth century, Suor Jacinta Fabbroni.[84] Particularly in the late Middle Ages, Florentines and Pistoians venerated their convents as powerhouses of sanctity, fueled by the precious prayers of virgin nuns: "Day and night they pray on behalf of the most worthy government of Florence."[85] Choir nuns and servant nuns had to turn their eyes away from heaven at times to attend to a variety of labors. They washed clothes, spun and wove, sewed, made jewelry, copied and illuminated manuscripts, and at San Jacopo a Ripoli assisted Friar Domenico of Pistoia in running a successful fifteenth-century humanist printing press. At some religious houses this work was pro forma, but in other cases it provided essential income, with the nuns depending only on their labors and public and private charity to sustain themselves.[86]

Christian monastic life had as its goal complete seclusion from the world, but in the Florentine dominion cloister did not always bar monastic residents from contact with the outside. Not every resident of a convent committed herself to a lifetime lived behind walls, professing the three monastic vows of poverty, chastity, and obedience to superiors or a rule. Instead, at progressive stages of the female life cycle, girls and women might stay temporarily in the convents of Tuscany. They spent time there as members of Third Orders (*pinzochere*) and as boarders (*commesse*), the latter sometimes seeking refuge from quarrels with relatives or husbands. Vitale de' Medici in 1587 requested help from his distant relative the grand duke, after Vitale's daughter had fled from her cruel and adulterous husband in Pistoia and asked to retreat to a convent.[87] Girls came for a few years to be educated, with their upkeep paid by their families. Some girls who had scholarly ambitions proceeded to become nuns. Taking religious orders offered the one legitimate way to be a female scholar, to have opportunities to write a history of the world, as Suor Fiammetta Frescobaldi did at the convent of San Jacopo a Ripoli.[88]

Both the temporary residents and the professed nuns sought to keep lines of communication open with their families outside. They received visits and gifts of money, books, and other items from their relatives.[89] Fissures in the symbolic barrier imposed by cloister permitted these brief contacts with the outside, as well as blatant abuses of the principle of seclusion. Ecclesiastical authorities constantly warred against breaches of cloister. The apostolic visitor of 1575, a papal inspector, demanded the sealing off of a chapel door at the Florentine convent Regina Coeli, and the abbess there noted, "May God concede us the grace that the door of Heaven not be closed to us!"[90]

But the convents of Florence and Pistoia held another category of confined women as well. Supplementing the function of jails like the Florentine Stinche, convents served as prisons for female criminals and women who lost out in disputes with powerful males over property or other issues. The historian Eric Cochrane unearthed one such telling incident: "In 1690 a wealthy widow named Elisabetta Mormorai was locked up in a convent simply because a disappointed suitor was influential enough to make the law into an instrument of personal vengeance."[91] In the previous century the Otto di Guardia, Florence's main criminal magistracy, sentenced a girl to an indefinite term as a servant at the Monastero delle Vergini in Pistoia.[92] For such females, as for nuns, the theory of the convent as an enclosed institution where women would remain for their lifetimes came to be realized.

Periodic shock waves reverberated through this monastic sea of continuity. In the 1430s Popes Eugenius IV and Martin V conducted drives to tighten up the lax cloister at Florentine convents. Rumors of immoral behavior tarnished the reputations of certain convents in the late fifteenth century, and some of those religious houses were reformed by Girolamo Savonarola, the messianic friar who led the Florentine republic in 1494–98.[93] The Protestant Reformation brought disquiet by parading alternative options to past traditions. The Protestants eliminated monasticism for both sexes, exalted the status of the wife as a companion to her husband, opened opportunities for female education, and invited religious activism on the part of the female laity—iconoclasm in the streets and sometimes even preaching. Although the Reformation made few converts in Catholic Tuscany, most people there heard of the outrageous heresies of the Protestants.[94]

At the same time Catholic reformers mounted their campaign to update and strengthen the Church. Among the many issues considered at the Council of Trent (1545–63), the churchmen confronted the sad state of Christendom's overcrowded convents filled with girls forced into the religious life. As a countermeasure, they decreed that no one should profess monastic vows before the age of sixteen. The ecclesiastics at Trent produced regulations both to deter coerced professions of vows and to exact unblemished conduct from religious who had willingly professed vows. They demanded that neither professed monks nor nuns own private property. They called for strict cloister at female monasteries, although not at male monasteries. The council required regular visitations of convents to enforce the regulations.[95]

Just before the opening of the council, Grand Duke Cosimo I had launched his own sweeping reforms. To an unprecedented degree, he extended lay control over the monasteries, ordering that each convent submit administration of its temporal affairs to four respectable laymen, or *operai*.[96] After the Council of Trent, the Tuscan bishops and archbishops carried out the intent of the council's decrees by setting numerical limits on the memberships of specific convents, so that the houses would not accept more mouths than their resources could feed. Here and elsewhere, ducal and ecclesiastical aims coincided, but on other policies they clashed. When churchmen attempted to curtail nuns' worldly contacts related to conventual labors, they were opposed by lay authorities, who recognized the economic hardships this and other correctives would impose on the convents. The nuns at some Tuscan convents accepted the reforms, but others violently resisted. As a result of the ducal and Tridentine reforms, especially those pertaining to cloister and property, financial distress increased sharply at many Florentine and Pistoian convents from the midsixteenth century onward.[97] The convents of Tuscany were to meet one final onslaught from the outside when first Grand Duke Pietro Leopoldo and then Napoleon Bonaparte successfully consolidated scores of monastic houses during their conventual suppressions of 1785 and 1808.

The convent represented another strategy for economic survival that in theory took care of all of life's needs. The outcome hung on whether two conditions were fulfilled: at the outset, a girl or woman needed a certain amount of money in order to be accepted into the convent, and sufficient conventual income had to accrue to keep the residents nourished. The dowry of 200 scudi for a choir nun in the early seventeenth century represented about one month's income for her patrician family, a moderate expenditure. For plebeian women the dowry for becoming a servant nun (*conversa*) ranged from 25 to 70 scudi, representing a heftier outlay equivalent to about one eighth to one third of a plebeian family's annual income.[98] Plebeian women managed to enter as *converse* by acquiring benefactors or offering a token amount and paying off the rest later in service or with wages from conventual labors. Once accepted, nuns might receive ongoing support from their families or other patrons outside. However, relatives did not always help willingly or at all.[99] Merely living at a convent did not give women personal control over their own property or over any expected income. At least the women who had not taken vows still had to rely on a male representative, a *mundualdo*, for transactions involving property. For those who did swear vows, profession may have served as a form of tacit legal emancipation, eliminating the need for a *mundualdo*.[100] But one of the convent's administrators, the *procuratore*, usually acted as a representative for the business and legal affairs of professed nuns.

Income for the convent as a whole and for individual residents derived from endowments, charity, and the efforts of nuns who labored at piecework inside the convent and sometimes begged in the streets. The Tridentine reforms diminished the flow of income in two ways. The Church wished to eliminate the financial security of individual residents by forbidding the retention of private property, a regulation that was sporadically enforced. Also, it drastically interfered with conventual regimens of labor and with alms seeking on the part of nuns.[101] When Grand Duke Cosimo I tried to moderate the zeal of the ecclesiastical reformers by pleading the poverty of the nuns, Pope Gregory XIII replied that the nuns would have to trust in God: "Just as Divine Providence sent bread to Elijah, the desert hermit, and to Paul [in the beaks of] ravens, [God] will inspire benefactors to provide for these nuns."[102]

Prostitution

In Tuscany, as in most societies, women also took the dishonorable road of prostitution. Florentine and Pistoian women engaged in professional and occasional prostitution because it seemed a useful economic tactic, because sexual license may have held an appeal, because their families or husbands may have forced them into it, and because the state itself encouraged prostitution. Up to the early fifteenth century, the Florentine government loosely regulated prostitution with the aim of stigmatizing prostitutes (*meretrici*). The year 1403 inaugurated a major change in policy: the state became a sponsor of prostitution. "Desiring to eliminate a worse evil by means of a lesser one," the Florentine government commenced importing foreign prostitutes to reside in three municipally subsidized brothels and tempt men away from sexual relations with other men. Over the course of the fifteenth century, the number of registered prostitutes in the city more than doubled, reaching 150 in 1486 and prompting Pope Pius II to describe Florence as "La città mercatrice, ma che dico, meretrice!" ("The merchant city, or rather say: the prostitute city!").[103]

All along, however, both before and after the turnabout in policy, prostitution in the Florentine dominion was seen not only as a sin in the eyes of Christians but as dishonorable in the civic arena of social interaction. Municipal authorities, the guardians of civic honor, needed to distinguish who in the city was an honorable person and who was not, in order to bestow privileges. The purity of the polis's women—laywomen as well as nuns—was one repository of civic honor. The female associated with the shame of prostitution ([*il*] *biasmo del meretricio*) tarnished her family as well as herself and prevented her relatives from winning repute. Municipal and ecclesiastical counselors waged an endless battle to keep honorable and dishonorable females apart in terms of their definition and physical location. Tensions arose when the borderlines became unclear. In the early sixteenth century, Florentine leaders believed that the balance in the city-state between decent and indecent women was shifting, and they feared that the corruption of respectable women loomed. Desperately desirous of regaining control, they revised their policies and switched to castigating and trying to cut back prostitution, using the refuges for *convertite* as one weapon in their arsenal. From the sixteenth century onward, the Florentine state pursued a harsher policy toward prostitution. A parallel hardening of attitudes occurred simultaneously in cities elsewhere in Italy and Europe. Henceforth, state authorities in Florence again concentrated on stigmatizing prostitutes, while at the same time reaching out to divert innocent females, particularly plebeian and poor women, from falling into the abyss of whoredom.[104]

Prostitution was available to Tuscan women as one more economic strategy in the cultural sex/gender system.[105] When we consider just the economic motives that may have impelled Tuscan women to engage in prostitution, we find an array of possibilities. They sold their bodies to survive when they lost other work or were widowed, and they exchanged sex for profit in order to gain extra income beyond the level of subsistence. Sometimes women made the tactical gamble that prostitution would prove more lucrative than other modes of sustenance available to females. Late-fourteenth-century Florentine judiciary officials heard the case of Angela, a prostitute who was informed by people in her neighborhood that they would supply a weekly basket of bread if she would cease copulating for money: "Angela replied that she did not wish to give up prostitution unless her neighbors first gave her 2 florins. Otherwise she intended to pursue the whore's life since she earned much more money than the amount which her neighbors wished to give her."[106] By the seventeenth century authorities were greatly dismayed, as their predecessors had been in the previous century, over what they saw as the ever growing number of prostitutes. The Florentine census of 1631 showed that of the women with listed occupations, over 80 percent were involved in textile production and trade, 4 percent in prostitution, and 3 percent in domestic service.[107] For every twenty female textile workers, there was one full-time prostitute, and the census did not include the vaster number of women involved in occasional bartering of sex.

As an economic strategy prostitution could offer one advantage over other forms of paid labor: direct access to cash. If a woman's husband or family did not know that she was trading sex for gain, then the payment earned went directly to her. When relatives and husbands persuaded women to prostitute themselves, they usually collected the returns, as is illustrated in a case that came before a magistrate of Pisa in 1417. The judicial records claim that one Bartolomeo di Lorenzo offered his wife to a brothel keeper, saying "You know that I have a wife, Stella, and you will recall that a few days ago, we agreed that you would employ her in your brothel in Lucca. Now if you will give me 30 florins, I will consent to your keeping her in your bordello." Bartolomeo's plan did not go into effect, and he himself became Stella's pimp. According to the court, after one episode of intercourse, the client "gave Stella a Florentine silver *quattrino* and a silk jacket with a belt as the price for her labor. Stella gave the coin to her husband Bartolomeo."[108] Other than kin, however, pimps and bawds were not widely in evidence either in the fifteenth century or afterward. While the prostitute might get cash in hand, she still could not on her own enter into contracts with the property acquired. Prostitutes, like all secular women, had to depend on male intermediaries, *mundualdi*.[109]

Although some Tuscan prostitutes were comfortable financially, others were poor. Prostitution could be a viable full-time career only during the first half of the female life cycle. Women in their midforties successfully operated as prostitutes, but it became more difficult to earn a living in that fashion as they aged.[110] In 1603 the Otto di Guardia handled a case emblematic of the fate that in reality befell some prostitutes and was thought by the public to be the end awaiting all of them. Betta from Val di Castello, a rural girl who had been a prostitute since the age of thirteen, was brought before the magistrates. Mistress to two married men, she had borne children to them, and then they had abandoned her. Discovered acting strangely in the woods, she was said to be possessed by a demon.[111] By the seventeenth century the Tuscan prostitute might be doubly outcast, being vilified by the state and relegated to the swelling hordes of poor.

The Refuges for *Convertite* in Florence and Pistoia

In the early modern age the three institutions that are the subject of this study—the Monastero delle Convertite, the Casa delle Malmaritate, and Santa Maria Maddalena of Pistoia—became the focus of concerted attention from civic leaders and the public. Institutional conversion of wayward women seemed to offer a solution to what society perceived as the problem of rising prostitution. The cities of sixteenth-century Tuscany were filled with unmarriageable and widowed women. To the authorities, every Tuscan woman in economic need or with severed social affiliations courted a fall from virtue. Convents served as the age-old refuge but could not always be relied upon to take in needy women. In 1521 the father of the future Grand Duke Cosimo I received two telling letters, the first from lackeys of the bishop of Viterbo and the second from the bishop himself:

> [29 June 1521] [T]he Bishop tried to put [Signora Maria, the poor, pregnant woman you sent] in some monastery, but he could not put her anywhere. The nuns did not want to accept her without permission from their General, and she in no way wanted to stay there or remain here. [We have resolved] to put her here in a room with some old woman [until further instructions]. . . .

> [13 July 1521] [I]t is not my charge to manage women, and not for anything do I want to do it because I have too much to do. I pray you to remove her immediately because I cannot attend to her. . . . I await a reply soon about where I should send her. . . .[112]

The traditional institutions for women—convents—were not enough, Catholics in early modern Europe realized. Lay and clerical reformers, including ex-prostitutes themselves, took the lead in founding refuges for *convertite* and other new custodial asylums for females. The two sets of institutions overlapped in terms of the populations housed, and they had to face the same challenges in resolving difficult questions of policy.

The policies of social institutions in Tuscan municipalities set the tone for what women's role was to be in those societies, whether females were to take an active role in society's mainstream or were to be confined to domiciles and convents.[113] We must ask whether there was a point of intersection between the perspectives of early modern women and of societal authorities. It was not just former prostitutes who looked with hope to new institutions in the sixteenth century. Respectable women, too, in Florence and elsewhere were interested in developing avenues for life and action more satisfying than those their society had offered in the past. During the age of Catholic reform, excitement percolated among female spiritual luminaries. In the 1530s in Brescia, Angela Merici, a Franciscan tertiary, founded the Company of Saint Ursula, an uncloistered association for women who wanted to serve the causes of education and charity. The community consisted of 130 virgins and a number of widows supervising them. The Tuscan cleric Francesco Landini explained that Angela Merici's new group intended to

> assist and edify many young virgins, both rich and poor, who even though they feel a deep respect for the religious way of life, are nevertheless disinclined to shut themselves up within the narrow walls of cloisters, or bind themselves by vows; or who, again, cannot enter nunneries because of poverty, or do not wish to do so for other good reasons.[114]

Two issues lay at the core of this initiative: the economic contingencies defining women's choices and the degree to which women could move away from the monastic ethos and its restrictions. After 1566, at the invitation of Archbishop Carlo Borromeo, the group spread to Milan. In seventeenth-century Florence Eleonora Montalvo Landi formulated a plan to start a female branch of the Jesuits, as Mary Ward had done clandestinely in England.[115] These religious women longed to put the message of the Gospel to work in the world, not behind convent walls.

The civic activists who wished to ameliorate conditions for ex-prostitutes wrestled with the same questions. Veronica Franco, a well-known Venetian courtesan and poetess of the late sixteenth century, wrote in a petition she intended to present to the Venetian Senate:

> There are many women who, out of poverty or sensuality or for some other reason, lead a dishonorable life, but who are sometimes moved by the Holy Spirit to think of the miserable end, both in body and soul, to which for the most part they come by this means. They could easily withdraw from ill-doing if they had some reputable place to repair to, where they might maintain themselves and their children. For they are not allowed to enter among the Zitelle or Convertite if they have mothers, children, husbands, or other necessary responsibilities. It is, moreover, difficult for them to persuade themselves to pass, in a moment, from such a licentious existence to so strict and austere a way of life as that of the Convertite. Because there is no provision for such cases, they persist in . . . this abominable crime among others: that women in need sell the virginity of their own innocent daughters.[116]

Again we find reform-minded women supporting new institutions and attempting to come to terms with pressing issues: the feminine sex's limited choices, the economics of women's lives, the fate of girls in peril, and the unsatisfying aspects of the monastic milieu. The backers of the Casa delle Malmaritate in Florence, quoted at the opening of this chapter, and the founders of Santa Maria Maddalena in Pistoia articulated similar concerns.[117]

Social policy toward the converted prostitute had relevance for all women in her society. Tuscan authorities saw female character as inevitably tied to economic circumstances, and in every economically distressed woman they diagnosed a likely prostitute. Many women labeled as endangered in one way or another passed sojourns in the Tuscan refuges for *convertite*. The administrators of the refuges in Florence and Pistoia believed in theory and knew from experience, from repeated departures from the institutions, that even those women who did reform for a time could revert to sinful states. In exhorting Christians to convert prostitutes, Pope Leo X's bull of 1520 quoted Jesus' reply when he was asked how many times sinners should be forgiven: "Not seven times only, but seventy times seven."[118] The administrators of the refuges in Tuscany and elsewhere responded by countenancing recidivism, the readmission of former residents. They opened a cyclical path between the refuges and the world. This practice differed radically from the mainstream convents' orientation toward lifetime residence. The willingness to permit recidivism also characterized the other new custodial institutions for women.

A final question of policy that stirred debate was the mixed nature of the populations at the Tuscan refuges for *convertite* and custodial institutions. Former prostitutes and women who had committed crimes mingled under one roof with presumably innocent young girls and female victims. Women who had come voluntarily shared the space with women forced to enter and remain. The situation had always been so at Tuscany's convents, hospitals, and jails, all of which were institutions that functioned, primarily or secondarily, as holding grounds for the marginal. Sixteenth-century administrators, while perpetuating the mélange, at the same time manifested discomfort about this phenomenon. The diversity of the populations made the tasks of the administrators more difficult.[119] Were the institutions to function primarily to instill penitence, to discipline deviants, or to teach skills for getting on respectably in the world? Debates over how much freedom of action, mobility, and communication females should have inside the institutions necessarily involved consideration of the contrasting social statuses and characters of the institutional residents. At the heart of the matter lay the question of which residents would have to remain locked up and which ones could be permitted to return to society. The histories of the early modern institutions for women reveal that some civic welfare institutions came to care exclusively for precisely defined populations differentiated from the masses of needy, while others did not. They provide a wealth of evidence about how European social welfare institutions divided up the labor of their missions.

Each of the three Tuscan refuges for *convertite* represents a different institutional variant. The Monastero delle Convertite was the most traditional institutional model, a *monastery* for penitent prostitutes. In the 1330s the lay male confraternity Santa Maria delle Laudi and a band of *convertite,* inspired by the preacher Simone Fidati da Cascia, established the refuge in Via Chiara, a street of churches and convents located in the smaller of the two sections of Florence, which was bisected by the Arno river.[120] Within a few years, the refuge had become an Augustinian convent for *convertite.* The Monastero delle Convertite usually held between one hundred and two hundred women. The convent weathered financial peaks and troughs for centuries. A shortfall of funds in 1620 prompted the administrators to take a bold initiative and request that the convent's financial affairs be put under the permanent management of the grand duke's Chancery of Possessions. From then on, benefiting from ducal protection and largesse, the Monastero delle Convertite achieved a prosperity that lasted until the convent's suppression by Napoleon in 1808.[121]

The other two refuges embodied the experimental approach favored by the Catholic reformers of sixteenth- and seventeenth-century Italy. A Florentine male and female confraternity in 1579 founded the Casa delle Malmaritate to specialize in helping married prostitutes and other troubled married women. This establishment promoted the newest reform tried at the time, the vision of rehabilitating women for a return to society. The Casa delle Malmaritate could hold up to thirty women. Housed on Via della Scala, a centrally located area newly patronized by the Medici dukes, the Casa delle Malmaritate functioned as a distinct entity until the early nineteenth century. Similarly, in 1604 the burghers of Pistoia set up Santa Maria Maddalena at the perimeter of town as an innovative community for ex-prostitutes. Like the Casa delle Malmaritate, the Pistoian settlement at first hinted at a widening of women's options. But like many of the experimental institutions of that age, it eventually rejected certain freedoms and became a traditional cloistered convent. Generally sheltering between twenty and forty residents, Santa Maria Maddalena endured at the site of Ponte San Leonardo on the Brana river until the suppressions of 1808.[122]

The historical records for the three refuges are of contrasting types. For the Casa delle Malmaritate and Santa Maria Maddalena, parallel sources exist: statutes and constitutions that outline the intent of the institutions' patrons. For both the Monastero delle Convertite and Santa Maria Maddalena, extensive administrative and financial records provide evidence about the institutions' residents and development. Historians have not been able to find similar records for the Casa delle Malmaritate. But we can derive some knowledge about the women who lived at the Casa delle Malmaritate from magisterial and police records.

II

Refuges for Women
in Early Modern Tuscany

2

Prostitution and the Tuscan Refuges

By the late sixteenth century, Florentines could observe increasing numbers of women obtaining income through two means: wage labor in the textile industry and prostitution. Before the midfourteenth century, women had held a variety of positions in the Tuscan labor force, but after the Black Death of 1348 their participation greatly diminished and did not revive until the late sixteenth century. At that time structural changes in the Florentine economy opened new positions for women in textile manufacturing, and the city acted as a magnet drawing women from the countryside and providing them with considerable opportunities for employment throughout the seventeenth century. Earlier in the sixteenth century, lay and religious officials had begun to anguish over a perceived rise in prostitution. The authorities responded to this development conditioned by the imperatives of civic history and by their society's assumptions about the roles of the sexes.[1]

The authorities saw a link between prostitution and women's place in the economic life of the city-state. They realized that poor girls cut off from charitable assistance "out of necessity quickly became prostitutes." They often heard women summoned by magistrates defend their decision to prostitute themselves as a necessity to avoid starvation.[2] In seeking to understand women's economic needs, civic leaders considered the two avenues that could help secure a woman's economic subsistence: marriage and employment. At the bottom strata of society, marriage alone offered no assured security. Many plebeian married women had to work for wages, which they contributed toward accumulating an adequate family income. Married female workers outnumbered their single counterparts. Beginning in the late sixteenth century, a boom in the production of luxury goods siphoned skilled male workers away from the lowest ranks of jobs in the Florentine textile industry, and Tuscan females entered the paid labor force in greater numbers than ever before. They answered a demand for unskilled labor in the textile sector, especially in the growing area of silk production. By 1663, women constituted 38 percent of all wool workers and 84 percent of all silk workers in Florence.[3] However, throughout the Middle Ages and early modern era, women tended to work at the lowest-paying jobs in the economy. A Pistoian servant girl in 1427 earned about ten florins per year plus board. Her income, including the cost of the food, could have just mounted up to the fifteen florins necessary then to support someone for a year. But salaries at that time were inflated in the wake of the Black Death and would soon drop. In the seventeenth century as well, the women involved in textile production worked at unskilled tasks paying the lowest wages in that industry.[4]

Some working women chose to supplement their meager wages through prostitution, and other women without jobs also chose this means for procuring money. Many a rural migrant girl found that she could not afford the high prices of the city and opted to sell her body in order to put food in her stomach. Married as well as single women found their way into prostitution to augment their incomes or escape destitution. Widows sometimes turned to prostituting themselves. Medieval Florentine magistrates executed pimps preying on widows, as for instance Niccolò di Giunta, who had "with bland and deceptive phrases induced several married women and widows of Florence to lead a life of sin." In the early sixteenth century Florentine magistrates continued to receive accusations against evildoers, male and female, who lured "indigent widows" into selling sex.[5]

Prostitution operated in early modern Tuscany, as elsewhere in early modern Europe, at the intersection of economic exigencies, Christian moral strictures, and gender ideology.[6] Myriad conflicting interests and contradictions emerged. The phenomenon of prostitution in early modern Florence and Pistoia presented a set of vexing problems for the state, for families, and for individual women.

The State

The Florentine state endeavored to accommodate Christianity's repugnance for prostitution. Christianity condemned wanton fornication on the part of both sexes as an abomination in the eyes of God. Prostitution also made a travesty of the Christian woman's ideal role in life, to be a vessel of chastity. Throughout the Middle Ages, state officials hosted honored visiting preachers who lifted their voices in the cathedral and other public shrines to rage against prostitution as sinful and vile.[7] The preachers urged women engaged in prostitution to "convert" to decent ways of living. From at least the thirteenth century on, institutions designed to offer a haven to converted prostitutes sprang up and died out in the environs of Florence. Of all of these, the Monastero delle Convertite had the greatest longevity. In the early fourteenth century the Monastero delle Convertite arose out of a network of relationships between several preachers and the confraternity Santa Maria delle Laudi based at the church of Santo Spirito. It became a potent institutional symbol of the call of conversion in Florence.

Generations of civic leaders attempted to inculcate precepts of gender ideology in their capacity as secular guardians of moral order. Before developing a systematic apparatus for dealing with prostitution in 1403, the Florentine government issued sporadic laws to guard society from the moral pollution that prostitutes could cause.[8] The tenor of this legislation set up a dichotomy between good chaste women, and bad sexually loose females whose presence defiled anything decent or sacred. The two types of females were to be kept apart geographically, forbidden to live in the same neighborhoods, and not accorded equal or simultaneous access to holy sites. Prostitutes had to wear special "signs"—gloves, high-heeled slippers, and bells on their heads—as part of a visual code that distinguished them from respectable women. When prostitutes violated the ordinances, they incurred fines, which produced welcome revenue for the state.[9]

But from the start, Florentine state policy on prostitution grew out of a hodgepodge of inconsistent objectives. While they relegated prostitutes to an inferior status, at no time did the rulers of Florence strive for the complete elimination of prostitution. The financial benefit the state derived from prostitutes' fines pitted the state's interests against the Church's position of exhorting conversion for prostitutes. Even the Church bent doctrine sufficiently to tolerate prostitution under some circumstances, prepared as it was to excuse more readily fornication on the part of males.[10] In order to prevent the debacle of widespread promiscuity among women, a special class of devalued females had to divert men's illicit sexual impulses. Perpetuating the dichotomized classes of females served the government's twin interests: preserving the virtue of citizens' wives and collecting income. Thus both religion and social mores deemed prostitution a necessary evil.

The Florentine state embarked on a new path in the management of prostitution when, in 1403, it established the Onestà magistracy, or Office of Decency. Here we see an early instance of the communal government extending its control over added jurisdictions, as it was increasingly to do in the fifteenth century. The Onestà was the first magistracy in Florence instituted to deal exclusively with sexual morality. Ironically, its mission was to foster prostitution in public brothels as an alternative to sodomy between men. Worried by the drop in population after the plague of 1348, the preachers of the late fourteenth century harangued their audiences about the spreading iniquity of sodomy that deterred men from marriage. Influential Florentines urged the republic's chief executive body, the Signoria, to act on this matter. The Signoria initially envisioned that the new magistracy of the Onestà would concentrate on extirpating the "enormous crime which is the vice of sodomy." But within a few days the Signoria reformulated the mission of the Onestà as the regulation of prostitution.[11]

The new magistracy received a mandate to staff and regulate public brothels. The Onestà, consisting of eight magistrates and their assistants, licensed foreign prostitutes and pimps to come to Florence and ply their trade in three brothel districts. The arrangements between pimps and prostitutes were usually domestic one-to-one bonds, and the majority of prostitutes did not have pimps. Entrepreneurial brothel keepers set up shop in the appointed neighborhoods in rented hostels, which were owned by Florence's greatest families—in one case, by a magistrate of the Onestà. The brothel keepers rented rooms to prostitutes. By 1436 the three brothel districts together offered seventy women to proclaim the pleasures of heterosexuality to the legions of men living in and passing through Florence. Pistoia too had its public brothel.[12]

The Onestà also administered a whole structure of ancillary regulations. In its first year of operation, it set forth the core of a system that would last for the next three centuries, with some important later additions. Prostitutes in Florence, and later in Pistoia and Pisa, were to be licensed and registered by the Onestà. They could not appear in public without wearing the special identifying signs designated by officials of the Onestà. They had to confine themselves to living in the brothel districts and appointed neighborhoods. Prostitutes who violated the ordinances would incur fines, whipping, or ritual humiliation. The Onestà acted as both a regulatory agency and a tribunal that adjudicated disputes involving prostitutes, pimps, and their clients.[13]

In order to recruit and keep the personnel that staffed brothels, the Onestà had to represent more than a slate of restrictions. It offered prostitutes certain protections as well: the right to be in Florence unmolested by other magistracies; immunity from prosecution for debt; and the promise of just treatment. By providing justice to prostitutes, the Onestà flew in the face of canon and Roman law, which denied the harlot's right to complain about wrongs done to her. Prostitutes themselves constituted 80 percent of the plaintiffs bringing complaints to the Onestà. The magistracy attended to the cases of about one hundred women per decade in the fifteenth century. Through their right to bring injustices before the Onestà, prostitutes enjoyed more direct access to the courts than did their respectable female contemporaries, who had to rely on male representatives to bring their causes to court.[14]

In the early sixteenth century, Florentine arbiters of moral life began to question the wisdom of their predecessors in encouraging prostitution. By this point civic authorities had come to regard prostitution as a source of corruption for good women, rather than as a needed counterweight to the lure of sodomy. A rise in population from the midfifteenth century onward may have diminished some of the fears that preachers and civic authorities had concerning sexual relations between men. Instead, they became increasingly agitated to see high dowry rates create a pool of unmarriageable females and to witness the simultaneous expansion of prostitution. Commentators expressed concern about the growing numbers of poor women and servant girls taking up prostitution or procuring. They feared that women of good families who could not find husbands would fall prey to prostitution. People denounced prostitutes for infiltrating respectable quarters of the city and for dressing in a manner "such that they conformed to the good women of the neighborhood, and were indistinguishable [from them]."[15] For the first time in five decades, the situation prompted Florentine lawmakers to act on the issue of prostitutes' dress. In April 1511 Piero Soderini's regime, intensely moralistic and beset by fear of enemies outside Florentine borders, attempted to put its house in order by managing the women of the city. The Soderini government enacted laws compelling prostitutes to adhere to the dress code and regulating dowries. In June 1527 legislation to uphold the dress code and to ensure the registration of prostitutes formed part of the moral reforms promulgated by the newly restored republic eager to implement its pious religious values. Other measures instituting a more stringent regulatory regimen toward prostitution were to follow.[16]

This early-sixteenth-century shift marked another watershed in the regulation of Tuscan prostitution. The anxiety in Tuscany coincided with a pan-European reevaluation of prostitution. In the late fifteenth century increasing moralism and growing fears of contagious diseases prompted civic authorities to start closing municipal brothels. The spread of the horrifying new disease of syphilis in the first half of the sixteenth century intensified the crackdown against prostitution on the part of Catholic and Protestant officials.[17] From 1511 on, the ruling regimes in Florence promulgated law after law and issued frequent demands for diligent enforcement. The state, whether republic or principate, had two intentions, to enhance its regulatory power and to cut back the numbers of prostitutes by promoting conversion. Out of these motivations, a financial partnership was born between the Onestà and the Monastero delle Convertite, and to a lesser extent between the magistracy and the later refuges for *convertite,* the Casa delle Malmaritate and Santa Maria Maddalena. By functioning as repositories for troublesome females, the refuges aided the government in its quest for order. The fines and taxes the Onestà levied on prostitutes in Florence, Pistoia, and Pisa in turn helped to finance the refuges that facilitated conversion.[18] Although a certain oddity may appear in the spectacle of a state licensing prostitution and then using prostitutes' fines and taxes to fund the reform of harlots, the system found echoes in Renaissance cultural assumptions. This approach reflected the bifurcated theology of Catholicism, a framework that rested as much on sin as on absolution. A minor tradition in canon law had always justified the use of prostitutes' ill-gotten gains for good causes such as giving alms or paying the tithe.[19]

Prostitutes found themselves confronted by a series of behavioral and fiscal constraints. Similar to a requirement that Pope Leo X had decreed for Roman prostitutes in 1520, the Florentine inheritance law of 1553 stipulated that throughout the dominion one quarter of the estate of a deceased prostitute must go to support the Monastero delle Convertite. Administrators of the convent complained that income from prostitutes' estates trickled in slowly at first. But some prostitutes did comply with the stipulation, employing in their wills the common formula for religious bequests with a slight variation at the end: "For the love of God and repose of her soul . . . and according to the statutes of the city of Florence."[20] In 1577, two years after the apostolic visitors had brought the full force of the Counter Reformation to Tuscany, and a few months after the archbishop had issued an antiprostitution directive, the Onestà undertook an internal revamping meant to sharpen its efficiency. The reform of the magistracy may have come at the urging of ecclesiastical officials eager to root out vice. It was also certainly a continuation of policies begun not long before by the first of the grand dukes, Cosimo I, to strengthen the state and its bureaucracies.[21]

The Onestà's all-encompassing Reform of 1577 codified policies that had been in effect in the recent past and established others anew. It required that prostitutes henceforth assemble for their annual roll call at the traditional Lenten sermon on Mary Magdalen, so that the event would also serve as an opportunity for conversion. Public prostitutes had to pay taxes every four months, and in order to be on the streets at night, they had to buy "bulletins" valid for fifteen days. The Monastero delle Convertite received a portion of the income from taxes and bulletins.[22] A rule barred prostitutes from riding in coaches and carriages, new status symbols then gaining in popularity. The sixteenth-century Florentine learned gentleman Scipione Ammirato complained that even Cleopatra had not ridden about in carriages as brazenly as did the prostitutes of Florence. Henceforth, if prostitutes dared to employ the vehicles, they were liable for punitive fines, which went in part to the Monastero delle Convertite.[23] Throughout the next century the magistracy tried in principle and in individual cases to implement more rigorous punishments than ever before: eviction, incarceration in the Stinche prison, institutional confinement, confiscation, and exile.[24]

In echoing the Church's hue and cry for conversion, the government owed *converted* prostitutes liberation from the regulations of the Onestà and cancellation of the stigma of being listed as a public prostitute. When a prostitute demonstrated that she had reformed, she could arrange to be removed from the registers of the Onestà.[25] Writing to the grand duke in 1558, the chancellor of the Onestà had noted the "custom" of cancellation and observed that it had no legal basis. He requested and obtained a new law of 1558 articulating the policy. In the past, the chancellor explained, prostitutes wishing to be canceled from the registers had to supply proof that they had been confessed, and then had to undergo probation. In the future, just supplying proof of confession and communion would no longer suffice, because, as a ducal counselor stated, "these simple guarantees they bring in nowadays are usually counterfeit, and they can't be believed."[26] Prostitutes would also have to produce three witnesses to certify their reformed behavior. The Onestà would investigate on its own and clear the women if they persevered for six months.[27] The magistracy particularly wanted to restore married prostitutes to a state of virtuous monogamous wedlock, and within a decade it reiterated the cancellation policy especially for them. They were subject to the same conditions and to verification by "respectable neighbors."[28]

Though girded by the most fervent intentions, the Florentine officials encountered abundant dilemmas in enforcing their new policies. With the explosion in the number of prostitutes, the magistrates faced the basic problem of "who is a *meretrice,* or prostitute, and who is not?" Early modern Tuscans recognized several variations on the general term *meretrice*. They spoke of streetwalkers (*cantoniere*), brothel prostitutes (*meretrici in postribulo*), parlor whores (*donne di partito*), and courtesans (*cortigiane*). But did the erring weaver's wife judged to be a "whore" (*puttana*) by the Otto di Guardia in 1503 merit one of those classifications? In some cases the court decided that such women did deserve the same treatment as registered prostitutes and meted out punishment accordingly, while in other cases it exonerated them. Eventually the magistrates had to decide if loose-living wives and spinsters were to be counted as public prostitutes. Tuscan men and women could leave anonymous denunciations of reputed prostitutes in a drum. The Onestà would then investigate by examining witnesses, including those accused women summoned to their defense. The civic governors had to develop criteria for distinguishing between good and bad women. Duty impelled them to try to prevent honorable females from turning into dishonorable ones.[29]

Social critics castigated prostitutes for presenting poor role models to other women. The notion of an influential model made a deep impression on educated Tuscans schooled in the humanist veneration for the models of antiquity. The seventeenth-century Florentine magistrate and legal scholar Marc'Antonio Savelli boasted that Florentine regulation of prostitution followed a classical Roman precedent. For Savelli, tutored in Roman and canon law, the idea of the model carried over to the persons of prostitutes. Women who sold themselves for money could justifiably be evicted from neighborhoods on the grounds that they paraded a "bad example," according to Savelli.[30] By the early seventeenth century, civic leaders had ample reason to worry about "bad examples," because the one to two hundred registered prostitutes in the city tended by then to be native Florentines or Tuscans and not, like their fifteenth-century counterparts, migrants from foreign territories.[31] The magistrates of the Onestà, whether drawing from the humanist notion of classical models or from the older tradition of Christian exemplars, voiced views similar to Savelli's. They bemoaned the fact that "the example and bad habits of a few often do harm to many." The authorities said of prostitutes that it was as if

> they are enamored of living indecently . . . and thus want to grow in number and be imitated by others. . . . Today, these prostitutes live in the most honorable and frequented streets of the city . . . without restraint, a thing that with time could infest the good women.[32]

In this case the Christian and humanist positive topos of imitation is reversed. The contagion of the model could be checked only by closing off intimacy and communication. Scandalous women would be removed from respectable neighborhoods so that upstanding people could not "hear or see the shameful, indecent things done by prostitutes."[33]

The civic authorities worried about innocent females who might "fall into trouble" and inadvertently cross the line into prostitution. They recognized the paradoxical role of the Onestà, an office that by its definition legitimized prostitution and yet could not be allowed to encourage the phenomenon too much.[34] The magistrates of the Onestà understood that by recruiting pimps and prostitutes, their predecessors bore at least partial responsibility for the problem of increased prostitution. Conscience sometimes moved those in charge to question the assumptions and mission of the Onestà. In 1520 Florentine leaders had tried to clear the city of all pimps.[35] In 1558 they pondered what to do about female pimps: "We do not know which procuresses (*ruffiane*) to tolerate in order to avoid a greater ill, and which ones we should condemn and punish." The government decided that it would continue to license procuresses who actually ran brothels. But it decreed penalties for "those persons who lead astray girls and women who are not already public prostitutes registered with the Onestà."[36]

Officials had to assess in a number of circumstances if young girls had lost their presumed innocence and gone over the brink into prostitution. After the Onestà's Reform of 1577, prostitutes incurred heavy penalties if the magistracy determined that they employed as servants young girls who were not themselves registered as prostitutes. The magistrates had imposed this condition in order to ward off corruption of the young. Some prostitutes adopted a similar preventive outlook toward their own daughters and tried to put them in the Monastero delle Convertite or elsewhere to protect them.[37] However, the inheritance law of 1553 forbade admission to the Monastero delle Convertite of any women other than converted prostitutes. In practice, officials of church and state may have interpreted the stipulation broadly; to them, it meant the convent should admit only females "of shameless ways," a description of wide latitude that could encompass even the youngest wayward girl. By 1647, administrators of the Monastero delle Convertite requested governmental help in stopping a flow of young girls into the refuge. The youthful entrants claimed to be prostitutes but did not appear in the Onestà's taxation records. Although the ducal government responded by reaffirming the policy that only officially recognized prostitutes could enter the Monastero delle Convertite, it left much confusion in its wake as to whether the girls were indeed prostitutes in a private or a public sense.[38]

Disputes arose over whether a woman with only one lover should be considered a prostitute. In 1639 a revision of the edict on carriages sought to include among the prostitutes subject to the ordinance all females of "bad reputation." It extended to "any woman of indecent ways, so long as it seems that publicly or secretly she gives her body to another, even to only one person."[39] The contemporary jurist Savelli found this inclusive tenor harsher than Roman or canon law. He disapproved of labeling every woman in love a prostitute, particularly feeling that the charge should not be applied to patrician women. Even if a noblewoman should prostitute herself, according to law she did not deserve to lose her privileges, he explained. Savelli believed that women who took one lover should often be excused, owing to the innate frailty of their sex. A number of decades earlier, in one case before the Otto di Guardia, magistrates had dismissed charges for unlicensed prostitution because they thought the woman fragile and easily persuaded, and their successors may have continued to reason in that vein. Savelli, the precise jurist, while no sympathizer with prostitution, did not like to see extreme labels flung about loosely. He said that to apply the title of "prostitute" ubiquitously would only mean that "there would be more prostitutes than honorable women."[40] For him, honor was not an objective quality dependent on bodily sexual purity. Rather, it was a judgment of worth and status to be subjectively and subtly manipulated. Women might retain degrees of honor or good reputation even while behaving contrary to the sexual prescriptions of their society.

Civic and religious leaders wrung their hands over the number of married women involved in prostitution. Marriage, thought certain medieval canonists and popes, should offer women a means of avoiding or escaping prostitution. The patrons of refuges for wayward women expected to be able to find men willing to marry their charges and in many cases succeeded.[41] But in practice, marriage did not necessarily mean an end to prostitution. In the sixteenth century, governmental officials determined that married and widowed prostitutes should be registered with the Onestà in the same way as other prostitutes, and simultaneously be encouraged to return to "living decently." Lay activists founded the Casa delle Malmaritate in 1579 to specialize in converting married prostitutes. To the seventeenth-century ducal counselors, it seemed that a new policy was needed. In an ordinance of 1633 they ordered the Onestà to eliminate from its licensees any married prostitutes, so that those women would no longer be able to evade prosecution for adultery. They prohibited the Onestà from registering married women in the future. The criminal magistracy, the Otto di Guardia, followed through in implementing the more rigorous policy by prosecuting eight women for adultery in 1633.[42]

Grand Duke Ferdinando II, Archbishop Pietro Nicolini, and many clerics, however, came to feel that the ordinance of 1633 had been a mistake. It did not achieve its objective of spurring married prostitutes to convert. The result was spiritual and temporal scandal and financial loss for the Monastero delle Convertite. So in 1635 the government reversed itself and decreed that all married prostitutes must in fact register with the Onestà and submit to its regulations, this being the greater penalty for them. The state exhorted married harlots to retire from their lives of profligacy. Otherwise, notwithstanding the married prostitutes' registration with the Onestà, the Otto di Guardia could prosecute them for adultery either on charges brought by their husbands or ex officio.[43]

This reversal did not dispel the chaos characterizing the married prostitute's legal status in Tuscany. Experts on law noted contradictions regarding her standing within the authoritative legal corpus and between codified law and magisterial practice. Despite the fiat of 1635 declaring married prostitutes subject to prosecution for adultery, magistrates in the midseventeenth century did not press to enforce the letter or spirit of the ordinance. In 1673 the government amplified the law of 1635 to enable family members as well as husbands to initiate proceedings against adulteresses.[44]

Yet the supplemental edict seems to have done little to alter the situation. Eight years later the legal scholar Savelli concluded in disgust: "In Florence, they punish no married prostitutes of whatever sort. When these women register at the Office of Decency (which rather should be called the Office of Indecency), they cannot, according to common opinion, be accused or bothered by their husbands and relatives."[45] Perhaps both relatives and magistrates avoided delving deeply into the affairs of the married prostitute: too many sensitive chords could be struck. Prostitution might seem to be not a sin but a rational strategy, necessary along with marriage, for women to make economic ends meet. Families' complicity in prostitution could come to painful light. Or the equally troubling question might arise of why an aristocratic woman who partook in illicit liaisons deserved treatment any different from that of the plebeian streetwalker.

In addition to its difficulties in identifying and controlling prostitutes, the Florentine state had to cope with a constant barrage of pressure from the Monastero delle Convertite. The convent had a stake in having as many prostitutes as possible on the registers of the Onestà, in order to collect income from them. Throughout the sixteenth and seventeenth centuries, a series of appeals emanated from the Monastero delle Convertite requesting that more and more women be added to the registers or at least made subject to the magistracy's regulations. In 1559 the Monastero delle Convertite sought to extend the provisions of the inheritance law of 1553 to women "of bad reputation in the public eye" who were not yet listed with the Onestà. To benefit the Monastero delle Convertite, the Onestà proposed in 1625 that the state "tax . . . the unregistered prostitutes, who have today multiplied to a much greater number than the registered ones." The grand duke approved these requests, and in 1653 and 1665 he commanded officials of the Onestà to execute the laws vigilantly and to ignore any "protections" the women claimed.[46]

The state's interest in distinguishing between good and bad females was in fact undermined, because women could shield themselves from the Onestà's regulations. They could acquire two forms of protection: cancellation and immunities. Fiscal needs had forced the state into selling immunities. After the Monastero delle Convertite succeeded in extending the inheritance law like a net, the convent later requested in 1559 that unregistered prostitutes pay a new tax in exchange for certain immunities. Two purposes would be served: unregistered prostitutes would not go unpunished, and the Monastero delle Convertite could garner appreciated income. By paying the tax, suspect women could avoid wearing the prostitute's signs and could live in any quarter, as long as their neighbors tolerated them. The ducal administrators determined that suspect women should pay the Onestà's *traditional* tax for registered prostitutes, while retaining their immunities. The authorities intended to add the promiscuous women to the official registers in a gradual fashion.[47]

Once the state began granting immunities, the practice spread. In 1614 the nuns of the Monastero delle Convertite alerted Grand Duke Cosimo II of their awareness that the Onestà had a list of women it planned to register, both to purge particular neighborhoods and to raise the tax intake. Looking out for their cut of the taxes, the nuns urged the government to proceed with caution. Since the designated women were not already registered as public prostitutes subject to travel restrictions, they would be free to leave the duchy to evade paying. Others, the nuns feared, would retreat and live with men or with their husbands as a trick, but would in any case continue their scandalous ways. No governmental agent, they warned, would succeed in collecting the taxes; this reform would fall only on the shoulders of poor prostitutes who were not squeamish about being in the public stews. Instead, the convent asked the grand duke to impose a fee of twenty scudi, for one time only, to be paid for the favor of erasure from the list. The nuns stipulated that the money be paid directly to the abbess of the Monastero delle Convertite. Women who did not supplicate for the favor would become subject to the laws of the Onestà.[48]

By 1625, suspect women could pay a new tax of two scudi every four months to free themselves from harassment by agents of the Onestà or other magistracies; they would remain unregistered and immune from most regulations of the Onestà.[49] A percentage of the new taxes went to the Monastero delle Convertite. In 1638 the government conceded that registered and unregistered prostitutes could purchase licenses making them immune from the prohibition against riding in carriages. Those licenses too produced income for the Monastero delle Convertite. Prostitutes and suspect women generally handed over a few scudi for a half year's privileges, but some like Margherita Negri gave the convent a lump sum of sixty scudi for a lifetime immunity from the regulations of the Onestà. She paid an amount equivalent to the lowest-grade dowry necessary for becoming a nun at the Monastero delle Convertite, for what was a similar investment, the right to pursue a preferred way of life.[50] The state continued to grant tax dispensations to individual prostitutes who paid special fees to the convent. Notations of payments by "privileged women" and "favors" (*gratie*) abounded in the seventeenth-century records of the Monastero delle Convertite and the Onestà. The sixteenth-century ducal successes in reforming the judicial system by cutting off the flow of *gratie* had not persisted into the subsequent century, at least not in matters pertaining to prostitution.[51]

The accumulation of immunities invalidated the code the Florentines had devised for distinguishing between worthy and disreputable women. First, recognition of the difference between true virtue and sin gave way to an emphasis on the illusion of virtue. Unlike medieval ordinances that unequivocally ordered prostitutes to keep their polluting presence far from holy sites, similar legislation of the midsixteenth century contained a new exception: "[prostitutes] can be tolerated residing even within a hundred yards of monasteries if they live in apparent modesty and decency." This focus on appearances was in keeping with the perspective of that quintessential Florentine strategist of public policy, Niccolò Machiavelli, who advised, "Everybody sees what you appear to be, few feel what you are."[52] But as the later immunities evolved, not even maintaining the appearance of virtue mattered anymore, so long as income could be made from women's lapses. The integrity of the system had broken down. It was corrupt as a moral code and as a vehicle for teaching gender ideology; it was also unjust in favoring rich prostitutes. The authorities acknowledged the ethical bankruptcy of their system. They constantly suspected that prostitutes' conversions were fraudulent and set up a mechanism for undoing the cancellation process.[53] The state and its female subjects engaged in an elaborate game, one that offered many opportunities for prostitutes to dodge the tentacles of state control extending toward them.

Although the Florentine state attempted to respond to the problem of growing prostitution, in the end its policies had little efficacy. Some of the difficulty lay in the institutional weakness of the magistracy. A slate of eight magistrates, four of whom rotated out of office every six months, and a staff of eight did not constitute a bureau that could fully supervise the activities of hundreds of registered and suspected prostitutes. In 1649 the permanent bureaucrats of the Onestà echoed a complaint they had made seven years earlier, that the magistrates who rotated in and out of office did not adequately fulfill their duties. To avoid creating ill will among their fellow citizens, the magistrates shirked the task of investigating charges against suspect women, "even the most notorious prostitutes."[54] Things had not improved much in terms of magisterial pursuit of duty since the previous century, when one official of the Otto di Guardia had explained his laxness in policing his fellow citizens by acknowledging, "When I am finished with my term in office, I want to be able to go home at nights without being wounded or murdered."[55] The financial solvency of the Monastero delle Convertite, however, depended on the funds that came by way of prostitutes. To boost the income flowing to the Monastero delle Convertite, the bureaucrats sought and obtained the power to authorize investigations and new registrations on their own, bypassing the magistrates. In such a context, Tuscany's grand duke must have readily understood the motivation behind a memorandum he received from an official of the convent or the government. The memo urged the duke, in the interest of greater efficiency and for the benefit of the Monastero delle Convertite, to diminish or eradicate the Onestà's role as a middleman.[56]

For Tuscan civic leaders, the whole course of the seventeenth century brought increasing frustration as they proved unable to enforce the laws on prostitution. Despite the state's attempt to stigmatize and reduce prostitution from the sixteenth century on, leading citizens still saw it as something that had to be tolerated "in order to avoid the worst." Perhaps because of the displacement of burgher respectability by a looser courtly morality as the ethos at the top of society, the clientele of prostitutes appeared to include a greater proportion of patrician men than it had in previous centuries. One moralist wrote: "The most noble and respectable men [have] commerce with these infamous women . . . and freely, yea shamelessly, [go] into their houses in broad daylight."[57]

By 1670 the important inheritance law, last renewed in 1619, had long "gone into oblivion," and its champions in the government called in desperation for concerted efforts to revive its observance. The next year officials of the Onestà disclosed that the sale of bulletins for nightwalking yielded the Monastero delle Convertite little revenue, although this income "once was considerable," and similarly, that a laughably small number of licenses for riding in carriages had been sold that year—five! Grand Duke Cosimo III agreed, among other measures, to reduce the prices of licenses for riding in carriages so that prostitutes could manage to purchase them. The Monastero delle Convertite, needing to build "capital" in 1672, asked the government, as it had in the past, to send deputies to collect taxes from Florentine prostitutes who had fled to other cities in the duchy. In 1680 the criminal magistracy, the Otto di Guardia, assumed the dwindling responsibilities of the Onestà.[58]

Reviewing the century in 1681, the jurist Marc'Antonio Savelli unleashed a tirade on how the laws had been abused and ignored in his time. Great numbers of married and single prostitutes swarmed everywhere, tempting women and men, the jurist wrote. He noted with distress that the Onestà issued licenses bestowing immunity from its own regulations. Perhaps, Savelli concurred, it is necessary to tolerate *unmarried* prostitutes in order to avoid greater ills, but these women must be made to obey the laws. To Savelli and certain of his concerned contemporaries, it was unconscionable to excuse neglect of the laws as custom or corruption. Theirs remained a faint voice. Despite subsequent attempts to implement the regulations, prostitution continued to thrive in Tuscany until 1780, when Grand Duke Pietro Leopoldo adopted a Draconian stance by attempting to ban all public prostitutes from the duchy, with the sole exception of the port of Livorno.[59]

The Family

Prostitution in Florence and its subject cities not only challenged the state; it strained family relationships as well. Civic authorities knew that women's relatives and husbands sometimes forced them into prostitution. Court records detail cases like that of Maddalena Gonelli, a seventeenth-century termagant of a procuress. She had her daughter Marietta wed in order to prostitute her more easily, locking out and chasing away with blows the new son-in-law as soon as possible.[60] Or families so mistreated daughters, wives, widows, and other female kin that the victims took flight and turned to prostitution when they had no other recourse.

Yet in the formulation of official policy, lawmakers took a rather one-sided view of prostitutes' relationships with their relatives. While aware that some women might prostitute themselves at their husbands' insistence, they saw almost all the potential damage as coming from the prostitutes.[61] The law of 1577 barring the employment of young girls or boys as servants in prostitutes' homes sought to prevent disreputable women from corrupting members of their own families.[62] Legislators and citizens believed that the stigma of prostitution blemished a woman's relatives as well as herself.[63] This sentiment appeared in an edict of 1688 seeking to prevent prostitutes from residing in

unauthorized areas of Florence and corrupting "decent persons." The measure aimed "to remove the occasion for honorable women [*donne onorate*] to
follow the sentinel of vice and offend the Madonna and their own honor and
that of their families."[64] Accordingly, the lawmakers aimed in part to protect
the honor of plebeian and patrician families, by keeping daughters from selling their bodies and by limiting prostitution so as not to tempt sons to expend
themselves and their patrimonies on wanton women. Yet whatever a prostitute's relatives may have felt they were owed in recompense for social shame,
they were not to interfere with the portions of prostitutes' estates due the
Monastero delle Convertite. Relatives did assert their claims. In 1617 Girolamo Stiattesi, a prostitute's widower, extracted from the Monastero delle
Convertite his share of his wife's estate, which the convent had taken, thinking him dead. Piera Martini, a prostitute's sister, retrieved confiscated property from Santa Maria Maddalena so as to furnish her own marital dowry.[65]

The possibility of conversion drew the attention not just of the prostitute
herself, but also of her family. In 1603 a cutler in Grosseto stabbed his wife, a
prostitute, for having reneged on her promise to reform. Roman law supported the rights of relatives to compel prostitutes to reform.[66] When relatives
sometimes sought the institutionalization of wayward women, Tuscan state
officials consented on the basis of a communal statute from the fourteenth
century stipulating that "relatives can arrange incarceration of kin behaving
immorally." Although this statute was usually employed against delinquent
sons, authorities occasionally permitted its use regarding unruly females.
They did so in a case of 1659, granting the request of Salvestro da Uzano that
his sister, a middle-aged widow and registered prostitute, be interned in the
Mendicanti poorhouse.[67] The ordinance of 1673 specifically amplified the law
on married prostitutes so that relatives—especially fathers, brothers, and
paternal and maternal uncles—in addition to husbands could initiate proceedings against such women for adultery.[68]

A family of the upper or middle strata of Tuscan society was likely to
characterize the presence of a whoring female in its midst as "dishonor."[69] The
implications of such association with a reputed whore could be similar for
patrician or plebeian families: diminishment of prestige in the community,
possible loss of access to patronage, lessened chances of making advantageous
alliances with other families, and intrusion by the government into the family
patrimony through the state's claims to a quarter of the prostitute's property
at death. The stakes of finance and privilege were greater among patrician
families, but we cannot say that patricians felt more strongly than plebeian
families about the moral considerations involved when a female relative prostituted herself. Families from all social levels might wish to disown or punish
misbehaving female kin, although they did not universally feel this way. Both
patrician and plebeian families may have used the apparatus of church or state
to get their wayward female members into the refuges for *convertite*. When
prostitutes did enter the refuges, they found a sympathetic recognition of the
complexities of familial interaction. Especially at the Casa delle Malmaritate,

administrators understood, better than civic leaders seemed to, that the chances were as likely that relatives had caused a woman's fall as that she had dishonored a wholesome hearth. The administrators there felt that they should not return a woman to her relatives, "if one sees that they made her fall into trouble."[70]

The Women

Involvement in prostitution did not offer women a smooth path in life. The woman suspected of being a whore lost face and rank in the civic arena. For the magistrate and jurist Marc'Antonio Savelli, registered prostitutes were "marked off from other honorable women . . . [and] stripped of honor." In Tuscan ritual life, the prostitute played a public role as a symbolic presence who polluted others. Medieval Florentines paraded prostitutes past enemies' gates as a form of disrespect, and for the same reason had a condemned heretic march through the brothel district on his way to execution.[71] The registered prostitute occupied a marginal legal position. While prostitutes enjoyed freer access to the judicial system than did most women, they were also denied certain legal rights that other females possessed. One law of 1675 banned prostitutes but not other female travelers from staying at inns.[72] Prostitutes often suffered from persecution by rowdy youths, neighbors trying to oust them, and police of different magistracies competing to arrest or manhandle them. Many prostitutes figured as victims in the cases of rape that came before the Otto di Guardia in the seventeenth century. The Onestà operated with a notable lack of secrecy, and the names of registered or suspected prostitutes could become fodder for gossip in a society that counted reputation foremost.[73] Despite concern on the part of authorities to avoid impoverishing prostitutes, a life of selling one's body might mean meager subsistence and constant indebtedness.[74] Officials of the Onestà said that only the unregistered prostitutes had property; the registered prostitutes were "like the snail," owning so little they could carry it on their backs.[75] They divided prostitutes into three classes: the comfortable, women of mediocre status, and the poor, those of the first condition being the fewest in number.[76] The woman who prostituted herself risked becoming a spiritual outcast. Ever reviled, the figure of the prostitute was the target for countless moral fanatics and crusaders.

What was at stake for a woman engaged in prostitution vis-à-vis her immediate socioeconomic relationships in her community? If relatives and neighbors disapproved of her behavior, she might lose financial support from her family or the chance to make a good marriage. Certain convents would not accept her, since convents sometimes encountered censure from magistrates if they received females "of bad reputation." Girls and women known to be whores could not easily obtain jobs as servants. They "have difficulty finding gentlewomen who want them in the house," the founders of the Casa delle Malmaritate said.[77]

But involvement in prostitution did not necessarily wreck a woman's life or place in her community. Families were not always opposed. Pimping and prostitution often went together as a family enterprise. Some patrician families condoned female members' illicit liaisons with well-placed men in exchange for some form of social privilege. Known prostitutes could be popular with and perhaps protected by their neighbors. Involvement in prostitution did not prevent a woman from earning additional income through work in the textile trade, other piecework, or vending. Some prostitutes got along quite comfortably in economic terms, and, as we have seen in the case of fourteenth-century Angela, they may have preferred the monetary profits of sin to other modes of acquiring income. Professional or occasional prostitution was not inevitably an intolerable way of life for a Florentine or Pistoian woman. The founders of the Casa delle Malmaritate perceived a wide gulf between the social status of the known "public" prostitute registered with the Onestà and that of the "secret" or "hidden" prostitute whose activity remained unknown to the world. Especially if a woman could keep her illicit activity secret—admittedly a hard task in the intimate early modern civic environment—she might be able to avoid the social drawbacks of prostitution.[78]

Just as prostitution gained notoriety in sixteenth- and seventeenth-century Europe, so did the idea of conversion for prostitutes. Public awareness and concern vastly inflated the figure of the reformed whore, an image in the cultural domain since the time of the medieval orders of penitent prostitutes. For Catholic reformers before and after the Council of Trent, Mary Magdalen became a favorite symbol. She personified the moral regeneration of the Church itself, as well as a reborn commitment to faith on the part of the individual believer. To clergy and laypersons alike, the converted prostitute was a symbol of wider societal controversies about conversion and the allegiance of Catholic, Protestant, or non-Christian believers. In these centuries artists undertook countless commissions for patrons fascinated with Mary Magdalen's dual attributes of sensuality and spirituality. Literary themes centering on conversion found increasing popularity with audiences. The figures of the prostitute and the converted prostitute inspired both moral treatises exhorting repentance and satirical literature. A seventeenth-century Italian casuistical treatise contained a chapter entitled "Men Who Die Impenitent Because of Excessive Attachment to Whores." In 1633 a Florentine publisher printed Giulio Guazzini's poetic tract, *The heroic and Christian conversion of Maria Lunga, known as Carrettina, a famous Florentine prostitute. A sinner for more then twenty years, she gave away all that she had to Godly causes, in penitence for her sins. And then she retired to serve the miserable women in the pesthouse.* Later that same year, the author performed the rhetorician's trick of reversal and issued his *Palinode in retraction of the praises written about Maria Lunga.* As civic governments looking for answers to the problem of prostitution turned their hopes toward the refuges for *convertite,* some of the art works and published and private writings of the era also drew attention to the institutions and fired the public imagination about them.[79]

A Profile of Ex-Prostitutes in Two Refuges

	Monastero delle Convertite (1614–1700)		Santa Maria Maddalena (1603–1687)	
	Number	Sample[a]	Number	Sample
Origins				
Tuscany	12 (75%)	16	36 (86%)	37
Other Italian	3 (19%)	16	1 (14%)	37
Foreign	1 (6%)	16	0 (0%)	37
Married or widowed	10 (11%)	87	9 (21%)	43
Have children	0 (0%)	87	1 (2%)	43
Have benefactors or guarantors	28 (32%)	87	9 (21%)	43
Average age at entrance	24 yrs	32	24 yrs	9
Average age at death	62 yrs	22	57 yrs	11

SOURCES: Compiled from Acquisti e Doni 230:4 Ricordi; volumes of Debitori e Creditori, CS126:51–58; CS191:10 Memorie; CS191:35 Fogli; and CS191:36 Fogli.

[a]The "sample" is the number of cases for which particular information is available.

Voluntarily or involuntarily, many prostitutes did end up in the refuges for *convertite*. The records of the Monastero delle Convertite and Santa Maria Maddalena convey general characteristics of the ex-prostitutes who at times filled the refuges to capacity (see table). In the early fifteenth century the Onestà's recruitment policy had more than half filled Florence's brothels with non-Italian women, but by the sixteenth century almost all the city's registered prostitutes were from northern Italy.[80] The *convertite,* coming from the ranks of registered and unregistered prostitutes, were also predominantly Italian and in large proportion Tuscan. Santa Maria Maddalena drew more than 50 percent of its residents from the environs of Pistoia and Florence. The *convertite* came from the respectable lower orders of Tuscan society. Their fathers had occupations such as mattress maker, footman, wood carver/ mason, and soldier. The *convertite* themselves left no indication of having done work other than prostitution, although some probably had tried various ways of securing a living. Contemporaries did not think it unusual for women to engage in both prostitution and other forms of wage earning. Michel de Montaigne, on a visit to Florence in 1581, noted in his journal that if a prostitute wanted to live outside the run-down lodgings available in the streets reserved for such females, she "must perform some other trade for concealment."[81] One in six of the women represented in the sample from the two refuges had been married. Perhaps typically, one *convertita* at Santa Maria Maddalena had a husband known as "il Meschino," or "Poor Shabby Fellow." Like the prostitutes of earlier centuries, very few of these women left evidence of having had children.[82] From a fifth to a third of the women in the sample had their paths to conversion eased by benefactors, who might be former lovers, charitable donors, or the state.

A little more than half (53 percent) of the *convertite* in the sample took up residence in the refuges between the ages of fifteen and twenty-five. Only a small number of prostitutes joined the communities at midlife, as if entering an old-age retirement home. The founders of the Casa delle Malmaritate wanted to reform and rehabilitate young women, and they discouraged admission of older prostitutes. Even at the Monastero delle Convertite, which as a convent was more likely to take in women of all ages, the administrators believed that older women could not easily adapt to the religious life. Women lived for long periods in the institutions, dying in their sixties and beyond.[83]

A look at individual cases can inform us as to why and how prostitutes enrolled in the refuges for *convertite*. Some women turned to the refuges because they grew weary of harassment by the Onestà. The registered prostitute Caterina Salvetti had a history of running into trouble with the Onestà. She figured in three separate cases in the year 1640. In one instance, the Onestà charged that Caterina had permitted a sixteen-year-old girl to live in her home, in violation of the statutes. Although Caterina helped the girl obtain a dowry and enter the Monastero delle Convertite, the magistracy still condemned her to be whipped and to pay a steep fine of twenty-five scudi. A few months later the Onestà levied on her a fine of two scudi for having been out at night without a bulletin. By the end of the 1640s, Caterina decided to try life in the Monastero delle Convertite. After one balked attempt, she entered in 1650 with the help of a benefactor, Signor Filippo Castellani. As a nun, Caterina adapted well, living in the Monastero delle Convertite in comfort for eleven years; at her death she bequeathed funds to start a chapel of Saint Catherine in the convent.[84]

Officials of the state, at their own initiative or at the request of families, sometimes coerced women into entering the refuges. The prostitute Margherita Pistorozzi from the countryside of Pistoia terminated troubles with the law by settling in Santa Maria Maddalena. She had formerly been in the refuge at its inception in 1604, stayed for a year or two, and then departed to return to her natal family. In 1613 Margherita offended the authorities and found herself in jail in Pistoia. Grand Duke Cosimo II's territorial government offered to absolve her, if she would accept admission to Santa Maria Maddalena and become a nun. A sponsor's donation of a dowry and oil, and perhaps also the presence of a sister in the convent, persuaded Margherita to agree to the proposition. The illiterate former prostitute enthusiastically embraced religious commitments, beginning with the habit of the Third Order of Saint Francis and progressing to the status of professed nun. Twenty-four years after her arrival, she served as the ministeress, or mother superior, of the convent.[85]

Other women, speaking for themselves or through intermediaries, emphasized spiritual reasons for seeking admission to the refuges. This was true of Maria Maddalena Niccolaini, a teenage prostitute originally from Livorno and bereft of her father, who sought admission to Santa Maria Maddalena in the mid- or late seventeenth century. Her entrance petition, which was probably inked onto paper by a cleric, described her as being "given over to a life of sensuality and sin," and on the verge of bringing about the damnation of her own soul and the souls of others who sinned with her. But as a Christian she heard "the continual pangs of conscience and knew that she would not be able to save her soul without changing her way of life." The Italian phrase used for "changing her way of life" was *mutar' vita,* which appeared as well in devotional texts concerning the conversion of prostitutes, including the convent's own constitutions. The girl begged Santa Maria Maddalena's administrators not to abandon her and to permit her to "live and die there repenting her sins." A male "friend" promised to contribute money for a dowry and expenses. Maria Maddalena asked the convent to grant her acceptance soon so that she would not lose the charitable offer, without which she had no hope of converting, since she had no property and as a consequence would always have to remain in the hands of the Devil to survive. The emphasis on sin and repentance in the petition may have been composed by a clergyman, but we still sense this young girl's lack of wherewithal, and her desire to leave the life of prostitution.[86]

Some women may have decided to enter the refuges because of financial incentives. They could take advantage of certain benefits available to them only if they converted and entered refuges. *Convertite* often received monetary aid from private benefactors or the state, and the refuges offered reductions in dowry rates for prostitutes who decided to enter on the day of the Lenten sermon on Mary Magdalen. In April 1669, Signor Dottore Pompilio Ticciati made an ample donation to Maria Maddalena Buontempi on the condition that she retire from her "immorality" (*mala vita*) and become a nun in the Monastero delle Convertite.[87] Tommasa Cerchiai resided at the Monastero delle Convertite as a servant for several weeks in 1626 while awaiting admission at the reduced dowry rate that prevailed on the day of the sermon.[88] From its foundation in the late sixteenth century, the Casa delle Malmaritate attracted converted prostitutes who sometimes entered on the day of the sermon and even transferred from that institution to the Monastero delle Convertite.[89] The refuges had various ways of aiding with financing in order to encourage prostitutes to enter. When the donation intended for the seventeenth-century *convertita* Margherita Giardinieri failed to materialize, the Monastero delle Convertite found a remedy. The convent located gentlewomen who contributed the dowry, enabling the twenty-three-year-old "parlor prostitute" to put on a novice nun's habit. Later Margherita sued her onetime lover, Lodovico Catastini, who had borrowed her money and sworn to help her get into the convent, only to revoke his pledge when he himself took religious orders.[90]

Numerous private donors promised support for prostitutes desirous of living the converted life in the refuges, and they generally fulfilled their obligations. The patrician benefactor of Suor Celeste Costa, a reformed prostitute, gave her a yearly allowance beginning in 1671 and left a copy of the pledge with his will to prevent his relatives from contesting it. Understandably, many women seized these opportunities for security and peace of mind. Some prospered in the refuges as a result. Suor Bartolomea Leonora Corsini, a *convertita* in the Monastero delle Convertite, received annual donations from a nobleman and another benefactor for twenty-six years. At her death she left legacies for the convent's confessor and for windows in its church.[91]

The institutions represented a sought-after refuge for some would-be *convertite*, but other prostitutes may have felt that they could maneuver more freely and with greater happiness in the outside world. Illustrative of the latter possibility is the history of Margherita Negri, whom we have encountered purchasing a lifetime immunity from prosecution by the Onestà. She was a sometime prostitute who supported other women in their desire to live in the refuges for *convertite*. Margherita had worked in the Monastero delle Convertite in the mid-1620s as a servant. In 1639 she paid the convent sixty scudi to obtain the lifetime immunity enabling her to ride in coaches and not otherwise be bothered by the Onestà. Margherita must have prospered and enjoyed a life filled with many coach rides, because we next meet her as a benefactor for an entrant to the Monastero delle Convertite—Marta, the daughter or wife of the coachman Francesco. In 1643 she pledged to pay Marta's dowry of 140 scudi and fulfilled the commitment in a series of payments. While Margherita herself never entered the refuge, she maintained her ties with the place and in 1655 left a testamentary donation of eighteen scudi annually to three nuns residing there.[92] Tuscan females involved in prostitution may have liked the idea of the refuge and recognized that the institutions might be able to help in certain circumstances. Ultimately, however, many of them—including women like Margherita, who had the money for a dowry— probably preferred the freedom to determine for themselves their contacts, actions, and mores.

Despite the inconveniences and annoyances endemic to a life of prostitution, the number of prostitutes in Tuscany appears to have climbed in the sixteenth and seventeenth centuries. The government's efforts to cope with this distressing turn of events did not stop with the attempted reinvigoration of the Onestà. Civic leaders also put credence in the institutional option embodied, at the outset, by the Monastero delle Convertite. From the late sixteenth century onward, the focus on conversion and institutionalization intensified. In 1579 lay Florentine activists set up the Casa delle Malmaritate, and in 1590 Archbishop Alessandro de' Medici urged the state to establish another refuge for abandoned prostitutes.[93] The foundation of Santa Maria Maddalena of Pistoia occurred in 1604. In chapter 4 we will examine the institutional programs proffered as a solution to the problem of rising prostitution. But before we reach that point, we must take up the question of who else beyond ex-prostitutes populated the refuges for *convertite*.

3

Anomalous Women and Girls
in the Tuscan Refuges

We would be in error to look at the refuges for *convertite* just as places for former public prostitutes. The refuges held a variety of other women to whom that classification did not apply. This chapter deals with who those women were, what circumstances they came from, and why they were in the institutions.

Females who were not prostitutes lived in the refuges in a variety of capacities. They stayed in the establishments as temporary guests, as long-term boarders (*commesse*), as employees (*fattoresse* and women *in serbo*), as internees sentenced there, and as members of religious communities (*suore* and *monache*). The reasons why they ended up in the institutions differed. The anthropologist Mary Douglas's writings on anomaly offer a helpful way of understanding the presence of many of these women and girls. She has explained how in societies with intricate networks of conceptual classification schemes and hierarchies, the anomalous entity that does not easily fit one accepted category or another can be disturbing, even threatening.[1] We can think of many of the residents of the refuges for *convertite* as anomalous females. Usually the state or their families sought to institutionalize them as a temporary or permanent measure, to confine the troublesome to a known environment where they could be controlled and even transformed. Sometimes the women themselves came to the institutions as places of refuge when life in the outside world became unbearable.

The nonprostitutes in the refuges for *convertite* were a motley assortment (see table). Their exact numbers are hard to pinpoint, because the scattered evidence in surviving records does not identify as prostitutes many residents who indeed came from that background. The nonprostitutes may have represented about one eighth to one quarter of the population of the refuges. The founders of the Casa delle Malmaritate expected to shelter a minor constituency of nonprostitutes. And at almost any given time, the Monastero delle Convertite and Santa Maria Maddalena held a certain small group of females who had not been prostitutes.[2]

As in the case of the former prostitutes in the refuges, most of the resident nonprostitutes were from Tuscany. The institutions offered a solution to *local*

A Profile of Nonprostitutes in Two Refuges[a]

	Monastero delle Convertite (1614–1706)		Santa Maria Maddalena (1604–1720)	
	Number	Sample	Number	Sample
Origins				
Tuscany	11 (64%)	17	12 (100%)	12
Other Italian	4 (24%)	17	0 (0%)	12
Foreign	2 (12%)	17	0 (0%)	12
Married or widowed	7 (5%)	141	4 (13%)	32
Have children	2 (1%)	141	1 (3%)	32
Have benefactors or guarantors	28 (20%)	141	5 (16%)	32
Average age at entrance	22 yrs	9	33 yrs[b]	2
Average age at death	64 yrs	62	55 yrs	1

SOURCES: See table in chapter 2; also, records of the Otto di Guardia.

[a]Although not identified as such, a number of these women probably had been prostitutes. The numbers in the table are therefore inflated and should not be taken as representative of the proportions of nonprostitutes actually present in the institutions.

[b]One was aged 52 years and the other was listed as a "maiden" (*fanciulla vergine*).

problems, although in many instances the factor of migration came into play. About half these women migrated to their immediate environs from small Tuscan villages, a fact contributing to their characteristic quality of being "out of place."

In terms of class, noblewomen as well as weavers' daughters were represented. The latter outnumbered the former, but noblewomen indeed appear in the institutions' plans and records in the fifteenth and sixteenth centuries. The founders of the Casa delle Malmaritate expected to receive noble or patrician girls who had been led astray and whose families wanted them interned. They also expected to welcome gentlewomen who came to serve as prioress out of necessity or piety. Similarly, the administrators of the Monastero delle Convertite sheltered problematic gentlewomen deposited there, and welcomed other women from Florence's upper echelons seeking membership. They proudly kept a list of the forty-one noblewomen and gentlewomen who had filled the office of abbess between 1455 and 1596.[3] Respectable women may have become nuns at convents for *convertite* like the Monastero delle Convertite and Santa Maria Maddalena because the notion of helping in the good work of reclaiming sinners appealed to them or their parents. Moreover, families perhaps sensed the relatively loose regimen at the Monastero delle Convertite. The convents for *convertite* may have offered the best all-round bargain among convents at a given time, in terms of the dowry rate, accommodations, and atmosphere. At least the Monastero delle Convertite by the midseventeenth century had prospered and could guarantee a comfortable life-style, perhaps owing to the considerable charity the cause of reform attracted.

The nonprostitutes entered the refuges at a wide range of ages, coming in as young girls or as women of fifty. Those who entered young often remained in the houses a remarkably long time. About two thirds of the women in this population at the Monastero delle Convertite died in their sixties or seventies or even older. Like many of the former prostitutes, a high proportion of these women did not return to the outside world and instead made the refuges their home.

The Monastero delle Convertite, Casa delle Malmaritate, and Santa Maria Maddalena took their place in a constellation of other socially useful institutions in Florence and Pistoia. Each city had its civil prisons, such as the Stinche in Florence for male and female criminals, and each also had Church-administered jails or sites for detention.[4] There were hospitals and orphanages for both sexes: to name just the largest, Santa Maria Nuova and the Innocenti in Florence and the Ospedale del Ceppo in Pistoia.[5] Florence had other important social institutions that drew residents from all over Tuscany, such as the Orbatello, a widows' asylum dating from the 1370s, and the Ospedale dei Mendicanti, a poorhouse opened in 1621.[6] Often, these other socially useful institutions served as "warehouses" for the deviant and marginal of early modern Tuscan society, just as anomalous women passed time in the refuges for *convertite* and *malmaritate*. Let us proceed to take a closer look at the nonprostitutes in the refuges, particularly those who represented anomalies vis-à-vis medieval and early modern values. The anomalous females in the refuges included young girls teetering on the precipice of lost innocence, women without reputable families to care for them, and women in quandaries related to marriage.

Juvenile Residents

In their first set of statutes in 1579, the founders of the Casa delle Malmaritate tried to formulate the conditions under which they would take in young girls. The founders advised against accepting virgins:

> We're not meant for everyone, but for those who've fallen into trouble. Yet not even for this reason should we accept virgins—even when their expenses will be paid and they come with *convertite* who are their mothers—because of the danger they'd be putting themselves in by being exposed to the conversation of the *convertite*.[7]

However, the founders did not look askance at accepting young girls who had lost their virginity or had it taken from them. This policy captures in essence the attitude of all the refuges for *convertite*. The establishments sought to avoid housing truly virtuous young girls, but would receive girls who put into question the innocence expected of them and thereby became anomalies in early modern Tuscan society.

Florentine civic authorities of the fifteenth century had no qualms that placing young rape victims in the Monastero delle Convertite would expose them to "danger." The victims' moral and physical integrity was already compromised. The Otto di Guardia magistracy ordered that Ginevra Angeli, a little pauper girl (*puella[m]* . . . *pauperculam*) about ten years old, be taken to the Monastero delle Convertite in 1487. She had been sodomized and raped by several men over a period of days at the home of the weaver Giovanni Francisci. The magistracy charged Giovanni with luring the girl to this debauchery. It sentenced him to undergo a public whipping and ten years' incarceration and to deposit in Santa Maria Nuova a dowry of one hundred lire for Ginevra.[8] The dowry might make possible for the girl an eventual marriage to someone of her own plebeian social level.

Ginevra's chance for a life in secular society was not irretrievably lost; her respectability could be redeemed. An observation made by a fifteenth-century contemporary, Florence's Archbishop Antonino Pierozzi, suggests that female honor did not consist solely of bodily purity: "[Regarding] virginity lost either legitimately . . . or illegitimately . . . , it is not possible to reacquire lost corporeal virginity nor the crown it merits; it is possible through true penitence to reacquire mental virginity and the crown it merits."[9] Ginevra was not a penitent, as described by Archbishop Antonino, although she did enter among the penitent *convertite*. Her situation corresponds to Antonino's view in that she could eventually emerge from the Monastero delle Convertite and be thought to have a pure state of mind and character, even if her body had been violated: she could go on and tread the honorable path of marriage. She was merely to be left in the Monastero delle Convertite until she recuperated, grew to adulthood, and reemerged to pick up the threads of a more normal life.

Thirteen-year-old Bella di Francesco met with the same resolution of her fate in 1503. The Otto di Guardia judged that she had been "abused" and had "grave damage" done to her by her mother's lover, the dyer Baldassare Niccolai, who raped and sodomized her. The magistrates absolved the girl on the grounds that she was a minor (*puella*) and sent her to the Monastero delle Convertite. They held her mother, Benedicta, and Baldassare responsible and decreed stiff punishments for them. Baldassare's sentence contained the condition that he could escape fifteen years' imprisonment by paying 150 florins and 100 lire to the Monastero delle Convertite to feed Bella for two years, and by depositing 100 lire as a dowry with which she could later marry or become a nun. Thus another crime against decent morality (*bonos mores*) was resolved, with guilt and innocence clearly allotted, and the perpetrator's payment making possible a period of spiritual and bodily healing for the victim. Bella too could proceed onto the honorable paths of marriage or monasticism.[10]

More perplexing to the authorities were cases in which the question of guilt and innocence was difficult to resolve. In 1531 the Otto di Guardia confronted such a puzzle regarding sixteen-year-old Lucretia Alvisi. They accused her and her father Giacomo of having an incestuous relationship and of aborting the pregnancy that had resulted from their polluted union. For these two heinous crimes the judges sentenced Giacomo to decapitation. They arrived at a mixed evaluation of Lucretia: "Partly by blandishments and partly by threats or fear of her father, she was induced to consent wickedly to this desire of his." The tribunal ordered the girl to the Monastero delle Convertite to be "bricked up," which probably meant isolated in solitary confinement with only two small windows for food and air. After five years, she could obtain release at the discretion of the Otto di Guardia.[11] The magistrates had lacked sufficient certainty of Lucretia's guilt to condemn her to death. Unlike the two other girls just discussed, Lucretia was not identified as a *puella,* and as someone past the age of puberty she could conceivably consent to intercourse.[12] The hint of her complicity evoked a troubling juxtaposition of two cultural tenets. Which was she—the dependent female in need of protection, or the female as temptress? Either one could create situations that disrupted social order. In this instance, shutting the problem away did not suffice. It had to be deeply buried and forgotten until its power to disturb had dissipated.

The administrators of the refuges for *convertite* debated over whether to house the daughters of prostitutes. This category of young girls, like that of rape victims, bore an ambiguous moral status. The administrators feared that they might be trapped into abetting the ruination of the young. Typical of the developments they wished to avoid was a case that came before the Otto di Guardia in 1515. The tribunal accused Madam Laura, a prostitute of Ferrara, of abducting a ten-year-old Ferrarese girl and leaving her in the Monastero delle Convertite with the intention of returning for her later to prostitute her.[13] The administrators had to tread a fine line between vigilance against such schemes and readiness to accept the girls whom they could truly help. As a preventive measure, the ducal government stipulated in the law of 1553 regulating prostitutes' legacies that the Monastero delle Convertite could no longer accept anyone who was not a converted prostitute.[14] The decree became a source of great inconvenience in the years ahead.

In many instances prostitutes wanted to put young girls in the institutions for the girls' genuine benefit, and the new law obstructed their aims. Piera de Levaldini, prostitute of Prato, wrote to Grand Duke Francesco I in 1576 requesting that her two daughters, Silvia, fifteen years old, and Antonia, thirteen years old, be dowered and permitted to enter the Monastero delle Convertite. With Piera, we find an instance of a presumably plebeian woman herself employing the terminology of honor. She said:

> Up to now, they have lived most honestly, and I want to bring them *honor* by making them nuns. . . . I beg you on bended knee because you are a fountain of piety and charity. . . . I ask from my heart so that they won't fall into trouble and so that this holy pious house will acquire two servants of God, who will always pray to the highest God that he concede your every wish.[15]

However, the ducal officials who oversaw monasteries advised the grand duke not to grant Piera's request because it contravened the law of 1553. They noted in addition that Florence's Archbishop Alessandro de' Medici had expressly written from Rome to urge that the Monastero delle Convertite accept no entrants other than *convertite*.

Nonetheless, people constantly attempted to circumvent the law. Spurred by "many friends at court," Antonio Serguidi in 1577 asked Archbishop Alessandro de' Medici for a favor. He asked on behalf of the courtesan Maria Marzochini that her two daughters, both under ten years of age, be admitted to the Monastero delle Convertite. Serguidi obviously felt pity and concern for the girls, who were betwixt and between, thus far innocent but on the threshold of a sinful world. He tried to persuade the archbishop with the argument that "these girls will improve their condition more there than they would staying with their mother." Nor would the convent suffer: it would receive the same payment adult nuns gave, three scudi per year.[16]

In the last quarter of the sixteenth century, the nuns of the Monastero delle Convertite themselves approached the grand duke for permission to accept as a nun the daughter of a prostitute they had taken in as a servant much earlier. Her mother had deposited 100 scudi to serve as a marital dowry for the girl and then absconded to Rome, leaving the fourteen-year-old "without any recourse." The girl now wanted to become a nun in the convent. An intercessor communicated on behalf of the nuns: "Notwithstanding the law, they say they are moved by charity for the girl to act, so that she won't leave here and follow the path of her mother. They say that in another case of 1562, this concession was granted."[17] The nuns knew that other times the law had been overlooked and that it would be overlooked again in the future, when doing so could benefit the institution.

Two centuries later, girls who did not conform to normative expectations were still taken to the refuges. At the request of state authorities in Milan, officials in Livorno in 1792 arrested Carolina Zappa, a girl who had run away from her paternal home in Milan with a man. The Livornese officials sent Carolina to the Casa delle Malmaritate, which she found not to her liking, and she asked to be put in "a more pleasant and airy conservatory."[18]

Anomalous young females were not the only very young members of the female sex who lived at the refuges for *convertite*. Despite policies discouraging the acceptance of the young and innocent, girls about whom no taint lurked entered the institutions, too. Throughout its history the Monastero delle Convertite served as a way station for girls dropped off there for some finite period of time. Girls joined the households as boarders (*commesse*), as did one Lisabetta di Marco Fantoni in 1506. Others, like Benedetta di Bastiano at the Monastero delle Convertite in 1617, lived and worked in the refuges as servants. One "maiden" came to Santa Maria Maddalena of Pistoia not as a servant but to serve God and the *convertite* as a teacher. Marietta Tamburini, the daughter of a local weaver, entered the refuge in its second year to instruct the other residents in the art of weaving. She, along with the *convertite*, became Franciscan tertiaries in 1607, and as Suor Verginia she may have remained in the house as long as twenty years. In this case practical necessity, and in other cases individual circumstances, outweighed the authorities' habitual concern about the wisdom of exposing impressionable young girls to *convertite*.[19]

Broken Bonds of Kinship

The strength and worth of a woman's kinship (*parentado*) could determine to what degree she fulfilled a normative role in her society. The administrators of the Tuscan refuges manifested constant concern for the variable of family in their charges' lives. Renaissance society fostered the ideal that from cradle to grave a woman's natal family and her marital family should provide financial support, hold the reins of moral discipline, and ably manage her affairs in the world. But the administrators knew that reality often did not match up with this ideal. The founders of the Casa delle Malmaritate warned against returning residents to relatives who may have prostituted or mistreated their own kin: "Many times, the relatives make these women such grand promises to get them in their hands, and when they have them, they kill them." The administrators of the refuge for *convertite* in Milan, the house of Soccorso in Bologna, and the Mendicanti poorhouse in seventeenth-century Florence were likewise experienced in overseeing women who had contested with their relatives. Greed over property prompted intrafamilial violence, as in the case of a Pisan barber charged in 1603 with killing his sister over 300 scudi inherited from their uncle and intended for her dowry. In many instances, females' sexual escapades and the perception of family disgrace or dishonor also prompted intrafamilial violence.[20]

Tuscan elites and officials believed that civic honor depended in part on the honor of families in the polis. The behavior of female family members held one key to whether or not families had honorable reputations. The Italian custodial institutions of the early modern era often served the ends of burghers who felt that they had to hide away a misbehaving female relative in order to preserve the family's honor.[21] Plebeian families, without necessarily articulating their needs in terms of *onore,* may have sought help from magistracies to deal with their unruly female members and achieved the same result of institutionalization. The Medici rulers and their entourage, operating under their own aristocratic code of honor, involved themselves in the affairs of their employees from the middle and lower ranks of society and arranged the institutionalization of their servitors' wayward female kin with the greatest "secrecy and decorum."[22]

Although Tuscan magistrates and patricians spoke both of individual female honor (parallel to individual male honor) and of family honor, the latter often overshadowed the former. Fifteenth-century Tuscan patricians might bestow on their womenfolk the appellation "a woman of honor" or the criticism that "her behavior in this matter does honor neither to her nor to us."[23] In other instances they introduced *onore* not in reference to the character of the woman in question but in a manner that reflected on the reputations of her family or of associated males. Florentine magisterial records of 1381 yield the charge that a magnate had tried to rape a peasant woman, "thus bringing obliquy upon her and dishonor upon her husband."[24] A late-fifteenth-century Florentine patrician breathed a sigh of relief when the man who had impregnated his unmarried Pistoian servant girl offered a dowry so that she could marry "and thus save [my brother-in-law]'s honor, since he had been responsible for [obtaining her father's permission and bringing] her to me."[25] In the first years of the eighteenth century Camillo Lanfranchi, a Pisan nobleman, did not speak of the honor of his postparturient mistress, gone to reside at the refuge for *convertite* in Pisa, but said in reference to his bastard child that he wished eventually to "put it in honor with the world."[26] We can find civic leaders of early modern Tuscany applying the terminology of *onore* to plebeian prostitutes as well as to aristocratic women, yet the woman herself and any concept of honor attached to her person often became instrumental to a focus on the reputation of patrician or plebeian families as a whole.[27] The Tuscan elites used the early modern institutions for women to protect their own family honor and to oversee the affairs of plebeian families in a fashion that seemed optimal for public morality and civic honor.

When the administrators of the refuges for *convertite* saw cases of families able to support female members, they frequently welcomed the opportunity to restore their charges to relatives who were decent and honest and had adequate incomes. Administrators approached the matter of residents' wishes to leave the institutions by seeking relatives "who wanted to take care of them." But girls and women of the lower social ranks had often lost contact with their natal families, whether because of migration, marriage, or the fragmentation of a household through poverty. In 1446 the seventy-two women in the Monastero delle Convertite were described as having "no relatives or only the poorest relatives" and no means of sustenance. A century later the founders of the Casa delle Malmaritate suspected that immoral females might be left at the institution and then abandoned by those who should have sustained them financially. When women sought to leave the refuges, the absence of reliable relatives posed a problem. If the women in question were of dubious reputation, the administrators might have them exiled from the diocese, as happened at Santa Maria Maddalena in 1621.[28]

The refuges for *convertite* served as a de facto alternative to family care. In the 1470s Ginevra de' Medici, a member of the Florentine ruling family, requested that the Monastero delle Convertite temporarily house a young member of her circle who with her willful behavior had been compounding a generally unhappy family situation. The girl's comportment at the convent was so intolerable that the abbess had to shirk her commitment to Madam Ginevra and return the girl to her father. The abbess begged pardon, saying, "With a hundred tongues, I could not tell you the craziness she brought here." By the early sixteenth century the Monastero delle Convertite provided a haven to many young women of the propertied class whose parents found themselves in tightened financial straits. The young women entered as charity cases or because their parents could better afford the dowries of the convent for *convertite* than those of other convents. Administrators said that the membership of the household swelled with "daughters of the once prosperous now made poor." What a reversal of expectations these girls underwent, how lost and at odds in their society they must have felt![29]

The breakdown of family bonds could be difficult for early modern women both in terms of how others viewed them and in terms of their own attitudes and options. When their families in the world failed them, many females turned to institutions such as convents, hospitals, conservatories, and refuges for *convertite*. With no families outside to care for them, some girls and women entered institutions in which relatives of theirs resided. In 1577 the courtesan Maria Marzochini, seeking a home for her daughters, chose the Monastero delle Convertite because she had two sisters who were nuns there. As the girls' aunts, the two nuns at the convent for *convertite* "could instill the virtues in them with more love than would others elsewhere." In the 1680s four sisters named Maddalena, Francesca, Maria Angiola, and Caterin'Angiola Spiombi entered the Monastero delle Convertite within three years of one another.[30]

Such familial connections within the refuge could provide the financial support and nurture that was lacking on the outside. When Margherita Guarnieri entered the Monastero delle Convertite in 1644 to become Suor Agata Caterina, her aunt already living in the house, Suor Maria Prudenza Soldani, contributed 15 scudi toward her dowry of 140 scudi.[31] Siblings pooled their resources and purchased single or multiple rooms to serve as joint living quarters. Some sets of relatives at the Monastero delle Convertite made pacts to share their *spoglie,* a scheme akin to life insurance. *Spoglie,* the assets left after a member of the household had died and creditors had been paid, normally reverted to the institution. However, residents could bond together and pay a onetime fee to the refuge for the privilege of sharing their *spoglie* among themselves. In 1695 the three Migliori sisters and their niece, a converted prostitute whose mother had also been in the convent, worked out such an arrangement and paid the refuge 60 scudi.[32] Women who made these pacts did not intend to leave the institutions for the precarious world; instead, they forged anew familial patrimonies for themselves.

A sense of partaking in bonds that had been sundered in the world sometimes carried over even to the relationships of residents not related by blood. Acting out of need, the women in the refuges created artificial families. The institutional authorities encouraged this phenomenon by using familial imagery and seeking to create a familial atmosphere. Household relationships at the Casa delle Malmaritate were to be as among "sisters." The administrators' view that they themselves served *in loco parentis* was given voice in a comment made by an administrator of Santa Maria Maddalena who said of the *convertite,* "With paternal love we treat them as daughters."[33] The administrators permitted related and unrelated women to undertake financial care and responsibility for one another, sometimes including the final gesture of paying for burial expenses. The predominantly childless women who came to the refuges for *convertite* would not have been permitted to keep young children with them, unlike the widows at the Orbatello asylum. But among fellow residents they found kindred souls to treat as family.[34] The administrators knew that the institutions filled a vacuum. The residents of the refuges for *convertite* sought to replicate inside an alternative world the norms that had not been met for them in society.

Dilemmas of Betrothal, Marriage, and Widowhood

The arrangements by which medieval and early modern Tuscans became betrothed were among the most sensitive and tense negotiations in their society. Pacts to establish marital alliances hung in a delicate balance that, if disturbed, could set off interpersonal or interclan rancor. The civil government often intervened, either on its own initiative or in response to pleas, to straighten out matters. In 1494 officials in the countryside ordered to the Monastero delle Convertite for a one-month stay Dorothea of Cascina, a runaway fiancée. Crying "Alarm, alarm!," an armed band led by Dorothea's betrothed, Vespa, had galloped up to extract her from the hands of the man with whom she had run away. The furious command "Send out Dorothea" produced the woman, and she was whisked off to the house of the local representative of government, the *podestà*. There she remained "obstinate," insisting that she wanted no other husband than her inamorato. The authorities resolved to send her to the Monastero delle Convertite, where she would have to decide either to return to Vespa or become a nun. While Dorothea delayed her departure as long as possible, telling everyone within earshot that she "would rather have any husband than become a nun," Vespa took a different woman as his wife.[35]

The bonds of matrimony in this era could be highly ambiguous and subject to challenge. In 1493 provincial authorities sent to the Monastero delle Convertite, until they could ascertain the truth, a young woman of good family they suspected of having been coerced into marriage. Pregnant, she had fled to the home of her lover, whose father arranged for the couple to wed. The father's move aroused enmity and a flurry of attempts by other concerned parties to dissolve the marriage. The impromptu alliance had offended the community and caught the woman involved in an untenable position. Bigamy or concubinage also frequently plagued Tuscan civil authorities. In 1527 the Otto di Guardia considered the accusation that Carlo de' Medici unjustly held two women, keeping one with him and lodging the other one in a monastery where she continuously cried "Vendetta before Christ!" Marco Lastri, a late-eighteenth-century observer, noted that the Casa delle Malmaritate received, among other females, young girls whose marriages were in doubt or the subject of litigation.[36]

Moreover, early modern Tuscan magisterial records are filled with tales of troubled marriages. In every generation, civil and ecclesiastical officials tackled case after case of warring couples, both counseling and disciplining the battling spouses. Marriage was supposed to be for life, and the Church did not permit divorce. The late-sixteenth-century magistrates with jurisdiction over Pistoia grieved over a wife who had been badly beaten by her husband, who was enamored of another woman. But they made it clear that her escape lay not in this world: "The poor thing didn't die." Spouses in medieval and early modern Tuscany had few officially recognized means of retreating from miserable marriages. Those with property sometimes could procure ecclesiastical annulments or Church-licensed separations. Other unhappy wives and husbands cut the marriage bond through de facto separations. For wives, separation might well mean loss of financial support from a husband. In some cases women won the protection of civil authorities who coerced the women's husbands, if still in the vicinity, to continue contributing to their maintenance.[37] Tuscan officials and the anomalous Tuscan women whose marriages had broken down looked to the refuges for *convertite* and custodial institutions as at least an interim solution.

Many wives who had clashed with their husbands landed in the refuges for *convertite*. Throughout this era authorities sentenced disobedient wives to a stay in the Monastero delle Convertite. As they stipulated in the late-fifteenth-century case of Lisabetta, wife of Carlo the goldsmith, there was to be no release "except by license of the magistrates or her husband." But the institutions also played host to maltreated wives. The Otto di Guardia placed women like an otherwise unidentified "Antonia" in the Monastero delle Convertite until "her husband satisfied us that he would not offend her and that he could keep her with him in peace." They commanded one obstreperous sixteenth-century woman to stay put in the Monastero delle Convertite, threatening that if she left they would send her back to her spouse.[38]

Women themselves chose the institutions as refuges from their unsuccessful marriages. Wives abandoned by their husbands came to the communities of *convertite,* particularly in periods of economic crisis and war. The plight of abandoned wives greatly distressed civic leaders. In the early sixteenth century the commune of Florence granted permission for abandoned wives and women separated from their husbands to live alongside widows in the Orbatello asylum. Lucrezia Ferrini, the wife of Franceso Fabbri, was luckier than most women in her situation. Months after her husband had abandoned her, she benefited from the aid of no less than a marquis. The nobleman Giovanbatista Borbone dal Monte, explaining that he acted from motives of piety and in exchange for prayers on his behalf, made a donation in 1684 to enable Lucrezia to enter the Monastero delle Convertite as Suor Maria Giovanna Benigna Gaetana.[39] The archbishop's office granted marital separation licenses permitting married women to enter the refuges for *convertite* in cases of domestic misery. We find Caterina Bottazi licensed in 1648 to take up residence in the Monastero delle Convertite "notwithstanding that she had a living husband," Anibale Riccioli. In her case it was stipulated that upon the death of her husband she was supposed to take the nun's habit within two months. If she failed to do so or departed, she would forfeit to the convent the dowry of 160 scudi she had paid at her entrance.[40]

Married women contrived to join the institutions without admitting that they had husbands. In particular, women coming from the countryside to the city, where they were not known, could manage this. Lucrezia Bozi of Cireglio carried out the subterfuge when she entered Santa Maria Maddalena of Pistoia about 1607. Twelve years passed while Lucretia, as Suor Caterina, wore the habit of the Third Order of Saint Francis. Then in 1619, when the convent was about to become cloistered, Lucretia preferred to depart rather than submit to monastic vows. Her desire to leave plunged her into a year of controversy that did not end until she finally told the administrators that she had a husband in Cireglio. Discovering that her spouse, Bernardino Belluomini, was a "person of means" who could "keep her in good custody as a wife," the administrators consigned her into his hands and those of her male relatives in Cireglio. Lucretia had come full circle. She had bucked tradition and comfort in leaving Cireglio only to become a woman at odds with the environment she chose. Then, ironically, the fate held in store for her was passage back to Cireglio. Similar events unfolded in 1618 at Bologna's house of Soccorso, which granted admission to Caterina Lanzini for a second time because she was "beautiful and in great peril, being in disgrace with her husband and other relatives." She asked to stay for three months and hoped for a quick reconciliation with her spouse. This was not to be. Even after Caterina asked repeatedly to leave, the administrators did not grant her request until 1621, because either they or her relatives wanted her retained.[41] Another woman had run into a no-win situation, caught between turmoil in marriage and unhappiness in an institution.

Widows figured among the large population of unwanted, homeless women in sixteenth-century Tuscany. Tuscan societies, with their characteristic late male ages of marriage, overflowed with both patrician and plebeian widows. We have already seen that in 1427 one in four adult women in the city of Florence was a widow, and in the countryside one in six. There is no reason to believe that these proportions decreased in the sixteenth and seventeenth centuries, since the pattern of late male marital ages continued. Widows in Florence in 1427 outnumbered widowers six to one. Widowers of all social ranks, urban and rural, tended to remarry more easily than did their female counterparts, with the possible exception of widows in the countryside. The widowers thus did not need to turn as much as widows did to institutional settings as places of residence. Plebeian widows, who as girls had often migrated from their villages to marry, out of necessity were quite mobile, moving about looking for work or sometimes returning to their native village to seek sustenance. The metropolis of Florence drew widows in great numbers especially in times of political strife or natural disaster, such as the years 1494 to 1530, which engulfed most of the Italian cities in war, and the periods of local Tuscan famines (1590–91, 1617–22, 1670–71, 1677–78), plague (1630), and depression (1647–49).[42]

Insolvency, creditors, and reluctance on the part of their husbands' families to return their dowries all militated against the well-being of widows. A woman who had conformed to normative expectations and as a dutiful wife had turned her holdings over to her husband could wind up a propertyless widow dependent on help from kin who resented her. The early-fifteenth-century Florentine merchant Giovanni Morelli recorded in a family diary his anger at having to help his widowed sister:

> Seeing [her husband Jacopo] in need, [Sandra] went too far in her obedience and pledged several farms that were in her name, without saying a word of this to us, her brothers, or to any other friend or relative. . . . The outcome is that she has been living in our house for some time now . . . as a young widow with a twelve-year-old son and no dowry, and if God doesn't send us some remedy, she is likely to be here another long while. I decided to write this down for the benefit of whoever reads it . . . as a warning that no one, man or woman, should ever divest himself of his property or rights either from fear, flattery, or any other motive.[43]

Widows encountered substantial difficulties guaranteeing their subsistence in Tuscan societies.

A succession of Florentine governments promulgated laws addressing the needs of widows and helping them to steward whatever property remained to them. From 1400 on, the Parte Guelfa, a quasi-governmental corporate association, assumed sponsorship of the Orbatello widows' asylum, originally a privately endowed institution. But by the late sixteenth century the Orbatello offered less space to Tuscan widows, because it had started to receive the overflow of orphan girls that the overcrowded Innocenti foundling hospital could not contain.[44] Many widows of this era could not afford to live by themselves, and plebeian widows could not depend on the Orbatello as earlier generations of their peers had done. Officials of the state and philanthropists endeavored to protect widows, so that the women would not have to prostitute themselves. It was in part in response to the needs of unaffiliated widows that the custodial institutions and refuges for *convertite* grew up or filled up anew.

The Monastero delle Convertite and Santa Maria Maddalena attracted not only women with living husbands but also widows. From the Middle Ages throughout the early modern centuries, Tuscan widows had, as one alternative, entered mainstream convents after their husbands' deaths. Propertied widows handed over some form of payment and became *commesse* (long-term boarders), *suore* in Third Orders, or professed nuns. Even poor widows might scrape together the funds to support themselves while living at a convent in part as an employee, such as a servant or factoress. Widows also sought admission to the refuges for *convertite,* perhaps drawn by the establishments' reputations of not being overly exacting. Some widows preferred to become *commesse,* as did "Lucrezia, formerly the wife of Niccolò di Antonio Fini," at the Monastero delle Convertite in 1494. Becoming a *commessa* was an option halfway between donning the nun's habit and continuing to cope with the uncertainty of life in society. This choice permitted women the flexibility to make other arrangements if their circumstances changed.[45]

Other women bereft of their husbands had more circumscribed options laid before them. The widow, known to possess a mature sexuality and a new availability, represented a dangerous and volatile status. Widows may have been especially vulnerable to rape, a fate that befell Madam Vettoria, the Florentine widow of a tradesman, at the hands of an armed intruder in 1524. It was the sexual promiscuity of the widow Maddalena, the Otto di Guardia concluded in 1630, that drove her parents, innkeepers in Arezzo, to beat her and to try to make her poison herself.[46] Social authorities and the widow's relatives needed to gain control over this potentially explosive force for the safety of the community. They had to prevent widows from tempting youths and husbands and from shaming their own families or the city. In 1642 a resident of the Monastero delle Convertite, Suor Felice Angiola Bracciolini, had the condition set before her by a male benefactor willing to support her, that she either take the nun's habit or live "honorably" in a state of widowhood attested to by respectable people in her parish. This stipulation is reminiscent of an Onestà ordinance of 1569, which had required similar corroboration from neighbors regarding the behavior of married or widowed prostitutes who claimed to have reformed. Officials believed that little conduct remained private, sealed off from the public eye, and reliance on the parish or neighbors for evaluations of a woman's reputation was common in other seventeenth-century cases of institutionalization. Suor Felice Angiola had already been in the Monastero delle Convertite four years earlier, but had departed after six months. Despite whatever discontent she had experienced at that time, she found the thought of trying the convent again preferable to returning to her neighborhood.[47]

Suor Felice Angiola seemed to adjust well to institutional life the second time around. She became a professed nun and remained in the convent for four decades, until her death in 1681. In two installments, before and after her profession of vows, she formulated a will that was an exemplary document of religious life, stipulating that postmortem Masses for the benefit of her soul be performed in the convent's church and leaving her rooms to serve as part of the household's infirmary.[48]

Some widowed women tried to make their way in civil society and only after a struggle chose the greater security of the institution. Signora Agata Neri, the widow of Giovanni Lenzi, from 1662 to 1666 rented a house owned by the Monastero delle Convertite. The house was at Quattro Lioni, a neighborhood frequented by prostitutes, and perhaps Agata scrounged to make a living as a procuress for a while. Then in 1679 she entered the convent as Suor Margherita Fedele Candida Aurora. With a dispensation from the ducal government, she paid only sixty scudi, less than half the usual amount, to become a veiled nun. She remained in the house for twenty years or more, possibly until her death.[49]

Widows came to the refuges for *convertite* as servants. Maddalena of Lucca and Maddalena, the widow of the weaver Domenico, joined the

Monastero delle Convertite in this capacity in the first quarter of the seventeenth century. It could not have been easy for such women to pay the convent the thirty scudi required for their food each year. But the convent may have often found benefactors for them, just as it arranged for a longtime patron, Signora Maddalena Capponi, to subsidize Maddalena, the weaver's widow.[50]

Not all widows who entered the refuges were near destitution. Some, who were more fortunate than Giovanni Morelli's sister Sandra described earlier, became wealthy women at the death of their husbands. Because of difficulties with relatives or for other reasons, even propertied widows sometimes preferred a semiautonomous living situation within an institution. A townswoman named Eufrasia, raised and married in Pistoia, decided to enter Santa Maria Maddalena in 1646, and she brought with her considerable holdings. She had at her disposal a small farm inherited from her father that she planned to sell, funds from her husband's estate, and a portion of her mother's dowry, totaling over 400 scudi. A widow of more marginal status but also with a bit of property had joined the community at Santa Maria Maddalena earlier. This widow, Appollonia Andreuccetti, entered together with her daughter, a former public prostitute. Drawing upon her reserves of 450 scudi in the form of an annuity (*censo*) and cash, she provided the dowry for both of them.[51] With blemished reputation and displaced from her native Lucca, she nonetheless possessed the stake for a new life for her daughter and herself.

Although the Monastero delle Convertite and Santa Maria Maddalena accepted widows and anomalous married women much in the same way that convents had always done on a smaller scale, the Florentine Casa delle Malmaritate brought a new recognition and articulation to married women's problems. Founded in 1579, that establishment followed an institutional pattern that had been evolving for decades in Italian cities from the south to the north. The sixteenth century saw a proliferation of new Catholic charitable foundations, among them houses for *malmaritate* and *case di soccorso* specializing in helping troubled married women. The institutions grew out of the pre- and post-Tridentine Catholic concern with the health of the family. Early-sixteenth-century Catholic reformers had tried to engage family members in joint spiritual activities such as prayer, and extended practical help to families to prevent them from falling into material and moral deprivation. The Reformation threatened Catholic assumptions about the place of the family in the world. Protestantism set forth notions of companionate marriage and held up tantalizing visions of male and female evangelicals living together in a new order of harmony and spiritual bliss. The lure of Protestantism wrenched families apart. Those who implemented the Counter Reformation intensified the Catholic focus on the family and intended it to be one of the bulwarks on which they would refortify Catholicism.[52]

The theologians' concerns influenced and were shared by Florence's lay activists. The sponsors of the Casa delle Malmaritate sought to look behind the façades of troubled marriages. They wanted to understand why married women would need to, or be tempted to, prostitute themselves. And they hoped to counter the intrafamilial violence long a feature of their violent era. Medieval moralists such as the layman Paolo da Certaldo and the preacher Bernardino of Siena had tacitly or explicitly authorized physical chastisement of wives. In this area, prescription certainly found its behavioral counterpart, as we witness in the report of one Tuscan woman of 1427 who complained to the tax office, "my husband does great damage to me every time he returns, throwing me out of the house and beating me."[53] Later in that century, Friar Cherubino da Siena, in his book of advice the *Rules of Marriage,* still recommended: "You should beat [your wife] . . . if she likes being at the window and lends a ready ear to dishonest young men, or if she has taken to bad habits or bad company, or commits some other wrong that is a mortal sin."[54] By the early modern period, Florentine peacekeeping officials still believed that husbands had the right to discipline their wives with blows, but they disapproved of gratuitous mistreatment. When confronted with men who beat their wives without reasonable cause, authorities often warned them to stop under the threat of corporal punishment.[55]

The founders of the Casa delle Malmaritate said that they would receive, in addition to married prostitutes, women "who with danger to their lives stay with their husbands." So as not to encourage honest women to leave their spouses, two male members of the confraternity that supervised the institution would always seek to reconcile the couple. The founders saw their role as peacemaker to families or couples in conflict, but they would take care not to return a woman to relatives who might harm her. In theory, those to be accepted included women able to obtain from the archbishop separation licenses for just cause, adulteresses sentenced to be shut up in the house, and wives whose husbands wished to put them there "to make them more humble." Women in all these categories were to arrive with formal licenses and permissions in hand.[56]

In practice, the legal niceties may have fallen by the wayside. One of the few pieces of evidence we have regarding who really did end up in the Casa delle Malmaritate in its early decades tells the story of Margherita Pellegrini. As the Otto di Guardia discovered in 1615, a certain Giambatista Tozzi went for medical care to the Florentine apothecary Domenico Pellegrini, and after regaining his health became amorously involved with the man's wife, Margherita. The magistrates impugned Giàmbatista for having shown no regard for Domenico's honor or Margherita's. He trysted with the woman in her husband's house and seduced her into coming away with him, taking her from place to place and finally leaving her in the Casa delle Malmaritate without license from her husband![57]

In 1776 the Casa delle Malmaritate fell under the jurisdiction of a new supervisory body, the civil police ministry, but it continued its mission of sheltering predominantly married women who did not conform in one way or another to social norms. As the records of the police ministry reveal, the institution continued to house the different kinds of problematic females foreseen by the founders. Some women sought to enter it as a refuge from husbands who mistreated them. Violante Guidetti of Livorno passed two or more years apart from her unfaithful husband, whom she left about 1790. She divided this time between the Casa delle Malmaritate, to which she had sought admission, and two private houses in which she lived after illness forced her to leave the institution. Illness was one reason why voluntary entrants sometimes departed from the establishment for *malmaritate,* and inadequate financial support was another. In 1777 an unnamed woman upset with her spouse's behavior wanted to enter the establishment. She gained admittance, but her husband failed to pay for her maintenance as agreed, and the cleric who oversaw daily administration of the institution had to ask the state to make the husband pay or to authorize release of the resident.[58]

Other women found themselves detained or interned in the Casa delle Malmaritate to guarantee their respectable conduct. Since the sixteenth century, social authorities and private individuals could have women confined there for this purpose. Carmina Pucetti, an adulterous wife, failed in her attempt to get the ecclesiastical court to dissolve her marriage. She then in 1777 petitioned the civil government in Pisa to require her husband to provide funds for her to live apart from him. The officials declined to do so unless she agreed to live in the Casa delle Malmaritate, where presumably she could no longer behave immorally. Having inspired scandalous rumors concerning herself and a young man, Bastiana Grilli had to leave the home she shared with her husband in Gubbio in 1783 and go live with her in-laws in Florence. Her spouse, back at his job as a servitor to an abbot in Gubbio, asked the Florentine authorities to confine her to the Casa delle Malmaritate at his expense, if she attempted to leave Florence. He must have thought that he could avert further scandal by relying on the resources of the state to control his wife's actions. The patrician family of a young cleric, Ottaviano Ricasoli, succeeded in getting Giovine Santa Seracini, the daughter of a reputed prostitute, confined to the Casa delle Malmaritate in 1777 in order to prevent the cleric from carrying out his intention of marrying her. The cleric obtained Giovine's release after the passage of a week.[59]

For many females interned at the Casa delle Malmaritate, only a fine line separated detention and punishment. Authorities confined some women there in order to chastise them. In 1777 Jacopo Mazzetti persuaded officials to incarcerate his scolding wife in the institution for the second time. Many interned women indeed perceived the Casa delle Malmaritate as a punitive institution. In 1774 Maria Falcini Lotti, the daughter of a silversmith and wife of a butcher, obtained a legal separation granted by the archbishop because of her spouse's libertine ways. After failing to get the decision reversed in another ecclesiastical court, her husband managed to have her put in the Casa delle Malmaritate. In 1777 a spokesperson for Maria petitioned the police to release her, arguing that her institutionalization was "against the rules of good justice," and that a woman who had been granted two favorable decisions did not deserve "the severe consequence of having to be in a place of punishment." By agreeing to reside with a respectable matron, Maria won permission to leave the institution after half a year there.[60] Upon discovering that the widow Vittoria Valori led a "scandalous" life in Florence, in a manner "unworthy . . . of someone of respected old lineage," her siblings and relatives in Livorno had her confined to the Casa delle Malmaritate in 1778. Five years later she wrote state officials to seek release from what she viewed as a period of hellish incarceration: "I am here abandoned by all, without ever having had a chance to explain myself or defend myself, neither to authorities nor to relatives. Where is there a barbarity and a cruelty like this?"[61] Unfortunately for Vittoria, who felt that she was in "a pillory and not in a conservatory," the records indicate that she was still there a decade later.

Yet, at least in the late eighteenth century, civil authorities did not automatically incarcerate every woman whom a husband or relative wanted to confine. In 1783 the husband of Maria Antonia Assunta Gherardini of Pistoia tried to have his wife confined in the Casa delle Malmaritate as punishment for refusing to live with him and finding a job as a servant in Florence. Upon investigation, the police found no grounds for suspecting Maria of immorality. They discovered that her husband had beaten her and had not provided well for her. The police informed Maria's husband that he could take his request to judicial officials, but that they themselves would not accede to his demand.[62]

The Florentine Casa delle Malmaritate and some of the other institutions elsewhere that received *malmaritate* represented a significant modification of social attitudes and gender ideology. Pious reformers in this period had established the Casa Pia in Rome, the Soccorso in Mantua, and enclaves of *malmaritate* in Bologna with the intention of aiding married women whose marriages had gone awry. The founders of such houses made an institutional commitment to acknowledging as legitimate such women's dissatisfaction with their marriages. They recognized a formidable social problem that had been little considered previously, and they developed a new option as a solution to the problem.[63] At the very same time that the Church was reaffirming the sacredness of and shoring up marriage, these Catholic leaders admitted the possible failure of marriage as a social context for women's lives. In the sixteenth century another new option for unhappy spouses had appeared. Some of the Protestant reformers sanctioned divorce and the possibility of remarriage in cases of adultery or abandonment.[64] By institutionalizing marital grievance and separation, establishments like the Casa delle Malmaritate represented for Catholics an important new way of criticizing and sidestepping unsuccessful marriages. These institutions served as a social outlet that permitted the early modern Catholic Church to stave off ecclesiastical approval of divorce.

The Institution as Warehouse

The composition of the refuges for *convertite* turned out to be more diverse than that expected by their founders. The institutions' residents were hardly limited to prostitutes from the lowest strata of Florentine society. Young girls, including innocent young girls of the type authorities did not want to see living among the *convertite,* at times wound up there. Just as the Casa delle Malmaritate served as a de facto prison, so had the Monastero delle Convertite earlier. In 1537 the Otto di Guardia sentenced Betta di Michele, a young unmarried servant accused of having tried to poison her female employer, to two years in the prison of the Monastero delle Convertite. In one early-sixteenth-century instance, the Otto di Guardia dealt with two sisters literally "out of place"—female travelers who on their way to Rome had suffered harassment from armed youths—by assigning them to a stay in the Monastero delle Convertite. The institutions took in females with whom the authorities did not know what else to do, women out of resonance with expectations and ideals.[65]

Although the punitive institutionalization of suspected prostitutes increased from the early sixteenth century on, during the subsequent centuries the Tuscan refuges for *convertite* continued to house a variety of nonprostitutes as well. The Monastero delle Convertite and the Casa delle Malmaritate served as what sociologist Andrew T. Scull has called "custodial warehouses" or dumping grounds for the problematic females of early modern Tuscan society.[66] The Monastero delle Convertite performed this "warehousing" function especially from its origin through the sixteenth century. Since its foundation in 1579, the Casa delle Malmaritate began to draw off some of the deviant population that formerly might have been sheltered at the Monastero delle Convertite. Santa Maria Maddalena was less of a multifunctional institution, because in its early decades it began to conform to narrower Counter-Reformation ideals of rigorous conventual life focused on the fulfillment of spiritual vocation. Despite their oft-voiced desire to be able to distinguish clearly between good and bad women, Tuscan officials distributed their society's problematic females to different social institutions in a seemingly bemused, random fashion. They deposited a sodomized ten-year-old girl in the Monastero delle Convertite, confined a husband-killer to a convent, and sent kidnap victims to the Stinche prison. Authorities clearly viewed a sentence to the Monastero delle Convertite as less harsh than one to the Stinche. But if a consistency beyond patronage connections or financial considerations lay behind their dispersals of deviant females, it is hard to discern.[67] The arbiters of early modern society did not always perceive a difference between females as transgressors and females as victims. The authorities could use the notion of female vulnerability, central to Renaissance gender ideology, as a fallback for interpreting either phenomenon. Both transgressors and victims were simply anomalies rifting the fabric of the social order, and they had to be removed.

Yet even as they filled the institutions with the guilty and the innocent in a patchwork way, the officials themselves manifested displeasure at the resulting mélange. They groped to establish some sense of boundary. The Monastero delle Convertite sometimes refused to accept females sentenced to stay there, and the magistrates ordered others to keep their contaminating presence away from the convent. In the second edition of their statutes, published in 1583, the administrators of the Casa delle Malmaritate fretted because "experience demonstrates that putting together decent women and *convertite* is often a cause of great confusion"; they hoped to set up "a separate place for the decent married women."[68] The proliferation of differentiated social institutions was the way of the future. The refuges for *convertite* played a valuable role as pioneering experiments. The refuges were the fruits of efforts by concerned citizens who, while weighed by intimations of unease, coped as best they could and searched for feasible solutions to social problems. Theirs was a formidable task, both to enforce society's normative conventions for the female sex and yet still respond to the glaring needs of the women who did not live up to those norms.

Figure 1 Saint Mary Magdalen with Biblical inscription "Unless you repent, you will all of you come to the same end," from statute book for the Casa delle Malmaritate. (Frontispiece from *Sommario de capitoli*, 1583. Reprinted courtesy of Biblioteca Nazionale Centrale, Florence.)

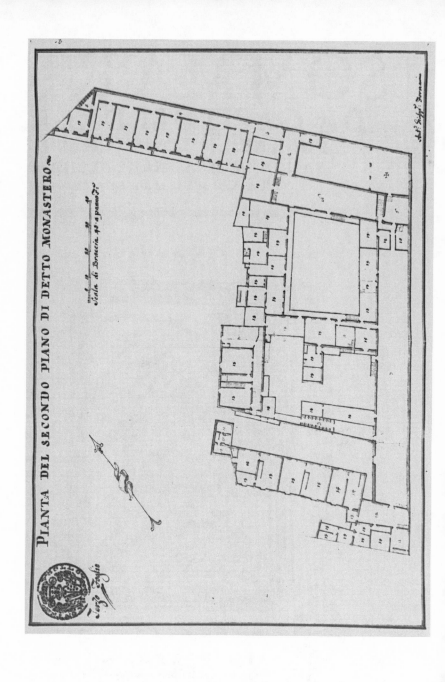

PIANTA DEL SECONDO PIANO DI DETTO MONASTERO

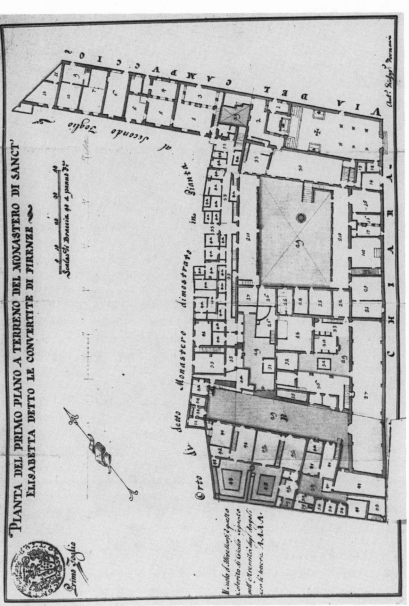

Figure 2 First floor (*bottom*) and second floor (*top*) of the Monastero delle Convertite, indicating that a large proportion (33 and 74 percent, respectively, on the first and second floors) of the convent's rooms were individual living quarters purchased by the nuns. On the first floor, the numbers 41 and 42 designate nuns' quarters, and on the second floor the number is 15. (Archivio di Stato, Florence, CS126:81 [1755]. Reprinted by permission.)

Figure 3 Etching of Saint Mary Magdalen in a record book of the Monastero delle Convertite. (Archivio di Stato, Florence, CS126:62 [1435–1620]. Reprinted by permission.)

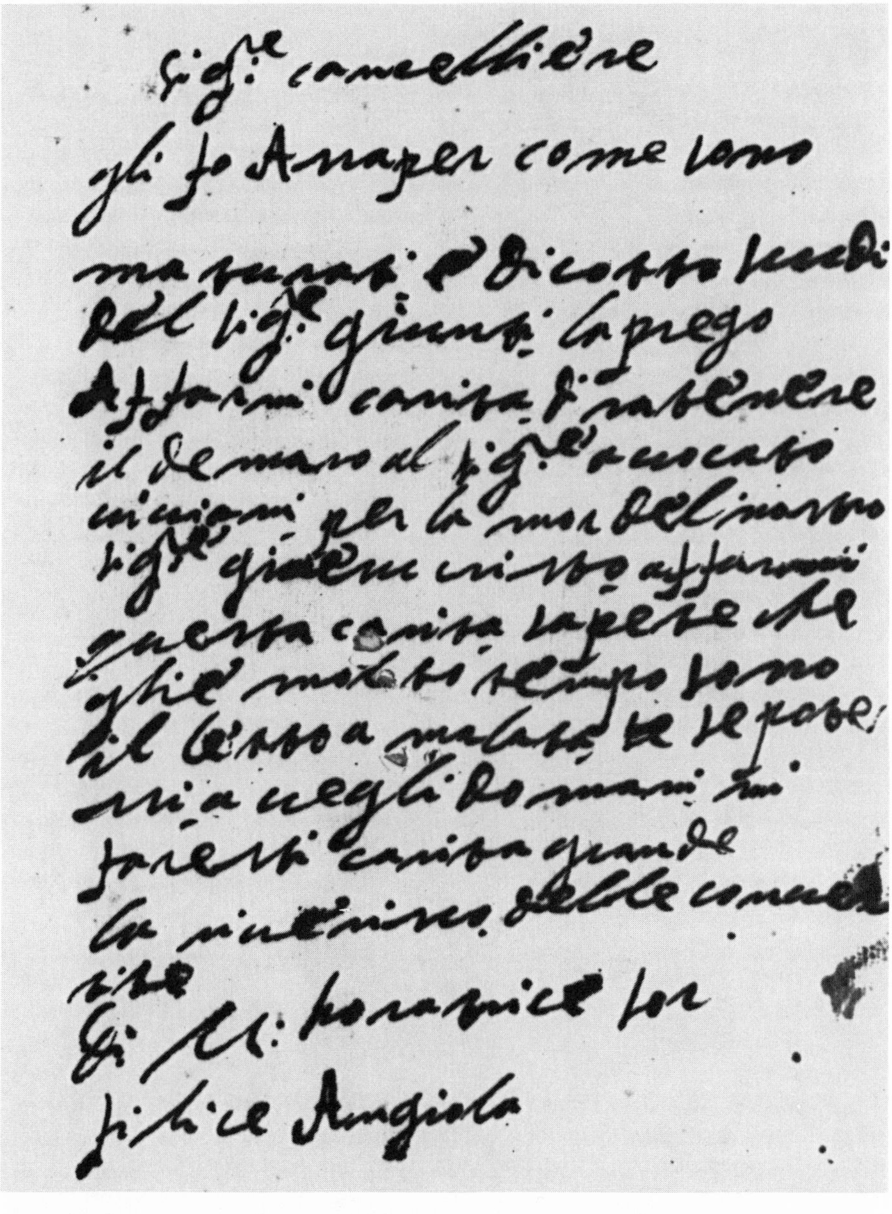

Figure 4 Women untrained in writing nonetheless wrote to arrange their financial affairs. This scrawled, ungrammatical letter from Suor Felice Angiola Bracciolini is typical. It reads: "Signor chancellor. I make you to know how the 18 scudi of Signor Giunti have matured. I beg you for the love of our Lord Jesus Christ to do me the favor of keeping the money with the lawyer Viviani. To do me this favor, you know that for a long time I have been sick in bed. If I could have [the scudi] tomorrow, you would do me a great favor. I send my respects, from the [Monastero delle] Convertite. From the one who prays for you, S[u]or Filice Angiola. (Archivio di Stato, Florence, CS126:66 [late seventeenth century]. Reprinted by permission.)

Figure 5 Reforming the body and soul at the Magdalen House: a spinning wheel, Table of Diet, Anglican Book of Common Prayer, and Bible. (Frontispiece from Hanway, *Thoughts on the Plan,* 1759. Reprinted courtesy of the Print Collection, Lewis Walpole Library, Yale University.)

Figure 6 Reformed prostitute, in uniform of the Magdalen House, before the institution's chapel. (Frontispiece from Dodd, *An Account,* 1770. Reprinted courtesy of the Library, University of California at Berkeley.)

4

"At Work and Recreation Together": Life Inside the Women's Refuges of Tuscany

What sort of life did ex-prostitutes and anomalous women lead within the Tuscan refuges? The tenor of life depended on both the objectives of each refuge's founders and on the residents' own actions and adaptations. In this chapter we will explore founders' ethics of reform and residents' responses concerning the life of the community and the disposition of property.

Economic and Spiritual Ethics of Reform

The Monastero delle Convertite, in existence from about the 1330s, embodied a traditional, rather haphazard approach to the conversion of sinful women. Fourteenth-century preachers, together with male members of a confraternity, had persuaded a number of prostitutes to repent and had founded the refuge that evolved into the Monastero delle Convertite, an Augustinian convent. The administrators of the Monastero delle Convertite expected repentant prostitutes to reform by becoming novices and nuns and conforming to a life of penitence and religious observance. In the fourteenth century the religious regimen at the Monastero delle Convertite was fairly moderate and loose, and so it remained in subsequent centuries.[1]

The later refuges for *convertite,* the Casa delle Malmaritate in Florence and Santa Maria Maddalena in Pistoia, however, arose in response to the perceived increase in prostitution in the sixteenth century and offered coherent programmatic solutions to the new social problem. At the Casa delle Malmaritate and Santa Maria Maddalena, starkly contrasting strategies emerged. The program at the Casa delle Malmaritate embodied an economically oriented ethic of reform, and the program at Santa Maria Maddalena a decidedly spiritual ethic of reform.

The prosperous male and female members of the confraternity that launched the Casa delle Malmaritate in 1579 envisioned a program of reform that can be characterized as economic behaviorism. The founders planned to offer ex-prostitutes financial prods and rewards. Recognizing that prostitution fed on women's economic needs, they hoped to eradicate it by an economic cure. The founders intended to convert former prostitutes into honest laborers and reinsert them into society. Residents in the house would labor at "what they knew" and at the piecework assigned by administrators. Those who had "some property" would be dowered and married off to men of substance. Others, the married prostitutes expected to predominate in the household, would return to the world as laborers or servants.[2]

Life in the Casa delle Malmaritate was to reflect the tone of sound business. The founders demanded that financially solvent entrants contribute toward the substantial charge for room and board of three scudi per month, so that the *convertite* would not "usurp charity." Women too poor to do this at entrance would pay monthly taxes on the fruits of their in-house labor and retain the rest of their earnings. The members of the confraternity that founded the institution took the view, more and more widespread in the sixteenth century, that they wished to aid only the laboring and deserving poor.[3] The founders of the Casa delle Malmaritate spoke the language of money; they were concerned, above all else, with questions of financing, which they took as indicators of other kinds of information. The founders believed that if an entrant honestly revealed her assets, so that they could apportion her contribution to her living expenses, they should view her financial cooperation as a sign of sincere desire to reform.[4] The backers of the house manifested great concern for the economic viability of their female charges. They tried to ensure that donors' promises to support *convertite* would be fulfilled. With a sharp acumen honed in the world of Florentine commerce, they analyzed the binding power of such promises and detected loopholes.[5] The statutes of the Casa delle Malmaritate permitted residents to retain possession of any goods or land they owned. In fact, the founders wanted the ex-prostitutes to receive help from administrators if they tried to reclaim property due them.[6]

The members of the confraternity would find residents piecework to do at a "just price." The statutes stipulated that the administrators should not permit the women to work without remuneration or when they could earn more at other tasks. The founders of the Casa delle Malmaritate believed that their program would produce a high level of motivation for labor. They warned administrators not to let *convertite* work all the time and neglect their duties in spiritual exercises and offices of the household. Nonetheless, the founders insisted in their practical way that the residents should not engage in excessive fasting. Overall, they believed that the optimal program of reform should emphasize a workhouselike severity over piety.[7]

The approach to moral reform taken by the founders of the Casa delle Malmaritate was reminiscent of a businessman's balanced ledger. Aware that relatives sometimes forced women into prostitution, the founders of the refuge intended to restore *convertite* to their families only upon receipt of monetary security for the women's welfare. They wanted to make the families, like the *convertite* themselves, financially responsible, which in Florence also connoted moral uprightness.[8] The founders' interest lay in inculcating a work ethic and in producing able-bodied young workers. Graduates of the refuge might receive monetary assistance and other forms of aid in reestablishing themselves outside the institution. The "daughters of this place" were like apprentices in trades who partook in the paternalistic networks of patronage and clientage that operated in the Florentine world of business. Only claims of inability to find "honest work" outside, not plaints of sickness or old age, would justify reentry into the refuge.[9] To control the conditions under which women departed, administrators developed a carrot-and-stick policy. They expected to reward good conduct with financial help and to punish inappropriate behavior by confiscating property or levying fines. In sum, the founders of the Casa delle Malmaritate held out the promise of absolution from this or that pecuniary penalty more often than they focused on the notion of absolution from sin.[10]

Reform wore a different face at Santa Maria Maddalena in Pistoia. Founded by a group of lay patricians in 1604, the Pistoian refuge demanded introspective penitence behind enclosed walls. Initially, life at Santa Maria Maddalena emphasized training for both labor and religion. The founders knew of many cases in which women had turned away from prostitution and then "had difficulty supporting themselves."[11] Sensitive to the ex-prostitutes' acute dependency and poverty, the backers enrolled a "maiden" who could teach weaving to the new *convertite*. They aimed to shelter and to educate women who renounced the life of sin.[12] They took incremental steps toward achieving their long-term goal of establishing a convent. In 1606 administrators of the refuge asked the bishop of Pistoia to permit the former prostitutes to cut their hair—"the instrument of the Devil"—and assume a monastic habit. When the bishop deferred the request, the *convertite* joined the Third Order of Saint Francis in 1607. By 1626 the administrators, the bishop, and many of the female residents all concurred in turning Santa Maria Maddalena into a cloistered Franciscan convent.[13]

The conventual constitutions emphasized the cloistered life as one key to reform. As nuns, the converts made vows of poverty, chastity, and obedience that would remove them from the "tyrannical liberty" of the secular world.[14] Cloister imposed an additional physical barrier against the outside world. The destiny of the nuns was not to return to the world or even to have contact with it. Instead, they were to withdraw into an inner world. The constitutions exhorted the *convertite* to look inside themselves, "take full custody of your heart and your sentiments," and regenerate themselves spiritually.[15]

Works of penance would help the prostitutes-turned-nuns to develop a sense of internal repentance, to accompany their external conformity to a life of chastity. The conventual administrators expected the nuns to carry out the penitential rites of fasting, vigil, discipline, and humiliation. Among other requisites of penitence, the nuns had the obligation to scourge themselves weekly. The constitutions urged that the nuns frequently contemplate the Last Judgment's punishments and rewards. Retiring to bed each night would entail a scrupulous examination of conscience, to be performed "as if entering your tomb."[16] The path of penitence required constant effort, and it had no easy exits. The ecclesiastical supervisors of the convent reminded the *convertite* that Christ had said in Matthew 24, "Not he who begins but he who perseveres until the end will be saved." The churchmen elaborated: "Although the prize of eternal happiness is promised to whoever begins to live right, it is given only to those who persevere up to the end."[17] The women at Santa Maria Maddalena would hear repeatedly of the conversions of Mary Magdalen, the desert fathers, the Prodigal Son, and the courtesan Thaïs.[18] The administrators hoped that the nuns would imitate these stalwart role models and gird themselves for the arduous lifelong course of penitential sacrifice.

Santa Maria Maddalena's founders planned a program of reform meant to engage ex-prostitutes in continuous occupation of the mind and body. The nuns had a schedule of duties, ranging from devotional tasks to paid labor at piecework. The constitutions recommended that the administrators of the convent encourage instruction in weaving and even reading.[19] At the convent, however, these activities would fulfill a different function than at the Florentine Casa delle Malmaritate. They would keep idle hands busy, unable to do the Devil's work, whereas in Florence the labor of *convertite* represented a blessed boon that productive hands could offer the commonwealth. Unlike the women at the Casa delle Malmaritate, Santa Maria Maddalena's nuns fully relinquished their earnings to the convent. The constitutions equated property with worldly carnality. The regimen at Santa Maria Maddalena promoted an ideal image of the penitent nun as selfless and propertyless.[20]

Life at Santa Maria Maddalena reflected Counter-Reformation values. The conventual constitutions echoed the notions of vocation and "calling" to religious life that had been demonstrated by the worthy figures of Catholic reform, the Capuchin monks, and carefully articulated by Ignatius Loyola. The constitutions urged the nuns to live up to their "double vocation, both of conversion and religion."[21] As nuns, the women at Santa Maria Maddalena would perform far more devotional observances than did their sister *convertite* at the Casa delle Malmaritate in Florence. At the Casa delle Malmaritate only the prioress had to have intimate knowledge of the statutes of the refuge. At the Pistoian convent all residents would hear a chapter of the constitutions read aloud every Friday.[22] The constitutions frequently cited official Church policy as guidelines. Yet even Santa Maria Maddalena's ecclesiastical supervisors had to acknowledge that their flock differed from other nuns, and they conceded to the *convertite* a version of the Franciscan monastic rule tailored to their presumed abilities.[23] Fervent as the desire for orthodoxy might be at Santa Maria Maddalena, the convent differed from other convents. Its mission was not simply to mold good women into God's servants, but rather to carry out the exacting challenge of reforming hardened sinners into devout penitents.

Why did the Casa delle Malmaritate and Santa Maria Maddalena offer such contrasting programs of reform? The difference in socioeconomic contexts for the two refuges provides one explanation. The concentration of growing industries in Florence demanded workers and supplied positions in a way that limited-scale production in Pistoia did not. The fact that the founders of the Casa delle Malmaritate hoped to reinsert residents into society as workers, while the founders of Santa Maria Maddalena favored retaining *convertite* at the convent, may reflect the disparate economic opportunities for women in these two locales. Another reason for the differences lay in who ran the institutions. The spiritual superseded the practical at Santa Maria Maddalena in large part because churchmen acceded to control of that refuge. Laymen retained power at the more secular Casa delle Malmaritate in Florence. As a noteworthy new institution in the small town of Pistoia, Santa Maria Maddalena drew a great deal of attention and personal involvement on the part of the local ecclesiastical establishment. Clerics and leaders of the Church in Pistoia lent on-the-spot advice and inspiration. The Casa delle Malmaritate, on the other hand, was one of scores of charitable organizations in Florence, where pressing concerns inside and outside the diocese competed for the attention of the ecclesiastical hierarchy. The relative strength and immediacy of ecclesiastical leadership in Pistoia, as opposed to a more distant ecclesiastical interest in Florence, played a significant role in setting the dissimilar tones of the two refuges. Finally, the Casa delle Malmaritate primarily intended to receive married prostitutes, predisposing that institution toward a worldly orientation. It could more easily reform such women by preparing them to return to husbands and secular life, rather than by attempting to make nuns of them.[24]

Responses to the Institutional Community

Newly admitted *convertite* had little choice but to adapt to certain features of the refuges, whereas in other matters they could respond to their new environments on an individual basis. One of the first conditions upon entering a refuge was that a woman had to ensure that she clothed herself in a mode deemed appropriate for her new life. This rite of passage represented the initial step toward achieving the founders' goals for the *convertite,* those of re-creating their self-identity and conforming to socially approved gender roles. Residents at the Casa delle Malmaritate clad themselves in whatever modest garments they had, while most women at the Monastero delle Convertite and Santa Maria Maddalena adopted a monastic habit. Administrators at the Casa delle Malmaritate had orders to confiscate any men's clothing the ex-prostitutes owned, articles that the women may have once worn on a lark or as tokens claimed from clients. Santa Maria Maddalena's constitutions commanded the nuns to wear plain black shoes and not shoes incised in the style favored by boys in the secular world. The new raiment became the outward and visible sign of a changed life. To foster a transformation that went more than skin deep, the Casa delle Malmaritate and Santa Maria Maddalena also made available hairshirts to reinforce an inner inclination toward penitence.[25]

Entrants encountered a second constraint in the form of the physical environments of the refuges. At their permanent sites in Florence and Pistoia respectively, the two monastic refuges, the Monastero delle Convertite and Santa Maria Maddalena, offered premises that were in some ways similar. Both refuges housed a church, kitchen, refectory, visitors' parlor, and prison. A major difference lay in sleeping arrangements. Santa Maria Maddalena had a communal dormitory, while the Monastero delle Convertite had a profusion of single rooms and suites used as living and sleeping quarters (see illustration insert, Figure 2). The Casa delle Malmaritate, located in its first few years in a newly constructed convent, included a kitchen, refectory, communal dormitory, novices' room, prison, and audience room where the confraternity met, and residents had access to the convent's ground-floor church. By 1582 the Casa delle Malmaritate moved to its own neighboring quarters, and sometime before the early nineteenth century it acquired a three-story building. All three refuges probably had specially designated work areas as well.[26] The refuges' physical premises posed obligations in day-to-day maintenance that had to be met in order for the institutions to function. The administrators of the refuges imposed systems of elective offices in administration and housekeeping that they expected residents to fulfill. Administrators viewed service in these offices as practically and morally beneficial. The residents indeed elected one another and filled the offices that kept the households operating.[27] As we shall see, the physical premises also presented opportunities for residents to act autonomously in manipulating their living situations and environment.

For entrants to the refuges, one of the changed facets of their lives that required the most adjustment was the degree of confinement they would have to endure. They did not have to face complete isolation from society. Male administrators, chaplains, confessors, preachers, and medical personnel made appearances. Gentlewomen called upon the residents to encourage them in their efforts at reform. At the grille or in the parlor, residents received visits from family members whom administrators considered respectable.[28] There were also unwelcome disturbances from outside, ranging from noisemaking to premeditated abductions and violence. In 1583 one Piero ("alias the Bee") Magnanini, a thug working for unknown others, tried to kill a woman who had just entered the Monastero delle Convertite. Asking for "Isabella," he delivered to her a forged letter, Greek wine, and a poisoned plant. Four days later, having heard that the poison had not done its job, the man returned with the lure of a basket of edibles, and a knife up his sleeve. When Isabella came to the door, he stabbed her and fled, leaving the woman with a knife stuck in her chest. The Otto di Guardia arrested the culprit, but whether Isabella lived or died was not recorded.[29]

Although, in the view of the founders, living in a confined environment could preserve one's chastity and save one's soul, the *convertite* found that the loss of personal freedom of movement and communication could also take its toll on the spirit. Women in the refuges for *convertite* developed ways of coping with the restrictions of living under lock and key. Like Suor Antonina

Ferrante Vannucci, a *convertita* and professed nun at the Monastero delle Convertite, they managed to maneuver somewhat within the limitations. In 1670, at the close of her first decade in the convent, Antonina received from a priest, Father Lorenzo Voltagli, an annual donation stipulating that she "live like a good nun and not go chatter at the grille with anyone who came to visit without [Father Lorenzo's] license." A few days after composing the donation, Father Lorenzo more reasonably amended it to say that Antonina could go to the grille to attend to necessities and that she could speak to certain relatives. Fourteen years passed without incident, and then the priest angrily ceased payment, charging that Antonina had violated his orders. With casuistry worthy of a Jesuit, Antonina denied that her action of writing a letter to a relative had contravened the conditions because, as she explained, the priest had not specifically prohibited letter writing. Father Lorenzo's stipulations "were erroneous and of no force" anyway, Antonina argued, because, being under the jurisdiction of her monastic superiors, she could not tie herself to such promises. Fulfilling the role of a religious meant that she owed obedience only to her conventual superiors, not to an outsider whose interference would generate resentment. And as a vulnerable female, she should not be "defrauded" by his imposition of a qualification through what was supposed to be charity.

Relying on one of the convent's supervisors in the ducal bureaucracy to convey her response, Antonina took her society's image of the ultimately dutiful nun and made it work to her advantage. She and the official turned the tables and put the priest on the defensive, demanding that he recommence payment or risk the displeasure of his ecclesiastical superiors and God.[30] Although perseverance in conversion meant being cut off from society and adjusting to having watchful eyes always over one's shoulder, the residents of the refuges nonetheless managed to salvage some personal autonomy and satisfactions.

The question of status at the monastic refuges allowed residents much leeway for manipulation. At the nonmonastic Casa delle Malmaritate, all residents had the same status in compliance with the statutes of the refuge.[31] But at the Monastero delle Convertite and Santa Maria Maddalena, women could manipulate their status on two overlapping tracks. One track concerned the route from acceptance into the convent to adoption of the monastic habit (investiture) to profession of the nun's binding vows of poverty, chastity, and obedience. The other track concerned the division of labor within the household and the type of nun one became—a *conversa* (or *servigiale*), who attended to the domestic needs of other nuns, or a *velata*, a veiled nun who benefited from the help of the servant nuns.[32]

A woman's degree of progression on these tracks depended on personal preference and on whether or not she could afford the dowries correlated with the statuses. At the Monastero delle Convertite and Santa Maria Maddalena, a wide gap lay between the dowry for *velata* and that for *servigiale,* with the higher status costing twice as much. If a prostitute could delay her entrance

until the day of the Lenten sermon on Mary Magdalen, she would find reduced prices—in 1628 at the Monastero delle Convertite, a cut from 160 to
140 scudi for *velata,* and from 70 to 30 scudi for *servigiale.* The dowries for
servigiale were within the same range as or more costly than those at other
contemporary Italian convents, but the dowries for *velata* were somewhat
lower than their analogues elsewhere.[33] As we have already seen, about the
same sum, sixty scudi, would enable a prostitute to become a *convertita* in a
monastic refuge or to purchase a lifetime immunity from harassment by the
Onestà.[34] At their acceptance or investiture, entrants to the monastic refuges
paid a single dowry, which covered both investiture and the possibility of
eventually making profession.[35] Only if in the future they decided to upgrade
their status, might they commit themselves to paying a second dowry.

Some women contrived to attain the status they desired even if funds were
lacking, while others scaled back their ambitions. Entrants found donors who
could help them, and they inveigled administrators of the convents into granting reductions or waiving dowries.[36] They persuaded the institutions to accept,
in lieu of cash, either payment in kind or long-term pledges backed by guarantors. In 1569 an ex-prostitute named Elisabetta, having already passed two
years in the Monastero delle Convertite, wished to become a nun and transferred title to her only property, her house, to defray the dowry.[37] Women
might scrounge and stint for twenty years or more to pay off their dowries.[38]
Aid from an entrant's peers could also underwrite accession to a higher status.
Piera Santini entered the Monastero delle Convertite in 1628 as a *servigiale,*
but "the nuns wanted her to become a *velata,*" and from one of the nuns who
was a relative of hers she obtained the funds to permit the upgrading.[39] Other
less fortunate women had to lower their expectations, as happened to
Margherita Giardinieri, who wanted to enter the Monastero delle Convertite
in the early seventeenth century. When her anticipated funding for the status
of *velata* did not materialize, this "poor little whore," as her contemporaries
called her, had to accept charity and settle for becoming a servant nun.[40]

Taking on a higher religious status often meant a great deal to *convertite,*
as an episode from the history of Santa Maria Maddalena illustrates. Over its
first two decades that refuge followed an uneven course toward becoming a
cloistered convent in 1626. In 1638 Suor Maria Francesca, Suor Maria Felice,
and the latter's daughter Suor Maria Jacinta, all ex-prostitutes who had undergone investiture, requested from the bishop of Pistoia permission to make
profession of their final vows before their year of probation had ended. These
novices declared that they were "moved by zeal . . . and eager to perfect
themselves in religion and to acquire greater merit in the service of [God]."
They contended that only custom, not stated policy, dictated that, in the past,
professions had been made after a year.[41] Their wish to bypass the custom
instigated a major controversy.

An investigation conducted by the bishop's vicar, Girolamo Godemini,
produced conflicting arguments. The vicar found Santa Maria Maddalena's
constitutions to be ambiguous on the timing of professions. But as he ascer-

tained from the convent's records and from conversations with all the professed nuns, in practice the administrators and religious had interpreted the
constitutions in such a way that nuns made professions only after a year's
probation. This was in fact the case at most female monastic houses, including
the Monastero delle Convertite. However, word had reached Girolamo
Godemini of recent resolutions on the part of papal and episcopal authorities
to grant to *convertite* the privilege of taking vows early, and he came to favor
amending the constitutions. Although the professed nuns had grumbled, "We
waited out the year, and so should others," the vicar believed that the change
would be for the better. The lay administrators of the convent, the *operai,* had
persuasively argued that while waiting out a year to take vows, many *convertite* had returned to lives of sin. The departures upset the other members of
the household and posed the danger that some of the professed nuns might
furtively follow those who had left. The vicar hoped that Bishop Alessandro
del Caccia, in deciding the matter, would act in such a way as to prevent
further departures.

Bishop Alessandro agreed to the request advanced by the novices. He
ordered that the constitutions be revised to permit the early profession of
monastic vows by *convertite.* By pressing for the shorter interval preceding
profession, the ex-prostitutes brought about a change in policy that could
encourage further reform on the part of their sisters still in a state of sin.
Because of the change that they initiated, *convertite* would more quickly be
able to span the chasm separating abhorred sinners from sanctified nuns. A
month after the controversy, the three Franciscan tertiaries responsible for the
revision in policy professed their vows together on a particularly holy occasion, the name day of their patron, Saint Francis.[42]

Ceremonies marking transitions in status, as well as the installation of new
officers in the household, punctuated the rhythm of life at the refuges and had
considerable symbolic significance. Taking on the title of *Suor,* usually a new
personal name, and the monastic habit at investiture impressed upon the
convertita that she had embarked upon a moral and spiritual rebirth.[43] Elaborate rites of acceptance welcomed entrants arriving on the day of the Lenten
sermon on Mary Magdalen and at other times.[44] Equally potent was the
velata's profession. The ceremonies and the commitment to a respectable and
communal life that they represented could hold a powerful allure. At the
Monastero delle Convertite in 1627, Suor Maddalena Costante asked on her
deathbed if she could make profession. A thirty-three-year-old married prostitute, she had undergone investiture, thanks to a Jesuit benefactor, two years
earlier. Acquiescing to her plea, the governor and abbess placed the just-
blessed black veil on her head four hours before she died.[45]

Freed from the exigencies of surviving in society, many of the *convertite*
devoted themselves to newfound activities in the refuges, just as the founders
had hoped they would. At all three of the Tuscan refuges, the administrators
required participation in prayer, with the hours of prayer being most numerous, naturally, at the monastic refuges. The constitutions of Santa Maria

Maddalena stipulated that nuns who failed to do their sacral duties would be punished. The *convertite* indeed carried out their sacral obligations. The two monastic refuges rang with the voices of *convertite* singing to fulfill contracts of prayer for the living and the dead, to accompany priests conducting Mass, and to participate in rites of the household.[46] During the depression of 1620, when Grand Duke Cosimo II sent the Monastero delle Convertite old Venetian gold pieces worth 163 scudi, "the nuns on the spot immediately went into the choir and sang the Te Deum Laudamus and prayed to God for the health of the Grand Duke." Through their ritualized acts, they expressed their gratitude for the ducal gift that could "purchase much bread."[47] The nuns also filled the office of *sagrestana,* caretaker of the church and of religious artifacts such as the relics from the head of Saint Cordula and arm of Saint Dionysius at the Monastero delle Convertite.[48]

Many residents went beyond doing what was required of them in sacral activity and showed a personal inclination toward devotions. One of the women at Santa Maria Maddalena preached "a most devout sermon" at the institution's first ceremony of investiture in 1607, when she and her fellow residents donned the habit of the Third Order of Saint Francis. Her oratory stirred the audience of *convertite,* clerics, and gentlefolk. But the churchmen who took charge of Santa Maria Maddalena in the 1620s could not close their eyes to such unorthodox practices and expressly forbade sermonizing on the part of *suore* receiving their habits.[49] Residents of the refuges found other channels as well for individual religious expression. Typically, a Suor Margherita at the Monastero delle Convertite funded a set of devotions for her protectress, Saint Margaret.[50] Participating in devotions could be quite important to the residents. Vittoria Valori, who had been interned in the Casa delle Malmaritate late in the eighteenth century, after the refuge had become an arm of the police ministry and less of a quasi-religious institution, strenuously protested when the confessor at the refuge barred her from taking communion for some time because of her misbehavior within the institution.[51]

Within a certain licit range, residents of the refuges could find opportunities for learning and creative expression. The residents were permitted, and at Santa Maria Maddalena even urged, to read appropriate material that would instill virtue. By the mid-1770s, as part of its education for novices, the Monastero delle Convertite paid a literate nun to teach newcomers to read and write. The sixteenth-century administrators of the Casa delle Malmaritate cautioned against the importation of lascivious writings and pictures, but they approved of and had on hand devotional images.[52] Likewise, the Monastero delle Convertite offered to its nuns an array of art works to contemplate (see illustration insert, Figure 3). These included an altarpiece of the Trinity, John the Baptist, and Mary Magdalen painted by Sandro Botticelli, and a centrally placed tree of saints that one of the convent's seventeenth-century confessors had given to the household.[53] In addition, some women at the refuges had personal devotional images. Suor Francesca Cammilla, an illiterate nun at the

Monastero delle Convertite in the late seventeenth century, possessed her own statue of the Madonna.[54]

A number of the women in the refuges took the initiative to enhance the environment around them. An early-seventeenth-century administrator new to his position wanted to determine the origins of two chapels in the Monastero delle Convertite, and to find out he interviewed the nuns. His oral survey revealed that past and present members of the convent had founded the chapels. In the future, too, members would found additional chapels, including one honoring "Santa Maria Maddalena Penitente."[55] The residents added to the store of spiritual riches at the refuges. In 1621 Suor Lorenza of the Monastero delle Convertite commissioned for the convent's garden a scene of Christ and Mary Magdalen, paying twelve scudi out of her pocket for it. She commissioned the work from Giovanni da San Giovanni, a "famous painter of our times," and under it his assistant painted a "little story" of the Nativity.[56]

The ex-prostitutes and anomalous women who entered refuges confronted an unavoidable corporate ethos and the profound desire on the part of the institutional supervisors that the life of the community be characterized by "peace." The founders of the Casa delle Malmaritate required residents to be "at work and recreation together," not "retired" and hidden away from one another. They said that the "common good" should always be a higher priority than the well-being of any one individual.[57] The residents had to cope with living communally in a group with a somewhat shifting composition. Throughout the early modern period, the number of women at the Monastero delle Convertite ranged between 100 and 200; at Santa Maria Maddalena, between 20 and 40; and at the Casa delle Malmaritate, between a few and 30. The Monastero delle Convertite at times received from 12 to 20 new entrants per year, twice as many as would enter a mainstream Tuscan convent in a year. Smaller numbers of women annually joined Santa Maria Maddalena.[58] Especially on the day of the annual Lenten sermon on Mary Magdalen, clusters of women applied for entrance to the refuges for *convertite*. To be suddenly thrown in close proximity with so many unknown people and to have to acclimate, taxed the residents' capacities for flexibility and tolerance.

In some cases close interpersonal bonds did evolve. The connection could grow through service. A servant nun (*conversa* or *servigiale*) usually attended to the needs of one particular veiled nun, who may have helped to pay the *servigiale*'s dowry. The veiled nun could come to feel a deep sense of caring and responsibility for the servant who stood by her. She might express her gratitude by trying to provide for the woman after the veiled nun's own death. Sometime before her death in 1661, Suor Caterina Salvetti at the Monastero delle Convertite bequeathed "the greater part of her goods" to her servant, Suor Filippa Caterina.[59]

In another form of service, more reciprocal, women nursed one another during sickness. At the Casa delle Malmaritate and Santa Maria Maddalena, residents had to take their turn at fulfilling the office of nurse. They had ample opportunity to tend to one another, for illness often befell the residents, and some of them suffered from long-term ailments.[60] At the Monastero delle Convertite as well, residents brought their friends through crises and appreciated the kindnesses done to them. They sought to repay individuals and the community. Suor Bartolomea Leonora Corsini in 1695 dictated a bedside will to her confessor and left twelve scudi to one nun and her room to another, because they had "ministered to her needs during her illness." In the preceding decade another nun had died and bequeathed her rooms to serve as quarters for the sick.[61]

The women in the institutions developed many kinds of relationships for mutual support and aid. A resident might take an entrant under her wing, in a gesture of protective rapport. Administrators at the Monastero delle Convertite, like their counterparts at other convents in Florence, sometimes alluded to the phenomenon of discipleship. Just as the male *discepoli* of thirteenth- and fourteenth-century Florentine guildsmen were apprentices, the female *discepole* of nuns at convents were spiritual apprentices, like Jesus' disciples. In 1628 Suor Lisabetta at the Monastero delle Convertite contributed sixteen scudi toward the dowry of "her disciple," Suor Margherita Argentina, an ex-prostitute signed up for the status of veiled nun. A contemporary, Suor Andrea Angelica, bequeathed a set of rooms to "one of her disciples."[62] These *discepole* may sometimes have been servant nuns, but as Suor Margherita Argentina's example demonstrates, they were not always so. Even when they were servants to the women who claimed them as disciples, they were clearly much more than that in psychological terms. Residents of the refuges for *convertite* formed friendships with fellow residents and showed how they valued these friends by remembering them in their wills, bequeathing money, property, or some small token of recognition.

Personal relationships developed through shared living quarters. Residents of the Casa delle Malmaritate and Santa Maria Maddalena occupied communal dormitories. While some members of the Monastero delle Convertite bought spacious suites of rooms and lived there by themselves, many others shared the one or two small chambers they could afford to purchase.[63] Veiled nuns and their servant nuns often shared rooms, as did residents who were related to one another. The convent's administrators occasionally tried to dissuade professed nuns from sharing their quarters with women not yet wearing the habit, but otherwise they did not interfere in the matter of who lived with whom.[64] However, lay and religious authorities did show concern over sleeping arrangements. They feared seeing friendships between the women veer into illicit sexual intimacies. At other early modern refuges for *convertite* and even mainstream convents, officials discovered women who were sexually involved with other women. Bishop Alfonso Binarino, the apostolic visitor who inspected the Monastero delle Convertite in 1575, felt the need to command in writing that "the nuns should sleep alone." From Santa Maria Maddalena's earliest days, the Pistoian administrators took pains to ensure an adequate supply of beds. Administrators at the Casa delle Malmaritate and Santa Maria Maddalena ordered residents to refrain from visiting one another's beds and sleeping two to a bed. The administrators of the Casa delle Malmaritate intended to conduct bed checks and insisted that some form of illumination be lit throughout the night. They asserted that they would deny permission for entrance to any applicant who could not be assured of having her own bed, supplied by either the house or herself. Despite the rules, the need for intimacy, physical warmth, and perhaps sexual solace could outweigh fears of punishment, and women may well have continued to sleep with companions at the Monastero delle Convertite or the other Tuscan refuges whenever they could do so undetected.[65]

A factor that mediated human relations at the refuges was the pervasive emphasis on role models. The administrators of the refuges feared that bad examples of conduct in the household would inspire imitation, and they tried to shame misbehaving residents. They welcomed *convertite* sincere in their reform who could set good examples.[66] Indeed, the good spirits of well-adjusted residents could be contagious and very much appreciated. The records kept by administrators at the Monastero delle Convertite note three fondly remembered gentleborn nuns nominated "for holy memory" because of their exemplary lives. The records eulogized the convent's Suor Lucretia Felice, deceased in 1630 after more than a year's illness, as "a great example of patience and perfection." And when Suor Feliciana Diez moved out of the refuge after four years to go to her relatives in Pisa, her departure left "everyone in the monastery saddened, for she was much loved because of all her good qualities."[67]

Immaterial and material links connected present residents to past and future ones. In addition to hearing inspiring stories of exemplary predecessors, the residents of the refuges for *convertite* also identified with the past in other ways. Entrants at the Monastero delle Convertite and at the other refuges took over the rooms and beds of recently deceased residents. In cases of extreme need, like that of Santa Maria Maddalena's Domenica Milocchi, who came in 1660 with "nothing of her own," the hand-me-downs extended to clothing.[68] The continuity also encompassed nomenclature. At their investitures, three seventeenth-century entrants to the Monastero delle Convertite, Suor Maria Antonia, Suor Batista Felice, and Suor Maria Oretta, assumed names that had belonged to recently deceased nuns whom the entrants probably had not known personally.[69] The deceased remained with the living in another sense, too, because they found their final resting place in the sepulchers of the refuges where they had lasted out the years.[70] Residents of the refuges knew that they held responsibility for making their microcosm livable. Santa Maria Maddalena's nuns diligently voted on the question of admittance for each applicant, deciding if she would fit in and whether or not the community ought to expand.[71]

The administrators of the refuges anticipated dissonance in the households and formulated punishments for those who disturbed the "unity and peace."

Santa Maria Maddalena's administrators devised penalties ranging from "being deprived of the company of others in the refectory" to public humiliation before the community. At the Casa delle Malmaritate, a resident who made a nuisance of herself might have to submit to the correction of standing before the others as they ate, with a stick in her mouth, enacting the recognizable image of the silent, virtuous female familiar from emblem books.[72] The fact that most of the residents in the refuges for *convertite,* unlike nuns in mainstream convents, had been social mavericks may have even intensified interpersonal conflicts at the refuges. They were women who knew how to rebel against authority by one means or another.

Most of the types of conflict envisioned by the administrators in fact occurred. Their experience of the *convertite* made administrators at Santa Maria Maddalena impress upon entrants that it was forbidden to speak injuriously to fellow residents or to taunt them about past excesses committed in the world.[73] An eighteenth-century administrator of the Casa delle Malmaritate commented about the interned Vittoria Valori, who complained of mistreatment by her fellow residents: "Regarding her sorrow that sometimes her faults were related to the new entrants, many times it happened because of her quarrels, since she is too ready to mock everyone. Consequently, gossiping occurs, which I believe is very hard to prevent among these sort of persons."[74] Administrators expected the worst behavior from the women under their roof. They feared that their charges would lay violent hands upon one another. Eighteenth-century police supervising the Casa delle Malmaritate received a report that a resident, infuriated at having been denied access to a notary to reply to a letter from her husband, had attacked a teacher or the prioress with a sharp iron implement. But upon investigation, they found that the angry woman had threatened only herself with various objects.[75]

Resentments arose over inequities. At all the refuges, even those with clear differentiations in status, administrators strove to inculcate a spirit of egalitarianism in such matters as dress and the assignment of piecework, in an effort to level and unify. The founders of the Casa delle Malmaritate believed that if they did not accord the *convertite* equitable financial treatment, no one would ever have a moment's peace in the house.[76] Their fears were reasonable: just such a situation developed at the Monastero delle Convertite.

Squabbling on the part of residents of the Monastero delle Convertite brought about two changes in policy, meant to improve morale. In December 1619 discord had polarized the residents of the convent. The nuns looked on with approval when their abbess, Suor Gostanza, adopted the policy of serving the same kind of wine to veiled nuns and servant nuns alike. Previously, she had served pure wine to the veiled nuns and diluted wine to the servants. Some received enough to drink, and others complained that they had too little. With the new practice equality reigned, and the nuns pronounced themselves happier at that state of affairs.[77]

Then a month later everyone at the Monastero delle Convertite agreed that they should eliminate the annual taxes paid by the nuns. The taxes of three scudi for veiled nuns and one scudo for servant nuns had procured for each nun a little extra meat, oil, and fuel. But the administrators of the convent lamented that every time they tried to collect taxes

> there was always a ruckus. Because someone would say, "I was and I am sick," or "I don't have work," or "I'm in office and exempt," and one thing and another such that there was always noise and contestation among them. One would get mad when another escaped paying. If one nun didn't pay, another would say, "I don't want to pay either."[78]

The residents of the Monastero delle Convertite approached tax time with the same connivance that Tuscans at large brought to reducing their tax assessments.[79] The elimination of the taxes and of the attendant friction pleased the administrators. Even though the nuns lost the guaranteed provision of extra material benefits, they too were "content with the change." Once amity descended again upon the house, some of the nuns may have continued to enjoy extra comforts provided or paid for by their personal benefactors.

Dislike of the regimen and the superiors who enforced it prompted dissension at the refuges. In the inaugural year of the Casa delle Malmaritate, the administrators and *convertite* relocated the household, and they stopped along the way to hear the day's first Mass at a nearby church. There the priest voiced the customary request that the *convertite* reconcile any differences among them. They took the opportunity, outside of confession, to pour out their hearts to the confessor and to object to what they felt were the tyrannizing ways of the prioress. They said they had borne this treatment for many months out of the desire to save their souls, but they could stand it no longer. The women asked the confessor to intercede on their behalf. Hearing them all say the same thing, he conferred with a colleague, and the latter consulted someone else. So, noted the governor of the refuge in recording this incident, outside there arose rumors that great dissention wracked the house, when in fact calm reigned once again because the residents had released their antagonism in the cathartic outburst. In his analysis, the women did not count upon further action on the part of the cleric, since they would not be seeing him again.

But reverberations of the episode carried beyond the encounter at the church. The governor had heard the rumors and sought their origins. He determined that the *convertite* had all agreed to complain in order to revenge themselves on the prioress for her efforts to make them dress more modestly. To prevent the recurrence of such gossip, the administrators of the Casa delle Malmaritate tried to ensure that the residents would not find members of the supervising confraternity, or other people, willing to listen to their charges against the prioress and other superiors. The administrators neither expected nor desired good feelings between the residents and the prioress all the time, for that would mean that the prioress was too weak. Instead they concluded that, "because in [good families] and between mothers and daughters there arise conflicts, it is not a big thing that they arise among our *convertite.* . . .

and in fact, it's a good sign for these upheavals to occur occasionally."[80] The implication was that if everyone kept a sense of proportion, the squalls could come and go without threatening the life of the community.

Disposition of Property

Living in the refuges for *convertite* also required adapting and maneuvering in terms of one's relationship to property. Administrators of the refuges expected residents to contribute toward their own support and that of the household with property they had owned before entrance, income that came by way of public or private benefactors, and wages for labor performed within the institutions. Residents had an active role in the economic administration of the Monastero delle Convertite and of Santa Maria Maddalena. They voiced opinions about whether proposed financial transactions would be to the refuge's advantage. The nuns at the Monastero delle Convertite gathered together in the refectory for such a discussion in 1585. The abbess explained to them the terms of an offer, and "all speaking at the same time, they concurred, with much contentment."[81] Contracts for sales and rentals of properties belonging to the Monastero delle Convertite and Santa Maria Maddalena were drawn up in the names of the professed nuns, and they cited the nuns' assent to the transaction, along with that of the *operai*. The nuns of Santa Maria Maddalena fulfilled some duties undertaken at other refuges by male administrators, the *procuratori*.[82] At Santa Maria Maddalena, and probably at the other refuges, too, residents who had received education aided the ministeress and female officers with their writing and accounting tasks.[83] Nuns volunteered to supply venture capital to assure the future prosperity of their institution. Two seventeenth-century residents of the Monastero delle Convertite, Suor Luisa Monti and Suor Beatrice Giunti, supplied cash for the convent's purchase of two houses, in return for shares in a public investment fund, the Monte di Graticole, and Masses performed on their behalf during their lifetimes and afterward.[84]

Many residents at the refuges for *convertite* also continued to steward their own property. *Convertite,* like all women, were supposed to have a male intermediary (*mundualdo*) authorizing their financial affairs. The Onestà acted as a *mundualdo* for many registered prostitutes. The *procuratori* of the monastic refuges would take over this function if *convertite* became professed nuns. The sixteenth-century ex-prostitute Elisabetta, whom we recall offering her house as a dowry to enter the Monastero delle Convertite, indeed obtained permission from the Onestà, which served as her *mundualdo*.[85] At the Casa delle Malmaritate, where the founders believed that possession of property made people responsible, they encouraged *convertite* to safeguard their own goods, after giving the house and fellow residents their due. With all entrants of the Casa delle Malmaritate listing possessions in inventories and storing them in individual locked chests, the women could trust that when it came time to depart, they would be able to take away what they had brought.[86] The first group of *convertite* at Santa Maria Maddalena received from the founders the promise that if the refuge lost all its residents, each woman could retrieve her property. After a year, though, the administrators declared that this policy would not be in force for future entrants, whose property would belong irrevocably to the institution.[87]

The matter of entrants' property became an issue for convents, because starting in the late sixteenth century apostolic visitors were supposed to determine whether convents "observed the Council of Trent's . . . decree forbidding nuns to retain personal property." The Tridentine regulations ordered that professed nuns must incorporate into the convent any income they received from holdings or legacies. Instructions given to the visitors noted that when nuns incorporated substantial property into the convent, the abbess could legitimately exercise "charity and discretion" and see to it that they lived comfortably. When an apostolic visitor inspected the Monastero delle Convertite in 1575, he reported nothing untoward concerning these matters.[88] The visitor may have missed some irregularities. For despite the rules, evidence from the decades after the Council of Trent and from the seventeenth century indicates that the professed nuns of the Monastero delle Convertite continued to retain individual title to their property.[89] In the late 1630s proceeds from the rental of a house owned by Suor Lavinia Barbigi accrued to her account in the conventual account books. An entry in the convent's administrative records stated that the *procuratore* rented Suor Lavinia's house "for that nun."[90] Nuns could draw on their own property in order to serve as guarantors or benefactors for new entrants. Some offered as collateral the rooms they had purchased from the convent. Others contributed cash, as Suor Maria Prudenza Soldani did in 1645, when she wanted to help pay her niece's dowry.[91] Nuns at the Monastero delle Convertite accumulated property in the form of rooms, income from donations or rents, and dividends from shares in the investment funds known as *monti,* and many of them bequeathed their property according to their personal preferences.[92] The convent inherited a large amount of property from its nuns but in some cases only after the property had first circulated as a legacy to a deceased nun's fellow nuns.[93]

Even at Santa Maria Maddalena, whose conventual constitutions vociferously echoed the Tridentine policy, women left behind personal property at death.[94] The theoretical ban on personal property there was modified to permit vestiges of privatism. Administrators in fact warned that if a nun harmed another nun's belongings, her own possessions would suffer the same damage.[95]

These *convertite* and anomalous women from mercantile cities, like their fellow Florentines and Pistoians, were tied into the advanced economic and financial systems of early modern Tuscany. They carried with them into the institutions the economic concerns that had weighed on their minds outside. Prostitutes and anomalous women accustomed to having their property under their own control or that of their families suddenly saw it placed within the

grasp of a many-membered corporation. The change may have been especially disconcerting for the prostitutes, who, more than most women of their
time, enjoyed greater freedom to acquire cash when they needed it, as well as
greater ability to protect their proprietary rights before magistrates.[96] Within
the circumscribed institutional universe, many of them maneuvered successfully to protect their interests.

At the Monastero delle Convertite the residents engaged in certain forms of
speculation. A number of the nuns there owned shares in the investment funds
called *monti* and received annual dividends, such as the five scudi per year that
went to the convent's abbess of the early seventeenth century, Suor Maria
Gratia Alberighi. The convent reaped a benefit when at the death of Suor
Maria Arcangiola Giorgi in 1674 it inherited her four valuable shares in the
Monte di Pietà, worth 400 scudi. Although sometimes the nuns' dividends
amounted to only a small sum—little more than a scudo annually—in general,
the shares proved good investments for the nuns, as for most Florentines.[97]

Other residents shepherded past loans or engaged in new lending. Before
her conversion the illiterate prostitute Caterina Salvetti had made interest-
free loans to several men. When she became Suor Caterina in the Monastero
delle Convertite in 1650, she and the administrators of the convent kept track
of the outstanding debts. Suor Caterina by no means died impoverished, but
when her soul passed on in 1661, the debts owed her remained unpaid. Once
in the convent, nuns lent funds to clients closer to home, their fellow nuns.
When one nun made an interest-free loan to another nun, as Suor Eleonora
de' Medici did for Suor Margherita Fedele Candida Aurora in the mid-1680s,
she might be more assured of repayment.[98] Through their lending, such
women may have hoped to gain some hidden form of interest or a nonmaterial
favor. In two separate transactions in the second half of the seventeenth
century, Suor Bartolomea Leonora Corsini and Suor Francesca Zenobia
Strozzi each loaned money to male acquaintances, who planned to engage in
monetary and financial speculation at fairs and pay interest to the nuns. Suor
Francesca's involvement as a lender was touched by scandal when she posthu-
mously figured in a lawsuit concerned in part with forgery.[99]

Members of the Monastero delle Convertite showed a spirit of entrepre-
neurism. Suor Laura Francesca Gotti and her three aunts, all nuns in the
refuge in the second half of the seventeenth century, made a pact with the
convent that they would share in one another's intestate assets (*spoglie*). Even
before and after coming up with this version of a tontine, Suor Laura Francesca, an ex-prostitute, seemed familiar with shrewd finance. She acquired
most of the dowry for upgrading her status from her aunts; inherited dividends
from the Monte di Pietà from another nun; sought to collect on a donation
made to her deceased mother, Suor Maria Diodata; and purchased joint living
quarters with an aunt.[100]

The widow Agata Neri, whom we have met earlier as Suor Margherita
Fedele Candida Aurora, who borrowed from another nun, tried an inventive
strategy before her entry into the convent. Apparently fearing confiscation of

her property when she became a nun, she attempted to outsmart the system by depositing certain goods with a male acquaintance. But once she discovered the laxness at the Monastero delle Convertite and tried to retrieve her possessions, she encountered difficulty in doing so and had to enlist the assistance of a magistrate.[101]

Complications often arose to plague the lives of women in the unfamiliar circumstance of having to rely on sponsors' pledges of support. The *convertita* had to adjust to living on a sort of retirement pension, since neither by selling her body nor by working sporadically at cottage industry in the convent could she easily acquire extra cash when she wanted it. Benefactors, who ranged from shopkeepers to nobles, sometimes failed to produce the funds to cover their promises. When this situation developed, the best-intentioned of the donors planned to redeem their pledges as soon as possible and simply asked the expectant recipients to be patient, as one seventeenth-century gentlewoman wrote to Suor Maria Lorenza Giordani at the Monastero delle Convertite.[102]

Patience did not always lead to results, and then the women had to pin their hopes on litigation and petitions to authorities. Every year the Monastero delle Convertite paid for litigation in the civil and ecclesiastical courts; the nuns on whose behalf the convent lodged suits reimbursed the refuge when they could.[103] The women had to find the means to stymie scoundrels out to cheat them. In a complaint lodged probably in the late 1640s, Suor Maria Innocenza Berti asked the convent's supervisors in the ducal bureaucracy to enforce payment of an annual donation that Signor Anton Berti had promised her twenty years before. As she explained in a plaintive letter, Berti's heir, Filippo Ginori, had requested the contract and "I gave him the original," thinking that he wanted it in order to fulfill the pledge. But after handing over the contract, she never saw a single scudo in payment and realized that the heir had tricked her.[104]

Suor Felice Angiola Bracciolini likewise had to beseech powerful protectors for aid (see illustration insert, Figure 4). She suffered Job's trials in trying to collect on the annual donation to her initiated almost forty years earlier when she was a young widow. In the 1660s her donor's heirs or tenants, who now bore responsibility for the remittance, continually stalled and avoided payment. Twice in 1679 the aged Suor Felice Angiola, who described herself as "always sick," sent letters to ducal officials complaining that payment on the donation had ceased despite the fact that she "had infinitely requested it." She asked them to "wield your authority to get satisfaction for me."[105] At least on occasion, the suits and supplications brought justice, as in the case of Suor Maddalenangiola Fabiani in 1639. She won from Grand Duke Ferdinando II a decree that would help her to acquire the funds due her from the sale of her benefactor's estate.[106]

The residents of the refuges for *convertite* faced the dilemma of keeping themselves financially secure and comfortable despite numerous obstacles. Women unaccustomed to writing took up pen and paper to document their plaints, struggling with vocabulary and leaving ink blots. The illiterate persuaded others to write for them. They coped with the challenges, sometimes in farsighted strategies, other times in desperate attempts to respond to a crisis. Some of them may even have found inside the institutions opportunities for financial machinations and management that they would not have been afforded in the outside world.

For many of the women at the refuges, institutional life involved a balance between conforming to what administrators required of them and manipulating those aspects of their environment on which they could have an effect. As we shall see, however, some women never acclimated themselves to institutional life and wanted, more than anything, to leave the refuges.

5

The Tuscan Refuges as Social Institutions

Contemporaries viewed the foundation of refuges for *convertite* as being in the "public interest" (*essere utile publico*).[1] This chapter will examine the refuges for *convertite* as social institutions in the immediate context of their civic communities and in the larger context of the historical development of Western institutions.

Civic Dynamics and Values

Like other social institutions in medieval and early modern cities, the Tuscan refuges contributed in various ways to a sense of civic identity. In an incident reminiscent of the civic humanism that had flourished in Italian cities of the Renaissance, the inspiration for founding Santa Maria Maddalena connected the past and present. As the Pistoian sponsors informed Grand Duke Ferdinando I, they desired to imitate a fourteenth-century refuge for ex-prostitutes: "There was in olden days in this city a monastery for *convertite*. . . . Thus it is not surprising that in the year 1604 we are trying to do the same thing." The backers unearthed records almost three hundred years old and closely investigated the foundation of the fourteenth-century monastery and the support it had received from communal funds. The aged parchments held the same Biblical quotation that Pope Leo X had cited in his bull of 1520 renewing the call for the conversion of prostitutes: "there is more joy in heaven over one sinner turned to penitence than over ninety-nine righteous people."[2] The Tuscan refuges constituted links in civic networks for philanthropy and piety. They shared duties, economic arrangements, and personnel with other civic institutions. In the early seventeenth century the Monastero delle Convertite co-owned an urban rental property with the nuns of the Bigallo. In subsequent decades Father Gregorio Dezzi, a former chancellor of the Onestà magistracy, served as the convent's confessor, and Girolamo Salvatichi, a canon of the cathedral in Pistoia, served as the first governor of Santa Maria Maddalena.[3]

The institutions for *convertite* played a vital role in the civic economy of status based on honor and shame. The refuges were embedded in and meant to sustain the cultural sex/gender system based on the notion of female duality. The *meretrice convertita* (converted prostitute) was a conundrum that epitomized the dual image of the female's twin capacities: *meretrice* signified all that was vile and sinful, but *convertita* signified the promise of redemption and holiness. The institutions functioned as a sort of purification plant of the sex/gender system, by aiding women attempting to make the transition from disapproved to approved behavior. The refuges also provided a place for women lacking clearcut statuses and identities—women who were temporarily or permanently unclassifiable as honorable or dishonorable. The unclassifiable might threaten the symbolic weight of the two dichotomous images of feminine behavior unless there was some structural way of encompassing it, some give at the interstices of the ideological system. It was precisely this elasticity that the institutions permitted.

The rehabilitation of prostitutes unfolded as a morality play enacted on the public stage. The redeemed prostitutes joined the ranks of the city's holy figures, who were thought to be sources of protection and power in civic ritual life. Over the course of the seventeenth century, the Monastero delle Convertite drew public visitors to witness its internal ceremonies and venerate its holy image of the Virgin known as the Madonna of Love.[4] In 1620 the abbess of the convent, Suor Gostanza Niccolini, organized a particularly grand sacred spectacle that brought Florence's ruling family together with a portion of the civic populace. She had the idea of rallying the citizenry to pray for Florence's most important personage and the convent's nearby neighbor at the Palazzo Pitti, Grand Duke Cosimo II, who had been struck by an illness. "All the city," reported the convent's chronicler, came to visit the chapel of the Monastero delle Convertite, where a revered crucifix stood on view for five days. Then a torchlight procession with the crucifix at its head wound its way from the Monastero delle Convertite to four other monasteries in the neighborhood of Santo Spirito, in a two-hour rite. The procession visited the square outside the Palazzo Pitti, where the ailing grand duke and his duchess appeared to see the crucifix. The chronicler claimed with pride that the assembled crowd had credited the convent's crucifix with a miracle when it seemed to quell a hailstorm at the moment the procession was to begin.[5]

The Casa delle Malmaritate and Santa Maria Maddalena enjoyed public acclaim as well. Michele Poccianti, who authored a sixteenth-century compendium of Florence's religious treasures, cultivated the reputation of the Casa delle Malmaritate, praising its patrons who "provided everything needed out of their own pockets . . . a thing truly pious and full of infinite charity."[6] In Pistoia much attention focused on the band of *convertite* establishing a community in the early seventeenth century, especially as they switched locations several times. Moving in 1609 into the building in which they would settle permanently, the *suore* staged an elaborate rite of passage. Accompanied by the convent's male spiritual director and administrators, two closed carriages carried the *convertite* through the streets in full view of well-wishers. It was a dazzling testament to the power of respectability for transforming status. The women, formerly as prostitutes forbidden to occupy carriages, by virtue of their conversion now merited the honor of riding at the center of the solemn and holy procession. The Pistoian *convertite* continued to attract numerous visitors to ceremonies at the convent's new site.[7]

The Tuscan refuges figured among their cities' central social welfare institutions and reflected changing attitudes toward poor relief in the early modern period. Because the refuges for *convertite* had a certain resemblance to the medieval religious orders of penitent prostitutes, to some extent they still mirrored the traditional concept of Catholic charity in which the faithful performed the "good work" of giving to the Christlike "holy poor" and were rewarded by God's grace. The "holy poor" might be lay beggars in the streets or religious in monasteries, both in their different ways being living representations of Christ's sacrifice. The notion of refuges for *convertite* attracted supporters when the Catholic reform movement and post-Tridentine Church tried to revitalize Catholicism in part by turning religion toward solving deficiencies in social welfare.[8] Among other preoccupations, the reformers developed an intense concern about female virtue, about trying to make women, particularly poor women, adhere to the prevailing standards of morality. They wanted to prevent women on the one hand from becoming presumptuous Protestant harridans speaking out in church, and on the other from joining the widening ranks of prostitutes.

Yet at a time when respect for the Church and its doctrine of good works was at a low ebb, people no longer had confidence that the random gift of a coin to a beggar would automatically yield grace. If the poor could not by virtue of *who they were* be the vehicles by which their richer fellows obtained grace, they would have to find some other justification for soliciting alms. And if the prosperous were to continue to help the weak, they would have to have some other motivation. In the sixteenth century the upper orders continued to provide poor relief to the impotent poor—the ill and old—because of who those indigent poor *were,* but the elite also started to provide rationalized institutional relief to one group of needy, the "deserving poor," who merited help because of *what they did.* With aid, the deserving poor could improve their lot and moral standing in life, thus becoming more responsible members of the polity, better able to serve and obey their superiors. Donors now gave charity with the expectation of producing in return a beneficial change in the recipient, such as the transformation from prostitute to decent, honorable woman. But if the deserving poor failed to live up to the conditions for meriting aid, then instead they were said to "usurp charity," the phrase used by the founders of the Casa delle Malmaritate to describe entrants who might refuse to pay fees toward their upkeep.[9] This charge would have been inappropriate for the holy poor of former times.

The Tridentine Church did not follow the example of the Protestant churches, which rejected the concept of the "holy poor," as well as the concept of monasticism. Even though the Tridentine Church did not alter its doctrine on the holy poor, many Catholic laypersons had earlier, like Protestants, adopted a discriminating stance toward poor relief. They preferred to give to the deserving rather than to the undeserving poor. The result was a spectrum of Catholic institutions, some embodying the old and some the new perspectives, and, within many individual Catholic institutions, a plethora of mixed attitudes. The founders of the Casa delle Malmaritate spoke constantly of wanting to help women who were alone and "abandoned" in society. Yet at the same time they feared that "some people will bring us *convertite* [for whom they are responsible], not to help them but to abandon them covertly and turn over the burden to us." This fear of being exploited represented a considerable shift from the outlook that had prevailed at the Monastero delle Convertite in the fifteenth century, when administrators took in more and more females and then appealed to the government for aid.[10] It was the difference between traditional Church-run charity and the privately sponsored or municipal institutions for poor relief that became more widespread in the sixteenth century. The shift reflected the end of the single-religion Christian commonwealth and the multiplication of European society's charitable agencies into new institutions, many of which were more secular than those of the past.

A letter written by the benefactor of one of the nuns at the Monastero delle Convertite in 1693 illustrates the changed ambience concerning charity. Signor Giovanni Nardi, who came from a family that had ties to the Monastero delle Convertite, sent the communication to an overseer of the convent. Signor Nardi was enraged by the charges made by a *convertita,* Suor Vittoria Pistilli, that he owed her money from a pledge made by his late brother. He asserted:

> I do not owe anything. I gave her charity, in good times and bad, purely out of courtesy, not because I was bound. The nun knows this well; I wanted her to declare that she received it as such, which if I need to I can prove. . . . I gave it to her even though I was not obligated. You'll understand this when you realize that I have a credit with this nun for many scudi from a rent of more than ten years. The nun's mother lives on one floor of a house in Via del Campuccio near the convent of the Convertite, a space that rents for 4½ scudi. The location was chosen by the nun, who wanted her mother nearby so that she could feed her easily. I want to say that this is a liquid account, of which I have never received one penny. Thus Your Excellency should consider whether I can be the debtor of this nun, toward whom I've always had only one intention—to give charity, in remembrance of the soul of my brother. But not now, when she pretends that I'm obligated. In that case, I intend to justify and defend myself and collect my credit. Then when she asks me for charity, that which she pretends is justly due, I will see about consoling her. But this has to depend on my choice, not on her pretension. Because I do not wish to tie myself up with obligations, and I want to give charity when I can.[11]

Earlier in the seventeenth century charity still came to the Monastero delle Convertite from "secret persons"; but donors like Giovanni Nardi had no use for anonymous good works and instead demanded recognition and appreciation for their charity.[12] Giovanni Nardi had more in common with the founders of the Casa delle Malmaritate, who feared that charity could be "usurped." The rationale for giving had long receded from the medieval notion of charity as an unwritten obligation between the Christian believer and God. People continued to give, but to deserving recipients and when tangible social returns were in the offing.

New Social Institutions

Among the early modern women's institutions, the custodial establishments and some of the refuges for *convertite* represented an important new kind of social institution that was closer in form to a lay asylum than to a convent. Of the three Tuscan refuges, the Casa delle Malmaritate best epitomizes the new-style lay asylum. The members of the confraternity that founded the Casa delle Malmaritate argued that the existing Monastero delle Convertite failed to enlarge upon the limited choices available to women because, like mainstream convents, it accepted only women without husbands who would agree to become nuns. The patrons of the Casa delle Malmaritate felt that the times required a different kind of refuge:

> [M]any [immoral women] . . . remain in sin since they are unable to become nuns because they have husbands and, for various reasons, cannot return to their husbands. Or even if they're free, they may not want to become nuns. . . . For lack of help, they stay tied to the Devil. Or they convert and then quickly return to immorality. If things were otherwise, they would convert and persevere.[13]

The founders of the Casa delle Malmaritate believed that they filled the gap by setting up a lay house (*casa*) in which women did not have to become nuns and could instead return to society, or, if they genuinely wished to, could eventually transfer to convents and adopt a religious habit.

For the public and some participants, an aura of monasticism nonetheless hovered about both the Casa delle Malmaritate and Santa Maria Maddalena. Although the founders of the Casa delle Malmaritate differentiated between traditional "religious" houses and their new refuge, they referred to "cloister" at their institution. In 1589, even after the decade-old community of *malmaritate* had moved from the Monastero della Santissima Concezione to its own secular site, Michele Poccianti offered this description of the Casa delle Malmaritate: "there, troubled and sinful married women are maintained as if they were in a cloistered monastery of nuns." Although the *convertite* of Santa Maria Maddalena lived for their first five years in a series of lay residences, the founders of the Pistoian refuge from the outset had a vague intention of eventually forming a convent. They occasionally referred to the refuge as "this monastery" although usually as "this place." Some of those who applied the terminology of monasticism to the refuges for *convertite* did so because they saw little reason to make fine distinctions about institutional definition, and others did so because they placed a positive value on the respectability

and security that monasticism connoted. The uncertainty of linguistic classification bears witness to the novelty of the institutions and to the anomaly of
women living in neither family home nor nunnery.[14]

The administrators of the refuges were unsure to what degree they should
adopt or reject a policy of monastic-style seclusion. In Santa Maria Maddalena's initial months, officials permitted groups of *convertite,* accompanied by
administrators, to go to Mass at a church in town. But after obtaining the use of
a nearby chapel, they curtailed the practice, fretting that it was not "decent" for
the ex-prostitutes to be outside the refuge and probably fearing that their
charges might use the occasion to flee. In 1606 the administrators asked the
bishop of Pistoia, Alessandro del Caccia, to allow the *convertite* to cut their
hair, wear a monastic habit, and become novices. They also asked him to take
over supervision of the refuge himself. When the bishop refused, the administrators secured permission for the local Franciscan friars to invest the women as
suore in the Third Order of Saint Francis. By 1608 the administrators petitioned
the ducal government to grant them use of a hospital they wished to turn into a
"convent" in order to "segregate" the *convertite.*[15] Some leeway in granting the
convertite freedom of mobility and communication might serve the interests of
reform, whereas too much would be an impediment. The Casa delle Malmaritate and Santa Maria Maddalena reluctantly allowed residents to venture outside for unavoidable travel due to illness or other circumstances, but only when
accompanied by respectable companions.[16] Some male benefactors who had
been sexually involved with *convertite* made evident their displeasure at being
cut off from contact with their former inamoratas. The Florentine citizen Pier
Francesco da Diacceto arranged and possibly funded a prostitute's enrollment
in the Casa delle Malmaritate in 1580, and when he discovered that he would
not be allowed to speak to her as was his wont, he hurled rocks at the house's
windows in protest.[17] Reform in some cases turned out to be more rigorous than
sponsors or *convertite* expected.

The question of when women could or could not depart from the refuges
was the key issue in the development of new social institutions that offered
women greater options. The Casa delle Malmaritate embodied the most experimental approach to the reform of prostitutes, in which residents were
expected to leave the institution to return to society. Nonetheless, the founders still wanted to control the circumstances under which residents departed.
They intended to release residents when they had faith that the women had
been genuinely reformed and could be trusted to lead Christian lives elsewhere. They planned to offer financial aid to *convertite* who departed under
the proper auspices to go to respectable guardians, into service, or into a
convent. But they intended to dun those who left unregenerate. The founders
of the Casa delle Malmaritate had said that while no one was to be retained by
force, imprisonment could serve as one method of encouraging perseverance
in residents seeking to go prematurely. Escapees who left without a license
voted by the confraternity, if found, were to be thrust into prison for the
"scandal" they brought to the house.[18]

The founders of the Casa delle Malmaritate foresaw that some *convertite* would want to leave before their reform had been completed, so as "not to be so shut in." In the house's early months a few *convertite* resented being admonished by two gentlewomen of the confraternity, and the *convertite* protested to the other gentlewomen that they "could not stand to be there any longer." They, and perhaps other residents inspired by them, asserted that they did not want to remain. The house's governor called their bluff: "We don't want you here so surly. Whoever wants to go can pay up and leave." When this response silenced the *convertite,* the governor and administrators concluded that the women kept quiet out of fear of being thrown out and interpreted their threats as a sham to get more indulgent treatment. In their statutes the founders of the refuge also envisioned that they might take the initiative themselves and evict disruptive residents, recommending that it should be done surreptitiously so as not to inspire empathetic desires to go among the other women.[19] Because of the lack of records, we cannot evaluate the program of reinsertion at the Casa delle Malmaritate, although we know that analogous institutions elsewhere did fulfill their intention to reinsert errant women into society.[20]

Departures from the Monastero delle Convertite occurred in a different atmosphere. In contrast to the Casa delle Malmaritate and Santa Maria Maddalena, the Monastero delle Convertite was not part of the new wave of foundations of institutions for women in the early modern period. It had evolved from a lay refuge into a monastery in the fourteenth century. Like mainstream convents, the Monastero delle Convertite sent peacekeeping officers to recapture escaped professed nuns.[21] But, because of its special population of ex-prostitutes, it had to cope regularly with demands for release on the part of entrants and novices who could not accustom themselves to life behind the walls of the Florentine convent.

In the midseventeenth century, and probably in other periods, too, the Monastero delle Convertite licensed one or two departures annually. Sometimes the convent granted refunds on payments toward dowries, and other times the women had to forfeit their payments in order to depart.[22] The administrators there tried to ensure that departing residents would be placed with worthy guardians, such as relatives, spouses, or the administrators of other institutions for *convertite*.[23] Husbands appeared at the door to retrieve entrants, and purported widows who had entered the convent conveniently discovered, when they wanted to leave, that their husbands were in faċt alive. After about a month's stay, the *convertita* Gostanza Albertini left "because she could not be certain of the death of her husband, and instead had heard for sure that he was alive."[24] The authorities licensed the departures of residents so that the women could wed, as they did for Maddalena Martini in 1633. Maddalena refused to carry through her investiture as a veiled nun, saying that she "could not stand to be shut up so," and left to marry instead.[25]

The administrators at the Monastero delle Convertite even released women whom they hoped would live virtuously on their own. They recorded about the ex-prostitute nicknamed "la Rossa," who left after a short time: "She explained that she could not bear or sustain life under cloister, but she goes with a good desire to live in a Christian fashion and may God concede her the grace to do so."[26] They inscribed about Caterina Bentivogli, who departed after three months: "She intends to conduct herself in a Christian manner outside, being unable to live the life of a nun because of her advanced age."[27] Without rancor, the administrators also released invested *suore* who simply declared that they had no bent for religion: "Because she had never been inclined toward religion, she was conceded license to go."[28] Upon releasing Suor Lucretia Alessandra, an ex-prostitute who had stayed for a year and three quarters, they wrote: "She did not like monastic life. She asked for license from the governor and finally, after repeated pleas and reminders, obtained it."[29] When confronted with applications for release, the convent's administrators evidently weighed the circumstances and characters of the women involved, before deciding who could be released and who ought to be retained.

The refuge for *convertite* in Pistoia, Santa Maria Maddalena, presents a fascinating case study of how the question of departures provoked institutional and social controversy. When the refuge opened in 1604, the administrators immediately had to come to terms with how they would deal with requests for release. To attract *convertite* to the institution, the founders promised the first twelve residents that, if ever the refuge emptied to the extent that not one *convertita* remained, their property would be returned to them and no penalties imposed. By the time the second year commenced, the backers awakened to the potential deleterious consequences of allowing their failed converts to roam nearby streets. They stipulated that future entrants who departed would both forfeit their property and be banned from the environs of Pistoia.[30] Of the refuge's fourteen ex-prostitutes, almost half were permitted to leave between 1605 and 1608. The periods of residence of the six women who left ranged from perhaps half a year up to two years. As events unfolded, the administrators indeed enforced their regulation on property. But in most departures, the sentence of banning seems not to have been carried out; the administrators were content with simply placing the *convertite* in the custody of reputable relatives or spouses in Pistoia and elsewhere.[31] During the house's first half decade, residents took their leave fairly casually, like Margherita of Sambuca who left in late 1605 or in 1606: "She forfeits what she brought and she goes to her mother and her brother in Pistoia."[32] Maria of Statigliana, and Sabatina of Bologna, residents for two years and several months respectively, left several months after the other residents joined the Third Order of Saint Francis in 1607, which they declined to do. The women who left Santa Maria Maddalena were so determined to manage their own destinies that they incurred financial losses in order to extricate themselves.[33]

Controversies over the issue of departure came to the fore at Santa Maria Maddalena in the years 1619–21. Suor Caterina, an invested nun who had been in the refuge for twelve years, began in early August 1619 to "stir up disquiet." The male administrators, the *operai,* reported to the grand duke's counselors in Florence that "every day she says she wants to leave the convent" and asked what they should do. The counselors denied permission for the *suora* to leave. Within a few weeks of the disquiet and hardly by coincidence, the *operai* resolved to repeat their earlier request to the bishop of Pistoia to put Santa Maria Maddalena under ecclesiastical supervision. They wanted to conform to the Tridentine decree that even Third Order communities should be subject to cloister, and they doubted that laymen could adequately govern female religious. The state policy dating from 1545 that placed greater responsibility for conventual supervision in the hands of lay *operai* was still a relatively new phenomenon. By mid-September a ducal minister wrote to Santa Maria Maddalena's *operai* to convey that the grand duchess was very disturbed by Suor Caterina's "caprice and unrest." Her Highness "recognized the damage and scandal that would arise for the woman herself and for all those connected with the institution inside and out," in the event of such a departure. For the "public good" and the welfare of the institution, the grand duchess commanded that Suor Caterina not be released and instead be imprisoned "for months or years" until she came to a greater fear of God. Conventual authorities were not to free her until they believed that she had formed a firm resolution to endure in conversion. The *operai* locked Suor Caterina in the convent's prison and read to the other residents the minister's letter expressing the grand duchess's sentiments.

Pleas to depart continued to surface. Within a few months another invested nun, the Sienese Suor Francesca Jacinta, who had been in the house for two years, repeatedly asked for her release, with her brother echoing the demands. When efforts to make Suor Francesca Jacinta persevere proved to no avail, the administrators relented and let her go to her brother on July 27, 1620. Finally, at the end of November 1620, despite all the tactics employed to retain the incarcerated Suor Caterina, she too secured her exit by admitting that she had a husband. The *operai* verified this fact and sent the beleaguered woman on to her husband and relatives in Cireglio.[34] In January 1621 the *operai* agreed to liberate a resident of thirteen years' standing, Suor Maria Angela, after many pleas put forth by the woman herself and by her father in Viterbo. They trusted that, "given her character and her plans to reside with her father, she leaves with a mind to live in a Christian manner."[35]

The transformation of Santa Maria Maddalena into a cloistered convent prompted residents to make further attempts to leave the community. Some women thought initially that they could live with the new policy and then revised their opinions. One such *convertita,* Suor Gostanza, had joined the institution in 1617, which may have been her second entrance after an earlier sojourn and exit. She underwent investiture in 1619. On a petition sent to the bishop of Pistoia on August 25, 1621, to request official cloister, Suor Gostanza's name appeared among those of the *suore* favoring the alteration. After allowing the *suore* three months for deliberation, the bishop's vicar, Jacopo Panciatichi, visited the house on November 28 to confirm their intentions. In the course of individual interviews, every woman on the list reiterated her assent, except for Suor Gostanza, who "responded deliberately that she wanted to leave and that she did not want to become a nun." When Gostanza's superiors could not budge her from this position, the vicar ordered that she be punished for her "obstinacy." Gostanza had to kneel before him in the presence of the other *suore* and the *operai,* and Santa Maria Maddalena's vicaress, Suor Marta, stripped her of her novice's veil and habit. After the ritual humiliation, the vicar rang down the curtain on the emotion-fraught day by authorizing claustration for the convent, with the nuns' professions of final vows to follow after a year of probation. Apparently Gostanza decided, in the end, not to leave. She remained, and went on to hold elective household offices and to make profession with twelve of her peers in 1626. She was still in the refuge in the mid-1630s and perhaps beyond.[36]

Other women knew immediately that they wanted to have no part of a cloistered convent. When the petition with the names of the *suore* favoring cloister went to the bishop in late August 1621, four other *suore* and one *convertita* who had not yet undergone investiture made it clear that they did not wish to live as nuns under cloister. By the beginning of September, the mutineers voiced a desire to leave. The bishop's chancellor went to interview them to try to obtain information on relatives to whom they could be sent. He explained that the intention was to concede them to relatives "so that they could live honorably and in order to remedy the scandals that could arise because of them." If relatives could not be located, the recalcitrant women would be exiled from the diocese. The women listened to this plan and avowed that they did not have families who wanted to take care of them. Via the chancellor, they requested from the bishopric immediate license to go. The episcopal authorities, dismayed to find that the women "persisted in their evil deliberation," decided to end the matter by evicting the nay-sayers from the house. On September 15 police from the Bargello escorted the five women to the diocese of Pescia and gave each a written order commanding that she not return to the diocese of Pistoia for a year, under the threat of whipping.[37]

The banning did not end the troubles. One of the exiled women, Agnola of Maremma, who had been invested as Suor Margherita Dorini, returned to Pistoia on December 16, exactly two months after her eviction. Santa Maria Maddalena's *operaio* Lodovico Pazaglia informed the bishop's vicar of her presence at the home of a priest, the rector of a neighboring church associated with the convent. The vicar had Agnola arrested there and incarcerated in a secret cell guarded by the secular authorities. Facing the vicar the next day, Agnola defended herself by saying that she had been brought to Pistoia by Cecco of Montagnana, who had promised to marry her and, as she could prove with documentation, had in fact done so. With her documentation as evidence, she had supplicated Grand Duke Ferdinando II for permission to live in Pistoia again. The ruler had granted it, and she had thought herself able to return to the town, having wed precisely so that she could "live honorably."

In this instance a plebeian woman used the language of *onore* not to describe her dishonor but to communicate with officials in terms that she knew were meaningful to them. If she erred, she did so out of ignorance, she explained, and asked to be freed. On the 18th the vicar released Agnola. However, he made her leave the environs of Pistoia.[38]

Agnola of Maremma, the former Suor Margherita Dorini, was caught in one of the no-win situations that befell women of her day. Neither as a *suora convertita* nor as a married woman could she live up to what officials wanted from her. The result for Agnola was a barrier to her freedom wherever she turned. She could not bring herself to continue as a *convertita* in 1621, when to do so meant accepting cloister. And when she tried to conform to the code of gender ideology—the cultural tenet that the honorable state of marriage could restore good character to a prostitute—her act of marriage did not succeed in guaranteeing her respectability in society. To the authorities, Agnola appeared not to be living as a faithful, honorable married woman, but rather to be sinning with a priest. Agnola raised the specter in their minds that she would continue to act immorally even while married, for the officials knew that some married women committed the double sin of adultery and prostitution. So she was impeded from living where she desired to live, both as a *convertita* evicted and exiled from Santa Maria Maddalena and Pistoia, and as a married woman once again barred from living in the town.

In the month of Agnola's return, two of the convent's four *operai*, Lodovico Pazaglia and Francesco Gatteschi, resigned their posts over the incident. Agnola's arrest at the priest's home had caused "great scandal to the convent." The return of the exiled *convertita* had generated scandal because it implied that Santa Maria Maddalena operated inefficiently in converting prostitutes. The two officials felt overwhelming "disgust" for "those who, contrary to the conventual statutes and in violation of God's honor and the convent's reputation, enabled these women to get out and to return to their lives of sin in the city." By February 1622 Pazaglia and Gatteschi had tempered their bitterness and resumed their posts at the request of civic officials. The contretemps concerning the departures of the five *convertite* evidently provoked a certain amount of soul-searching among Santa Maria Maddalena's backers about the nature and identity of the institution and its success in fulfilling its mission.[39]

One episode of 1623 may have reassured Santa Maria Maddalena's backers and convinced them that the institution was on the right track. In that year the administrators bade a fond farewell to Maria Francesca of Cireglio, the daughter of a provincial soldier who had been in the refuge as a *convertita* for ten years but had not undergone investiture. On what he thought was his deathbed, her former lover, a nobleman, sent for Maria in order to marry her and legitimate their children. The *operai* who accompanied Maria to the man's home expressed their pleasure: "Although she was not of noble blood equal to his, for her goodness and modesty and the honesty with which she had lived in the convent, she deserved to have him thus restore her honor."[40]

This was what the founders of Santa Maria Maddalena had in mind when they started the institution: the redemption of dishonored women.

The year 1626 brought an end to the tensions at Santa Maria Maddalena over what the nature of the institution should be. In May 1625 the *suore,* either acting on their own desire or pressed by male administrators, asked the episcopate to authorize claustration a second time. The first authorization, in November 1621, had not been followed by the expected professions of vows after the passage of one year of probation. The failure of the first attempt to enclose the convent may have had something to do with a sense of ambiguity caused by the mass exodus of the five *convertite* and the ensuing scandal. Between 1621 and mid-1626, two other women seem to have left. One of them was Cammilla Tamburini, a married prostitute who had been permitted to stay in 1621 after the authorization of claustration, even though she expected her husband to return to Pistoia and retrieve her eventually. In July 1626 the *suore* at Santa Maria Maddalena made a group profession of their final vows, assuming a commitment to remain within the cloistered convent "until the end of their lives," and thereby determined the fate of their institution.[41]

As a corollary to the question of departure, the administrators of all the refuges for *convertite* had to confront the issue of recidivism. The founders of the Casa delle Malmaritate planned to welcome back women who lost honest jobs in the world. They anticipated that some of the *convertite* who received license to leave and even some who became nuns would revert to sin out of either financial need or impiety, and they intended to readmit these women as well. But the founders would readmit former members who had departed in disfavor only if the women proved themselves more humble next time, ready to perform the lowliest chores in penance.[42]

The administrators at the Monastero delle Convertite and at Santa Maria Maddalena showed by their practices that they, too, were willing to take in recidivists. The prostitute Caterina Giani left the Monastero delle Convertite in 1638 after less than a year, saying that she "could not get used to monastic life," but she returned within four months and repeated her investiture. She remained there nearly forty years. A group of *convertite* that entered the Monastero delle Convertite on the day of the Lenten sermon on Mary Magdalen in 1661 included the prostitute Luisa Donnini, who had been in the convent "other times."[43] The Florentine state sometimes granted reduced dowry rates to prostitutes reentering the Monastero delle Convertite for a second try.[44] The constitutions of Santa Maria Maddalena, approved in 1626, required questioning of would-be entrants to determine if they had ever been nuns or professed nuns in any convent. The administrators there readmitted at least their own former members. One of Santa Maria Maddalena's original *convertite,* Margherita of Sambuca, who had been released to her brother after spending over a year in the refuge, rejoined the household in 1613. Jailed in Pistoia and given the ultimatum that she either become a nun or remain imprisoned, she decided to try the convent again and went on to make profession.[45] Suor Annalena Landi, who had preached a vivid sermon at the Pistoian refuge in 1607, soured on institutional life and was one of the notorious five residents exiled in 1621. However, her resistance decreased, and by 1634 she had rejoined the convent and proclaimed her vows.[46] Some women may have returned not so much to avoid succumbing to sin, but because the refuge seemed like a secure haven, perhaps more like home than any place else. Maria Francesca of Cireglio, the woman who had redeemed her honor through marriage to her noble ex-lover, reappeared as a widow in 1642 at Santa Maria Maddalena, from which she had departed, well esteemed, nineteen years earlier. She reentered the convent and, this time, underwent investiture.[47]

As social institutions, the refuges for *convertite* were faced, in the sixteenth and seventeenth centuries, with women's determined claims to greater liberty in the ordering of their own lives. These women did not articulate challenges to the ideology of female inferiority and subordination. They were not participants in the era's *querelle des femmes,* its debate about whether females should have greater freedoms. However, they pitted themselves against attempts to keep them enclosed. While the administrators of the refuges were not enthusiastic about allowing egress, they did permit departures because the residents persisted in their efforts to have that freedom. The fear that men would kidnap residents or entice them out lurked in the minds of administrators, but the officials acknowledged that women often left at their own discretion.[48] In 1603 the Otto di Guardia charged Bastiano the tailor with having stolen from the Monastero delle Convertite not only his former lover, the ex-prostitute Maria, but also the money intended for her dowry. The Otto di Guardia concluded that Maria exited "of her own volition," and institutional administrators used this phrase again and again in describing departures.[49] Authorities ultimately recognized that some women quit the institutions not because they were lured out by men or, on their own, were perversely drawn to sin, but because institutional life had never suited them or had ceased to suit them at present. Although benefactors of *convertite* who entered monastic refuges made contractual stipulations that the entrants should not leave the cloister (*smonacassi[no]*), *convertite* violated the strictures, choosing to trade in financial security for a passport to the outside world.[50]

The sixteenth-century refuges for *convertite* and custodial institutions elsewhere in Italy confronted the same difficult policy decisions that the Florentine and Pistoian refuges faced. They had to resolve what sorts of freedoms, especially in the matter of egress, could be permitted for residents. All through the sixteenth century, new social institutions for females sprang up based on the premise that residents could or would exit eventually. This ethos characterized some of the era's custodial establishments for girls, institutions for *malmaritate* and women in need of assistance (*soccorso*), and refuges for *convertite*.[51] Certain institutional administrators may have agreed with the view of an official at Florence's seventeenth-century poorhouse, who commented that troublesome women "perhaps commit more and worse sins being forcibly locked up, than those they would commit if they were at liberty."[52] Lay and ecclesiastical reformers continued in the seventeenth century to found institutions with innovative policies concerning temporary sojourns. Yet during these two centuries, other refuges for *convertite* and custodial institutions either were founded as convents or turned into convents.[53] What explains these simultaneous but opposite trends?

One of the trends, the continuing prominence of the monastic model for institutional life, paralleled Counter-Reformation campaigns to heighten discipline at mainstream convents and in religious life generally. In the latter half of the sixteenth century, Angela Merici's uncloistered association of women engaged in teaching and charity, the Ursulines, began to draw reactions of distrust as well as praise. By the seventeenth century, in most places the group had been diverted from its original intent onto the safer path of formalization as a cloistered religious order.[54] Everywhere in Catholic Europe, churchmen tried to enforce claustration at convents and to make female Third Order communities take monastic vows, as Archbishop Alessandro de' Medici attempted to do at the Florentine community of Annalena in 1586. Many women at convents, communities of tertiaries, and other institutions vigorously fought the efforts to clamp down. They feared being cut off from their families and the outside, and some enlisted the aid of powerful relatives to resist the directives emanating from the Church.[55]

Officials of church and state were cognizant that many women disliked regimens of claustration, whether at mainstream convents, refuges for *convertite,* or custodial institutions. Most of the residents at the refuge for *convertite* in Siena had not made vows and believed that they could depart, but Suor Maddalena, the only professed nun in the household, had this to say to the apostolic visitor of 1575: "I have never been [here willingly], because when they brought me, I came with sighs and weeping. I do not have the heart to observe the rule, and as I stay here I believe it will be my damnation. . . . I have made a vow not to sully my body."[56] In the seventeenth century Arcangela Tarabotti, an unwilling nun in a Venetian convent since the age of eleven, published a tirade accusing the male sex of having locked women in monasteries out of greed and made of them "miserable captives."[57] Churchmen at the Council of Trent and afterward tried to address such grievances. They legislated to deter coerced professions by young girls and set ceilings on memberships in convents to counter overpopulation and material hardship.[58] The post-Tridentine Church sought to end the compulsory institutionalization of women in convents and thereby hoped to purify convents as spiritual institutions. But churchmen were not opposed in general to the forced institutionalization of women. They just wanted it to occur in nonmonastic institutions.[59] Unlike mainstream convents, refuges for *convertite* and custodial institutions often had no limitations on their size except spatial ones. Religious and secular authorities expected the institutionalization of women to expand. The Roman Zitelle Disperse (1595) had a satellite convent whose population was limited to twenty in order to leave as much room as possible for the two hundred or more girls who might fill the Zitelle itself. Santa Valeria, Milan's refuge for *convertite,* had no limits on its membership during the 1570s and

1580s, decades of increased compulsory confinements there. The apostolic visitor in fact recommended larger quarters for Santa Valeria in order to accommodate more residents.[60]

The simultaneous but opposite trends evident among women's institutions occurred because, for every step toward more open institutions, societal authorities grew frightened and took a step back toward what they knew from the past. Sixteenth- and seventeenth-century ecclesiastical and civil authorities could not stretch their outlook sufficiently to countenance a thoroughgoing freedom for women to come and go from institutional communities as they pleased and to live at their own self-direction. Many families and benefactors viewed the matter in the same light as the authorities. Even the institutions that were not officially convents had cloisterlike environments and regimens. The founders of the Casa delle Malmaritate, who conceded that marriages might fail women and promoted the reinsertion of women into the world, established a novel institution. But their innovativeness had limits: they wanted to keep the residents shut in and under guard. Like institutional administrators in other cities, they wished to release residents only to reputable custodians and wanted to supervise "daughters" of the institution after their departure.[61] The brakes put on experimentation did not arise simply from looking backward. They appeared also because in Catholic reform the drive to centralize triumphed over the instinct to experiment. By 1729 Pope Benedict XIII was so offended at seeing a flow of evictees from Bologna's Casa del Soccorso return to sin that he shut down the establishment.[62] In addition, since the midsixteenth century Spain had exercised a kind of political overlordship over Italy and fostered a sense of conservatism in religious and moral affairs, which may have influenced the thrust of some lay initiatives.

Yet the new wave of foundations of institutions for females in early modern Italy, taken as a whole, did add flexibility to women's residential choices and possibilities. Alongside marriage and the convent, females now had the new option of temporary residence in a lay institution. In the preceding era convents had allowed some de facto flow between the institution and society for females of different conditions (girls receiving education, secular boarders, internees, novice nuns who decided not to make profession). However, in its essence the convent was a place of segregation from the world. After the Tridentine Church ordered strict observance of claustration, professed nuns could not flee cloistered convents for the world without being subject to recapture and retribution.[63] In an era when many females were placed in convents quite young, this meant that great numbers of women had no choice but to remain in the convent for life. The refuges for *convertite* and custodial institutions, in contrast, introduced a model of more open and flexible institutions for women. Notwithstanding the fact that females were often compulsorily interned or retained in such establishments, these asylums were in essence premised upon the idea of movement back and forth between the institution and society. Even those asylums that eventually became convents contributed in their initial phases to the experimentation with institutional forms. The voluntary and compulsory facets of the refuges for *convertite* and custodial institutions were always in tension at two levels of institutional operation: some residents came voluntarily, and others under duress; administrators had notions that their establishments should be both voluntary and compulsory in different aspects of their policies.

The further evolution of a model of flexible institutions for women in Italy—specifically, the emergence of lay schools for females—was related to the increasing differentiation of early modern social institutions. Social institutions became more differentiated from one another in terms of their functions, specializations, and voluntary or compulsory natures. In the post-Tridentine decades, refuges for *convertite* and custodial establishments took over from the respiritualized convents the function of serving as sites of confinement for errant women, reinforcing their own separate institutional identity. Some of the women's institutions of the sixteenth century were designed at the outset to specialize in specific groups such as young girls or ex-prostitutes.[64] Other institutions, after a period of operation, attempted to increase their specialization. In the mid-1580s, a decade after the Soccorso in Cremona had opened to serve *convertite, malmaritate,* and imperiled girls, that house restricted entrance solely to imperiled girls in order to shield them from sources of corruption. For the same reason, when a second edition of statutes for the Casa delle Malmaritate was printed in 1583 it deplored the refuge's practice of mixing sinful prostitutes and maltreated wives, and urged the opening of an annex for the innocent group. At the beginning of the eighteenth century, the conservatory of Saint Francis de Sales, which had grown up in Florence's Mendicanti, or poorhouse, detached itself from the poorhouse in order to concentrate on educating honest girls without subjecting them to the contaminating presence of the female deviants who had come to make up the population of the Mendicanti.[65]

In the course of the eighteenth century, Italians increasingly differentiated among social institutions, recognizing convents as being for voluntary religious pursuit, schools for voluntary education, and houses of correction for compulsory punishment. Although social institutions became generally more differentiated in the modern centuries, many women's asylums remained multifunctional and contained a blend of voluntary and compulsory elements.[66] Chapter 7 will relate how the voluntary facets of the early modern refuges for ex-prostitutes and custodial institutions for females had an influence on the spread of girls' schools, and how the compulsory facets influenced the development of women's prisons.

Such influences were evident in Tuscany under the rule of Grand Duke Pietro Leopoldo (1765–90), who launched a series of educational reforms that expanded significantly the options available to females in Tuscany. In creating numerous new schools and educational conservatories for girls, he built upon two centuries' worth of institutional models offered by the refuges for *convertite* and custodial institutions, particularly the earlier conservatories. A member of the ruling Habsburg family of Austria who was later crowned

Emperor Leopold II, Pietro Leopoldo was one of the most efficient of the Enlightenment modernizers of his era. After having opened a number of day schools in the early 1780s to teach work skills to plebeian girls, in 1785 Pietro Leopoldo consolidated many of Tuscany's convents in order to transform or incorporate them into lay conservatories whose mission was to educate girls. The ruler also asked the conservatories to accept as paying boarders needy women such as widows or *malmaritate*. He transformed at least twenty-two convents into conservatories and sponsored the foundation of other new conservatories. The grand duke gave to all nuns in his realm the choice of taking on an activist teaching role outside of cloister or continuing in a traditional monastic life-style. Those who chose to teach at the conservatories would have the status of "oblate," wear a habit, and pay a dowry toward their maintenance, but would not take any sort of vows. At the existing conservatories, such as the Conservatorio delle Abbandonate (1584) in Pistoia, and the new conservatories, Pietro Leopoldo guaranteed that "there will be liberty for the oblates to leave the community, without any other reason than their own inclination." The freedom granted women was not complete, since oblates were prohibited from reentering a conservatory they had left. Presumably, former oblates could enter a different conservatory in the dominion. Through his creation of sixty-six conservatories in all, Pietro Leopoldo extended official recognition to the fact that women's freedom of mobility had been drastically constrained in the past, and he sought to enlarge the scope of their liberty.[67]

The history of the Casa delle Malmaritate illustrates a different development in the history of social institutions. Although originally supervised by a devotional confraternity and the archbishop, the Casa delle Malmaritate was always a lay institution and never a monastery. Being in essence a lay but religiously oriented reformatory for married prostitutes and maladapted wives, the Casa delle Malmaritate in 1776 came under the supervision of the police ministry serving Grand Duke Pietro Leopoldo. In the succeeding decades most women at the institution were compulsorily interned by the police, but a few still came voluntarily. This change in supervision of the institution coincided with other Leopoldine reforms aimed at enhancing the state's power and its ability to promote civil and moral order. Among other administrative reorganizations, Pietro Leopoldo streamlined and professionalized the judiciary, simultaneously removing many matters from the realm of adjudication and reserving them for the police to handle through preventive tactics or detention. Influenced by the penal theorist Cesare Beccaria, the grand duke strove to rationalize punishment in Tuscany and to make it less expiatory and more corrective. The establishment in 1782 of a new prison for both sexes, the Casa di Correzione, exemplified this aim.[68] Within this context of social reforms, the ducal bureaucrats who took charge of the Casa delle Malmaritate tried to heighten the "discipline of the place and of the individuals there" and improve the institution, so that "it can serve the moral purification of the city."[69]

The Casa delle Malmaritate, as well as the houses of correction elsewhere in continental Europe and in England, offered a model for the new Casa di Correzione. Some members of the public called the Casa delle Malmaritate "a house of correction" even before the opening of the official Casa di Correzione.[70] The refuges for *convertite* had long been sites of internment for occasional prostitutes, and the newly established Casa di Correzione also performed this function. In the eyes of the officials, the Casa delle Malmaritate and Casa di Correzione equally served to intern immoral women, and when the latter closed in 1793, officials declared that the Casa delle Malmaritate would be its substitute in various cases.[71] Under the jurisdiction of the civil police, the Casa delle Malmaritate became an organ of the secular state's penal system for incarcerating and correcting socially troublesome women.

The Institutions, Women's Economic Strategies, and Female Honor

Did the refuges for *convertite* and the custodial institutions offer women a viable alternative to prostituting themselves and courting dishonor? The refuges in Florence and Pistoia and those in other Italian cities offered old and new answers to this problem. They gave concerted aid toward putting women on the traditional paths of honor—the convent, marriage, and employment as workers or servants. For some women, having social and financial support helping them to embark on these paths may have made them more economically secure than they had been in their previous lives. But these paths provided no guarantees that women would remain virtuous or adequately sustained economically.

Many of the refuges for *convertite* and custodial institutions also offered a very important new answer—the option of a temporary or long-term sojourn in a nonmonastic residential community. The founders of the refuges for *convertite* and custodial institutions intended for their establishments to cancel or prevent "sin" and to restore or conserve respectable social reputation. Yet both the founders and the residents realized that for some females a stay in an institution could worsen their reputations. The founders of the Casa delle Malmaritate urged extreme caution in receiving "hidden sinners" since, "coming from us, they make themselves infamous and will always have the name of prostitute." The prioress of Venice's convent for *convertite* pined in 1597 that no relatives or friends came to see her nuns: "they disdain to come and visit the nunnery of the Convertite, for they do not like anyone to know that their sisters or other relatives are in there." At the Soccorso in Bologna in the early seventeenth century, administrators refused a longtime resident's request to be joined by her daughter, saying that residence in the institution would "prejudice" the girl. In contrast, one former resident of Bologna's Soccorso believed that return to the house would "better her reputation" as a prelude to marriage. The administrator of Florence's Mendicanti, or poorhouse, which by the late seventeenth century had become an institution for unruly females, felt that women who were not hardened in vice and not publicly shamed would benefit from a stay at his institution: "with time and their retreat into seclusion, the memory of their indiscretion will be absolutely canceled." But in 1738 two recently orphaned sisters successfully resisted their relatives' plan to put them in the Mendicanti because the girls wanted to avert "the weight of infamy that they would bear if they were enclosed in that place."[72]

As the historian Lucia Ferrante has suggested, the refuges for *convertite* and custodial institutions, as well as unofficial asylums for women such as the Mendicanti became, had a distinctly double valence. They could either enhance or detract from a woman's reputation. In many cities some of the women's institutions had greater honor attached to them than others. However, whether females were materially or symbolically aided by their residence in the institutions depended not so much on the institution's characteristics as on the circumstances behind their admittance and their particular familial and social connections.[73]

For all their innovation, the refuges for *convertite* and custodial institutions in early modern Italy did not solve a significant controversy that festered inside these asylums and resonated in society at large: the question of how responsibility for female welfare was to be efficaciously divided between the public and women themselves. Although the poorest women entered gratis or with dowries furnished by public and private benefactors, all residents were expected to help pay for their own unkeep through their labor. The founders of Venice's sixteenth-century Zitelle, for instance, intended for the girls there to do handiwork to contribute toward the maintenance of the institution and to accumulate money for their marital dowries. At the moment of a resident's reinsertion into society, the same joint responsibility prevailed. The institutions provided aid in securing dowries or employment, while the women were expected to work for wages that would sustain them.[74]

Ecclesiastical and civil authorities constantly boasted of the patriarchal system in which relatives and benefactors took care of women, but never did they stop requiring money and labor from women themselves, and herein lay the grounds for conflict. The same churchmen who wanted females to have ways of supporting themselves other than prostitution ironically interfered with the nonsexual avenues of obtaining income that women found. Archiepiscopal officials tried to ban the individual wages that traditionally went to the women at Milan's refuge for *convertite,* Santa Valeria, just as the Tridentine reformers prohibited nuns everywhere from retaining individual incomes.[75] Determined to impose cloister, Counter-Reformation leaders limited the contact that institutional residents could have with the outside to arrange labors or solicit charity. In 1646 they stopped the members of Rome's Zitelle Disperse from contracting out as servants and from begging in the streets as *cercatrici.* Ecclesiastical officials in Milan had barred begging by the women at Santa Valeria in the 1570s. For some female communities, the charity collected by nuns or institutional residents had sometimes made the difference between misery and subsistence.[76]

A single impetus lay behind the Church's issuance of these restrictions touching upon economic matters—the desire to bring all institutions into closer conformance with the monastic model highest in honor. Religious authorities knew that income-producing activities at the institutions might interfere with spiritual exercises. The *suore* at Santa Valeria had admitted to the archiepiscopal vicar in 1579 that often they were too tired from spinning and housework to awake early and recite the first divine office of the day.[77] As a general policy, the Church moved to replace an active means by which women in institutions gleaned income with a more passive one. Rather than having women go to jobs outside or send their lay administrators to bring back piecework, the Church preferred to see institutional residents adopt more of a religious function and await benefactions requiring devotional acts in return.[78]

For institutional residents to have real earning power would confer a degree of independence, something that the officials viewed with trepidation. The contrasting economic and spiritual ethics of reform at Florence's Casa delle Malmaritate and Pistoia's Santa Maria Maddalena reflect a difference that we usually find between lay and ecclesiastical reformers in Italy as a whole. Although the ecclesiastical administrators of women's institutions, as well as the lay administrators, ran work programs like the instruction in weaving at Santa Maria Maddalena, they manifested greater ambivalence toward this facet of the regimen than did their lay counterparts. Under ecclesiastical supervisors, labor was sometimes meant more to keep bodies busy than to train workers to earn a living wage.

At another level, however, all male leaders, whether of church or state, shared one assumption. They felt that, although women should labor and earn income to benefit themselves and society, females should not themselves control this process or its profits. Prostitution offended religious and lay authorities not only because women violated the virtue of female chastity many times over, but because in exchange for sex the women acquired money in hand, which was a form of power. Female control over property went against the grain of early modern gender ideology and the laws of early modern societies. Stretching an old aphorism a bit, we could say that the city-state of Florence fostered both the world's oldest profession and the Western world's oldest capitalism. What were the implications for the future, when the rest of Europe became mercantile-capitalist Florence writ large? The very same controversy over women's potential economic empowerment versus the dictates of gender ideology would arise again in an overt way with nineteenth-century industrialization and the debates that accompanied women's entry into factory work. Then, authorities of church and state would again become alarmed lest securing their own wage outside the home would confer upon women a sense of independence that could lead them to sexual promiscuity.[79]

The multiplication of refuges for *convertite* and custodial institutions in the sixteenth century did not stop large numbers of women from prostituting themselves and thereby putting their reputation at risk in the eyes of their contemporaries. We have seen a few Tuscan plebeian females perhaps on their own employing the language of honor and shame and of sin (*peccato*).[80] And we have seen extensive evidence of Tuscan magistrates, clerics, and notaries using this terminology to describe the actions of females at all levels of society. As articulated by males, female "honor" was often instrumental, reflecting more on the honor of affiliated males and families than on the woman herself.

Although the elite called the state of being sexually violated and illegitimate sexual activity on the part of females "dishonor," these conditions did not *permanently* stigmatize plebeian women before members of their own class, who willingly married them, or before their social superiors. For both sexes, socioeconomic variables affected the mutable status of honor/dishonor. Social status made a difference in how subtly definitions of honor might be shaded. As we have seen, the seventeenth-century jurist Marc'Antonio Savelli felt that women of his own rank who succumbed to immorality owing to some "fault" or "frailty" did not deserve to be called prostitutes. For Savelli "honor," to some extent, was a matter of semantics. He warned against labeling so many women "prostitutes" that they would outnumber the honorable women.[81] Another important variable, property, did not in itself confer honor upon a woman; rich prostitutes did not merit classification as honorable. What redeemed honor for the disgraced woman who acquired a dowry was not the money per se but the monastic, institutional, or marital life-style the dowry would allow, plus in many cases patronage from respectable social superiors.[82] Female honor was not simply corporeal purity or possession of enough money, but a recognized intention to live according to socioreligious notions of morality, corroborated by verification from the community. *Onore* for a patrician woman or *onestà* (decency) for a plebeian woman was not so much a matter of actual behavior, as one of what her community knew and said about her.

The lay and ecclesiastical leaders of Tuscan societies promulgated laws to restrain female behavior, and promoted gender ideology to suggest to women how to think about themselves. They discovered that the laws did not deter prostitution. Nor were the authorities confident about the efficacy of the social shame, religious penitence, and guilt that they tried to instill in erring females. Women had ways of evading the pressures. Social dishonor could be eradicated and sin absolved in the here and now, if not in the hereafter, by rites of penance. The slate appeared to be wiped clean, so why amend character? From the officials' perspective, at least institutionalization cleansed society by removing prostitutes from the streets. Societal authorities gradually put diminished emphasis on the religious nature of penitence and transformed the notion of penitence into secular expiation for the commission of social crimes. Increasingly, they concentrated on social analyses of deficiencies in the community and formulated social cures: the program at the Casa delle Malmaritate of training residents for employment, or the approach of disciplinary incarceration represented by Florence's wholly secular seventeenth-century poorhouse, the Mendicanti.[83]

Did the Tuscan ruling class's ethic of *onore* impinge on the lives of plebeian women? The code held relevance for the plebeian woman in determining how the state treated her—whether or not the Onestà hounded her as a prostitute, or another magistracy confined her to an institution as a dishonorable woman. Some Tuscan women who prostituted themselves seemed to conceive of this activity in practical terms without any sort of ill feeling. The fourteenth-century freelancer Angela was reported to have remarked to a neighbor, "I am and I wish to remain a public whore, and I will sell my body to you for money."[84] Even if other prostitutes, particularly those of subsequent centuries, conceived of selling their bodies as sin or dishonor, for many of them the ultimate priority of surviving outweighed whatever spiritual guilt or social discomfort they may have felt. Indubitably, how a woman secured a living affected her reputation. But as we have seen, a woman's reputation, even if dishonored, did not necessarily impair her ability to obtain economic security through marriage, entrance into a convent, residence in an institution, or wage earning as a laborer or prostitute. What had life-and-death meaning for most women's lives in early modern Florence and Pistoia was access to income, not the immediate state of their reputations.

Epilogue

In 1808–10 the Napoleonic occupation of Italy confiscated the property of the Monastero delle Convertite and Santa Maria Maddalena and shut down their operations. The occupation incorporated the Casa delle Malmaritate into the Conservatorio di San Felice, which was predominantly a girls' school but henceforth received a small number of maladjusted wives in order to carry on the socially beneficial service offered by the Casa delle Malmaritate.[85]

The increasing institutionalization of women that began in the sixteenth century was not simply synonymous with confinement. The proliferation of institutions opened opportunities as well. Over the course of several centuries, the refuges for *convertite* and custodial institutions afforded women expanded extradomestic roles. Among the founders and outstanding patrons of the early modern institutions for females were many women, including Lodovica Torelli, Paola Negri, Isabella Gosa de Cardona, and Rosa Govone.[86] As in the case of the *beguines* of northern Europe, a few fortunate females who had access to property bought or endowed sites and set up communities for themselves or other women. Well-to-do women showed great interest in the refuges for *convertite,* from Madam Bice, who donated buildings for Pistoia's fourteenth-century settlement for *convertite,* to the seventeenth-century female benefactors and grand duchesses of Tuscany who involved themselves in the affairs of the Monastero delle Convertite and Santa Maria Maddalena. Some of the ex-prostitutes themselves embraced the chance to shape their new environments, even to preach sermons. At the death of Suor Maria Teresia, who had lived in Santa Maria Maddalena for over thirty years, administrators referred to her as "one of the founders."[87] Like other Catholic women in other settings, some of the females involved with the refuges for *convertite* and custodial institutions were eager for a more active role in religious participation. The gentlewomen who visited residents at the Casa delle Malmaritate, Santa Maria Maddalena, Venice's Soccorso, and other establishments drew many kinds of comfort from the institutions: the merit of doing a good work, a sense of protecting class interests (their own identities, men, and patrimonies), and the knowledge that a refuge was there waiting if their own circumstances should unexpectedly deteriorate. When women—both the philanthropic gentlewomen and the residents—overcame the antipathy of male authorities to female leadership, they managed to exert control over many aspects of life in these communities.[88]

The refuges for *convertite* and custodial institutions offered women of the early modern era a new residential option. Many of the women's institutions were able to thrive for long periods of time because civic communities gave considerable ideological and charitable support to the establishments and generally viewed them as socially useful. Such early modern asylums as Tuscany's Casa delle Malmaritate and Santa Maria Maddalena lasted for over two hundred years, and the conservatory Santa Maria del Baraccano of Bologna endured from 1553 until 1968! Although the refuges for *convertite* did not produce any notable decrease in the number of prostitutes in seventeenth- and eighteenth-century Tuscany, their ability to attract recidivists suggests that the institutions held a certain appeal for women. The fact of recidivism also demonstrates how authorities experimented in order to make social institutions more congruent with women's needs. Despite having to defuse the "scandals" that sometimes arose when they permitted departures from the refuges for *convertite* and custodial institutions, lay and clerical activists groped to accommodate women's needs in a changing world. For at least some of these social activists, stewarding women in society could no longer consist solely of forcibly confining the females, locking them up in the home or in convents to guarantee their chastity. Civil governments and lay and clerical patrons wanted women to enter or voluntarily reenter residential communities that permitted a certain degree of fluidity. Concern for the public interest had been joined by a wary accommodation of women's desires to have greater liberty and exercise greater autonomy.[89]

III

From Early Modern
to Modern Women's Asylums

6

The Adaptation of an Institutional Model: From the Monastero delle Convertite to the Mary Magdalene Project

The various types of asylums created for women in early modern Europe—refuges for *convertite,* preventive conservatories for girls, and depositories for *malmaritate* and other females in need of assistance—had an important long-term impact on Western societies. This impact was not a function of the numbers of women affected in any given time or place. Rather, it was in the realm of social knowledge: the influence cast by institutional models.[1] Part III of this book will trace the ways in which early modern Catholic institutional models were adapted over time to suit the culturally different requisites of Protestant societies as well as the shifting socioeconomic needs of later Catholic societies. This chapter analyzes the interrelationships among sixteenth-century refuges for the reform of prostitutes, eighteenth- and nineteenth-century Magdalen houses, and twentieth-century homes for ex-prostitutes. Chapter 7 explores the influence of early modern women's asylums upon later social institutions concerned with corrections, education, or housing.

Asylums for ex-prostitutes flourished in the sixteenth century and have continued to exist up to the present day. Cutting across the theological and political differences among Western societies over the centuries, a shared tradition of Judeo-Christian gender ideology—one based on the subordination of women and a sexual double standard—played a crucial role in encouraging the repeated foundations of asylums to reform prostitutes. In retrospect, marked continuities are clearly evident among the ex-prostitutes' asylums that have been established in past Western societies and the areas of the world influenced by such societies. Many of the founders of asylums for ex-prostitutes were equally aware of the continuities. They knew that they were building upon models, learning from and reacting against earlier institutions. The founders of early modern and modern women's asylums often studied the statutes of, and recruited personnel from, similar institutions elsewhere.[2]

In addition to continuities, significant differences are also evident among the various asylums for ex-prostitutes that emerged during the time under consideration. As we track the evolution of ex-prostitutes' asylums, we will find ongoing contention over the degree of compulsion or freedom that characterized these enterprises. At times this contrast between compulsion and freedom was identified as a difference between Catholicism and Protestantism. Even before the Reformation, within the Catholic tradition alone, groups favoring an encloistering monastic program to reform prostitutes had clashed with groups favoring a more secular program of reinsertion into society. The former believed in compulsory confinement and the swearing of vows; the latter upheld women's voluntary choice to enter a refuge and to depart from it. After the Reformation this split was often reflected in a sectarian division between Catholics and Protestants. At other times the contrast between compulsion and freedom has been identified with competing nonsectarian political outlooks. Independent of what broader referent was involved, a key question that constantly arose was whether or not women should have the same freedom and mobility generally accorded to adult males.

The deepest roots of ex-prostitutes' asylums hark back to the fundamental Christian motifs of sin, penitence, conversion, and redemption. Monastic as well as lay communities that were designed to convert sinful prostitutes to lives of penitence and redemption sprang up sporadically in Europe during the Middle Ages. In sixteenth-century Italy, as this study has shown, the Catholic reform movement and the Counter-Reformation Church fostered a great wave of new foundations of refuges for converted prostitutes.

Refuges for ex-prostitutes began to multiply in the sixteenth and seventeenth centuries in the other Catholic societies of Europe as well. From its base in Italy, the Church campaigned for the establishment of the institutions. The new religious orders and congregations of the Catholic reform movement and Counter Reformation, such as the male Barnabites, Jesuits, and Oratorians and the female Angeliche, took a leading role in founding the institutions for ex-prostitutes. Many of the peripatetic members of these orders brought direct evidence of the operation of such institutions in Italian cities.

Counter-Reformation Spain was one society that experienced a rise in the number of asylums for ex-prostitutes. Jesuits in early-seventeenth-century Seville founded the Casa Pía as a transitional refuge for ex-prostitutes that was meant to be less ascetic than a convent. Ex-prostitutes' asylums in Spanish cities were often known as *casas de recogidas* (houses of the redeemed), as was the refuge Santa María Magdalena de la Penitencia, which was incorporated in Madrid in 1619. Some of the Spanish refuges were closer in form to convents where women might remain for life, while others were closer to houses of correction where women were interned for finite periods. From the sixteenth century onward, Spanish officials exported the institutions for penitent women to their territories in the New World, particularly to Mexico.[3]

In France some of the medieval refuges for penitent prostitutes, the communities of *repenties,* endured in one form or another for centuries, like the one in Avignon. Other institutions to reform prostitutes, like Marseilles's Hôpital du Refuge (1640) and Clermont's Refuge (1668), were new foundations. The powerful confraternity devoted to enforcing Counter-Reformation orthodoxy, the Company of the Holy Sacrament, founded two ex-prostitutes' asylums, the Recluses (1689) and the Filles Pénitentes, in Lyons and played a role in creating ex-prostitutes' refuges in other French cities, too. One of the most important of the new foundations was the convent Notre-Dame de Charité du Refuge in Caen (1641), which came to be known as Bon Pasteur (Good Shepherd). The appellation "Bon Pasteur" adhered to many ex-prostitutes' asylums, even those not connected with the Caen order, and this designation spread in the nineteenth century. The Oratorian preacher Jean Eudes, who founded the Caen order, consciously drew from Italian precedents, substituting the Roman usage of *converties* for the local term *repenties*. In general, however, the French institutions were harsher and more repressive than their analogues in Italy. Although the French asylums attracted small contingents of voluntary entrants, they also had characteristics that historians have associated with the "great confinement" in seventeenth-century France: nonjudicial confinement effected by royal decree (*lettre de cachet*) and intertwined functions with the prisonlike poorhouses (*hôpitaux généraux*) and military prisons for camp followers. Because they were considered religious institutions, at least some of the French refuges for ex-prostitutes fell victim to the anticlerical revolutionary authorities in the years after 1789 and had their property given to hospitals. Others managed to survive the Revolution.[4]

The Reformation created a schism in Christendom's treatment of ex-prostitutes. Some scholars have argued that in the sixteenth century both Catholics and Protestants partook of a similar moralism that was behind the massive closings of formerly tolerated brothels all over Europe. Whether this was the case or not, the two religious groups clearly differed in their general treatment of ex-prostitutes. In contrast to the Catholic wave of establishments for penitent prostitutes, Protestants in German cities and Anglicans in London simply closed the brothels and told the prostitutes to go elsewhere. Protestants and Anglicans transformed both theology and the social roles available to believers. They abandoned or deemphasized the Catholic panoply of intercessory saints and rejected the institution of monasticism. In downplaying Mary Magdalen's role as a saint at the very time that the Catholic Church was emphasizing her importance, Protestants and Anglicans removed an appealing symbolic lure for prostitutes to convert. They offered ex-prostitutes neither monastic-style refuges nor lay refuges, but expected the former prostitutes either to marry or to live as respectable single women. The Protestants and Anglicans provided no institutional alternative, except prison, for those women who persisted in prostituting themselves.[5]

It became clear to some socially minded Protestants, however, that they could adapt Catholic institutions for the reform of prostitutes to suit their own needs. Freelance prostitution had by no means disappeared from Protestant societies after the closings of brothels in the wake of the Reformation. Civil authorities in English, Dutch, and German cities tried to discourage individual dissolute women and prostitutes by sentencing them to short stays in the cities' main carceral institutions, the houses of correction. Amsterdam's

Spinhouse was such an institution, and a well-known one in its time. Dutch authorities first established the Rasphouse, a house of correction for males, in 1596 and then the similar Spinhouse in 1597. They sent suspected prostitutes there to spin wool and reflect on the folly of their promiscuity.[6] Prostitution became a particularly troubling issue for a certain commercial and philanthropic sector of society in eighteenth-century London. With England involved in a series of wars, this sector believed that prostitution corrupted the armed forces, diverted women from more useful production and reproduction, and generally threatened the continuation of the nation's prosperity. Public discussion of the problem began at midcentury in the cosmopolitan gentlemen's magazines. Although suspicious of mainstream "popish convents" that seemed to be "sacred prisons" enclosing unwilling nuns, correspondents were nonetheless attracted to the idea of reforming prostitutes in monastic-style asylums similar to those in "foreign countries."[7]

Having possibly participated in this correspondence or at least been attentive to it, a group of philanthropists, including Robert Dingley and Jonas Hanway, founded the London Magdalen House in 1758 (see illustration insert, Figures 5 and 6). These men were widely traveled merchants quite familiar with and interested in the charitable practices of other countries. Amid their own milieu of practically oriented Anglican Christianity, they were keenly aware of earlier Catholic institutional models, both emulating and rejecting different aspects of the antecedent institutions.[8] Jonas Hanway, who was involved in a range of philanthropic projects, wrote numerous letters and tracts to publicize and raise funds for the charities he supported. In a published letter to a prospective patron entitled "The practice of other nations, with regard to houses for the reception of penitent prostitutes," he explained the lineage of the new Magdalen House. Nothing that, among the many current charitable proposals for the "public good," many would not be practicable, Hanway declared:

> Such is not the case of the Magdalane charity, nor is the undertaking so new as your Lordship seems to imagine. I have turned over some volumes on the subject, and made several enquiries, and I find the same thing has been adopted by almost every christian country in the world. . . .
> . . . though we think ourselves much wiser than other nations, we are many centuries behind several of them. Motives of policy, as well as a sense of moral and religious obligation, have erected many institutions of this kind, which have been supported by some of the greatest, and noblest minded persons of both sexes, in Italy, France, Spain, the United Provinces, and several other countries.[9]

Considering whether other countries had institutions that could be "recommend[ed] . . . as a model to us," Hanway proceeded to describe a number of institutions in different settings. He began with the Dutch late-sixteenth-century Spinhuys (Spinhouse) and Verbeetering Huys (Reformatory) and then discussed monastic orders for penitent prostitutes, frequently called Magdalanes, established between the thirteenth and sixteenth centuries in Marseilles, Metz, Naples, Paris, Rouen, and Bordeaux. He identified another order of the same type in midsixteenth-century Seville and informed his reader that the "discipline" of confinement in a penitential house for erring women had spread to New Spain as well.

Hanway devoted lengthy commentary to the country with the longest history of magdalen institutions, Italy:

> In Rome, a convent of this sort was established so long since as 626, dedicated to Mary Magdalane, who is considered as the patroness of penitents. [He notes the support of Popes Leo X and Clement VIII.] There are charities of this kind in almost every city in Italy. In some of these retreats there are of three distinctions; one of St. Magdalane, who makes vows; one of St. Martha, who are not admitted to make vows; and one of St. Lazarus, who are detained by force.
>
> Thus we see what the practice of christians has long been in popish countries.[10]

The English philanthropist was struck by the facts that the Italian refuges were widespread and that they varied in their form. He went on to discuss the role that the refuges (in his words, "Le Convertite") played in Italian systems of regulating prostitution.

Hanway detected one of the most significant differences among women's asylums—their voluntary or compulsory nature. He ascribed this difference to religious orientations:

> It is one of the absurd tenets of the Romish church, to engage people to make vows, and to shut them entirely from the world, whether their hearts subscribe to such seclusion or not; but this is not the case in all instances, even with that church, as appears from what I have mentioned above; and it cannot be the less agreeable to the purity of genuine christianity, nor the less consistent with the wisest policy, to afford unhappy women a temporary voluntary retreat, where piety may be supported by labor, and where the united force of both will qualify them effectually for both worlds.[11]

Hanway implicitly contrasted the Catholic impetus toward monasticism and the segregation of women with his own Protestant faith's stress on the responsibility of individuals to behave morally while in the midst of worldly society. But another nonreligious component also ran through Hanway's view of the difference between voluntary and compulsory institutions. He pitted the concept of the English "free country" against implied continental practices of unlawful confinement and authoritarian regulation. In another letter on the subject of prostitution, he wrote of corporal punishment in the asylum: "it is as contrary to a voluntary confinement, as compulsive measures would be inconsistent with real penitence."[12] These perplexing questions about the purpose and nature of institutions were addressed within two discourses, the one of Catholic versus Protestant and the other of civil liberty versus unbridled authoritarianism.

The English example of the Magdalen House spread in the early nineteenth century to the United States, where philanthropists and religious activists continued to develop a Protestant institutional model for the reform of prostitutes. During the colonial period prostitutes arrested for immoral or criminal behavior generally faced banishment and sometimes confinement in jails or workhouses.[13] In 1800 a group of prominent men in Philadelphia made the first effort to set up a penitential asylum for prostitutes in the United States. Among them were many who had supported the birth of the American republic and who wished to instill moral and socially beneficial traits in its people. Acting from concerns blending political ideology and paternalistic humanitarianism, they sponsored a number of charitable and reformist efforts, including the formation of the Magdalen Society of Philadelphia. Counting among them the city's mayor and a bishop of the Episcopal Church, these gentlemen wanted to restore errant women "to the paths of virtue" and to transform them into "useful members of Society," preferably good mothers capable of inculcating republican values in their sons. They desired to run a voluntary asylum for depraved females who "wish[ed] to be rescued." The gentlemen corresponded with the Magdalen Society of London and obtained advice on how to administer an asylum designed to reform penitent prostitutes. By 1808 this group had established Philadelphia's Magdalen Society Asylum, which operated until 1917.[14]

Moral reformers in New York City were also inspired by the models of ex-prostitutes' asylums abroad. In 1811–12 Ezra Stiles Ely, an evangelical Presbyterian clergyman who ministered to the poor in the municipal almshouse, led the drive to establish an asylum like "the Magdalen of London." Income from Ely's publications financed the founding of the Magdalen Society of New York, which administered an asylum from 1812 to 1818. Ely wrote: "Should that institution be conducted on the principles of similar charities in Europe, it will undoubtedly be productive of much good."[15]

A subsequent attempt to set up a Magdalen asylum in New York City arose in 1831 at the initiative of John R. McDowall, a Presbyterian missionary, and his male and female supporters. The missionary joined forces with the New York Magdalen Society, which had been reconstituted in 1830. Like Ezra Stiles Ely, McDowall and his supporters were evangelicals caught up in the religious revivalism of the times known as the Second Great Awakening. In an "Address" to the public, the board of directors of the fledgling New York Magdalen Asylum argued that the practicality and efficiency of such an asylum could be demonstrated by "multitudes of facts, of long and fair experiment":

> Institutions of this description are said to have existed at a remote period on various parts of the continent of Europe. However this may be, so early as 1758 the Magdalen charity, at the head of which were the Earl of Hertford, Lord Romney, and others of distinguished rank, was instituted, and commenced its operations in the city of London. And although it then labored under the disadvantage of being somewhat novel, yet within the first forty-

four years of its existence, it rescued from debasement, as appears from its report, 2,238 who were reconciled to their friends, or placed out at service. Since that period, such institutions have been greatly multiplied, and have fully answered the most sanguine expectations of their projectors.[16]

Both McDowall and Ezra Stiles Ely met with skepticism from their Presbyterian ecclesiastical superiors, who suspected them of pruriently consorting with prostitutes and formally denounced them. By publishing the names of men who patronized prostitutes, McDowall also incurred condemnation from many respectable families and a New York State Grand Jury.[17]

Public hostility to McDowall's aggressive antiprostitution crusade made the early 1830s a period of flux for the New York Magdalen Asylum and similar institutions founded at the same time. Asylums for ex-prostitutes, or attempts to launch such asylums, had begun to surface in other American cities, too. Among them was the Boston Penitent Females' Refuge, dating from about 1821. Baltimore's Magdalen Society also tried, but failed, to open a refuge before 1831. Some of the refuges quickly succumbed, and others persisted, sometimes under changed names and sponsorship. In New York City, for instance, in the early 1830s the Female Benevolent Society opened a "Magdalen Institution," and the New York Female Moral Reform Society took over John R. McDowall's antiprostitution newspaper and revived the cause of the asylum that he had fostered.[18]

The Protestant mission to "rescue" prostitutes thrived in modern Britain, North America, other English-speaking lands, and certain parts of Europe. Fueled by evangelical Christian revivals, crusades for moral reform drew intense public interest in the nineteenth century. At the same time, prostitution increased noticeably because of industrialization and urbanization. Prostitution came to be viewed as a highly disturbing problem, the great "social evil," and in Britain, continental Europe, and to a lesser extent the United States, it inspired forms of official licensed regulation to keep it under control. Asylums to rescue "fallen women," as well as institutions to aid females at risk of falling into prostitution, proliferated. Many of the rescue homes resembled the London Magdalen House, which continued to operate into the second half of the twentieth century. In early Victorian England many middle-class men and women, including William Gladstone and Charles Dickens, helped to establish and sustain rescue homes. Rescue institutions sprang from all Protestant denominations, from Quakers to Unitarians to Methodists; from organizations like the Young Women's Christian Association; and from Jewish groups as well. The Salvation Army, from its inception in the mid-1860s, sponsored refuges ranging from Glasgow's Home of Help and Love (1886) to London's Faith House of the early 1970s. British abolitionist organizations seeking to end state regulation of prostitution, like the Ladies' National Association led by Josephine Butler, also ran rescue homes in a Protestant religious vein. By 1900 Britain alone had over three hundred rescue homes sheltering about six thousand women annually. The Protestant associations of deaconesses and sisterhoods that emerged during the nineteenth century in continental Europe, England, and the United States involved themselves in the reform of prostitutes. They administered Houses of Mercy and other asylums for penitent prostitutes. The most influential group of deaconesses, those at Kaiserswerth in Prussia, instituted a retreat for ex-prostitutes in 1833.[19]

In 1847 a group of middle-class women, including Quakers and evangelical Protestants of other denominations, founded Philadelphia's second major refuge for ex-prostitutes and immoral females. They made an interesting choice in deciding to model their asylum upon the Rosine refuges of eighteenth- and nineteenth-century Italy. They were attracted to this Italian Catholic institutional predecessor because it offered a unique model of female leadership. Rosa Govone (1716–76), a devout lay Catholic reformer, had founded the Rosine institutions in and near Turin in order to provide plebeian girls with an opportunity to support themselves through honest labor without turning to prostitution. Instead of imitating Philadelphia's Magdalen Society Asylum or other Protestant institutions for ex-prostitutes, the founders of the Rosine House in Philadelphia specifically reacted against the male management of the Magdalen Society Asylum and believed that, as females, they were better equipped to run a refuge to reform ex-prostitutes. They regarded Rosa Govone, whom they learned about from the journal of a women's organization for moral reform, as a "great . . . benefactor of her sex." The Rosine House in Philadelphia adopted the motto of the Italian Rosine institutions, "You shall support yourself honestly by the labor of your own hands." The motto reflected an understanding that women's sources of support outside themselves were not always adequate, and embraced the goal of self-reliance. It struck a chord with the founding group in Philadelphia, which included many single self-supporting women.[20]

Like the English reformer Jonas Hanway a century earlier, the female philanthropists in Philadelphia found appeal in one of the several types of Catholic institutional models: the lay refuge, which was not a convent and did not require vows. They were still, however, quite selective about which features of the model they did and did not want to emulate. One difference lay in the fact that, although Rosa Govone had founded preventive institutions for imperiled girls, the women in Philadelphia launched an asylum to redeem fallen females. The Philadelphians noted another difference in the way that local American customs

> prevent such institutions here as exist in Catholic populations, where the influence of the priests leads females to lives of seclusion and devotion, . . .
> . . . The object of this Society, is not to keep those it seeks to benefit cloistered for life, but to prepare them for usefulness, and send them forth to take their portion of the world's work, that they may redeem the past misspent time, and become a blessing instead of a curse to society.[21]

From the report of an acquaintance who visited the Rosine institution in Turin, the philanthropists in Philadelphia knew that a number of women spent their entire lives in the Italian Rosine, because of either their own inclinations or impediments to departure. The women in Philadelphia clearly recognized that, although the Italian Rosine was not a convent, it nonetheless encouraged residents to remain for life, while the Philadelphians claimed for themselves the very different goal of reinsertion.[22]

Americans in the past century and the current one have devoted considerable efforts to developing the Protestant institutional model for the reform of prostitutes. Beginning in the early 1890s, the wealthy American merchant-evangelist Charles N. Crittenton and the physician Kate Waller Barrett organized a nationwide network of sixty-five Florence Crittenton homes for ex-prostitutes and other fallen women. Otto Wilson, the Crittenton organization's historian, saw the homes as following in the tradition of refuges for "Magdalens." The Florence Crittenton homes emphasized a noncompulsory ethos. In both theory and practice they took pains to avoid prisonlike quarters and regimens. More recently the Mary Magdalene Project, funded by a Presbyterian church, opened its doors in Los Angeles in 1980. Linked to a long tradition of Protestant rescue asylums and highly publicized in the 1980s, the Mary Magdalene Project offered shelter and training to a small number of former prostitutes who voluntarily sought to change their lives.[23]

The Catholic tradition of ex-prostitutes' refuges that appeared in force in Europe in the early modern period continued into modern times. The nineteenth century, with its vociferous antiprostitution movement, brought a resurgence in the founding of Catholic refuges in Europe and elsewhere. Most prominent among the Catholic rescue institutions was the congregation of nuns of Bon Pasteur d'Angers, a newly invigorated offshoot of the oldest seventeenth-century Bon Pasteur order. Between its 1831 origin and 1868, this order multiplied into 110 convents in France, with branches in Italy, Belgium, Germany, England, the Austrian Empire, North America, and several non-Western sites. By 1940 the Bon Pasteur order had substantial institutional representation in South America, Asia, Africa, and Oceania, and its work went on in subsequent decades. Other Catholic organizations not affiliated with Bon Pasteur also administered prostitutes' refuges, such as the Miséricorde de Laval (1820), begun in France and extended to Poland with fifteen branches called Magdalenki, and the Legion of Mary in contemporary Ireland. The Dominican Sisters of Bethany, founded by a French cleric in 1866, continued to shelter fallen women into the midtwentieth century, with branches in the Netherlands, Belgium, and the United States.[24] In the 1840s the Spanish noblewoman Micaela Desmaisières founded the Hermanas Adoratrices to provide a refuge for immoral women, and today this order has two thousand nuns working worldwide to aid prostitutes in various ways.[25]

In some places the Catholic and Protestant models for the reform of prostitutes competed with each other. In Sydney, Australia, in the late nineteenth century, Catholic and Protestant asylums for ex-prostitutes, the Good Samaritan Refuge and the Sydney Female Refuge, stood side by side on the same street. Sectarian antagonisms swirled around them. Militant Protestants accused the Catholic refuge of forcible detainment, a charge that had been sensationally leveled in connection with mainstream Catholic convents in the preceding decades. But at both refuges the managers' desire to limit residents' communication with the outside world conflicted with recognition of the residents' legal rights. Again, it was not only religious differences that determined institutional regimens, but other standards that came into conflict, such as morality versus civil liberties.[26]

Apart from these two streams of Catholic and Protestant institutions, reformers established predominantly secular ex-prostitutes' asylums that do not squarely fit a religious model. Feminists sought to administer secular asylums, like the turn-of-the-century feminist socialists in Milan who founded the Asilo Mariuccia (1902), which continues to operate today. As chronicled in a superb study by Annarita Buttafuoco, these feminists saw themselves as pioneers of a lay form of asylum that could wean women away from prostitution without emphasizing notions of sin and without coercing ex-prostitutes into confinement. The directors of the Asilo Mariuccia resisted proposals for internal gates to foil escapes and held steadfast to the ideal of voluntary residence at the refuge. In the twentieth century a secular psychological approach gained popularity as a counterweight to the religious method of rehabilitating prostitutes. A range of asylums, such as the Foyers d'Accueil (Welcome Center) founded in 1953 in Brussels by the psychotherapist Nelly Verbeke, offered individual psychoanalysis or psychotherapy, as well as training in work skills, to ex-prostitutes who resided there.[27]

State and local governments also sponsored secular asylums for ex-prostitutes. As early as 1795 the reforming magistrate Patrick Colquhoun called for compulsory, publicly financed rescue homes in London, although the government did not then accede. In the nineteenth century, public authorities took on greater responsibility for social services generally. European anticlerical movements and social reformers pressed governments to supplant the Catholic Church in the provision of social and welfare services. Abolitionists and the feminists who ran the Asilo Mariuccia asked the Italian national government to assume the funding of prostitutes' refuges and to build new public asylums of this nature, but the state demurred, preferring to rely on private charity. With the enactment of the Merlin law of 1958, which abolished the regulation of prostitution, the Italian state pledged to fund secular reformatories for prostitutes. It fulfilled this pledge in a limited fashion by underwriting the Italian Committee for the Moral and Social Defense of Women. This national agency guided ex-prostitutes to private religious institutions, secular psychologically oriented asylums, or other sources of aid. Similarly, in 1991 the state of New York planned to give $250,000 to help realize a female physician's goal of turning a former brothel into a refuge for prostitutes in New York City.[28] Just as in the early modern period, and since then in many countries such as Spain, some public authorities have relied on collaboration with private religious institutions in order to reform prostitutes. The governments provide the funding and the institutions offer the services.[29]

Governments undertaking the administration of asylums confronted the question of whether the institutionalization should be voluntary or compulsory. Coercion could play a part both in terms of admission and in terms of the duration of the stay. Women's stays in asylums ran the gamut from a few days to a lifetime, but administrators often expected ex-prostitutes to remain for one year.[30]

A number of twentieth-century totalitarian governments have jettisoned the old view of prostitution as a necessary evil and used the great resources at their disposal to try to extirpate prostitution. Marxist-Leninist regimes have tended to revile prostitution both because it can yield income uncontrolled by the state, and because it is perceived as a vestige of capitalism's exploitation of individuals. From this perspective, society has caused prostitution and owes the prostitute rehabilitation.

In campaigns to end prostitution and rehabilitate prostitutes, the governments of the Soviet Union, China, and Cuba employed institutional programs that had compulsory features. All three of these societies could draw upon prerevolutionary experience with asylums to rescue prostitutes.[31] After the Bolshevik Revolution, from the early 1920s on, officials in cities of the Soviet Union set up ex-prostitutes' reeducational asylums called prophylactoria. They tried to persuade women to enter the prophylactoria voluntarily, but threatened incarceration or penal servitude as the alternative. Although the prophylactoria required residents to stay for a year, they permitted the women a fair degree of mobility and contacts outside the institution. In the People's Republic of China in the late 1940s and early 1950s, urban municipal authorities sent prostitutes to compulsory retraining institutions. One such asylum, the Women's Labor Training Institute (1951) in Shanghai, received close to two thousand unwilling prostitutes corraled in large groups by police, and began to release the rehabilitated women in 1953. Postrevolutionary Cuba chose a semicompulsory means of reforming prostitutes. In 1961 governmental officials there established makeshift asylums called "farms" and "schools" to retrain prostitutes. They asked the ex-prostitutes themselves whether the institutionalization should be voluntary or compulsory, and opted for a nominally voluntary policy to which exceptions were made for occasional detainments and imprisonment for noncooperation. The Cuban asylums granted passes for short leaves and retained their residents for about a year before releasing them to jobs.[32]

The 1956 congress of the International Abolitionist Federation issued guidelines for the rehabilitation of prostitutes, urging that admission into reformative institutions should be strictly voluntary. Yet compulsory rehabilitation continues to be a tempting solution for some reformers and governments. In 1964, a year after Britain's Wolfenden Committee rejected compulsory measures, the magazine *New Society* featured an article favorably reporting on a compulsory Danish asylum for young prostitutes and suggesting that such a system was preferable to the English practice of putting youthful prostitutes among general offenders in prison. In 1983 the government of Zimbabwe tried to enforce a new policy of institutionalization for prostitutes, who in the past had been fined but not jailed. Soldiers and police conducted a month-long roundup in cities, arresting an estimated two thousand suspected prostitutes with the intention of sending them to centers for training and rehabilitation. But many husbands and influential figures protested that innocent women had been arrested, forcing the authorities to release most, if not all, of the detainees. Just as in the case of the early modern refuges for former prostitutes, the contrast between voluntary and compulsory means of rehabilitating prostitutes continues to be evident in the twentieth century. Both positions have their adherents, and this century has brought a new systematization and thoroughness to the compulsory programs.[33]

What can we say about the overall effect of the asylums to reform prostitutes? To start with, they were not effective at reducing prostitution. The size of the asylums precluded that, because they could shelter only limited numbers of women, while the numbers of prostitutes in major cities ran into the thousands or tens of thousands. In the panorama of asylums over the centuries, the smaller ones accommodated less than thirty or forty residents, and the larger ones generally held one or two hundred.[34]

How effectively did the asylums reform their residents? The asylums made efforts to calculate their rates of success and failure. In terms of placing departing residents in jobs or with families, London's Magdalen House boasted a success rate as high as 82 percent from the mid-1770s to the mid-1780s, a rise from 57 percent in 1758–78. But such a high rate does not measure the long-term rehabilitation of prostitutes. One historian who has studied the Magdalen House believes that the rising success rate owed to increasing selectivity in admissions and also perhaps a gradual relaxing in standards about placement. Probably more representative of the asylums that I have examined was the late-nineteenth-century Sydney Female Refuge with its acknowledged failure rate of 72 percent. Several decades later, looking back upon thirty-three years of operation, the Asilo Mariuccia traced the subsequent whereabouts of less than half of its former residents and, for a group of 376 living alumnae, determined that 280 women, or 74 percent, were "successes." However, a markedly different story emerged from correspondence sent to the Asilo by former residents, many of whom apparently returned to prostitution. The placement rates were snapshots at one moment in time. They reveal nothing about the notorious difficulty in arranging placements, about how the former residents frequently left or were forced out of their placements after a short time, or about how many of the former residents subsequently became prostitutes again.[35]

Residents of the ex-prostitutes' asylums often returned to the world only to confront again the poverty in which they had lived before entering the institutions. The major failure of the asylums, as measured by their stated goals, was their inability to train women to be economically self-sufficient without resorting to prostitution. The Rosine House in nineteenth-century Philadelphia based its identity on promoting the notion of female self-maintenance through honest labor. Yet the Rosine institution, like almost all the other ex-prostitutes' asylums over the sweep of centuries, did not venture beyond offering its residents training in the traditionally low-paid, high-layoff women's employments in textile and needle trades, domestic service, handicrafts, or laundering. In many cases the economic insecurities of these occupations were what had prompted residents to turn to prostitution in the first place. These choices of areas for training can be attributed in part to the broader social structures, which offered neither high-paying occupational opportunities for women nor supports for training women in more remunerative work within the asylums.[36]

But it was not only social limitations that determined the narrow scope of employments foreseen for the residents of ex-prostitutes' asylums. The female managers of the Rosine House rejected the idea of preparing residents for shopwork: "We have had sorrowful proofs of the temptations that surround those who depend on that kind of employment."[37] The women who ran the Asilo Mariuccia in early-twentieth-century Milan insisted on placing reformed residents at rural factories with annexed dormitories supervised by nuns. They preferred to send their charges away from what they viewed as the corrupting atmosphere of the city. Some residents believed that removal into the countryside blighted their opportunities. One wrote to the female administrators of the Asilo:

> . . . my intention is to come to Milan because now it is five years since I have seen Milan. I am already twenty-one years old and I wish to go be with my mother and brother. . . . Understand that I really have a need to learn a trade, because the work that I do here is not available in Milan. You can see the need I have in order to earn my bread honestly in the future.[38]

The administrators of the asylums put a higher value on morality than on other circumstances that might contribute to women's economic self-sufficiency.

Although many of the asylums had the goal of reinserting residents into society, the Catholic refuges also tolerated or encouraged permanent residence at the institution. As we have seen, asylums might fulfill their goal of reinsertion without teaching the ex-prostitutes the work skills that would enable them to avoid reprostituting themselves. Only in the case of the women who chose to remain indefinitely at the Catholic refuges either as nuns or laywomen was the question of economic self-support seemingly skirted. But contemporaries wondered whether the Catholic refuges trained residents sufficiently to afford them a genuine choice of whether to rejoin society or not. Visiting a number of Bon Pasteur asylums in early-twentieth-century France, the social critic Henri Joly considered whether it would not be more "useful" to return women to society rather than permitting them to remain in the asylums:

> "Useful," yes; but the question is precisely to know whether those who ask to stay at the convent don't have the sense that, without family, without supports, without other memories than those of their past misfortunes, they would not succeed in providing for themselves or marrying.[39]

The asylums may have failed these women as well, because they may have remained not so much out of inherent desire, but because they felt that they had not been trained to support themselves in the world.

The enduring influence of certain central features of traditional Judeo-Christian gender ideology gave the institutions for ex-prostitutes a repressive character that was common among these asylums throughout the centuries. One constant was a punitive attitude toward female sexual license. It found expression in the haircropping rituals to which entrants to many asylums were subjected, even in secular twentieth-century establishments.[40] Another continuity emphasized marriage as the optimal rehabilitation for the prostitute. Single women could be trusted to manage their own sexual behavior no more in twentieth-century Italy than in seventeenth-century France.[41] If not marriage, then surveillance was to ensure single women's proper deportment. Even the feminists who conceived the Asilo Mariuccia envisioned from the outset releasing their charges into supervised situations of residence and work, not to their own autonomous inclinations.[42] Also striking in its longevity was a stress on the need to confine females to maintain their chastity. Many of the asylums espousing voluntary admission relied on fences, walls, and locks to deter residents from leaving or having unauthorized contacts.[43] As will be discussed further in the following chapter, some Catholic and Protestant asylums started out preferring to take voluntary entrants and then retreated from these principles by receiving females compulsorily interned there by public authorities.[44]

It is equally clear that the residents commonly chafed under the oppressive nature of the institutions for the reform of prostitutes. Nineteenth-century residents of ex-prostitutes' asylums echoed the same protests against confinement made by those in early modern Italian asylums. "I did not fancy being shut up in such a place as that," wrote one woman who fled from a House of Mercy in Victorian England. Expressing hostility toward ex-prostitutes' asylums, some prostitutes of the modern era shunned the institutions because their children usually could not accompany them or chose terms in jail over longer sojourns in the asylums.[45]

But other women truly sought refuge in the asylums and appreciated the assistance they received there. Some former residents of the York Refuge in late-nineteenth-century England returned to it for their "holidays" or when they were temporarily unemployed. One woman who had been in that asylum wrote to the matron after her departure: "It was a kindness you did me if you only knew how the thought of it lives me [sic] as it cured me a great deal of my bad temper. I feel it just the same but it is a relief to go and tell some of the Ladies."[46] Despite the dreary regimen at the York Refuge, this former resident took comfort in the mere fact that someone was there caring and paying attention to her. A young ex-prostitute at the early-twentieth-century Asilo Mariuccia wrote to her mother that "the sweet existence I have led for six years [in the asylum] was for me a resurrection." Former prostitutes, ranging from Veronica Franco in sixteenth-century Venice to Maimie Pinzer in twentieth-century Montreal, sometimes took the initiative to set up refuges because they believed in the value of such institutions to serve the needs of women like themselves. The modern refuges for ex-prostitutes, like the early modern ones before them, took in girls and women who had not necessarily been prostitutes. Girls who had experienced incest constituted 7 percent of the residents at the Asilo Mariuccia in its first decade and å half, and for these females the asylum undoubtedly represented an improvement over living with exploitative and abusive relatives. One victim of incest described the administrators of the Asilo as "ladies who have done me much good in the time of my disgrace." The fact that former residents voluntarily sought readmission to the asylums corroborates the value of the institutions for some of the women there.[47]

Ex-prostitutes' asylums provided thousands of girls and women with the respite to get through a hard time or helped set them on a less stigmatized, more law-abiding path in the long run. The asylums were important as both the symbol and the reality of enlarged options for all females in Western societies, who traditionally had highly limited choices. Moreover, they gave rise to numerous offshoots, as we will explore.

7

Social Legacies of the Early Modern
Women's Asylums

... and so ended [that asylum] too, swept away in the vortex of time,
which transformed monasteries and the old charitable institutions into
new institutions called for by new times.
— SERAFINO BIFFI, *Sui riformatori pei giovani* (1870)[1]

The asylums for women and girls that flourished in the early modern era left a
rich social legacy. They influenced the development of later social institutions
for the populace at large, as well as social institutions specifically for women.
The ex-prostitutes' refuges and custodial institutions of the early modern era,
taken together, produced what we might best describe as the institutional
model of the women's reformatory/conservatory. This institutional form was
essentially a new product of the early modern period, and by the end of that
age it was firmly etched in the public consciousness. The early modern asylums for females had been multifunctional. Yet these asylums influenced the
development of later social institutions with more specialized functions in the
realms of corrections, education, and housing.

Correctional Institutions

Asylums for women played a formative role in the elaboration of Western
penal institutions. First, refuges for penitent prostitutes offered the primary
model that posited rehabilitation as the goal of custody, a goal that was
adopted by the modern penitentiary prison. Second, women's asylums of all
kinds helped to spawn specialized reformatories for youth that became widespread in the nineteenth century. Third, women's asylums were, in part, early
exemplars of single-sex prisons for women.

The histories of women's asylums and prisons are very much intertwined.
The history of the prison has been charted as a trajectory of changing functions. In the Middle Ages, when most punishments ranged from corporal
inflictions to fines to public humiliations, prisons generally served to detain
offenders awaiting trial or punishment. During the Renaissance, social au-

thorities began with increasing frequency to sentence offenders to prison terms as punishment. Under the influence of Enlightenment theorists like Cesare Beccaria who recommended more humane and rational penal systems, incarceration itself became the standard punishment. Reformers of the same epoch devised another innovative form of prison, the penitentiary, to rehabilitate. Penologists believe that the modern prison has several progenitors, including an ancestor shared with women's asylums—the monastery. Monasteries proffered the example of seclusion in individual cells and contained prisons wherein erring monks and nuns performed penance. In addition, they often served as places of confinement for transgressing women, and a small number of men, who were neither nuns nor monks. While the monastery represented an informal site of confinement for secular persons, prisons and women's asylums specialized in the function of confinement and evolved along parallel and sometimes intersecting tracks of institutional development. Prisons also developed in connection with yet other institutions that were related to women's asylums: almshouses, workhouses, and houses of correction.[2]

The Penitentiary Prison

Originated by the early modern ex-prostitutes' asylums, the penal model of incarceration, penitence, and rehabilitation was extended to the male sex in the form of the modern penitentiary prison. It is noteworthy that both historians of Catholic refuges for the reform of prostitutes, and historians of Protestant institutions for ex-prostitutes, have viewed those asylums as prototypes of the modern penitentiary prison.[3] The significant characteristic of the asylums was not their differing religious affiliations, but rather their commonality in being institutions designed to cope with deviant women. It was the female sex that first inspired the institutional response of confinement and spurred the creation of techniques to control and guide an enclosed population. The mission of the ex-prostitutes' refuges was to inspire sentiments of penitence in ex-prostitutes and wayward girls. In Catholic thought, "penitence" holds the dual connotation of feeling regret for sins and enacting the penance that will expiate the sins. Penance may take the form of acts that honor God, punish the sinner, or decrease the likelihood of future sinning. "Penitence" bears the promise of conversion to a purified status, or what later came to be called "rehabilitation."[4] The reforming house for prostitutes paved the way for society's reforming houses for criminals in general.

The causes of moral reform and prison reform in England were interrelated. From 1758 on—the date of the opening of the London Magdalen House—the English public grew familiar with the notion of the "penitent" prostitute through the many publications about the new institution, and through visits by the city's elite to its chapel. Two decades later the English penal reformers John Howard, William Eden, and William Blackstone first officially used the term "penitentiary" to designate a new form of prison in the Penitentiary Act of 1779. "Penitentiary" prisons for male criminals and "penitentiary" asylums for wayward females became popular in England in roughly the same period, the late eighteenth and early nineteenth centuries. Even before John Howard published his exposé *The State of the Prisons* (1777), Jonas Hanway, one of the chief sponsors of the Magdalen House, had urged construction of a new penal "reformatory" that would impose solitary confinement upon two hundred convicted offenders of both sexes. To Hanway and to Howard, confinement of offenders should not simply punish but rather cultivate "repentance" and rehabilitate character. Although Howard later claimed that Amsterdam's Rasphouse for men and Spinhouse for women served as the immediate models for the Penitentiary Act, he had also visited two other penal institutions for "licentious" and "loose" women. One was part of the Roman correctional asylum of San Michele, which deeply impressed Howard, and the other was the prison of Saint-Martin in Paris. The first English prisons to embody the ideals of the penitentiary prison appeared in the mid-1770s and the next two decades. The Penitentiary Act of 1779 had stipulated the construction of separate penitentiary prisons for men and women in London, but neither was built immediately. In 1807, however, activists on another front of social reform founded an ex-prostitutes' asylum called the London Female Penitentiary. In subsequent years so many ex-prostitutes' asylums named "penitentiaries" cropped up in England that the Anglican Church organized the Church Penitentiary Association in 1851 to oversee their operations.[5]

Penal reformers around the world expressed enthusiasm for the penitentiary prison. In the late eighteenth and early nineteenth centuries, American authorities developed the competing models of penitentiaries at Philadelphia and Auburn, N.Y., which differed in their degrees of solitary confinement. As in the case of the English reformers, the same prominent Philadelphians were involved in establishing the penitentiary prison and the Magdalen Asylum. The Quaker Benjamin Rush, who had spent time with John Howard's circle in England, and the Episcopal bishop William White were founding members of both the Philadelphia Society for Alleviating the Miseries of Public Prisons and the Magdalen Society. They had ample opportunity for cross-fertilization of ideas with their colleagues abroad and among themselves.[6]

The penitentiary prison attracted interest in France. In *De la réforme des prisons* (1838), the well-known reformer Léon Faucher charged: "Punishment today is humane; but it is not Christian; it subordinates amendment of character to deterrence, and holds up chastisement as a means of deterrence instead of focusing on *repentance*."[7] Faucher valued asylums for penitent prostitutes. He urged the state to establish asylums in every administrative territory of the nation. In his drive to infuse the French penal system with the spirit of penitence, Faucher cited, among others, "Magdalen the sinner" as one of Catholicism's most moving examples of conversion and echoed the Biblical topos that had been used in connection with both Catholic and Protestant refuges for ex-prostitutes, "There is more joy in heaven over one sinner who repents than over ten of the elect."[8]

Administrators in Europe launched numerous experiments to put into operation the penitentiary prison stressing conversion and rehabilitation. By the late 1840s there were separate corrective facilities for females in France, Germany, and Tuscany that were considered part of the new penitentiary prison system. Some women's asylums in these societies also bore the designation "penitentiary," such as the Roman "Penitenziario Pio del Buon Pastore" for ex-prostitutes and errant girls, mentioned by a reformer in 1870.[9] One historian has singled out as the chief features of the early penitentiary prison "the solitary confinement of inmates, the rule of silence, meditation and worship."[10] Compulsory labor also figured in the regimens of penitentiaries. In different prisons its role might be weighted more toward discipline, rehabilitative training, financial sustenance of the institution, or maneuvers related to the economy outside the prison. The early modern women's asylums constituted a model for the overall rehabilitative and religious ethos of the penitentiary prison, although not a source for the practice of solitary confinement. The idea of solitary confinement derived from a variety of sources, including Catholic monasticism, Dutch houses of correction, and English social critiques.[11]

Having adapted the rehabilitative model offered by women's asylums by making solitary confinement a central feature, penal reformers in Europe debated about whether the penitentiary prison and its regimen were suitable for females. By the late nineteenth century the leading current of European penal theory came to support solitary confinement for females. European penitentiary prisons indeed housed female offenders, but only some of them—notably in Belgium, France, and England—kept the women in solitary confinement for varying portions of their sentences.[12]

American administrators of penitentiary prisons, particularly the one at Auburn, N.Y., further adapted the rehabilitative model offered by the women's asylums by emphasizing external behavior as much as internal reformation. To exact conformity in external behavior, they relied on disciplinary techniques such as marches in lockstep and corporal punishments inflicted by lash. American penologists, like their European counterparts, were unsure about whether women should be incarcerated in the penitentiary prison. In the period before single-sex prisons for women existed, American judges were reluctant to sentence women to mixed-sex penitentiaries. A criminologist has written about the United States:

> Penitentiaries were designed for men. Given nineteenth-century beliefs about the nature of women (or, at least, white women) [i.e., their frailty], there could have been no widespread movement to subject women to the lockstep and lash. Although small numbers of female convicts were held in penitentiaries, they were treated differently in some respects just because they were women.[13]

In view of the influence that women's asylums had on the development of the penitentiary prison, there is irony in the fact that women in American penitentiary prisons "were not fully subjected to the routines considered remedial for men."[14]

The reasons for the different treatment of female prisoners were manifold. Solitary confinement entailed expensive construction of cells. Male offenders eclipsed female offenders in number and in perceived danger to society, so in some settings in the United States and abroad female offenders were not seen to warrant the same expenditure for solitary confinement. Although males were arrested for crimes against persons, property, labor regulations, and national security, females tended to be arrested for violations of public and moral order and for crimes against property. Because female deviants did not pose the same threat to society's sociopolitical infrastructure or to the internal security of the prison that men did, judges and administrators of prisons had less incentive to submit them to solitary confinement. The supposed benefit of solitary confinement—the inculcation of penitence—could be achieved by other means in Italian and French prisons: the common practice of having nuns guard female prisoners. Theory also played a role in determining penal practice. In different times and places in the nineteenth century, certain currents of thought suggested that deviant women could not be rehabilitated. Early in the century some moralists saw "ruined" prostitutes as irredeemable. Later, followers of the criminologist Cesare Lombroso argued that rehabilitative techniques would have no effect on "born" female criminals and "born" prostitutes, although *mild* rehabilitative regimens could help less deviant women whose misbehavior stemmed from environmental causes. Other views, generally coming from religious or feminist circles, projected greater optimism about using gentle methods to reform all types of female offenders. None of these theories, different as they were, lent much support to the idea of placing female offenders in solitary confinement. Most Western societies, moreover, held a wider range of reformative institutions outside the penal system for women than for men, lessening the need to concentrate women's rehabilitation in the penitentiary prison.[15]

Women's asylums influenced another important dimension of the rehabilitative penal regimen: postinstitutional surveillance and aid. The women's asylums over the centuries had long sought to offer moral guidance and socioeconomic assistance to released residents.[16] In nineteenth-century Britain, continental Europe, and the United States, organizations emerged to smooth the way for juvenile and adult released prisoners of both sexes. The patronage organizations for released female prisoners closely resembled and sometimes overlapped in activity with women's asylums. At Kaiserswerth in Prussia, Protestant deaconesses administered the House of Refuge for Released Female Prisoners and Magdalens (1833). Madame de Lamartine cofounded a committee (1836) for the patronage of delinquents and prostitutes released from Paris's Saint-Lazare prison and helped establish for these young women two asylums later affiliated with the Bon Pasteur order. The nuns of Marie-Joseph, who guarded women in French prisons, administered their own refuges for released female prisoners, as well as their own asylums for wayward girls, juvenile delinquents, and former prostitutes. The organizations for postinstitutional surveillance and aid set the stage for the parole system, a penal innovation that took shape between the midnineteenth and early twentieth centuries.[17]

Reformatories for Youth

The early modern women's asylums anticipated not only the nineteenth-century emphasis on rehabilitation but also the far-reaching scope of modern rehabilitative institutions. What Michel Foucault has called the "carceral archipelago"—the web of interrelated penal, welfare, and educational institutions that emerged in the nineteenth century—was preceded by the vast network of women's institutions that grew up in early modern Europe. Foucault believed that the carceral archipelago blurred the distinction between "the least irregularity" and "the greatest crime." It heightened the significance of "the departure from the norm," and because of it, "the social enemy was transformed into a deviant."[18] Centuries earlier, as we have seen, women's asylums had identified nonconforming females as deviants and had separated them from society to resocialize them. The institutions for females developed the techniques of surveillance and discipline that Foucault portrays as so essential to the institutions of the carceral archipelago.

Women's asylums helped to inspire the nineteenth-century reformatory for youth, a central institution in the carceral archipelago. In Western culture since antiquity, there has long been a symbolic association between women and children, with both groups perceived as being in need of male protection and subject to male authority. The linkage between reform and prevention that developed in the early modern women's asylums gave rise to nineteenth-century institutions to correct and assist young males.

The Italian reformer Serafino Biffi believed that his era's reformatories for youth owed their genealogy to the early modern women's asylums. Citing the example of his own city, Biffi wrote that "at the turn of the sixteenth century there began to appear in Milan special asylums for helping endangered or wayward youth." Calling these early modern asylums "reformatories" (*riformatori*), he divided them into three categories:

> the houses for *convertite* that offered asylum to girls and women who had already transgressed . . . the conservatories that were simple houses of preservation and sheltered girls in danger of losing their virtue . . . and mixed asylums that held persons of both categories. . . . Thus . . . Milan has for a long time had on a grand scale the useful institutions with which present-day society aids the wayward. It is, however, curious that the reformatories of those days were only for the female sex.[19]

Biffi's surprise was not at the existence of reformatories for women in the early modern era, but at the lack of such institutions for errant male youth in that era. Females represented one of society's most problematic groups in the early modern period, in view of the turn of public sentiment against prostitution. Although the early modern world had a small number of institutions for the correctional confinement of young males, the expansion of such institutions did not occur until the nineteenth century.[20] In the modern era, the great changes brought by a steep rise in population, industrialization, and urbanization upset traditional patterns of growing to adulthood and exposed youths to an increased risk of committing deviant acts. Adolescents and their potential for virtue or vice began to seem problematic in different ways than they had in the past. Instead of relying upon traditional sodalities and confraternities to keep the behavior of male adolescents within acceptable bounds, civic and social leaders decided to establish new public and private institutions to perform this function. They created reformatories for youth, such as Mettray in France, to serve as alternatives to adult prisons. The reformatories offered preventive detention to keep adolescents from getting into trouble. Other new institutions helped the young to obtain lodging, employment, education, and innocent recreation.[21]

The women's asylums initiated the process of identifying and defining youthful "delinquency." Many of the ex-prostitutes' asylums in existence over the centuries underwent a common pattern of shifting emphasis. They found it too hard to reform experienced prostitutes steeped in immorality and came to concentrate instead on young wayward girls. The administrators of the asylums believed they could more easily put young girls on the path to virtue, find them suitable employment in society, and prevent their deeper fall into vice. This same shift in emphasis occurred at the sixteenth-century house of Soccorso (Assistance) in Cremona, the eighteenth-century Magdalen House in London, and the nineteenth-century Magdalen Asylum in Philadelphia.[22] Both before and after the appearance of the reformatories for youth, the women's asylums helped to hone the emerging public image of the delinquent adolescent. Alongside young girls admitted voluntarily, a number of women's asylums held girls committed by judicial or administrative order, as punishment for an offense or as preventive detention. French civil authorities in the nineteenth century relied heavily on ex-prostitutes' refuges and women's asylums to incarcerate female juvenile delinquents. Asylums like the one on the rue de Reuilly in Paris, run by a group of French Protestant deaconesses, housed girls committed by their families under the right of "paternal correction," and girls acquitted of offenses but sentenced to preventive detention. The nineteenth-century Casa di Riabilitazione in Venice, an asylum for released female prisoners, and the early-twentieth-century Florence Crittenton homes in the United States, performed a similar service of attempting to reform juvenile delinquents sent by the courts. As one staff member in the Florence Crittenton organization noted, many of the interned girls "have not broken laws of the land—they have transgressed the laws of God." The penal function performed by women's asylums shaded over into the execution of educational and welfare functions. Bon Pasteur asylums in France acted as the state's deputy in sheltering poor girls whose board was paid by the regional welfare administration.[23]

Single-Sex Prisons for Women

Women's asylums also contributed significantly to the development of women's prisons. Many women's asylums in early modern Europe served as de facto prisons for certain women who were committed there at the discretion of their families, the Church, or secular officials. Such women may or may not have violated laws. Mainstream convents had occasionally fulfilled this carceral function, but the women's asylums in early modern Catholic societies did so on a greatly enlarged scale. Officials sentenced girls and women to the women's institutions not only for short-term sojourns like three months, but also for periods as long as one year. Authorities also ordered indeterminate detention, to be concluded when an administrator decided that the woman could be trusted to behave well outside. In 1687, for example, the brothers of Françoise Couchet, who had "scandalously prostituted" herself, succeeded in obtaining a life sentence to confine her to the Refuge of Clermont. In the eighteenth century the royal government tried to extend the carceral function of the Refuge by establishing within it a true prison for camp followers.[24]

Because of the sexual double standard, females in early modern Europe were punished for moral offenses for which males were much less often held accountable. And for these offenses, females were more likely to receive terms of incarceration in asylums rather than other punishments such as fines or public humiliation. Incarceration had practical and symbolic value. On a practical level it ensured what was seen as a female's most important asset for her and her family: her chastity. On a symbolic level it reinforced the prevailing gender ideology. Incarceration halted the public insubordination of loose-living women whose behavior breached the code of deportment for their sex. The religious character of the institutions emphasized that the women's transgressions were not just socially dishonorable but sinful as well.[25]

In addition to serving as de facto prisons, women's asylums also inspired the establishment of, and sometimes became, *official* prisons for women. The first women's prison in Spain arose in part from the efforts of the nun Magdalena de San Gerónimo to convert prostitutes in refuges in Valladolid and Madrid. In 1608 she published a tract calling for a new single-sex women's prison to coerce the reform of incorrigible prostitutes and safeguard their behavior by isolating them from males. She seems to have initiated the policies that transformed Madrid's House of Santa Isabel, a multipurpose asylum for poor children and repentant prostitutes, into a more rigorous women's prison (*galera*). Governing authorities in revolutionary France strove to ensure that women and men would be segregated in single-sex penal facilities. Intending for the Parisian hospital Salpêtrière to continue its longtime service as a site of incarceration and forced cure for prostitutes and wayward girls, they officially renamed it the National House for Women. Revolutionary authorities also turned Madelonnettes, a convent for repentant prostitutes, into a prison for women.[26]

The internment of prostitutes in many of the early modern women's asylums foreshadowed and provided a model for the later widespread incarceration of prostitutes in various kinds of institutions. Some prisons like the Petite Force in nineteenth-century Paris specialized in prostitutes. Lock hospitals, like those in Victorian England at the time of the Contagious Diseases Acts, received prostitutes forcibly subjected to treatment for venereal disease. Infirmary-prisons, such as the nineteenth-century *sifilicomi* in Italy and the Hospital de la Magdalena in early-twentieth-century Barcelona, did the same.[27] Women's asylums in the modern era continued to serve as de facto prisons in some circumstances. During World War I the Florence Crittenton homes in the United States served as alternative sites of internment for some of the 30,000 women whom military authorities arrested as suspected prostitutes. In the last year of the war, the Florence Crittenton home in Chattanooga stewarded 667 camp followers in its hastily established farm facility.[28]

Women's asylums figured in the nineteenth-century reformist movement to create single-sex prisons for women in Europe and the United States. Penal reformers wanted to stop the intermingling of the sexes in prisons, because female prisoners in mixed-sex prisons usually had to endure conditions far inferior to those of the male prisoners, as well as sexual exploitation and abuse. In the early nineteenth century the internationally renowned English Quaker Elizabeth Fry regularly visited female inmates in mixed-sex prisons and called for the development of single-sex prisons for women. The campaigns for single-sex prisons for women in Britain and the United States were related to moral reformers' efforts to rescue prostitutes and other "fallen women," as reformers branded all women incarcerated in the existing mixed-sex prisons. A high proportion of the females in mixed-sex prisons were indeed there on charges of prostitution or immorality. The moral reformers, usually females themselves, founded shelters for discharged female prisoners that often overlapped in goals and functions with rescue homes for ex-prostitutes. Reformers popularized the notion that women should have their own institutions, including prisons, especially tailored to gender-specific needs. The reformers wanted women's prisons to have milder regimens emphasizing moral and religious suasion toward reform, and female staff who would be best equipped to rehabilitate other females.[29]

By the end of the nineteenth century, single-sex prisons for women had been established in continental European societies, Britain, and the United States. In Rome in 1870, a new wing of the Buon Pastore asylum for penitent prostitutes and erring females became the city's custodial prison for women.[30] Those in the United States seeking to improve conditions for female prisoners strove to create "reformatories" for females, akin to the European reformatories for youth. The American philanthropist Josephine Shaw Lowell also looked directly to women's asylums for guidance. She successfully lobbied for the construction of the Hudson House of Refuge for Women (1887), one of her country's first reformatory prisons for females. Lowell recommended that

the House of Refuge emulate the staffing practices and approach to rehabilitation described in an English account of reforming penitent prostitutes, *Thirty-
two Years in a House of Mercy.* Lowell's desire "to convert" female prisoners
was echoed in this declaration from Jessie Hodder, the superintendent of the
turn-of-the-century Massachusetts Reformatory for Women: "Sin is the cause
of crime and conversion the cure; there should be industrial training, school
work and medical care as assistants to the central purpose of religious conversion."[31] The American women's reformatories mirrored ex-prostitutes' asylums in their emphasis on contrition and conversion.

The story of the American women's reformatory prison and indeterminate
sentencing epitomizes the way in which women were the trying grounds for
innovations in penology that had wide reverberations. What had been a longtime common practice in Western societies—the confinement of females in
asylums for indefinite periods of time until they seemed reformed—became
official penological practice with the enactment of indeterminate sentencing
and its eventual extension from female to male offenders. The experimental
House of Shelter for females (1868–74) at the Detroit House of Correction,
which has been called "the first women's reformatory in America," led the
way in employing rehabilitative techniques that became the norm for both
sexes in American prisons. Superintendent Zebulon Brockway took inspiration for the House of Shelter from another precedent-setting institution, the
State Industrial School for Girls (1856) in Lancaster, Mass., which in turn had
been modeled on European reformatories for youth. He also drew upon
European penological theories favoring the individualization of punishment,
indeterminate sentencing, and graduated stages of prison discipline. In 1869
Brockway drafted and won passage of America's first indeterminate sentencing law. The Michigan statute made convicted prostitutes subject to a longer
period of incarceration than previously (up to three years), on the premise
that the longer confinement would permit rehabilitation and that the women
could secure release on parole by demonstrating their reformation. The Michigan legislature rejected proposals to extend indeterminate sentencing to men.
Indeterminate sentencing represented an increase in state authority over prisoners, and as one criminologist has noted, "Officials were more hesitant to
impose on men the most radical forms of control."[32]

In the last quarter of the nineteenth century, Brockway honed his rehabilitative regimen in the newly constructed New York State Reformatory at Elmira, which rose alongside other new women's reformatories for misdemean-
ants and men's reformatories for felons in the various states. In New York,
Brockway persuaded the legislature to enact indeterminate sentencing for
male offenders. By 1923 nearly half of the offenders sentenced to American
state prisons were committed under indeterminate sentences. Whereas the
penitentiary prison posited internal penitence as the key to moral regeneration, the reformatory prison emphasized external cooperative conduct as the
route to a shorter incarceration. The American reformatory prisons, particularly Elmira, became internationally famous and contributed to the establish-

ment of similar penal institutions elsewhere, such as the English Borstal system based on indeterminate sentencing.[33]

By the 1930s, enthusiasm for fully implementing the program of women's reformatories had ebbed in the United States. In weakened form, however, the ethos of the reformatories has colored the entire prison system for females down to the present day. Sentencing laws enacted contemporaneously with the reformatories permitted women to receive longer sentences than men convicted of the same crime. Such statutes remained in force for long periods of time and succumbed to court decisions in Pennsylvania, Connecticut, and New Jersey only in the 1960s and 1970s.[34] In women's prisons in contemporary Italy, secular female guards in some cases now work alongside the nuns, but the penitential regime administered by nuns that was common to the nineteenth century still prevails. In the view of a young political prisoner of the 1970s, "the sisters are harmful because they conflate all problems, bringing everything back to the question of penitence."[35] Women's prisons today in both the United States and Italy inculcate a traditional gender ideology of female subordination, perpetuate differential treatment of male and female offenders, and fail to offer inmates training in high-paid work skills that might enable them to support themselves adequately and conduct themselves in a licit manner in society. Women's prisons perpetuate much of the regimen of the women's asylums that helped to spawn them.[36]

Educational Institutions

Just as the compulsory facets of the early modern women's asylums influenced the nature of prisons, the voluntary facets of the asylums played a notable role in the development of educational institutions for females. The women's asylums in Catholic societies fostered women's education in two ways. In some instances the founders of refuges for ex-prostitutes began by carrying out a mission of reform but then turned toward offering a more general kind of education. In other instances the asylums, such as the Italian conservatories, were essentially educational institutions from the outset.

In medieval and early modern Catholic societies, monasteries and the Church dominated primary and higher education. Male and female monastic houses provided education to boys and girls whose families paid to board them there, and ecclesiastical authorities licensed lay teachers who taught urban and village children for a fee. Alternatively or in addition, children of the lower and middle social ranks might undertake formal or informal apprenticeship in an occupation. Generally, families of all social levels did not consider education outside the home to be as useful for girls as for boys and sent far fewer girls than boys to school.[37] Although convents continued to be central providers of schooling for girls in the early modern centuries, the women's asylums that rose in that period furthered female education in their own fashion.

Certain patrons and administrators of early modern refuges for ex-prostitutes discovered a secondary mission: providing education to imperiled girls so as to enable them to support themselves without resorting to prostitution. In France in 1630 the devout laywomen Madame de Polaillon and Madame de Villeneuve, who had previously striven to reform prostitutes in asylums, respectively organized the congregations of the Providence of God and Daughters of the Cross to educate poor girls. These congregations, composed of pious women, taught poor girls Catholic doctrine, basic elementary education, and work skills. The congregations were part of a broad movement. In France between 1600 and 1720, laywomen and a few male clerics organized ninety-one female teaching congregations. Although the earliest congregations focused on running boarding schools to teach elite girls Catholic doctrine and keep them untainted by Protestantism, the later congregations concentrated on offering day schooling to poor girls with the aim of preserving their virtue.[38]

Financial need also prompted asylums for ex-prostitutes to undertake educational work. In the mideighteenth century the Refuge of Clermont in France, which had sheltered ex-prostitutes since 1668, additionally began to house poor girls in order to give them free or low-cost education in moral decorum and work skills. The nuns of the Refuge decided to provide preventive education as an outgrowth of their efforts at reform. However, a financial crisis in the 1760s led the nuns to cease teaching poor girls and to start offering education for elite girls, whose families could afford tuition and who would be segregated from the penitents. The boarding school for patrician girls proved quite profitable, and the nuns continued to operate it, as well as guide penitent women, until the institution was suppressed by the Revolution. The male administrators always regretted that educating elite girls had superseded preventively educating poor girls, which had been more in keeping with the institution's original reformative aims. Whereas the male administrators cared most about having the institution carry out its moralizing mission, the nuns, unlike the administrators, had to live at the Refuge, and for them avoiding starvation may have been the foremost consideration.[39]

Similar transformations befell other women's asylums. In Milan in 1555, Isabella Gosa de Cardona, a fervent nun who had founded refuges for *convertite* elsewhere and had been permitted to preach in churches, established the house of Soccorso (Assistance) to shelter ex-prostitutes and imperiled females. In the next decade Isabella left Milan, and the Soccorso moved under the aegis of Archbishop Carlo Borromeo, who imposed upon it a more monastic form. Although Borromeo reaffirmed the institution's original mission of aiding sinful women, the nuns administering the Soccorso had other preferences. They tried to eliminate the disreputable women and replace them with respectable girls whom they promised to educate for a fee. Given the financial precariousness of many communities of women in the sixteenth century, the motivation for this shift may well have been a desire to increase the income of the Soccorso. Further, having seen their house become more monastic, the nuns, like their counterparts in other institutions, would have found it appropriate to assume the traditional monastic duty of providing education. Despite repeated and long-term insistence from the Soccorso's lay and ecclesiastical supervisors that the institution return to its original intent, the nuns succeeded in transforming the asylum into predominantly a school. A mixture of reformist and financial motives continued to make it plausible for administrators of ex-prostitutes' asylums to move into educational work. The nineteenth-century Sisters of the Good Samaritan, who managed a Catholic asylum for ex-prostitutes in Sydney, additionally began to offer schooling to girls shortly after their first decade of operation.[40]

Many of the women's asylums in early modern Italy—the conservatories—were largely devoted to education. Funded by lay or religious supporters, these institutions aimed to "conserve" the virtue of girls by housing and educating them. Some conservatories exclusively accepted the virgin daughters of the upper and middle social ranks, while others devoted their efforts to the endangered girls of the lower echelons. In the sixteenth and seventeenth centuries the conservatories, along with convents, offered the main form of schooling available to females. Many residents of conservatories adopted the semimonastic status and habit of an oblate. The conservatories were characterized by a kind of institutional fluidity. From the early modern period through the nineteenth century, because of the paucity of options open to them in society, women often wanted to remain in the conservatories for their entire lives. Oblates asked to take nuns' vows and pressed for their conservatories to become convents. In addition, at conservatories that housed a mix of females from different strata of society, the more respectable residents or the administrators sometimes tried to stop the admission of poorer girls by transforming the institution into a convent or into a school for middle- and upper-class girls only.[41] This kind of shift occurred at the Conservatorio della Divina Provvidenza in Rome, which originated as an institution for imperiled girls in 1672. Probably seeking to reinforce the conservatory's rapid growth in size and financial endowment, by 1703 the administrators changed it into a school for well-to-do girls.[42]

The conservatories considerably advanced girls' education in Italy, particularly from the late eighteenth century onward. Intellectual, political, and economic theories circulating during the Enlightenment led certain Italian rulers to view the education of all classes as a civil duty and inspired them to try to lessen the Church's control over education. As chapter 5 detailed, Grand Duke Pietro Leopoldo of Tuscany reduced the number of convents, augmented the number of conservatories, and required the conservatories to provide secular education to girls in the form of either boarding schools, or free day schooling for girls who could not afford to board. In the kingdom of Naples, a region abounding in conservatories, Ferdinando IV attempted in the 1780s to turn these institutions toward public education. He tried to foster state-supported education for all classes by requiring the conservatories and other religious institutions to open schools, and by promoting a standardized pedagogy. These measures resulted in a few new schools for girls in the next decade, but the innovative schools in Naples lost their state financing and closed in the wake of the French Revolution.[43]

In the nineteenth century the conservatories in various ways continued to further the development of female education. Conservatories designed to convey work skills to poor girls served as models for the transmission of practical skills to girls from the better-off classes. This was the case at the Conservatorio delle Pericolanti (Conservatory for Endangered Girls) founded in 1688 in Prato, which opened day schools to teach handicrafts to external students in 1816. After operating in Turin for nearly a century to train imperiled girls in work skills, and after serving as the inspiration for an ex-prostitutes' asylum in Philadelphia, the Rosine institution began to offer practical and elementary schooling for girls and women of the bourgeoisie in the midnineteenth century. Conservatories had a role in training teachers. A seventeenth-century Conservatorio in Como that was founded for wayward girls and women was later fused with two female orphanages; then, toward the end of the nineteenth century, it opened a school for well-to-do girls where orphans who had thrived in their schooling could serve as teachers.[44]

Nineteenth-century conservatories also became battlegrounds in church-state conflicts over the laicization of education. For reasons related to the growth of nationalism, liberalism, republicanism, and anticlericalism, more and more nineteenth-century states started to provide alternatives to Church-run schools. After the unification of Italy in 1860, the liberal leaders of the civil polity did not want to see their daughters and other girls educated by a monarchist Catholic Church, which they believed prepared girls only for the cloister and failed to train them in the arts of being a "good housewife" and "good mother" of republican citizens. Although the designation *conservatorio* was starting to give way to *educatorio* or *educandato* in the nineteenth century, the change in terminology did not represent any change in the orientation of "conserving." Girls at boarding schools were subject to a great many restrictions affecting their behavior and mobility. In Catholic thought and culture, the emphasis on confining females to keep them chaste was seen as equally valid for nuns pursuing a spiritual vocation, ex-prostitutes undergoing reform, and girls being educated. Proposed laws of the 1860s and 1870s sought to bring schools at convents and conservatories under state control, but they met with strong opposition. By the early twentieth century Italy, like most Western European countries and the United States, had universal free education for boys and girls, and Italian girls increasingly attended secular secondary schools and universities. Yet debate over whether females were best educated by the state or by religious institutions continued to rage well into this century, particularly during the Fascist regime, which with the Concordat of 1929 returned responsibility for educating girls to the Church.[45]

In the Protestant societies of early modern Europe, the education of girls advanced without the institutional bases of convents and asylums for women. The Protestant Reformation and Catholic Counter Reformation brought new opportunities for free schooling for boys and girls. Earnest Protestants in Germany, England, and Scandinavia, like their Catholic counterparts elsewhere, saw education as a key to religious adherence in belief and conduct, and they set up numerous schools. Religious denominations and civil governments in the Protestant lands sponsored a variety of schools serving children of different social ranks and of both sexes.[46] Even with all these local traditions supporting education, Protestants occasionally looked approvingly to Catholic institutions as models. Men familiar to the reformer Jonas Hanway founded the Lambeth Asylum in London in 1759 as an orphanage-school for poor girls. While skeptical of the effort, Hanway nonetheless summoned up a model:

> In Rome they have an establishment for poor female orphans, called the order of the holy sacrament, where they are taught such trades, as they can live by, when they come into the world: they manufacture wool, both in cloth and stuffs, and at the same time observe great exactness in their devotions. There is hardly any country, protestant or popish, mahommedan or pagan, but shews tenderness for such young girls as wander about the streets in filth and rags.[47]

Prior to the mideighteenth century, institutions for females in Protestant societies were neither numerous nor varied. They consisted largely of scattered orphanages and boarding schools for girls. They also included sporadic communities of pious women, many of which were carryovers from pre-Reformation times.[48] Hanway and his associates inaugurated a Protestant tradition of greater experimentation with a spectrum of women's asylums, ranging from refuges for ex-prostitutes to schools to other kinds of institutions. This experimentation took hold in other Protestant societies as well.

To a lesser extent than in the Catholic cases, some of the women's asylums established in modern Protestant societies also became involved in educational work. In 1916 the Magdalen Society of Philadelphia sold the Magdalen Asylum and phased out its residential sheltering of ex-prostitutes and promiscuous girls. Renamed the White-Williams Foundation, it redirected its efforts toward education, specifically toward providing guidance counseling to girls in public and parochial schools. A little more than a decade later, the Florence Crittenton homes for reformed prostitutes and wayward girls added educational services to their original mission. Staff members of the Florence Crittenton homes addressed teenagers in public high schools and lobbied for public schools to provide some form of sex education.[49] Protestants perceived the same merits in linking correction and preventive education as did Catholics, although among Catholics this dyad was more intimately bound up with notions of confinement. The linkage of correction and prevention emerged from the cultural gender ideology common to Catholic and Protestant societies, an ideology that defined the moral female as one who was not sexually promiscuous.

Residential Institutions for Problematic Women

The early modern women's asylums were the ancestors of a wide range of residential institutions established to respond to the perceived needs of women. The asylums directly spawned institutions of this nature, and they also represented an inherited lexicon of forms and models out of which new institutions grew. Such institutions as women's hostels, homes for unwed mothers, and battered women's shelters offered new residential options to solve the problems unique to or most critically faced by women. In different times and places, different groups of females were seen as problematic: working women in need of housing, unmarried women about to give birth, and victims of domestic violence. The responses often took institutional form, and they often arose out of women's own initiatives. The responses came from all the major religious denominations in Western societies. Some of the problems that women confronted tended to be particular to their sex, such as unwed pregnancy or domestic violence, whose victims are usually female because of women's generally greater physical vulnerability. The residential institutions set up to ameliorate these problems were designed for women; hardly any such institutions were created for men. Lack of housing and work was a problem that beset men as well as women. Organizations like the Young Men's Christian Association (YMCA) and Young Women's Christian Association (YWCA) of the Victorian era established residential institutions for both young men and young women who lacked adequate housing or employment. However, women's residences sprang up on a much larger scale than men's, and the reasons for their creation were different in degree. Aside from crusaders for social purity, society in general did not care as much about keeping men sexually virtuous as it did women. And males did not confront as great barriers to finding employment and supporting themselves as did women.[50]

Women's Housing

Since early modern times, socially minded reformers of diverse nationalities, religions, and ethnicities have tried to address the difficulties resulting from women's sexual and economic vulnerability by creating special housing for females. Reformers found the sexual and economic vulnerability of women extremely problematic. As a contributor to an African-American newspaper stated in 1920, "the Y.W.C.A. is playing and will play a great part in helping Chicago solve one of her greatest problems, 'THE GIRL.' "[51] Residential units reserved for females served two purposes. They encouraged chastity, protecting women from male sexual aggressiveness and from their own sexual inclinations. One enthusiastic American writer at the turn of the century called residences for working women "veritable virtue-saving stations." The residences also offered a secure refuge where residents might better equip themselves to be financially self-sufficient. The Toronto YWCA said in the

1870s that the purpose of providing cheap housing to working women was to "inculcate self-dependence."[52] Housing for women arose at the hands of various sponsors. It took different forms, such as company housing and private housing for working women, lodgings for female travelers, dormitories for female students, and homes for aging women.[53]

In many cases, special housing for women was a by-product of efforts to reform prostitutes. The devout laywomen and clerics who founded refuges for ex-prostitutes and teaching congregations in seventeenth-century France also organized residential ateliers to train lower-class females in work skills. Madame de Miramion, who established two ex-prostitutes' asylums, set up a workshop in Paris that accepted poor girls and, later, homeless women. Noël Chomel, responsible for opening the Bon Pasteur asylum in Lyons, founded the House of Saint Vincent to shelter unemployed female workers. Nineteenth-century reformers who organized rescue homes for prostitutes, like the New York Female Moral Reform Society and the English proponent of social purity Ellice Hopkins, also launched other institutions to offer shelter and employment to respectable working women. A manager of Philadelphia's Rosine House for ex-prostitutes, which spurred the founding of a Temporary Home Association for working women, noted, "We wish not only to save the lost, but to preserve the innocent." Some of the nineteenth-century Bon Pasteur asylums for ex-prostitutes administered nearby halfway houses where released residents resided, obtained further training in work skills, and received help in finding employment as they made the transition from asylum back to society. One halfway house affiliated with the Bon Pasteur institution in Sens was known as the "asile Sainte-Marthe," an echo of certain similar early modern refuges in Italy and France also named after Saint Martha, who epitomized an active life in secular society.[54]

In England, continental Europe, and North America from the nineteenth century onward, local YWCA groups, Jewish women's leagues, and other women's associations founded thousands of "organized homes" or residences for working women and other females.[55] A number of the sponsors of the organized homes had been involved in rescue work with prostitutes and female delinquents, and they tried to differentiate the organized homes from other institutions that they seemed to resemble. Of its new Women's Boarding Home, the Minneapolis Woman's Christian Association said in 1874 that it was not "to be a Magdalen home, as some think." "The YWCA [hostel] is not a corrective institution," declared an administrator of the residence for African-American working women in Philadelphia in 1942. The YWCA criticized the Women's Hotel in New York in the 1870s for having overly strict rules that made it "not a *home,* but an asylum."[56] Two of the main Italian asylums involved in the reform of wayward girls, the Asilo Mariuccia in Milan and the Rosine institution in Turin, branched into operating boarding houses. During 1936–40 the Asilo Mariuccia administered a residence for its own alumnae and for female workers, clerks, and teachers. Since 1955 the Rosine institution has been running residences for female students and clerks and for aging women.[57] Although many of the organized homes were run by sponsors intent on guiding the lives of residents, some of the women's homes were meant to be managed by peers on an egalitarian basis. English and American feminists, working-class women, and students organized a number of cooperative boarding clubs of this type, such as the Jane Club, named after social worker Jane Addams, in Progressive-era Chicago.[58]

Women's housing is still very much alive today in many countries, ranging from YWCA residences and other homes for female boarders to women's hotels and cooperatives. Some of the same dilemmas regarding long-term residence that plagued the Italian conservatories arise at these hostels. The religious order than ran Saint Mary's Residence for Working Girls in New York City tried in 1985 to oust older residents staying on in violation of the house rules, so that the nuns could resume their mission of shepherding young working women. Contemporary Canada has advocates of special women's housing who want to create housing for groups they have identified as in need of it: working women, single mothers, and poor women. Arguing that women's wages do not permit them to buy homes, the Canadian advocates make the gender-based claim that "women need safe, affordable housing." Sexual and economic vulnerability are still seen today, just as in early modern Europe, to create a need on the part of women that merits an institutional response in the form of special housing.[59]

Maternity Homes

Unwed mothers constituted another category of females identified as problematic in Western societies. A few asylums for unmarried mothers were founded during the early modern period, but they began to appear in substantial numbers only in the nineteenth century.[60] Concern for unwed mothers deepened in the nineteenth century as a result of several sociocultural changes. Formerly, all females had been seen as the lustier sex, but nineteenth-century gender ideology portrayed normal females as asexual, a view that widened the symbolic gulf between moral and immoral women. Furthermore, illegitimacy rates in Europe and the United States rose, owing in part to two phenomena. First, industrialization and urbanization drew growing numbers of young women away from their family households and home communities, which traditionally would have legitimized premarital pregnancies by bringing about marriages. Second, changing social attitudes discouraged reliance on the once common practices of infant abandonment, infanticide, and abortion. Thus increasingly, unwed mothers posed problems in terms of social values and in terms of their own lives. The existence of the unwed mother undermined the high value accorded to marriage as a stabilizing socioeconomic force. The unwed mother and her child represented a drain on the economic resources of families and localities that were called upon to support them. Reformers believed that unmarried pregnant and postparturient women needed respectable patronage to redeem their social dishonor and guarantee their future sexual probity, and that they needed aid in finding a reliable means of self-support for themselves and their babies.[61]

Sheltering unwed mothers often developed out of rescue work with prostitutes. Boston's Temporary Home for Fallen Women (1838) and London's Homes of Hope (1860) were among the first rescue organizations to provide accommodation to wayward unmarried women with babies.[62] From the late nineteenth century onward, as a parallel service to its rescue efforts with prostitutes, the Salvation Army in Britain and the United States established "maternity homes" or "confinement homes" for antenatal and postnatal unmarried women and other expectant mothers. In early-twentieth-century Germany, Christian and Jewish feminist groups, seeking to end prostitution and modernize sexual ethics, founded homes that sheltered unwed mothers. Other organizations active in protecting and reforming women, such as the YWCA, also became involved in this endeavor.[63]

The Florence Crittenton confederation of homes for ex-prostitutes turned into the best-known American association of maternity homes, a shift in clientele that occurred in the 1920s and coincided with rising financial prosperity for the homes. After states closed red-light districts during the Progressive era, American social reformers believed prostitution to be on the verge of disappearing. The Florence Crittenton homes, sponsored by evangelical Protestants, then began to focus on a "problem [that] remained as pressing as ever," that of unmarried mothers. Asking residents for a six-month commitment, the homes tried to persuade the women to keep their babies rather than give them up for adoption. Armed with the pamphlet *Motherhood: A Means of Regeneration* by the association's cofounder, Kate Waller Barrett, the staff of the homes sought to prepare the residents to support themselves and their babies. They tried to change society as well, by seeking to decrease the legal and social stigma of illegitimacy, advocating paternal child support, and remarking approvingly on the spreading usage of contraception.[64]

In a few cases maternity homes reflected not only the close connection between ex-prostitutes and unwed mothers, but also the relationships we have uncovered among women's asylums and schools. A Protestant complex of reformatory institutions for females.in late-nineteenth-century Holland included one building, called "Magdalen," that was a home for unwed mothers who would promise to stay for six months. The complex further housed a normal school for training teachers, which meritorious residents of any of its constituent institutions could attend. The Anchorage, a maternity home in upstate New York founded by the Women's Christian Temperance Union in 1890, adopted a new name and a new mission in 1907. The maternity home became the Helen L. Bullock Industrial School for Girls, an institution devoted to the vocational training of adolescent girls.[65]

Nineteenth- and twentieth-century Catholic societies developed various ways of aiding unwed mothers. From the midnineteenth century on, religious and secular institutions to help unmarried mothers existed in Italy and Spain. In the mid-1970s Italy had a spectrum of maternity homes. They ranged from

Turin's Church-founded Pozzo di Sicar, whose name evoked Jesus' conversion of an immoral woman at the well of Sychar, to secular shelters run by public entities. The asylums for wayward women in Catholic countries often encouraged the foundation of specialized institutions for unwed mothers and sometimes themselves admitted females in that predicament. In such asylums, the unmarried mother commonly encountered an aura of secrecy long characteristic of attitudes toward illegitimate pregnancy in Catholic milieus. In 1902 a visitor called the refuge of Notre-Dame des Roches in Montpellier, which housed unwed mothers among other wayward females, "the most closed, most mysterious, most cloistered" institution he had seen. Seclusion of the unwed mother performed the twin functions of hiding a woman's personal dishonor and segregating from society the offending sight of the female who had violated its norms. Similar attitudes toward the unwed mother were evident in Protestant societies as well, where maternity homes urged residents not to reveal publicly their past histories.[66]

Homes for unwed mothers have undergone a recent revival in the United States. The number of maternity homes shrank in the 1960s, but antiabortion organizations began to revive them after the 1973 legalization of abortion, and they achieved a 40 percent increase between 1980 and 1989. The new maternity homes aid residents in keeping their babies or having them adopted, in obtaining work and education, and in solving other dilemmas. The homes have names such as Heritage Home in California, Madonna House in Kentucky, and Mom's House, in a former convent in Pennsylvania. Like the majority of maternity homes in the past, the new American homes for unwed mothers are funded primarily by evangelical Protestants and devout Catholics and seek to convert residents to a Christian way of life.[67]

Battered Women's Shelters

Much has been written in the United States about how in recent decades wife battery was "transformed from the status of an unfortunate personal pathology to that of a social problem requiring structural change." As one expert stated, "Wife abuse has been endemic for centuries; the women's movement made it a social problem."[68] However, the concept of the unhappy wife as problematic, and efforts to create asylums to help her, have a long history. Medieval songs featured the figure of the unhappy wife, known as the *malmariée* in French and as the *malmaritata* in Italian. The unhappy wife also appeared in early modern songs and writings. The women's asylums of early modern Italy, Spain, and France received maladapted wives, and Italians in the sixteenth century established asylums specifically for *malmaritate*. The *malmaritata* was a Janus-faced figure, being either the wife who fled an abusive husband or the wife whose husband institutionalized her for correction. The late-eighteenth-century Florentine commentator Marco Lastri viewed asylums for *malmaritate* as a useful alternative to civil divorce, which Catholic societies prohibited. The *malmaritata* or *malmariée* did not wholly disappear as a conceptual category in Catholic societies even in modern times.[69]

In the second half of the nineteenth century, Protestant social reformers came up with a different conceptualization of the unhappy wife as problematic. Anticrime reformers, feminists, and proponents of social purity in England and the United States sought to change relations between the sexes in their societies. They denounced wife beating, prostitution, and rape inside and outside of marriage, all of which they deemed abuses of women. In this nineteenth-century Anglo-Saxon version, the unhappy wife seen as problematic was not the two-sided figure of centuries past, but rather the beaten wife, an unambiguous victim. The solutions considered by reformers included making legal separation and divorce more accessible, mandating financial support by the wife beater, and punishing him. Reformist groups, such as the English Society for the Protection of Women and Children and the Chicago-based Protective Agency for Women and Children, also fostered a few asylums to shelter abused wives.[70]

In Britain and North America, places where advocacy against wife beating had taken root in the nineteenth century, feminist movements concerned with wife abuse reemerged in the 1970s. They established innovative shelters for battered wives and their children.[71] On a lesser scale, the movement to organize battered women's shelters has made inroads in Australia, the Netherlands, Germany, Switzerland, Belgium, France, Spain, Italy, and South America, as well as in developing countries.[72] The battered women's shelters of the 1970s had immediate institutional models as well as historical links with the earlier asylums for unhappy wives. In the United States the new refuges for battered women looked to shelters for abused families of alcoholics as models, and some of the antialcoholism shelters began to accept battered women in general. In Lausanne a home for unwed mothers extended its services to battered wives and their children.[73] Alongside the "reformist" and "radical" feminist collectives that sponsored shelters, mainstream organizations like the Salvation Army, the YWCA, and social service agencies established their own asylums for battered women. In the United States today, residence in a battered women's shelter is often viewed as a path toward divorce.[74]

It is interesting to consider the battered women's shelter qua institution. As we can see from the nineteenth-century background, it was not inevitable that solutions to the problem of the battered wife take the form of shelters. Why did shelters become so popular, and why were the women involved, and not the men, institutionalized? An American civil libertarian writing in the 1970s noted that attorney Marjory Fields, a leader in the movement against wife beating, felt uncomfortable with the idea of hiding away female victims while the abusive husbands were free. But, as the civil libertarian reported, Fields had "received too many calls from women huddled in phone booths with their children, asking where they should go, to question the movement for shelters." Although Chiswick Women's Aid, the group that led the drive to open battered women's shelters in Britain in 1971, also provided a separate house where male batterers could meet and live if they wished, institutions for abusive husbands have not become widespread anywhere in the world. Outside of court orders barring harmful action and the rare instances of incarceration, the treatment generally extended to wife batterers has been psychological counseling.[75] The creation of battered women's shelters reflects the historical tendency to institutionalize women in order to solve their problems. One social scientist explained: "Responses to complainants' reports that 'the victim has no place to go' tended to support the development of shelters rather than legislation penalizing the batterer or changing the sexist social structure."[76] Reformers of the 1970s, like those of the past, resorted to the creation of a protective environment, a residential institution, to compensate for women's vulnerability and lack of resources in the social arena.

Like earlier women's asylums, battered women's shelters both aid residents and restrict them. The shelters are premised upon the physical, economic, and social vulnerabilities of women today, which in certain respects are remarkably similar to the vulnerabilities of females in early modern societies. The feminist founders of shelters, following in a long tradition of women who created asylums for females of lower social ranks or for their peers, understood these weaknesses in the position of women in present-day societies. Like other female and male founders of asylums for women, they acted from a defensive, protective impulse. Shelters, which usually keep their addresses secret, serve as sanctuaries that hide women escaping from abuse. But another impulse also drove the feminist shelter movement, the desire to empower battered wives to overcome and seek to change the gender inequalities of the social structures in which they live. Each feminist shelter somehow has to reconcile the seclusion of women with the aim of promoting women's liberation. Susan B. Murray's case study, "The Unhappy Marriage of Theory and Practice: An Analysis of a Battered Women's Shelter," is suggestive about the limitations and benefits of the shelters. She demonstrates that, despite the wishes of the feminist founders to create an egalitarian shelter with an ethos of self-help, actual operating policies fomented class tensions. Hierarchical stratification appeared, and priorities diverged between staff members who stressed ideological consciousness and residents who stressed their glaring practical needs for employment and future housing. On the positive side, Murray believed that residents benefited from their informal interaction with fellow battered women, an exchange that countered the sense of isolation common to abused wives.[77]

In past centuries and the present one, unhappy wives have posed problems at a societal level by revealing the flaws in marriages and by providing grounds that could justify the legitimacy of divorce. Such women further posed problems at the individual level of restructuring their own lives. Because Catholic societies prohibited civil divorce and put great trust in institutional solutions, asylums that sheltered unhappy wives substituted for divorce for three or more centuries in Italy and other Catholic countries. In Protestant societies, which permitted a limited form of civil divorce and did not have much of a tradition of asylums before the mideighteenth century, the few asylums for unhappy wives that sprang up in the nineteenth century and the larger number in the late twentieth century have encouraged dissatisfied wives to think in terms of divorce. Since most Catholic countries have in recent decades legalized civil divorce, the asylums for unhappy wives that exist at present in those societies may in fact facilitate divorce there, too.[78]

Surveying the evolution from early modern to modern women's asylums, one sees the close connections among different types of women's institutions. Onetime convents became the sites for ex-prostitutes' asylums, women's prisons, girls' schools, and other residences for females. Critics called the first American women's colleges "Protestant nunneries."[79] Ex-prostitutes' refuges turned into prisons and schools. In one typical transition, a late-nineteenth-century asylum in Montpellier that had long held repentant prostitutes and been known as the "house of Magdalens" opened an orphanage, conservatory, and boarding school and began calling itself the "institution of Saint Martha." Reformers who believed that women were in need of moral guidance, protection, housing, economic assistance, or education saw these needs as interdependent. The institutional forms in which reformers attempted to address such needs were also interrelated. A young secretary boarding at Saint Mary's Residence for Working Girls in contemporary New York City remarked, "My friends at work think I live in a convent." The members of a female housing cooperative in present-day Vancouver remember about their new neighbors: "Their first theory was that we were a home for unwed mothers." These anecdotes are emblematic of the intimate links among women's asylums. Indeed, the evolution from sixteenth-century refuges for ex-prostitutes to modern residences for problematic women comes full circle in this recent statement by an advocate for battered women's shelters: "the principles of self-empowerment and personal transformation on which the feminist-based battered women's shelter is built, [is] a model which planners can use for new shelters, whether for battered women, the homeless, runaways or *prostitutes*."[80]

CONCLUSION

This book has traced the emergence of an extensive network of asylums for women in early modern Europe. The asylums grew up because of a combination of socioeconomic circumstances and the dictates of the era's gender ideology, which prompted reformers to attempt to control, protect, and help females. The study has further analyzed how the early modern women's asylums served as models for the creation or refinement of other social institutions that responded to changing societal needs in the areas of corrections, education, and social welfare. The asylums influenced the development of prisons and reformatories, schools for girls, and residences for problematic females.

One of the factors affecting how people regarded the women's asylums was the potent symbolism of prostitution. Throughout Western history the symbol of the prostitute has acted as a lodestone toward which perceptions of all female behavior were drawn. The prostitute has been a degraded and often criminalized figure. Every sexually active female risked being called a "whore," and every female who traded sexual favors for some sort of gain risked possible stigmatization, arrest, and punishment as a "prostitute."[1] Yet since the Middle Ages the figure of the prostitute has had a symbolic twin, the figure of the redeemed prostitute. Although religiously dominated culture has given way to more secularism in Western societies, the religious topos of conversion from the status of sinner has continued to be an inescapable motif in social life. The linkage of sin and penitence, with its origins in the Judeo-Christian Bible, has provided a paradigm for human behavior to which women in particular have been pressed to conform.

The prominence of the sin-penitence tandem as a standard for female behavior is most evident in Catholic societies. In Italy, for example, this paradigm has been employed across a vast span of time to portray females in very different situations. Moving three hundred years forward in time from the sixteenth-century *convertita pentita,* we find a model inmate in a nineteenth-century Italian women's prison being characterized by a nun as "resigned, repentant [*pentita*]." During the same period, a male social reformer who criticized the education provided by nuns in conservatories charged that the girls therein were unequipped to leave and had to remain "without means and repentant." A hundred years later, in 1982, the feminist leader Betty Friedan spoke in Italy after publishing a book with a newfound emphasis on the family. To her horror, she was introduced as a "repentant feminist."[2] Although deriving from Catholic culture, the sin-penitence paradigm for female behavior and its continuing strength have not been limited to Catholic societies. The paradigm of sin-penitence exists in another form in the magdalen house as an institutional model for the reform of prostitutes. Institutions similar to the original English Magdalen House have long thrived in Protestant milieus, and they continue to be founded.

As the preceding investigations have shown, from the sixteenth century onward more and more women became subject to institutionalization. The onset of the "great confinement" in the seventeenth century meant that the heightened institutionalization applied to men as well, but to a lesser extent and for different reasons than in the case of women. The growing institutionalization of women in Europe had begun as far back as the fifteenth century, during an expansion in both female and male monasteries. Florence in 1336 had a 2 to 1 ratio of male to female religious, which by 1552 shifted to a 4 to 1 ratio of female to male religious.[3] In the sixteenth century the networks of new reformatory and preventive asylums for females made their appearance. We have examined at length the institutionalization of women in the new asylums designed specifically for women. Our own century by no means brought an end to the practice of locking up women in gender-specific institutions like convents. In 1919 the reformer Margarita Nelken wrote about an incident in Madrid that appalled her: the Ladies' Committee for the Repression of the White Slave Trade tried to have a teenage girl confined for five years to a convent for ex-prostitutes to prevent her from prostituting herself. As Nelken said pointedly, "This did not happen in Africa or in the Middle Ages; it happened in Madrid in the month of July in 1919." And in the far-removed milieu of San Francisco in 1981, a judge sentenced a prostitute to a stay in a convent![4]

The increasing institutionalization of women occurred in two distinct forms: (1) in women's asylums, and (2) in institutions whose defining purpose was not gender-specific. From the sixteenth century onward, greater numbers of women were also confined in institutions intended for the general populace. Many early modern poorhouses in Italy and elsewhere, for example, predominantly sheltered women. From its origins in the 1620s, the Ospedale dei Mendicanti (Beggars' Hospital) in Florence held a population that was 65 percent female; by 1681, the 407 women at the establishment constituted nearly 100 percent of its population. The chief administrator of the Mendicanti futilely tried to prevent the poorhouse from becoming a "seraglio of worthless women."[5]

Moreover, correctional authorities have discriminated in the imprisonment of females and males by sending females to jail for offenses that did not result in incarceration when committed by males. Since the nineteenth century, penal institutions in a number of Western societies have housed girls sentenced not because they broke laws but because they committed violations of normative sexual morality—offenses for which young males were not incarcerated. In France and Italy girls who were not charged with crimes were committed to reformatories by courts acting upon the wishes of fathers, who held the legal right of paternal correction. Of the cases of paternal correction in French prisons in 1881, three fourths were girls.[6] American juvenile courts of the Progressive era—a new judicial system widely copied around the world—sentenced thousands of girls to reformatories for what has aptly been called "the crime of precocious sexuality." At a time when some social reformers were growing less enthusiastic about the institutionalization of delinquent boys, the authorities sent disproportionate numbers of girls into institutions and viewed custody itself as a form of treatment. Between 1910 and 1917, of the females and males who appeared before the Memphis Juvenile Court for all offenses, the court committed almost twice the proportion of females as males, sending the majority of the girls to the House of the Good Shepherd. Research shows that this discriminatory pattern of institutionalization still prevailed for juvenile female "status" offenders in the United States, Canada, and many European countries at least through the 1970s.[7] In a growing trend of the present day, American substance abusers who are pregnant have been jailed until they deliver their babies, and women fitting this profile have been imprisoned postnatally as punishment for purported prenatal child abuse.[8]

Long or indeterminate sentences increased the numbers of women in correctional institutions. Burdened by laws and customs developed in the last century, women in American prisons until quite recently received longer sentences than men charged with comparable crimes. In 1890, following a visit to the United States, the superintendent of a Canadian women's reformatory prison, a Mrs. O'Reilly, advocated extending women's sentences to make them like the American ones of up to ten years. She observed that the American inmates "look upon the Reformatory as their home." Her comment evokes not only the reformatories' attempts to be familial and homelike, but also the fact that sentences were so long as to make the carceral institution seem like a permanent residence. Josephine Shaw Lowell, a cofounder of several American women's reformatories, provided the reasoning behind the lengthy sentences: "it would cost the State less in the end to take these girls and women and keep them long enough to train them so that a reasonable percentage could go out as respectable and self-supporting women."[9] From the perspectives of both the individual prisoner and society, the reformer's motives are laudable, but the methods exacted a heavy toll in terms of freedom and gender equality.

Another social institution that incarcerated vast numbers of females was the mental asylum. Building upon humanitarian reforms of madhouses in the preceding century, social reformers and the emerging profession of psychiatry spurred the construction of numerous mental asylums in the nineteenth century. By midcentury, women outnumbered men among the patients in English public lunatic asylums. Of 58,640 certified lunatics committed to asylums in England and Wales in 1872, 31,822 were female. Between the late 1840s and 1871 the number of women in French mental institutions nearly doubled, rising from 9,930 to 19,692, and fewer of these women left the asylums than did male patients. In this period police increasingly initiated commitments to Salpêtrière, the Parisian insane asylum for females that had once, significantly, been a center for the compulsory treatment of diseased prostitutes.

Among the groups of women prominently represented at Salpêtrière were prostitutes and *mal mariées,* the same types of problematic females who had filled the women's asylums.[10]

In a description applicable not only to Italy but to other societies as well, Angela Groppi sums up the way in which mental asylums formed one link in networks of institutions used for the internment of unruly females:

> The system of reclusion for centuries played a relevant role in the tutelage of female honor and in the structures that sustained the social definition of "orderly" comportment by women. In pontifical Rome, between the late sixteenth century and late nineteenth century, places like convents, conservatories, poorhouses, houses of penitence, insane asylums, and prisons were used—with knowing plays upon the distinctions and confusions among them—to manage women's destinies that were deviant compared to the common destiny of normality, in turn defined and attributed in the social sphere.[11]

Groppi's research revealed that rebellious women were transferred back and forth between nineteenth-century Rome's Buon Pastore refuge and the insane asylum.[12] In the United States of the Progressive era, officials and families committed females who fit the diagnosis of "hypersexual" or "mentally deficient" to psychopathic hospitals and asylums for the feebleminded. Some of the women committed to American mental institutions arrived via a reformatory or prison, where they had been tested for mental aberrations and then, in the interests of eugenics, sent to the asylum. Testing two thousand prostitutes, the State Reformatory for Women in New York found fully 35.5 percent to be "subnormal." Concerning the shuttling among institutions, a historian concluded: "One consequence of this proliferation of institutions was that it ensnared some girls in the state's institutional web."[13]

Feminist commentators have observed that in the modern age psychosocial techniques of control over women have replaced religious methods. Because females more often than males tend to be under psychiatric care, women form a high percentage of the population—sometimes the majority—in twentieth-century mental institutions. Along with women diagnosed with specific maladies, American and Irish mental asylums have held battered wives committed by their husbands, and Italian mental asylums have held unwed mothers committed by their families.[14] A noted Italian expert on women and mental institutions writes that a woman's "internment and the motives for that internment are always tied to the narrowness and sparseness of the space conceded to her in our culture."[15] Certainly it is clear that violations of prescriptions concerning gender roles have often precipitated the commitment of women to mental institutions.

How do we evaluate the little-known history of women's asylums and women's institutionalization? First, we have to revise the historiography of institutions. One of the foremost scholars of social institutions, Michael B. Katz, believes that, notwithstanding the evidence of a "great confinement" in the seventeenth century, the sociopolitical deployment of institutions was essentially a modern invention: "the use of institutions as deliberate agencies of social policy, their specialization, and their emphasis upon the formation or reformation of character represented a new departure in modern history."[16] Yet the women's asylums of the centuries preceding the modern era meet each of Katz's criteria. These asylums carried out the publicly and privately sponsored social policies of removing prostitutes from the streets and preserving the virtue of young girls. They specialized in sheltering the female sex, and some of the asylums focused on certain subcategories of females such as ex-prostitutes or endangered girls. The prostitute in need of reform was, in fact, the prototype for all social outcasts in need of reform. The women's asylums implanted in the public consciousness the model of a reformatory institution.

We must revise the historiography of institutions not only by recognizing landmark developments further back in time, but also by acknowledging the importance of gender ideology in stimulating the emergence of major social institutions. This study has shown that the female gender was frequently the trying grounds for experiments in institution building that reverberated widely. Concerns about gender roles spurred the creation of women's asylums, and those asylums pioneered techniques of correction, education, and assistance that spread to the population at large. This investigation bears out what Joan Wallach Scott has urged regarding the usefulness of analyzing history from the perspective of gender. She argues that studying "the ways societies represent gender, *use it to articulate the rules of social relationships,* or construct the meaning of experience" can shed considerable light on social structures, social change, and contests over power in its various forms in past societies.[17]

In addition, the history of the women's asylums can help to reshape a debate within the historiography of institutions. Among scholars of institutions there have been clashes between those who have viewed institutions as embodying humanitarian advances and those who have seen social control as the primary feature of institutions. Weighing this debate in the context of women's asylums leads to the conclusion that both the humanitarian and social-control interpretations are valid. In terms of both the intentions of the founders and the practical outcomes, we find a blend of elements of humanitarian melioration and social control. The founders of women's asylums genuinely tried to help women surmount socioeconomic difficulties, yet they also wanted to steer women's sexual and reproductive behavior. The asylums provided some women with true havens of escape from abuse or deprivation, but they also constricted women's freedom of mobility and action. It may be more productive to admit that both the humanitarian and the social-control interpretations can be valid for the same institution than to believe that they have to be mutually exclusive.

Next, it is important to ask why women's experiences of institutionalization have been so different from those of men. Institutions were not invented just for women; institutionalization was and is a phenomenon that affects both sexes. Nor were greater numbers of women than men institutionalized in the past, if we take into account all kinds of institutions, especially prisons. What *is* striking is that far more gender-specific institutions were created for women than for men, and that the patterns of women's institutionalization differed significantly from those of men. The explanation of these experiences lies in the facts of both women's biological sex and their socially constructed gender identity.[18] Being female in Western societies meant facing the efforts of others to channel one's own sexual and reproductive capacities, and having little autonomous access to political and economic resources. In societies premised upon women's subordination, females were vulnerable to physical abuses and to economic inequities. They further risked being stigmatized if they violated the numerous prescriptions regulating their comportment.

In analyzing the "why" of women's experiences of institutionalization, we have to keep in mind their diversity. Females were institutionalized for a wide array of reasons: to be protected and assisted, to be punished, to be rehabilitated, or for a mixture of these reasons. We need to remember as well that, although many women were committed involuntarily, other women sought institutionalization. One partial explanation for the historical patterns of women's institutionalization has to do with the paucity of options for residence and sustenance available to females in Western societies. A justification for institutionalizing a woman that came up again and again over the centuries was that there was "no other place" for her. A female ward of the state in seventeenth-century Florence found herself interned in the poorhouse for a few months not because she was poor but because state bureaucrats had "no other place to conserve her." In early-nineteenth-century Paris a woman just released from the prostitutes' prison came to the police saying that she "had no place to go" and was held overnight. Concerned citizens in Saint Petersburg, Florida, opened a Florence Crittenton home in the 1920s for "girls who had no place to go except the county poorhouse or city hospital." In a 1977 article entitled "No Place to Go," an American sociologist charted the lack of places for escape available to abused wives, and cited battered women's shelters as necessary first steps toward a solution.[19] Historically, asylums have supplied another option for fulfilling women's pressing needs for room and board.

Western societies established institutions to respond to women's socioeconomic and physical vulnerabilities. Institutions have seemed to offer accessible and appropriate redress for women's economic privations. But institutions were not the inevitable response to women's socioeconomic needs. Noninstitutional solutions such as marriage, other economic partnerships, employment, and public assistance could also address those needs. The lure of institutionalization was even greater as a solution to women's physical and sexual vulnerability. Segregation in an institution protected females from the corporal and social dangers of rape, battering, and physical coercion. Although past epochs have brought greater specialization on the part of social institutions in general, including women's asylums, some women's institutions of the present century were still characterized by the same mélange of internees that was found in early modern women's refuges. Like the fifteenth-century Florentine Monastero delle Convertite, the twentieth-century Asilo Mariuccia in Milan and the American Florence Crittenton homes have also served as way stations for anomalous females, in addition to housing ex-prostitutes. The Asilo sheltered victims of rape and female minors involved in judiciary proceedings as witnesses, plaintiffs, or defendants. Crittenton homes received girls testifying in white slavery cases and women "who did not really belong in jail." Neither social authorities nor administrators of asylums made distinctions about whether females went astray by choice or not. The common denominator, and the significant circumstance that precipitated their institutionalization, was the females' state of being corrupted or fallen, or potentially so.[20] The women and girls owed their institutionalization to their female sex, which caused them to be perceived as socially and sexually vulnerable. As long as women remain the more physically vulnerable sex and sociocultural measures do not compensate for this difference, the tendency to rely on institutionalization to solve women's problems will continue.

Another facet of the explanation for women's historical experience with institutions is that Western gender ideology inspired authorities to punish women in a discriminatory fashion. Although both sexes violated religious and moral codes as well as civil laws dealing with sexuality, usually only the females and not the males were punished.[21] Women and girls drew punishment because the specter of an anarchic reproductive capacity among females greatly threatened the social structures and values of Western societies.

Annie Winsor Allen, the administrator of a late-nineteenth-century American women's reformatory, provided this justification for the discriminatory treatment of deviant females:

> Boys are committed to public guardianship for a great variety of misdeeds, "murder," "assault," "theft," "larceny," "forgery," "malicious mischief," "drunkenness," "improper guardianship," "troublesome child," etc., but never for sexual sins.
>
> Girls are committed—girls of twelve to sixteen, such as are sent to us— for "prostitution," "associating with vicious persons," "disorderly conduct," "improper guardianship," "unmanageable child," but very seldom for theft or any other crime, or for drunkenness. That is to say, what society most dreads and reprobates in a boy is crime; what it most dreads in a girl is sexual irregularity. . . . A girl wants to go about carelessly, thinking only of herself, just as a boy does. But the special feature of a girl's physical construction is such that she cannot go carelessly and unguardedly among lax and self-indulgent men without their making her very soon physically subject to them. So there scarcely is a woman criminal who is not also of a loose life. The men criminals are, of course, all loose-lived too; but society never has counted that, *for consequences in them are not immediate and glaringly social*—they are merely such things as disease, weakened will, and the like. On the other hand many loose-lived women are not criminals at all. . . .

> Why is our ideal for girls so different from our ideal for boys? Why do we dread and reprobate so intensely the only sin to which girls are very prone, and pass it over so without comment in a boy? We do it because this ideal, this dread and reprobation, are absolutely essential to the preservation and advance of the race. Ideals of conduct and definitions of crime and wrongdoing have always been made in the interests of society as a whole, entirely on the basis of consequences to society. Sex irregularity in girls has been deeply condemned because of its ill effect upon the development of the race. Society in the long run understands, and classes these injuries first of all, as moral offenses. Hence the types of the Pure and the Sinful. The race could never have advanced without this idea.[22]

In keeping with the eugenic theories and nativist sentiments circulating in her time, Allen was concerned with deterring pregnancies on the part of unmarried women and on the part of feebleminded women.[23] From her perspective, unrestrained women harmed American society and values by raising the number of illegitimate births and lowering the genetic stock of the race through their production of mentally deficient babies. In earlier eras different theories lay behind justifications for restraining women's reproductive capacity, but the impulse to control this capacity by institutionalizing women was just as great. Traditional gender ideology placed high value on women's chastity—the off-valve of their reproductive capacity. Female sexual honor was a cornerstone for the building of marital alliances that could bring economic, social, and political benefits to all parties involved. Patriarchy and family patrimonies depended upon the honorable sexual behavior of wives, daughters, and sisters. Women's abuse of this asset—in other words, women's sexual activity in illicit channels—drew retribution in the form of institutionalization. When women of later periods behaved in other ways that rejected such female gender roles as subordinate wife or self-sacrificing mother, this too sometimes earned them punishment in the form of institutionalization in mental asylums.

The criminologist Sonia Ambroset has argued that the Italian women's asylums preceded the nineteenth-century emergence of theories of deviance and played a role in that theoretical construction:

> The innumerable women's institutions . . . contributed to the process of defining the problem of female deviance. In analyzing the historical reality of the epoch, it is surprising to realize that all women were potentially institutionalizable. Prostitutes, vagabonds, ruined girls, but also virtuous girls, rich girls, and poor girls risked being put in institutions to be educated or reeducated.[24]

Even before the term "deviance" circulated, women "out of place"—those literally lacking a place to be, or not yet in their proper social place—were assigned a place in institutions. Social scientists have described two kinds of deviant status attributed to females. The first is a kind of generalized deviance resulting from a female's sex alone: "Males as a group constitute the dominant class and females are the deviant class. . . . In our society, male is normal (not merely different) and female is deviant, or Other."[25] The second kind of attributed deviance results from disapproved behaviors such as prostitution. The generalized deviance of being female in a male-dominated society, which meant being economically and sexually vulnerable, made all females subject to the pull of institutionalization. The sociologist Howard S. Becker noted that defining deviant behavior is a function of political and economic power.[26] Because women in Western societies have largely been excluded from political and economic power, they have generally not been the definers of deviance but more often those who were labeled deviant. Western social structures put the female sex in a position to become "deviants" by violating the many social prescriptions concerning female behavior, and this too led to women's institutionalization.

Finally, we have to comprehend what value the women's asylums had for the people residing in them and for society. Certain historians of social institutions have urged that it is time to move beyond interpreting institutions as humanitarian advances or as agencies of social control. The alternative they propose is to recognize that "the people at whom institutions were directed were not inert or passive," and to look at the ways people may have used institutions for their own ends.[27] Throughout this study, we have seen evidence that women did use asylums to give themselves fuller options concerning their roles in life and means of support. One memorable illustration is preserved in a farewell note left by an ex-prostitute who voluntarily entered the early-twentieth-century Asilo Mariuccia in Milan: "I am leaving the Asilo Mariuccia because it is not the place I believed it to be; I came to learn, and this is not a place where one can acquire a trade; I will think and look elsewhere. However, I thank you for all the attention and kindness that was given to me."[28] In fact, she had learned at the asylum to read and write, but she did not acquire practical training that she considered adequate to help her obtain remunerative employment in society. Both inside and outside the asylums, women encountered similar barriers: low pay and a minuscule range of occupational activities considered suitable for their sex. Residents of asylums also had to confront the hostility of workers in the free-market economy who charged that the labor force in the asylum undercut them by working for lower wages. This tense competition could have serious consequences, as it did during the Revolution of 1848 in France, when a group of laborers in Lyons set afire the silk-making machines and expelled the residents at the asylum of Notre-Dame-de-Compassion.[29] Faced with the asylums' limitations in equipping women to earn an adequate wage in society, residents sometimes found that it was simply easier to remain for one's lifetime in the asylum.

The asylums could enrich women's lives in certain ways. Despite their tendency to mirror society's narrow spectrum of occupational options for females, they did foster as new roles for women the positions of teacher within a school and administrator or counselor within an asylum. Some of the new careers arose in institutions that women founded for fellow females, such as the teaching congregations of seventeenth-century France and the battered women's shelters of twentieth-century Britain and the United States. In fostering new employment for women, the latter institutions had something in common with better-known examples of "female institution building": the girls' schools, women's colleges, nursing schools, religious sisterhoods, and settlement houses founded by women like Florence Nightingale and Jane Addams. Of the women's asylums discussed in this book, some had male founders and some had female founders. The evidence examined does not lead to generalizations differentiating the male and female founders or their institutions. But it is noteworthy that the development of new occupational and public roles occurred most frequently in female-founded asylums. The concern with this issue was shared by the other group of female institution builders mentioned above. Nightingale, Addams, and educators like Mary Lyon and Emily Davies yearned to create extradomestic roles for themselves and to serve others.

We can also speak of the women's asylums and the institutions founded by women like Nightingale and Addams in terms of what it meant to reside in a "women's community." Florence Nightingale and women like her sought to live in a female community. They thought that they would benefit from living with others of the same sex who, regardless of differences in class and wealth, confronted the same strictures of gender ideology. The women of the colleges and settlement houses attested that they did find the sort of community that they craved.[30] A few of the scholars who have studied women's asylums believe that residents there also benefited from the female community surrounding them. Alumnae of the Asilo Mariuccia communicated with or aided one another years after their sojourn in the institution. Similarly, residents of battered women's shelters often counsel one another and compare their difficulties and strategies for coping. Some residents of the asylums may have found therein what Annarita Buttafuoco, historian of the Asilo Mariuccia, called the "inestimable gift . . . [of] reciprocal solidarity."[31]

The ostensible value of asylums to societies was that they were supposed to convert inmates for society's benefit. Just as sociologist Erving Goffman called total institutions "forcing houses for changing persons," Italian social commentators had earlier characterized conservatories and other asylums as "transformatories."[32] But because asylums did not always appear to succeed at their rehabilitative goals, Western societies' enthusiasm for the institutional solution has waxed and waned. The nineteenth century, called "the age of the asylum," also brought currents of disaffection with institutions after they failed to live up to the founders' high hopes. Anti-institutional sentiments were especially strong in the United States in the late nineteenth century and the subsequent Progressive era. In Italy women and minors were the first to undergo a relative deinstitutionalization in the late nineteenth and early twentieth centuries, as the focal point for regulating their behavior shifted away from asylums and toward social services, schools, families, and neighborhoods. Deinstitutionalizing the mentally ill with the aim of offering them community-based treatment became popular in the United States, Britain, and the continental European countries in the 1960s and 1970s. American penologists also experimented with deinstitutionalization during that period. In contrast, the United States has recently experienced a surge in institution building to serve the needs of the expanding numbers of homeless people and recovering drug addicts in the 1980s and 1990s.[33]

Although the historical record does not reveal impressive successes by social institutions in rehabilitating inmates, we have seen that institutions may help certain individuals to return to society changed for the better, and that they can provide a needed temporary or permanent refuge even when no change is involved. Gender-specific institutions are in themselves neither good nor bad. The key variable in evaluating them is whether residents have the liberty to come and go as they please and to use institutions for their own self-determined ends.

What will be the future uses and deployments of institutions vis-à-vis women? The history of women's asylums that we have examined provides a few clues. One powerful influence will be the genealogical legacy of women's asylums. A line of institutional prototypes stretches back into history: battered women's shelters, homes for unwed mothers, women's residences, women's prisons, girls' schools, ex-prostitutes' asylums, convents. The structural relationships and resemblances among these institutions are the building blocks out of which new asylums for women will be formed. Another determinant is that many of the social structures and ideological prescriptions that governed gender roles in the past are still operating today.

To address the socioeconomic barriers and dilemmas that contemporary women face, social activists and reformers continue to turn to institutions as solutions. As we have seen, religious groups in particular find appeal in an environmental solution that provides a site conducive to the conversion of character or orientation. In the United States two kinds of asylums for women have multiplied in recent years. Beginning in the 1980s, antiabortion groups revived maternity homes. The 1990s have brought another experiment in institution building: the creation of residences for female drug addicts who are pregnant or have young children. While these homes for addicted women may offer residents valuable services, their spread poses the question of whether social authorities will compel women to enter and remain in the asylums, as they so often have done in the past.[34]

The new institutions for women that have arisen in the United States in the 1980s and 1990s, like those of the past, are social sites where the agendas of social reformers and the agendas of female residents meet. On one side are groups that promote ideologies like the antiabortion philosophy or wish to counter the rising number of babies who will be dependent on state support. On the other side are those women who try to improve their lives through a stay in an institution. In some instances, the differing agendas of reformers and residents may be complementary. In other cases they may result in a conflict of interests and perhaps the exacerbation of gender inequalities. The ideologies and institutions that have shaped the roles of females in Western societies have a deep-rooted history. As this study has shown, these ideologies and institutions have changed and adapted to social circumstances. Those who seek to understand these phenomena today must fully comprehend their causes and be aware of long-term continuities.

NOTES

Introduction

1. Erving Goffman, *Asylums: Essays on the Social Situation of Mental Patients and Other Inmates* (Garden City, N.Y.: Doubleday, 1961), pp. xiii, 3–124; "Humanitarianism or Control? A Symposium on Aspects of Nineteenth-Century Social Reform in Britain and America," *Rice University Studies* 67 (Winter 1981): 1–75; Michel Foucault, *Madness and Civilization: A History of Insanity in the Age of Reason,* trans. Richard Howard (New York: Random House, 1965), pp. 38–64 (originally published as *Histoire de la folie* [Paris: Plon, 1961]); Michel Foucault, *Discipline and Punish: The Birth of the Prison,* trans. Alan Sheridan (New York: Random House, 1979) (originally published as *Surveiller et punir: naissance de la prison* [Paris: Gallimard, 1975]); David J. Rothman, *The Discovery of the Asylum: Social Order and Disorder in the New Republic* (Boston: Little, Brown, 1971); Gerald N. Grob, *Mental Institutions in America: Social Policy to 1875* (New York: Free Press, 1973), pp. 48–49.

2. Michael B. Katz, "Origins of the Institutional State," *Marxist Perspectives* 1 (Winter 1978): 6. See also Grob, *Mental Institutions,* p. 42; Rothman, *Discovery of the Asylum,* p. xiii; and Foucault, *Madness and Civilization,* p. 64.

3. Herbert Blumer, "Social Problems as Collective Behavior," *Social Problems* 18 (Winter 1971): 298; Andrew T. Scull, *Decarceration: Community Treatment and the Deviant—a Radical View,* 2d ed., enl. (New Brunswick, N.J.: Rutgers University Press, 1984), p. 4, which discusses the mentally disturbed as a "problem population."

4. On monasteries that became prisons, see Patricia O'Brien, *The Promise of Punishment: Prisons in Nineteenth-Century France* (Princeton, N.J.: Princeton University Press, 1982), pp. 14, 63. For the institutions in Milan, see A. Bellini, "Misure di prevenzione e di redenzione risguardanti la prostituzione dalle epoche remote ai tempi nostri," *Giornale italiano di dermatologia e sifilologia* 82 (1941): 1185. For the institutions in Normandy, see Robert M. Schwartz, *Policing the Poor in Eighteenth-Century France* (Chapel Hill: University of North Carolina Press, 1988), p. 195.

5. Rothman, *Discovery of the Asylum,* p. xv.

6. Quoted by Rothman, *Discovery of the Asylum,* p. 84.

7. In addition to the works cited in n. 1, see Dario Melossi and Massimo Pavarini, *The Prison and the Factory: Origins of the Penitentiary System,* trans. Glynis Cousin (London: Macmillan, 1981) (originally published as *Carcere e fabbrica* [Bologna: Il Mulino, 1977]).

8. Christopher Lasch, *The World of Nations: Reflections on American History, Politics, and Culture* (New York: Knopf, 1973), pp. 12–13, 15, which reflect the influence of Foucault.

9. Katz, "Institutional State," p. 13.

10. Foucault, *Madness and Civilization,* pp. 38–64. Foucault's later focus, in *Discipline and Punish,* on the rise of carceral institutions in the nineteenth century was not a disavowal of his earlier thesis of the seventeenth-century "great confinement." In the later work he stated that the two explosions of institution building were "different projects . . . but not incompatible ones"(pp. 198–99). For a stimulating critique of

Foucault's arguments, see Lawrence Stone, "Madness," *New York Review of Books* 29 (16 December 1982): 28–36, and, in vol. 30 of the same publication, (31 March 1983): 42–44, "An Exchange with Michel Foucault."

11. Rothman, *Discovery of the Asylum,* p. xiii; Michael B. Katz, "The Origins of Public Education: A Reassessment," *History of Education Quarterly* 16 (Winter 1976): 403. For another discussion of the periodization of confinement, see Pieter Spierenburg, Introduction to *The Emergence of Carceral Institutions: Prisons, Galleys and Lunatic Asylums, 1550–1900,* ed. Pieter Spierenburg (Rotterdam: Erasmus Universiteit, 1984), pp. 2–8.

12. See Foucault, *Discipline and Punish,* p. 297, on the "carceral archipelago," and p. 305 on the "panoptic regime."

13. On the links between correction and social welfare, see Catherine Duprat, "Punir et guérir. En 1819, la prison des philanthropes," in *L'Impossible prison: recherches sur le système pénitentiaire au XIXᵉ siècle,* ed. Michelle Perrot (Paris: Editions du Seuil, 1980), pp. 64–122; David Garland, *Punishment and Welfare: A History of Penal Strategies* (Brookfield, Vt.: Gower, 1985).

14. Edwin M. Schur, *Labeling Women Deviant: Gender, Stigma, and Social Control* (New York: Random House, 1984), p. 5, quoting Howard S. Becker. In this source the quoted phrase was in italics, which I have deleted.

15. Ibid., p. 51.

16. Martha Vicinus, *Independent Women: Work and Community for Single Women, 1850–1920* (Chicago: University of Chicago Press, 1985), p. 12.

17. Estelle Freedman, "Separatism as Strategy: Female Institution Building and American Feminism, 1870–1930," *Feminist Studies* 5 (Fall 1979): 512–29.

18. Foucault, *Madness and Civilization,* p. 38; Rothman, *Discovery of the Asylum,* p. xiv.

19. Brian Pullan, "Support and Redeem: Charity and Poor Relief in Italian Cities from the Fourteenth to the Seventeenth Century," *Continuity and Change* 3 (1988): 177–208. For general background on the two Italian locales central to this study, see Gene A. Brucker, *Renaissance Florence* (New York: John Wiley & Sons, 1969) and David Herlihy, *Medieval and Renaissance Pistoia: The Social History of an Italian Town, 1200–1430* (New Haven, Conn.: Yale University Press, 1967).

20. Gregory Martin, *Roma Sancta,* ed. George Bruner Parks (Rome: Edizioni di Storia e Letteratura, 1969), p. 132.

21. On Beccaria and Leopold II (Pietro Leopoldo's later title), see Richard R. Korn and Lloyd W. McCorkle, *Criminology and Penology* (New York: Holt, Rinehart & Winston, 1959), p. 403. On Lombroso and Ottolenghi, see Mary Gibson, "The 'Female Offender' and the Italian School of Criminal Anthropology," *Journal of European Studies* 12 (1982): 155–59.

22. Michael Ignatieff, "Total Institutions and Working Classes: A Review Essay," *History Workshop Journal* 15 (Spring 1983): 169–73.

23. Some of the institutions for women in early modern Italy and France were denominated *rifugio* or *refuge.* For an early-seventeenth-century *refugio* in Siena, see Domenico Moreni, *Bibliografia storico-ragionata della Toscana,* 2 vols. (Florence: Domenico Ciardetti, 1805; Bologna: Forni, 1967), 1: 65–66. For a *casa del rifugio* in early-seventeenth-century Rome, see Guerrino Pelliccia, Introduction to *Motivi storici dell'educazione femminile (1500–1650)* by Gian Ludovico Masetti Zannini (Bari: EditorialeBari, 1980), n. 30. For French examples, see chapter 6.

24. Foucault, *Discipline and Punish,* p. 31.

Chapter 1

1. Archivio di Stato, Florence (hereafter ASF), Bigallo 1691, ff. 1–2v.

2. Medieval contemporaries perceived women's options as falling within a narrow range. Margaret L. King, "Personal, Domestic, and Republican Values in the Moral Philosophy of Giovanni Caldiera," *Renaissance Quarterly* 28 (Winter 1975): 554–57, elaborates how the fifteenth-century Venetian patrician writer Giovanni Caldiera described the conditions of women in society: married women, virgin nuns and widows in convents, virgin girls awaiting marriage, widows in the world, domestic servants, and prostitutes. Four of the six conditions relate to marriage or monasticism. As King notes, Caldiera distinguished between categories of men by their societal functions, but he distinguished between categories of women by their sexual status or behavior. For a useful overview of the position of women in medieval societies, see Jo Ann McNamara and Suzanne F. Wemple, "Sanctity and Power: Medieval Women," in *Becoming Visible: Women in European History,* ed. Renate Bridenthal and Claudia Koonz (Boston: Houghton Mifflin, 1977), pp. 92–118.

3. Bernardino da Siena, *Le prediche volgari* [Sienese sermons, 1427], ed. Piero Bargellini (Milan: Rizzoli, [c. 1936]), p. 679.

4. Guido Ruggiero, *The Boundaries of Eros: Sex Crime and Sexuality in Renaissance Venice* (New York: Oxford University Press, 1985), offers a comprehensive view of sexual mores in this epoch. On the adjudication of sex crimes in seventeenth-century Tuscany, see Lucrezia Troiano, "Moralità e confini dell'eros nel seicento Toscano," *Ricerche storiche* 17 (May–December 1987): 237–59.

5. McNamara and Wemple, "Sanctity and Power," pp. 98–99, 105–6; Pieter Spierenburg, "The Sociogenesis of Confinement and Its Development in Early Modern Europe," in *Emergence of Carceral Institutions,* ed. Pieter Spierenburg, pp. 10–11. The theme of the disproportionate institutionalization of females, as it applied to women in the early modern period, is developed in chapter 7, section on Reformatories for Youth, and in the Conclusion.

6. James A. Brundage, "Prostitution in the Medieval Canon Law," *Signs* 1 (1976): 825–28, 830, 833–35, 840–43.

7. Brundage, "Prostitution in Canon Law," pp. 829–30, 833, 835, 844; Jacques Rossiaud, *La prostituzione nel Medioevo* (Rome: Laterza, 1984), pp. 77–78, 7–9, 15; Leah Lydia Otis, *Prostitution in Medieval Society: The History of an Urban Institution in Languedoc* (Chicago: University of Chicago Press, 1985), pp. 55–56; Dora R. Stiefelmeier, "Sacro e profano: Note sulla prostituzione nella Germania medievale," *NuovaDWF: donnawomanfemme,* no. 3 (April–June 1977), pp. 34–50; Elisabeth Pavan, "Police des mœurs, société et politique à Venise à la fin du moyen âge," *Revue historique,* no. 264 (1980), pp. 241–88; Ruth Mazo Karras, "The Regulation of Brothels in Late Medieval England," *Signs* 14 (Winter 1989): 399–433. See also Keith Thomas, "The Double Standard," *Journal of the History of Ideas* 20 (1959): 195–216.

8. Matt. 21:31–33, cited by Brundage, "Prostitution in Canon Law," p. 841.

9. On usury, see Julius Kirshner, *Pursuing Honor While Avoiding Sin: The Monte delle Doti of Florence* (Milan: A. Giuffrè, 1978), pp. 30–58; Raymond De Roover, *San Bernardino of Siena and Sant'Antonino of Florence: The Two Great Economic Thinkers of the Middle Ages* (Boston: Baker Library, Harvard Graduate School of Business Administration, 1967).

10. On penitential confinement for religious, see Thorsten Sellin, "Dom Jean Mabillon—A Prison Reformer of the Seventeenth Century," *Journal of the American*

Institute of Criminal Law and Criminology 17 (1926–27): 583–92. Generally, on efforts to reform prostitutes, see Bellini, "Misure di prevenzione," pp. 1115–1202; Brundage, "Prostitution in Canon Law," pp. 841–44; Otis, *Prostitution in Medieval Society,* pp. 72–76. For Santa Maria Maddalena Penitente in Borgo Pinti, see Walther Limburger, *Die Gebäude von Florenz* (Leipzig: F. A. Brockhaus, 1910), p. 107. In addition to the Monastero delle Convertite, Florence had a number of other establishments for penitent prostitutes in the late Middle Ages. They would coalesce, remain on the scene for a few years, and then break up. For such groups as the Compagnia della Pietà delle Convertite di Fiesole and the Monastero di Santa Maria Maddalena delle Convertite di Cafaggiuolo, see ASF, Carte Strozziane, series III, vol. 233 (Raccolta di memorie, fondazioni e padronati di diverse chiese, monasteri, spedali, compagnie e simili fatta dal Senatore Carlo di Tommaso Strozzi), ff. 17rv, 28–29, 119v.

11. On the subjects discussed in this paragraph and the preceding one, see R. W. Southern, *Western Society and the Church in the Middle Ages* (Harmondsworth: Penguin Books, 1970), pp. 309–34; Brenda M. Bolton, "Mulieres Sanctae," in *Women in Medieval Society,* ed. Susan Mosher Stuard (Philadelphia: University of Pennsylvania Press, 1976), pp. 141–58; Anna Benvenuti Papi, "Penitenza e santità femminile in ambiente cateriniano e bernardiniano," in *Atti del simposio internazionale Cateriniano-Bernardiniano,* ed. Domenico Maffei and Paolo Nardi (Siena: Accademia Senese degli Intronati, 1982), pp. 865–75; E. W. McDonnell, *The Beguines and Beghards in Medieval Culture* (New Brunswick, N.J.: Rutgers University Press, 1954).

12. Translated by Brian Pullan in *Rich and Poor in Renaissance Venice: The Social Institutions of a Catholic State, to 1620* (Cambridge, Mass.: Harvard University Press, 1971), p. 377. I have adapted his spelling to American usage. On pp. 372–94, Pullan provides a richly detailed overview of the attempts by the bishops and others to convert prostitutes.

13. Chapter 6 documents the growth of refuges for converted prostitutes in Catholic societies outside Italy.

14. Pio Paschini, *Tre ricerche sulla storia della chiesa nel Cinquecento* (Rome: Edizioni Liturgiche, 1945), pp. 27–28, 50–79. For a general survey of the Italian refuges for ex-prostitutes, see Romano Canosa and Isabella Colonnello, *Storia della prostituzione in Italia dal Quattrocento alla fine del Settecento* (Rome: Sapere 2000, 1989), pp. 113–30.

15. On the communities in the Venetian dominion, see Pullan, *Rich and Poor,* pp. 376–80; Giuliana Marcolini and Giulio Marcon, "Prostituzione e assistenza a Venezia nel secolo XVIII: Il pio loco delle povere peccatrici penitenti di S. Iob," *Studi veneziani* 10 (1985): 99–136. On the communities in Sicilian cities, see Antonino Cutrera, *Storia della prostituzione in Sicilia: Monografia storico-giuridica* (1903; Palermo: Editori Stampatori Associati, 1971), p. 89. On Naples, see Paschini, *Tre ricerche,* p. 56, and on Mantua, Ruth P. Liebowitz, "Conversion or Confinement? Houses for Repentant Prostitutes in Late Renaissance Italy," paper presented at the Sixteenth Century Studies Conference, St. Louis, Mo., 25 October 1980, n. 4.

16. On the Milanese institutions, see Ruth P. Liebowitz, "Prison, Workshop and Convent: A House of Convertite in Counter-Reformation Milan," paper presented at the 6th Berkshire Conference on the History of Women, Northampton, Mass., 1 June 1984, p. 2.

17. Liebowitz, "Conversion or Confinement," p. 2; Christopher F. Black, *Italian Confraternities in the Sixteenth Century* (Cambridge: Cambridge University Press,

1989), p. 207; Canosa and Colonnello, *Storia della prostituzione,* p. 115; Pullan, *Rich and Poor,* p. 380.

18. Lucia Ferrante, "L'onore ritrovato. Donne nella Casa del Soccorso di S. Paolo a Bologna (sec. XVI–XVII)," *Quaderni storici* 53 (August 1983): 500. On Siena, see Liebowitz, "Conversion or Confinement," pp. 2, 6, n. 22; on the Monastery of the Convertite at Pisa, see chapter 5, n. 23.

19. ASF, Conventi Soppressi (hereafter CS) 126:70 Contratti, unpaginated, 7 February 1504.

20. Pullan, *Rich and Poor,* pp. 385, 391, 393. For detailed discussion and documents pertaining to the refuge of Santa Marta, see Pietro Tacchi Venturi, *Storia della compagnia di Gesù in Italia,* 3 vols. (Rome: Edizioni "La civiltà Cattolica," 1950–51), 1/i:382–85; 1/ii:284–313; 2/ii:160–82.

21. Pullan, *Rich and Poor,* pp. 372, 630–42, and, for a summary of scholars' views on Catholic/Protestant differences in attitudes toward poor relief, pp. 11–12. See also Natalie Zemon Davis, "Poor Relief, Humanism, and Heresy," in *Society and Culture in Early Modern France* (Stanford, Calif.: Stanford University Press, 1975), pp. 17–64; Thomas Riis, ed., *Aspects of Poverty in Early Modern Europe* (Florence: Europäisches Hochschulinstitut, 1981).

22. For changes in policies toward the poor in sixteenth-century Tuscany and the Tuscan Monti di Pietà, see Luigi Passerini, *Storia degli stabilimenti di beneficenza e d'istruzione elementare gratuita della città di Firenze* (Florence: Le Monnier, 1853); Luigi Bargiacchi, *Storia degli istituti di beneficenza, d'istruzione ed educazione in Pistoia e suo circondario dalle respettive origini a tutto l'anno 1880,* 4 vols. (Florence: Tipografia della pia casa di patronato pei minorenni, 1883–84), 3:6–7, 76–78; Daniela Lombardi, "Poveri a Firenze. Programmi e realizzazioni della politica assistenziale dei Medici tra cinque e seicento," in *Timore e carità: I poveri nell' Italia moderna,* ed. Giorgio Politi, Mario Rosa, and Franco della Peruta (Cremona: Libreria del Convegno, 1982), pp. 165–84. See also the fuller study by Daniela Lombardi, *Povertà maschile, povertà femminile. L'ospedale dei Mendicanti nella Firenze dei Medici* (Bologna: Il Mulino, 1988). On the holy poor of the Middle Ages, see Michel Mollat, ed., *Etudes sur l'histoire de la pauvreté (moyen âge–XVIe siècle),* 2 vols. (Paris: Publications de la Sorbonne, 1974).

23. Maria Vasaio-Zambonini, "Miserable Virgins and Abandoned Maidens in Tridentine Rome: A Social History of Two Charitable Institutions in the Mid-Sixteenth and Early Seventeenth Centuries" (Ph.D. diss. prospectus, New York University, 1984), pp. 2, 7; Pullan, *Rich and Poor,* p. 372.

24. Ferrante, "L'onore ritrovato," p. 499.

25. Pullan, *Rich and Poor,* pp. 381–82; Vasaio-Zambonini, "Miserable Virgins," pp. 2–5. See also Maria Elena Vasaio, "Il tessuto della virtù. Le zitelle di S. Eufemia e di S. Caterina dei Funari nella Controriforma," *Memoria* 11–12 (1984): 53–64.

26. Pullan, *Rich and Poor,* pp. 382–93.

27. For Naples, see Bargiacchi, *Storia degli istituti,* 2:255. For Milan, see Liebowitz, "Prison, Workshop and Convent," pp. 2–3.

28. On Bologna, see Luisa Ciammitti, "Quanto costa essere normali. La dote nel Conservatorio femminile di Santa Maria del Baraccano (1630–1680)," *Quaderni storici* 53 (August 1983): 469–70, nn. 1, 6, 8, and Ferrante, "L'onore ritrovato," pp. 499, 501. On Cremona, see Daniela Lombardi, "L'ospedale dei mendicanti nella Firenze del seicento. 'Da inutile serraglio dei mendici a conservatorio e casa di forza

per le donne,' " *Società e storia* 24 (1984): n. 39; on Venice, see Pullan, *Rich and Poor,* p. 391.

29. On Brescia and Vicenza, see Pullan, *Rich and Poor,* pp. 393–94. On Rome, see Vasaio-Zambonini, "Miserable Virgins," pp. 4–6. On Turin, see Lombardi, "L'ospedale dei Mendicanti," n. 35.

30. Lombardi, "Poveri a Firenze," pp. 167–68, describes four Florentine establishments for abandoned girls, all founded in the mid- or late sixteenth century: the Monastero delle Fanciulle Abbandonate della Pietà, San Niccolò, the Monastero del Ceppo, and the convent of Santa Caterina. See also Arnaldo D'Addario, *Aspetti della Controriforma in Firenze* (Rome: Ministero dell'Interno, 1972), pp. 51–54, 87. On Florence's Monastero delle Stabilite, a residential community set up in 1589 for plebeian girls, see Enrica Viviani della Robbia, *Nei monasteri fiorentini* (Florence: Sansoni, 1946), pp. 48–50. Bargiacchi, *Storia degli istituti,* 2:253–56, gives an account of Pistoia's seventeenth-century Conservatorio detto Divina Provvidenza and a similar institution in Prato that was nurtured by Bishop Gherardi's appointees, the Deputies for Abandoned and Endangered Girls. Bargiacchi, *Storia degli istituti,* 3:223–53, also offers a long history of the Pistoian Conservatorio delle Abbandonate, begun in 1584 and lasting into the twentieth century.

31. Lombardi, "L'ospedale dei Mendicanti," especially pp. 289–92, 307–8.

32. Ferrante, "L'onore ritrovato," p. 510.

33. CS191:10 Memorie, f. 1.

34. Paraphrased by Kirshner, *Pursuing Honor,* p. 5. Anthropologically oriented studies of honor and shame in Mediterranean societies include: J. K. Campbell, *Honour, Family and Patronage: A Study of Institutions and Moral Values in a Greek Mountain Community* (Oxford: Oxford University Press, 1964); J. G. Peristiany, ed., *Honour and Shame: The Values of Mediterranean Society* (London: Weidenfeld, 1965); Giovanna Fiume, ed., *Onore e storia nelle società mediterranee* (Palermo: La Luna, 1989); Jane Schneider, "Of Vigilance and Virgins: Honor and Shame and Access to Resources in Mediterranean Societies," *Ethnology* 10 (1971): 1–23. See also Sandra Cavallo and Simona Cerutti, "Onore femminile e controllo sociale della riproduzione in Piemonte tra Sei e Settecento," *Quaderni storici* 44 (August 1980): 346–76.

35. Brucker, *Renaissance Florence,* pp. 101–9; Kirshner, *Pursuing Honor,* p. 6; Thomas Kuehn, "Honor and Conflict in a Fifteenth-Century Florentine Family," *Ricerche storiche* 10 (May–August 1980): 287–305. On social networks, see Ronald F. E. Weissman, *Ritual Brotherhood in Renaissance Florence* (New York: Academic Press, 1982), pp. 21–26, 35, 40.

36. In ASF, Acquisti e Doni 292, unpaginated, at the date September 1558, the nineteenth-century archivist Carlo Carnesecchi transcribed the conclusion reached by magistrates of the Otto di Guardia that a weaver had been dishonored by his whorish wife. (A word of explanation is in order concerning the use of Acquisti e Doni 291 and 292 throughout this book. These documents consist of Carnesecchi's transcriptions or descriptions of magisterial cases, some of which no longer can be consulted in their original form. Comparisons between Carnesecchi's transcriptions and extant records indicate that he is a reliable source.) Kirshner, *Pursuing Honor,* pp. 10–11, explicates usages of the phrase *condurre ad honore,* including an example provided by a midfifteenth-century bishop of Pistoia. For the use of "honor" in preaching, see Bernardino da Siena, *Prediche,* Sienese sermons, 1427, p. 673, "E tu, uomo, fai che tu pensi nell'onore de la tua figliuola: ripara che scandalo non ti ne segua." In this particular case, the preacher in question was highborn.

37. Lauro Martines, "A Way of Looking at Women in Renaissance Florence," *Journal of Medieval and Renaissance Studies* 4 (1974): 26, translates this passage from one of the letters of Alessandra Strozzi, a Florentine merchant's widow: "Get the jewels ready, beautiful ones, we have found a wife. Being beautiful and belonging to Filippo Strozzi, she must have beautiful jewels, for just as you [my son] have won honor in other things, you cannot fall short in this." For the second quoted example, see the case of Maria Martelli below, n. 68.

38. I have encountered only sporadic reliable evidence indicating that the lower classes used the vocabulary of *onore* to describe their own actions or objectives. They may have employed it instrumentally when addressing superiors so as to help gain a desired end. A relevant text is cited by Kirshner (*Pursuing Honor,* p. 10, n. 30): a petition presented to the Florentine governing body in 1442 by Stefano Consalvi de Ispania, who had worked for the civic commune as a constable. He sought his overdue salary in order to dower his daughter and "lead [her] to honor." The petition, which was undoubtedly formulated by a scribe and set down in Latin, contained the line "Et quod ipse Stefanus cuperet dictam eius filiam existentem quindecim annorum vel circa ad honorem conducere." For an interesting discussion of female chastity as a component of patrician familial honor and the transmission of such values to the lower classes in medieval Genoa, see Diane Owen Hughes, "Kinsmen and Neighbors in Medieval Genoa," in *The Medieval City,* ed. Harry A. Miskimin, David Herlihy, and A. L. Udovitch (New Haven, Conn.: Yale University Press, 1977), pp. 110–11.

39. "Patrician women" is shorthand for women of the upper and middle social ranks, those who came from families of nobles, learned professionals, bankers, merchants, landowners (including prosperous peasants), guildsmen, and shopkeepers. By "plebeian women" I mean females who came from the *popolo minuto,* what Samuel Cohn has called "the laboring classes" of Florence. This stratum would include urban wage earners, rural sharecroppers (*mezzadri*), and the marginal poor of city and countryside. See Samuel Kline Cohn, Jr., *The Laboring Classes in Renaissance Florence* (New York: Academic Press, 1980), pp. 48, 66–67. The most telling circumstance separating my two categories of women (as will be explained below) is that plebeian women, in addition to serving as unpaid adjuncts helping in their husbands' work, also worked for wages, which patrician women did not.

40. Paolo da Certaldo is quoted in David Herlihy and Christiane Klapisch-Zuber, *Les Toscans et leurs familles: une étude du catasto florentin de 1427* (Paris: Presses de la Fondation Nationale des Sciences Politiques, 1978), p. 586. On medieval and early modern gender ideology and women's roles in social affairs, see Eleanor Commo McLaughlin, "Equality of Souls, Inequality of Sexes: Woman in Medieval Theology," in *Religion and Sexism: Images of Woman in the Jewish and Christian Traditions,* ed. Rosemary Radford Ruether (New York: Simon & Schuster, 1974), pp. 213–66; Ian Maclean, *The Renaissance Notion of Woman: A Study in the Fortunes of Scholasticism and Medical Science in European Intellectual Life* (Cambridge: Cambridge University Press, 1980); Joan Kelly-Gadol, "Did Women Have a Renaissance?," in *Becoming Visible,* ed. Renate Bridenthal and Claudia Koonz, pp. 137–64.

41. McLaughlin, "Equality of Souls," in *Religion and Sexism,* ed. Rosemary Radford Ruether, p. 218.

42. Ferrante, "L'onore ritrovato," pp. 509–11, 513–17.

43. Translated from lawmakers' deliberations on sumptuary legislation by Gene Brucker, ed., *The Society of Renaissance Florence: A Documentary Study* (New York: Harper & Row, 1971), p. 181.

44. Herlihy and Klapisch-Zuber, *Les Toscans*, pp. 404–5. David Herlihy, "Some Psychological and Social Roots of Violence in the Tuscan Cities," in *Violence and Civil Disorder in Italian Cities, 1200–1500*, ed. Lauro Martines (Los Angeles: University of California Press, 1972), p. 146, relates that in 1427, in the city of Florence itself, nearly 85 percent of twenty-year-old women were already married. On the later period, see R. Burr Litchfield, "Demographic Characteristics of Florentine Patrician Families, Sixteenth to Nineteenth Centuries," *Journal of Economic History* 29 (June 1969): 197–98.

45. Bernardino da Siena, *Opera omnia*, 9 vols. (Florence: Patres Collegii S. Bonaventurae, 1950–[65]), 2:108.

46. See Manlio Bellomo, *La condizione giuridica della donna in Italia* (Turin: Eri, 1970), pp. 27–28, 36–78, and idem, *Ricerche sui rapporti patrimoniali tra conjugi* (Milan: Giuffrè, 1961), for information about dowries and other transactions of property related to marriage, with examples from Florence and Pistoia; Thomas Kuehn, "Women, Marriage, and *Patria Potestas* in Late Medieval Florence," *Tijdschrift voor Rechtsgeschiedenis* 49 (1981): 131–36, 138, and idem, " 'Cum Consensu Mundualdi': Legal Guardianship of Women in Quattrocento Florence," *Viator* 13 (1982): 309–33; Samuel K. Cohn, Jr., "Donne in piazza e donne in tribunale a Firenze nel Rinascimento," *Studi storici* 22 (April–June 1981): 526–27; Herlihy and Klapisch-Zuber, *Les Toscans*, pp. 61, 531–33, 590–609; Christiane Klapisch-Zuber, *Women, Family, and Ritual in Renaissance Italy*, trans. Lydia Cochrane (Chicago: University of Chicago Press, 1985); *Leges municipales pistoriensium, nuper mandante Serenissimo Ferdinando II, Magno Duce Etruriae V, Reformate & Approbate Anno MDCXLVII* (Florence: Ex Typographia Serenissimi Magni Ducis, 1647), pp. 91–103, 272; Marc'Antonio Savelli, *Pratica universale: Estratta in compendio per alfabeto dalle principali leggi, bandi, statuti, ordini, e consuetudini, massime criminali, e miste, che vegliano nelli stati del serenissimo Gran Duca di Toscana* (Florence: Vincenzo Vangelisti, 1681), pp. 131–36, 246.

47. Herlihy and Klapisch-Zuber, *Les Toscans*, pp. 508–9, 476–77, 162–64.

48. Quoted in Iris Origo, *The World of San Bernardino* (London: Jonathan Cape, 1963), p. 52.

49. Christiane Klapisch, "Household and Family in Tuscany in 1427," in *Household and Family in Past Time*, ed. Peter Laslett (Cambridge: Cambridge University Press, 1972), p. 272; Herlihy and Klapisch-Zuber, *Les Toscans*, pp. 194–98, 204–9, 394–400, 413, and p. 428 on marital ages in the mountains and upper hills of the Pistoian countryside. Because of poverty, males there too postponed marriage until the end of their twenties and then wed women a decade younger. See also David Herlihy, "Marriage at Pistoia in the Fifteenth Century," *Bullettino storico pistoiese*, 3d series, 7 (1972): 10–15.

50. Kirshner, *Pursuing Honor*, p. 2; Martines, "Way of Looking," n. 36.

51. Bernardino da Siena, *Opera omnia*, 2:83; Herlihy and Klapisch-Zuber, *Les Toscans*, pp. 412–17, 548–50; Julius Kirshner and Anthony Molho, "The Dowry Fund and the Marriage Market in Early *Quattrocento* Florence," *Journal of Modern History* 50 (September 1978): 406–7, 420; Kirshner, *Pursuing Honor*, pp. 4–5, 9–15, 24–25, 35; Litchfield, "Demographic Characteristics," pp. 197–203; Eric Cochrane, *Florence in the Forgotten Centuries, 1527–1800: A History of Florence and the Florentines in the Age of the Grand Dukes* (Chicago: University of Chicago Press, 1973), pp. 136, 277–78, 287. Herlihy, *Medieval and Renaissance Pistoia*, p. 171, n. 73, records that a member of a prominent Pistoian family, the Rospigliosi, made investments for his

daughters' dowries in Florence in 1427, presumably in the Monte delle Doti. See also in the same source p. 255 on the Opera di San Iacopo, which provided dowries for Pistoian girls.

52. Paolo da Certaldo's advice is translated in Julia O'Faolain and Lauro Martines, eds., *Not in God's Image: Women in History from the Greeks to the Victorians* (New York: Harper & Row, 1973), p. 169. For the advice passed on by Alberti, see Leon Battista Alberti, *The Family in Renaissance Florence: A Translation by Renee Neu Watkins of I Libri della Famiglia by Leon Battista Alberti* (Columbia: University of South Carolina Press, 1969), pp. 207–8. For a rare glimpse of a Medici wife performing a diplomatic mission, and for another patrician female's deprecation of an opportunity for women to play a greater public role, see F. William Kent, "A Proposal by Savonarola for the Self-Reform of Florentine Women (March 1496)," *Memorie domenicane,* n.s., 14 (1983): 339, 334–38.

53. Herlihy and Klapisch-Zuber, *Les Toscans,* pp. 579, 599–600; Anne Jacobson Schutte, " 'Trionfo delle donne': Tematiche di rovesciamento dei ruoli nella Firenze rinascimentale," *Quaderni storici* 44 (August 1980): 485–87; Richard C. Trexler, *Public Life in Renaissance Florence* (New York: Academic Press, 1980), pp. 14–16, 37, 117, 218–39, 252, 313–14, 356–66, 394–95, 479, 509, 541–44. Trexler believes that under Savonarola and the sixteenth-century Medici dukes, women participated somewhat more frequently in Florentine public ritual life than they had under the oligarchic republics. The traveler, Grangier de Liverdes, is quoted in Judith C. Brown, "A Woman's Place Was in the Home: Women's Work in Renaissance Tuscany," in *Rewriting the Renaissance: The Discourses of Sexual Difference in Early Modern Europe,* ed. Margaret W. Ferguson, Maureen Quilligan, and Nancy J. Vickers (Chicago: University of Chicago Press, 1986), p. 215.

54. Herlihy and Klapisch-Zuber, *Les Toscans,* pp. 332, 563–67, 604; Martines, "Way of Looking," pp. 16–19.

55. Brown, "Woman's Place," p. 213.

56. Paul Oskar Kristeller, "Learned Women of Early Modern Italy: Humanists and University Scholars," in *Beyond Their Sex: Learned Women of the European Past,* ed. Patricia A. Labalme (New York: New York University Press, 1980), p. 97, and p. 92 on two fifteenth-century Florentine patrician women who wrote notable religious poetry, Lucrezia Tornabuoni and Antonia Pulci. On the problems encountered by female humanist scholars, see also Margaret L. King, "Thwarted Ambitions: Six Learned Women of the Italian Renaissance," *Soundings* 59 (1976): 280–304.

57. Cochrane, *Florence in Forgotten Centuries,* pp. 78, 83, 131, 258, 277. Among the sixteenth-century Florentine literati who wrote on women were Agnolo Firenzuola, Giovan Battista Gelli, and Bernardo Davanzati, all cited by Cochrane. On the *querelle des femmes,* see Joan Kelly, "Early Feminist Theory and the *Querelle des Femmes,* 1400–1789," *Signs* 8 (Autumn 1982): 4–28.

58. Herlihy and Klapisch-Zuber, *Les Toscans,* p. 416, n. 45; Cohn, *Laboring Classes,* pp. 47–48, 51–53, 73, 92, 24–25. Cohn states that only the poorest members of the lower strata generally did not exchange dowries. For a summation of what marital alliances could offer to the laboring classes, see also in his book pp. 14–17. Diane Owen Hughes in her article "Domestic Ideals and Social Behavior: Evidence from Medieval Genoa," in *The Family in History,* ed. Charles E. Rosenberg (Philadelphia: University of Pennsylvania Press, 1975), p. 136, argues that the children of artisanal families had greater freedom than those of patrician families to choose their own marital partners. See this article in general for interesting comparisons between

the habits of artisanal and aristocratic families, including late ages of marriage for male artisans (p. 124).

59. Herlihy and Klapisch-Zuber, *Les Toscans,* pp. 411–13, 405.

60. Ibid., pp. 207–8, 428, 476–79, 508.

61. Cohn, "Donne in piazza," pp. 515–19, 523, 531–33. Although Cohn contends that plebeian women were involved in public altercations far less by the midfifteenth century than a hundred years earlier, it is still accurate to say that women of the laboring classes spent more time physically in the streets in the fifteenth through seventeenth centuries than did their patrician female contemporaries. On a late-fifteenth-century Florentine food riot instigated by plebeian women who manifested political partisanship, see Kent, "A Proposal," p. 340.

62. Herlihy and Klapisch-Zuber, *Les Toscans,* pp. 322–24; Cohn, *Laboring Classes,* pp. 91–96, 103–4; Herlihy, *Medieval and Renaissance Pistoia,* pp. 83–84.

63. Cohn, *Laboring Classes,* p. 12.

64. Brown, "Woman's Place," pp. 208–21; Christiane Klapisch-Zuber, "Women Servants in Florence During the Fourteenth and Fifteenth Centuries," in *Women and Work in Preindustrial Europe,* ed. Barbara A. Hanawalt (Bloomington: Indiana University Press, 1986), pp. 56–80.

65. Translated by Brucker, *Society of Renaissance Florence,* pp. 233–34.

66. *Leges pistoriensium,* pp. 209–10 (Rub. XLVIII, "Quod Maritus teneatur pro Uxore de tela data ad texendum"). For the data in 1663, see Judith C. Brown and Jordan Goodman, "Women and Industry in Florence," *Journal of Economic History* 40 (March 1980): 78. See also Brucker, *Renaissance Florence,* pp. 60–62; Herlihy, *Medieval and Renaissance Pistoia,* pp. 84, 98; Herlihy and Klapisch-Zuber, *Les Toscans,* pp. 162, 208, 286, 413, 574, 582–83, and p. 331 on the custom of having servant girls work for a promised dowry instead of for regular wages. See also Hughes, "Domestic Ideals," pp. 125, 127, 136, on Genoese plebeian women active in trades and commerce.

67. Kirshner and Molho, "Dowry Fund," p. 413; Herlihy and Klapisch-Zuber, *Les Toscans,* p. 587.

68. Brucker, *Society of Renaissance Florence,* p. 69, relates the tale of a broken marriage in 1377. Civic officials ordered an abusive husband to give "a certain amount of food each year" to his wife Monna Madelena, who had returned to the home of her father, a lower-level guildsman. Trexler, in *Public Life,* p. 185, describes the case of Giovanni Morelli, a patrician whose wife fled from him in 1421. The government forced Morelli to pay her 56½ florins a year. In Acquisti e Doni 292, unpaginated, at the date 1538–46 (Suppliche al Magistrato Supremo), see a transcription of Maria Martelli's supplication to Duke Cosimo I. She explained that she had left her cruel husband and returned to her mother. But, lacking funds, both women had to take refuge in a convent. In order to "live in the world with honor" Maria asked the duke to obligate her patrician husband to provide for her support "whatever is appropriate to her quality and to the amount of dowry she gave him." Also see Herlihy and Klapisch-Zuber, *Les Toscans,* pp. 602–3, on the related matter of wives' rights to wrest their dowries from adulterous husbands.

69. Herlihy, *Medieval and Renaissance Pistoia,* pp. 84, 257; Herlihy and Klapisch-Zuber, *Les Toscans,* pp. 287, 610–11. On prosperous aristocratic widows in Genoa, see Hughes, "Domestic Ideals," pp. 139–42.

70. Kirshner, *Pursuing Honor,* p. 15; Herlihy and Klapisch-Zuber, *Les Toscans,* pp. 406–7. See also Hughes, "Domestic Ideals," pp. 139–40.

71. Herlihy and Klapisch-Zuber, *Les Toscans,* pp. 61, 483–84, 546, 557–58, 610; Trexler, *Public Life,* pp. 165–66.

72. Herlihy and Klapisch-Zuber, *Les Toscans,* pp. 323, 348.

73. Thomas Kuehn, *Emancipation in Late Medieval Florence* (New Brunswick, N.J.: Rutgers University Press, 1982), pp. 79, 81, 87, 90–96, 116–20; Kuehn, "Women, Marriage," pp. 141–43; Herlihy and Klapisch-Zuber, *Les Toscans,* p. 571.

74. Herlihy and Klapisch-Zuber, *Les Toscans,* pp. 405–6, 74–75, 337, 348, 495–96. In the same source, see pp. 477 and 287 for the high proportions of female heads of households in the town of Pistoia (21.7 percent) and in the city of Florence (15.7 percent) in 1427.

75. Dante Alighieri, *The Divine Comedy,* trans. H. R. Huse (New York: Holt, Rinehart & Winston, 1954), p. 345 (Paradise, Canto III: 96). Piccarda Donati was a young Florentine woman of holy repute who preferred monastic life to marriage, but was forced to leave the convent to wed. On her, see Viviani della Robbia, *Nei monasteri fiorentini,* pp. 3–4, and D'Addario, *Aspetti della Controriforma,* p. 7.

76. Richard C. Trexler, "Le Célibat à la fin du Moyen Age: les religieuses de Florence," *Annales* 27 (November–December 1972): 1345; Viviani della Robbia, *Nei monasteri fiorentini,* p. 6, and p. 104 for the slightly higher figure of 69 Florentine convents; Bargiacchi, *Storia degli istituti,* 1:21.

77. Ruth P. Liebowitz, "Voices from Convents: Nuns and Repentant Prostitutes in Late Renaissance Italy," paper presented at the 4th Berkshire Conference on the History of Women, South Hadley, Mass., 23 August 1978, pp. 1–2; Trexler, "Le Célibat," pp. 1346–49, 1337; Litchfield, "Demographic Characteristics," p. 203. Herlihy and Klapisch-Zuber, *Les Toscans,* p. 157, demonstrate that in fifteenth-century Florence the number of female religious had been about equal to the number of male religious.

78. Herlihy and Klapisch-Zuber, *Les Toscans,* p. 417: "En 1412, lorsque Giovanni Corsini fit entrer sa fille aînée, âgée de 9 ans, dans le couvent de San Piero Maggiore, il dut payer 230 florins, somme plus de deux fois inférieure aux 600 florins qu'il aurait dû débourser pour la marier dans le siècle." Trexler, "Le Célibat," p. 1340: "Un montant [a conventual dowry] de cent florins est courant au XVᵉ siècle, là où les dots matrimoniales vont de 300 à 1000 florins pour une jeune fille de même classe sociale." We can surmise from our data in chapter 4 and from the evidence presented by Viviani della Robbia, *Nei monasteri fiorentini,* p. 143, that in the 1620s a common dowry for a middle-to-upper-range Florentine convent might be 200 scudi. Litchfield, "Demographic Characteristics," p. 203, informs us that, in the first half of the seventeenth century, Florentine patrician marital dowries reached a median of 10,000 scudi and remained at that level until 1750.

79. See Cohn, *Laboring Classes,* pp. 92–93, on the tendency for women, at least of the upper and middle social ranks, to marry downward in fifteenth-century Florence; Trexler, "Le Célibat," pp. 1339, 1345; Cochrane, *Florence in Forgotten Centuries,* p. 209.

80. Gabriella Zarri, "Monasteri femminili e città (secoli XV–XVIII)," *Storia di Italia: Annali* 9 (1986): 359–429, provides an overview of monastic life in these periods.

81. Viviani della Robbia, *Nei monasteri fiorentini,* pp. 277–87; Bargiacchi, *Storia degli istituti,* 1:124, 4:159–60; Brucker, *Renaissance Florence,* p. 191.

82. In some cases the *converse* serving at convents were lay sisters, as can be seen

in Trexler, "Le Célibat," pp. 1334–35, and Pullan, *Rich and Poor,* p. 378. At the two convents for ex-prostitutes that I have studied, *converse* were a particular type of nun, and they could proceed all the way up the scale of commitment and perfection to become professed *monache converse.*

83. Viviani della Robbia, *Nei monasteri fiorentini,* pp. 278–79, 16, 262, 194; Brucker, *Renaissance Florence,* p. 191; Herlihy and Klapisch-Zuber, *Les Toscans,* p. 155; Trexler, "Le Célibat," pp. 1334, 1341–42.

84. For foundresses, see Viviani della Robbia, *Nei monasteri fiorentini,* pp. 56, 61, 88, 105–8, 150, 277–78, 48, and for female holy figures, see pp. 88–89, 130–39, 199. On the female holy figures, see also D'Addario, *Aspetti della Controriforma,* pp. 43–45, and Cochrane, *Florence in Forgotten Centuries,* pp. 211, 100, 134, 373, 136–38, 295.

85. Quoted by Trexler, "Le Célibat," p. 1329, from a manuscript written by a late-fifteenth-century Florentine patrician. Viviani della Robbia, *Nei monasteri fiorentini,* p. 115, provides a similar example in which the Florentine civic government, in the first quarter of the sixteenth century, sent charity to the nuns of San Giovannino delle Cavalieresse di Malta "because they pray for the city."

86. Viviani della Robbia, *Nei monasteri fiorentini,* pp. 15, 21–22, 123, 17, 37, 77; Trexler, "Le Célibat," pp. 1329, 1331.

87. On members of Third Orders living in monastic communities, see Herlihy and Klapisch-Zuber, *Les Toscans,* p. 153; Brucker, *Renaissance Florence,* p. 191; Trexler, "Le Célibat," pp. 1330, 1334, n. 29. On boarders and women seeking refuge in convents, see Trexler, "Le Célibat," p. 1335; Herlihy and Klapisch-Zuber, *Les Toscans,* pp. 153–54; Viviani della Robbia, *Nei monasteri fiorentini,* pp. 28, 255–56, 298–99; D'Addario, *Aspetti della Controriforma,* p. 114. For Vitale de' Medici and his daughter, see Acquisti e Doni 292, unpaginated, at the date September 1587 (transcription from the Suppliche della Pratica per Pistoia).

88. See Viviani della Robbia, *Nei monasteri fiorentini,* pp. 121, 127, 139, 231, 281, on the placement of girls in convents for education; on Suor Fiammetta, see p. 196. She was a studious nun who grew sickly and became bedridden as a young woman. She taught herself Latin and during her long life wrote many works of history, including "Storia universale dal principio del mondo sino al suo tempo" and "Indie Orientali e Occidentali."

89. Liebowitz, "Voices from Convents," pp. 5, 8–9; Viviani della Robbia, *Nei monasteri fiorentini,* pp. 200–201, 196, 140.

90. Quoted in Viviani della Robbia, *Nei monasteri fiorentini,* p. 258. On violations of cloister at Florentine convents, see also pp. 68, 200–201, 296.

91. Cochrane, *Florence in Forgotten Centuries,* p. 271. Elisabetta Mormorai was eventually transferred to a municipal stockade. Viviani della Robbia, *Nei monasteri fiorentini,* p. 27, relates the fates of Camilla Martelli and Eleonora degli Albizi, respectively the widow and mistress of Grand Duke Cosimo I, who were both confined to convents, the former by her stepson.

92. Acquisti e Doni 292, unpaginated, at the date 30 January 1506.

93. Viviani della Robbia, *Nei monasteri fiorentini,* pp. 63–64, 236, 26; Brucker, *Renaissance Florence,* p. 192; Richard C. Trexler, "La Prostitution florentine au XVe siècle: patronages et clientèles," *Annales* 36 (November–December 1981): 1005.

94. Jane Dempsey Douglass, "Women and the Continental Reformation," in *Religion and Sexism,* ed. Rosemary Radford Ruether, pp. 292–318; Roland Bainton,

Women of the Reformation in Germany and Italy (Boston: Beacon Press, 1971), pp. 165–267; Natalie Zemon Davis, "City Women and Religious Change," in *Society and Culture*, pp. 65–95; Nancy L. Roelker, "The Appeal of Calvinism to French Noblewomen in the Sixteenth Century," *Journal of Interdisciplinary History* 2 (Spring 1972): 391–413; Patrick Collinson, "The Role of Women in the English Reformation, Illustrated by the Life and Friendships of Anne Locke," in *Studies in Church History,* vol. 2, ed. G. J. Cuming (London: Thomas Nelson & Sons, 1965), pp. 258–72. The recent study by Lyndal Roper, *The Holy Household: Women and Morals in Reformation Augsburg* (Oxford: Clarendon Press, 1989), perceives more losses than gains for women in the changes effected by Protestants. On awareness of Protestantism in Tuscany, see D'Addario, *Aspetti della Controriforma,* pp. 33–36, 199, 414–15; Cochrane, *Florence in Forgotten Centuries,* pp. 60, 78, 126, 138, 210, 299–300.

95. Jean Delumeau, *Catholicism Between Luther and Voltaire: A New View of the Counter-Reformation,* trans. Jeremy Moiser (London: Burns & Oates, 1977), pp. 21–23 (originally published as *Le Catholicisme entre Luther et Voltaire* [Paris: Presses Universitaires de France, 1971]).

96. D'Addario, *Aspetti della Controriforma,* pp. 132–44, 480–83; Viviani della Robbia, *Nei monasteri fiorentini,* p. 209. The latter, p. 159, indicates that some convents had lay *operai* in the early sixteenth century and probably before that time as well. Cosimo I created a new ministry, the Deputies of the Monasteries, to whom the *operai* would report. Governmental supervision of the convents had existed in earlier periods, too, but nothing so extensive as the innovations of the sixteenth century. In *Renaissance Florence,* pp. 192–93, and *Society of Renaissance Florence,* pp. 206–7, Brucker offers information about the nine-man ministry established in 1421, the Officials of the Curfew and the Convents, which, despite opposition from the pope, persisted. For interpretations of Cosimo's extension of lay control over the convents, see Trexler, "Le Célibat," p. 1349, and Cochrane, *Florence in Forgotten Centuries,* pp. 59–61. For an overview of Tuscan laws and jurisprudence regarding monasteries, see Savelli, *Pratica universale,* pp. 247–48.

97. Viviani della Robbia, *Nei monasteri fiorentini,* pp. 6–7, 75–78, 186–90; D'Addario, *Aspetti della Controriforma,* pp. 157–58, 484, 162–67, 171, 281–97; Liebowitz, "Voices from Convents," pp. 5, 7, 9–12.

98. Viviani della Robbia, *Nei monasteri fiorentini,* p. 143, notes that in 1623 the usual dowry at the convent San Giovannino delle Cavalieresse di Malta was 200 scudi. To conclude that this sum is equivalent to a bit more than one month's income for a patrician family, I draw upon Litchfield, "Demographic Characteristics," p. 203, who states that in the early seventeenth century "10,000 *scudi* represented some five years income" for a moderately wealthy family. My information on the range of dowries for *converse* comes from hints in Viviani della Robbia, *Nei monasteri fiorentini,* pp. 123, 223, and from the data concerning the Monastero delle Convertite and Santa Maria Maddalena in chapter 4, section on Responses to the Institutional Community. We find in Lombardi, "Poveri a Firenze," p. 175, that Florentine administrators of poor relief in 1621 believed that beggars could live on about 52 scudi a year. Extrapolating from this a subsistence-level income for a four-person plebeian family of approximately 200 scudi, we arrive at what expenditure for the dowry of a *conversa* (25 to 70 scudi) might have meant. As indicated by D'Addario, *Aspetti della Controriforma,* pp. 290–91, n. 78, in exceptional circumstances administrators of convents sometimes admitted females even when no dowry was paid. They might do so when pressured by

powerful citizens or out of compassion for a poor girl. Both religious and civil authorities tried to stop such practices on the part of convents in a precarious financial situation.

99. Herlihy and Klapisch-Zuber, *Les Toscans,* p. 572; Trexler, "Le Célibat," p. 1340.

100. Kuehn, *Emancipation in Florence,* pp. 10–11.

101. See chapter 5, section on The Institutions, Women's Economic Strategies, and Female Honor.

102. Quoted in Viviani della Robbia, *Nei monasteri fiorentini,* p. 78. The pope's reference to Elijah is from 1 Kings 17:6 (NEB).

103. The "worse evil . . . lesser one" formulation, long associated with prostitution, appeared in the opening lines of a decree of 1415 proposing the financing of two municipal brothels, translated in part in Brucker, *Society of Renaissance Florence,* p. 190. For the number of prostitutes and the quotation from Pope Pius II, see Trexler, "La Prostitution," pp. 992, 987–88, 983.

104. The phrase "[il] biasmo del meretricio" appeared in a fourteenth-century commentary on Dante's *Divine Comedy* and was quoted in Kirshner, *Pursuing Honor,* p. 11, n. 32. Also see Trexler, "La Prostitution," pp. 1003–6.

105. On the concept of "sex/gender system," see Gayle Rubin, "The Traffic in Women: Notes on the 'Political Economy' of Sex," in *Toward an Anthropology of Women,* ed. Rayna R. Reiter (New York: Monthly Review Press, 1975), p. 159: "As a preliminary definition, a 'sex/gender system' is the set of arrangements by which a society transforms biological sexuality into products of human activity, and in which these transformed sexual needs are satisfied." See also pp. 167–68, 203–5.

106. Translated by Brucker, *Society of Renaissance Florence,* pp. 191–92.

107. Brown and Goodman, "Women and Industry," p. 78.

108. Translated by Brucker, *Society of Renaissance Florence,* pp. 199–200. According to judicial officials, the brothel keeper replied to Stella's husband: "I will give you 12 florins, or 16 at the most, and no more. For she is poorly clothed and I will have to furnish her with a new wardrobe." When Bartolomeo pimped for his wife, he reaped in payment, in addition to money, on one occasion "a wine flask full of oil" and on another a doublet.

109. On the prostitute's *mundualdo,* see ASF, Onestà 3, f. 16rv and Savelli, *Pratica universale,* pp. 241–42.

110. On prostitutes and begging, see Pullan, *Rich and Poor,* p. 376, and Ferrante, "L'onore ritrovato," p. 499. Brucker, *Society of Renaissance Florence,* pp. 194–95, translates a magisterial case in which a Florentine woman forty to forty-five years old was declared to be a public prostitute in 1400. The common view saw older women as having passed beyond carnal pleasures and acceded to a state of dignified chastity, meriting respect. But not all older women were viewed in this light. See Herlihy and Klapisch-Zuber, *Les Toscans,* p. 582, n. 150, for a Pisan countryman's description of his sixty-year-old mother as "mute, deaf, and of little virtue."

111. Acquisti e Doni 292, unpaginated, at the date 1603.

112. Transcribed by Carlo Carnesecchi in Acquisti e Doni 292, unpaginated, at the dates 29 June and 13 July 1521. Although the tone of the bishop's minions suggests a cavalier attitude toward Maria's welfare, the bishop himself reported back to Florence that he had lodged her with "a woman of property" and that he was trying his best to provide for her sustenance while awaiting instructions for her removal.

113. In the nineteenth century, debates arose over similar questions regarding women's public and private roles. See Vicinus, *Independent Women,* pp. 1–9.

114. Translated by Pullan, *Rich and Poor,* p. 394. On Angela Merici and other female religious activists, see Ruth P. Liebowitz, "Virgins in the Service of Christ: The Dispute over an Active Apostolate for Women During the Counter-Reformation," in *Women of Spirit: Female Leadership in the Jewish and Christian Traditions,* ed. Rosemary Ruether and Eleanor McLaughlin (New York: Simon & Schuster, 1979), pp. 133–37, 141–43. Also see Sister M. Monica, *Angela Merici and Her Teaching Idea, 1474–1540* (New York: Longmans, Green, 1927).

115. Cochrane, *Florence in Forgotten Centuries,* p. 212. On Mary Ward, see Liebowitz, "Virgins in the Service," pp. 135–37, 139, 142–44.

116. Translated by Pullan, *Rich and Poor,* p. 392. I have changed his spelling to American usage. See also Margaret F. Rosenthal, "Veronica Franco's *Terze Rime:* The Venetian Courtesan's Defense," *Renaissance Quarterly* 42 (Summer 1989): 227–57.

117. In CS191:35 Fogli, unpaginated, 10 April 1604, the lists of benefactors' subscriptions to support Santa Maria Maddalena begin thus: "For lack of a place in which to retire and be rehabilitated, many would-be *convertite* persevere in wrongdoing. . . . [We want to help these women] because already we have seen that many who were inspired by the Madonna to retire from wrongdoing have had difficulty sustaining themselves."

118. Translated by Pullan, *Rich and Poor,* p. 377.

119. For the mixed populations at the Venetian hospital of the Incurabili and at Milanese institutions for women in the sixteenth century, see Pullan, *Rich and Poor,* p. 376, and Liebowitz, "Prison, Workshop and Convent," pp. 3–4.

120. One can still visit the Monastero delle Convertite, the only one of the three Tuscan refuges for which this is true. I am grateful to Patricia Soberman for indicating that the convent is described in Eve Borsook, *The Companion Guide to Florence* (London: Collins, 1966), p. 321. An example of the common reuse and transformation of institutions, the former convent is today the Istituto Pio X, a Catholic establishment containing a youth hostel and a theater. In 1989 an administrator of the hostel permitted me to explore the premises. At that time the city had begun a restoration of the convent's chapel, on the corner of present-day Via de' Serragli and Via Campuccio, and presumably it will be open to visitors in the future.

121. On the origins and early history of the Monastero delle Convertite (also known as Santa Elisabetta), see Acquisti e Doni 45, the two unpaginated prefatory leaves headed "Fondatione del Monastero delle Convertite della nostra compagnia"; CS126:63 Ricordi (1616–26), unpaginated prefatory folio; Carte Strozziane, series III, vol. 233, f. 34v; Limburger, *Die Gebäude,* p. 55. These sources relay vague accounts of the foundation of the refuge, differing on precise dating but all concurring that the establishment was set up in the 1320s or 1330s. On the number of residents typically there, see chapter 4, n. 58.

122. For the founding and history of the Casa delle Malmaritate, see Bigallo 1691, ff. 1–2v; Marco Lastri, *L'osservatore fiorentino sugli edifizi della sua patria,* 3d ed., 8 vols. (1776; Florence: G. Ricci, 1821), 3:125–28. On the history of Santa Maria Maddalena, see Giuseppe Dondori, *Della pietà di Pistoia in grazia della sua patria* (Pistoia: P. A. Fortunati, 1666), pp. 53–54; Bargiacchi, *Storia degli istituti,* 1:64–65, 3:226, 4:332. Bargiacchi incorrectly stated that the convent did not have a long life. The institution's surviving records, now located in Florence's Archivio di Stato, go to

1810. For sources concerning the number of residents in the two refuges, see below, chapter 4, n. 58.

Chapter 2

1. On the economic changes, see Brown and Goodman, "Women and Industry," pp. 74, 78. It is hard to corroborate from the available evidence whether the perception of increasing prostitution was indeed correct. Evidence on the volume of prostitution in different periods can be inconclusive because data sometimes may include only registered prostitutes, an underrepresentation of the total number of women engaged in prostitution. Trexler, "La Prostitution," p. 992, found that in 1436 the personnel of Florentine brothels (prostitutes registered with the Onestà) numbered 70. A decade earlier, the overall civic population had been approximately 40,000, as noted by David Herlihy, "Mapping Households in Medieval Italy," *Catholic Historical Review* 58 (April 1972): 5. We learn from Herlihy and Klapisch-Zuber, *Les Toscans,* p. 581, that in 1560 a special survey in Florence identified 200 prostitutes, of whom 79 were registered with the Onestà. The city at that time had 60,000 people. Unlike the nineteenth-century English towns of Plymouth and Southampton, where Judith Walkowitz found extensive prostitution, fifteenth-century Florence and Pistoia did not have sex ratios in which females outnumbered males. In fact, in Florence the opposite was the case until both sexes entered old age. The sex ratios in Florence became more balanced in the sixteenth century. See Judith R. Walkowitz, *Prostitution and Victorian Society: Women, Class, and the State* (Cambridge: Cambridge University Press, 1980), p. 154; Herlihy and Klapisch-Zuber, *Les Toscans,* pp. 327–28, 341, 348.

2. The remark about poor girls is quoted by D'Addario, *Aspetti della Controriforma,* p. 309, n. 105, and pertains to the fate of female orphans who in 1580 had to leave the financially strapped Innocenti orphanage to be on their own. For a typical instance of a woman justifying prostitution, see Acquisti e Doni 292, unpaginated, at the date 1631, description of a case heard by the Otto di Guardia involving Jacopo Brogi.

3. Brown and Goodman, "Women and Industry," pp. 79, 78.

4. Herlihy, *Medieval and Renaissance Pistoia,* p. 151; Herlihy and Klapisch-Zuber, *Les Toscans,* p. 19; Brown and Goodman, "Women and Industry," n. 18.

5. The story of Niccolò di Giunta is translated by Brucker, *Society of Renaissance Florence,* p. 198. For the "indigent widows" in a privately kept brothel of 1511, see Trexler, "La Prostitution," p. 1004.

6. A wide-ranging conceptual framework for the historical analysis of prostitution is offered by Walkowitz's *Prostitution and Victorian Society.* For studies of medieval prostitution, see above, chapter 1, n. 7. Selected studies of prostitution in early modern Catholic societies include Antonio Barzaghi, *Donne o cortigiane? La prostituzione a Venezia. Documenti di costume dal XVI al XVIII secolo* (Verona: Bertani, 1980); Mary Elizabeth Perry, " 'Lost Women' " in Early Modern Seville: The Politics of Prostitution," *Feminist Studies* 4 (February 1978): 195–214; idem, "Deviant Insiders: Legalized Prostitutes and a Consciousness of Women in Early Modern Seville," *Comparative Studies in Society and History* 27 (January 1985): 138–58; Lucia Ferrante, "Pro mercede carnali . . . Il giusto prezzo rivendicato in tribunale," *Memoria* 17 (1986): 42–58 (special issue on prostitution); Colin Jones, "Prostitution and the Ruling Class in 18th-Century Montpellier," *History Workshop Journal* 6 (Autumn 1978): 7–28.

7. On Simone Fidati's preaching against prostitution, see Acquisti e Doni 292,

unpaginated. See Trexler, "La Prostitution," p. 1006, nn. 4, 136, on Savonarola's sermons attacking prostitution.

8. On the notion of pollution to individuals, objects, and society, see Mary Douglas, *Purity and Danger: An Analysis of Concepts of Pollution and Taboo* (New York: Praeger, 1966), especially pp. 2–4, 34–36, 41, 113, 140–42.

9. Generally, on regulations concerning prostitutes before the fifteenth century, see Onestà 1, ff. 9–12v; Archivio di Stato, Pistoia (hereafter ASP), Statuti 5, f. xviiii. On access to holy sites, see Onestà 1, ff. 18v–19v. For the dress code, see Brucker, *Society of Renaissance Florence,* pp. 191, 195.

10. Brundage, "Prostitution in Canon Law," pp. 830–35.

11. John K. Brackett, "Bureaucracy and Female Marginality: The Florentine Onestà and the Control of Prostitution, 1403–1680" (Department of History, University of Cincinnati, 1991, photocopy), p. 12; Trexler, "La Prostitution," pp. 983–84; Michael J. Rocke, "Il controllo dell'omossesualità a Firenze nel XV secolo: Gli 'Ufficiali di Notte,' " *Quaderni storici* 66 (December 1987): n. 19. In 1432 the Signoria created the Ufficiali di Notte to focus on homosexuality.

12. Trexler, "La Prostitution," pp. 985–88, 990–94. On Pistoia, see Maria Serena Mazzi, "Il mondo della prostituzione nella Firenze tardo medievale," *Ricerche storiche* 14 (May–December 1984): 352–53. For further discussion of Florentine prostitution and the Onestà, see Canosa and Colonnello, *Storia della prostituzione,* pp. 27–34, 93–112.

13. For the diverse regulations, see Onestà 1, ff. 2–5, 10–13, and Trexler, "La Prostitution," pp. 990, 1003–4. Trexler, in the same source, pp. 995–1000, analyzes Onestà 2 (Libro di Condannazioni, 1441–1523), which records individual cases handled by the magistracy. Other specific cases handled by the magistracy appear in Onestà 4 (Libro di Condannazioni, 1593–1627), Onestà 6 (Libro di Sentenze, 1629–42), and Otto di Guardia Granducale 2709, November 1686–February 1706.

14. Onestà 1, f. 12; Brundage, "Prostitution in Canon Law," pp. 839–40; Trexler, "La Prostitution," pp. 998, 986, for the percentage of prostitutes as plaintiffs and for data on the number of women seen per decade, and also p. 997.

15. Giovanni Cambi, commenting on the year 1511 in his *Istorie fiorentine,* quoted by Trexler, "La Prostitution," p. 1006. I use Trexler's translation from an English version of his article.

16. Trexler, "La Prostitution," pp. 1003–6; Brackett, "Bureaucracy and Female Marginality," pp. 20–23. The *provvisioni* of 11 April and 28 April 1511 and 16 June 1527 are copied in Onestà 1, ff. 21rv, 23v. For the political and legislative context of the decrees of 1511, see Brucker, *Renaissance Florence,* pp. 272–73, and Luca Landucci, *A Florentine Diary from 1450 to 1516,* trans. Alice de Rosen Jervis (New York: Arno Press, 1969), pp. 244–45. For the background related to the directive of 1527, see Cecil Roth, *The Last Florentine Republic* (New York: Russell & Russell, 1925), p. 64.

17. Pullan, *Rich and Poor,* p. 380; Rossiaud, *Prostituzione nel Medioevo,* pp. 209–12; Otis, *Prostitution in Medieval Society,* pp. 40–45; Owsei Temkin, "Therapeutic Trends and the Treatment of Syphilis Before 1900," *Bulletin of the History of Medicine* 29 (July–August 1955): 309, 311; Stanislav Andreski, " 'The Syphilitic Shock': Puritanism, Capitalism, & a Medical Factor," *Encounter* 55 (October 1980):76–81, and idem, "The Syphilitic Shock: A New Explanation of the 'Great Witch Craze' of the 16th and 17th Centuries in the Light of Medicine and Psychiatry," *Encounter* 58 (May 1982): 15, 25. I am indebted to Elizabeth Gleason for directing me to the latter articles. For studies of the Protestant crackdown, see chapter 6, n. 5.

18. On the Monastero delle Convertite, see Onestà 3, f. 26v, for the statement, "per essere quel Monastero in certo modo sotto la protezzione delli prefati offiziali d'Honestà." For the relationship between the Onestà and the Casa delle Malmaritate, see Bigallo 1691, ff. 15v, 30, 32v, 37v–38, 39; Onestà 4, f. 143; Onestà 6, f. 71, 11 May 1638. It is explained in Onestà 3, f. 59, 23 January 1670, that the practice of registering and taxing prostitutes extends to Pistoia and Pisa.

19. Brundage, "Prostitution in Canon Law," pp. 838–39.

20. Emmanuel Rodocanachi, *Courtisanes et bouffons: étude de mœurs romaines au XVIᵉ siècle* (Paris: Ernest Flammarion, 1894), pp. 69–71; Onestà 1, ff. 40, 44; Onestà 3, ff. 26, 29v, 14v, 59; Savelli, *Pratica universale,* pp. 239, 243, 247; Brackett, "Bureaucracy and Female Marginality," n. 89. See CS126:70 Contratti, unpaginated, 10 February 1610, for the quoted will of Maddalena di Arcangiolo Stiattesi, and see in the same source a similar will made by Maddalena di Piero della Torre, dated 26 February 1577.

21. See D'Addario, *Aspetti della Controriforma,* p. 277, on Archbishop Alessandro de' Medici's order of early September 1577 barring prostitutes from entering Florence's churches of greatest sacral and ceremonial importance. See Cochrane, *Florence in Forgotten Centuries,* pp. 58–59, 62–63, on Cosimo I's campaign to rationalize the departments of state.

22. Onestà 3, ff. 1–19v, unfolds in detail the Reform of 1577. For the roll call, see Onestà 3, f. 15v; Trexler, "La Prostitution," n. 99. On the tax system, see Onestà 3, ff. 6, 16v. The taxes predated the Reform. We find mention of *tasse straordinarie* at least from 1544, as in Onestà 1, f. 28v, and of a *tassa ordinaria* at least from 1559, as in Onestà 1, f. 42. For the nighttime bulletins, see Onestà 3, ff. 14, 16v. On the income going to the Monastero delle Convertite, see Onestà 3, ff. 6rv, 32.

23. Onestà 3, f. 13v. For Ammirato's exasperation, see Cochrane, *Florence in Forgotten Centuries,* p. 150. On coachmaking as part of the new production of luxury items in seventeenth-century Florence, see Brown and Goodman, "Women and Industry," p. 75. In the fifteenth century the Monastero delle Convertite, like other convents, had received a little income from the fines of magistracies, including the Onestà, as in Provvisioni Registri 137, f. 318, 10 March 1446. However, the income that came to the Monastero delle Convertite from Onestà fines multiplied considerably in the sixteenth and seventeenth centuries. The convent profited when prostitutes failed to wear their identifying signs, when they committed other dress violations, and when they infringed on the residential rules, as stipulated in Onestà 1, f. 21; Onestà 3, f. 13v; and Onestà 3, ff. 25, 42. For examples of sentences levying fines that benefited the Monastero delle Convertite, see Onestà 6, ff. 1rv, 53v, 72, 135–37.

24. Some of these punishments had been authorized in earlier regulations but not often implemented. On eviction, see Onestà 3, ff. 27v–28v (Bando of 19 June 1568), and Savelli, *Pratica universale,* pp. 240–44. For imprisonment, see Onestà 1, ff. 36v–37 (Bando of 15 February 1555), and Onestà 6, f. 49rv. For confinement, confiscation, and exile, see Savelli, *Pratica universale,* p. 240 (citing Bando of 13 August 1630), and Onestà 4, f. 8v. Examples of sentencing based on these regulations can be found in n. 29 and in Acquisti e Doni 292, unpaginated, descriptions of cases heard by the Otto di Guardia, at the dates 28 September 1514 and June 1592 (the case of Anna di Piero da Saragozza). On prostitutes in the Stinche for nonpayment of fines, see John K. Brackett, "The Otto di Guardia e Bulia: Crime and Its Control in Florence, 1537–1609," (Ph.D. diss., University of California, 1986), p. 95.

25. Onestà 1, ff. 27v–28, 31v–33, 37v.

26. Acquisti e Doni 292, unpaginated, at the date December 1558 (transcription of a letter to the Auditore delle Riformagioni).

27. Onestà 3, ff. 30v–31 (Legge of 10 February 1558); Savelli, *Pratica universale,* p. 239. In the late seventeenth century an amendment in force for a brief period required that officials of the Onestà check ecclesiastical registers to verify that applicants for cancellation had indeed taken the sacraments. See Onestà 3, f. 63.

28. Onestà 3, f. 27rv. Even before the Onestà established this official policy, it stressed in individual cases that married prostitutes would not be canceled unless they returned to their husbands and reformed. See Onestà 1, ff. 32v–33.

29. For the terminology of prostitution, see Onestà 3, f. 28, and Trexler, "La Prostitution," n. 15. For the weaver's wife, Veronica, judged to be a *puttana,* see Otto di Guardia Repubblicana 128, ff. 200v–201, 20 March 1503. The Otto di Guardia dealt with Veronica by confining her to the Monastero delle Convertite for nine months, followed by a year of exile from Florence. On denunciations, see Onestà 1, ff. 21v, 31; Onestà 3, f. 4rv.

30. Savelli, *Pratica universale,* p. 242. On the same page Savelli described the antique antecedent of the Onestà: "questo Ufizio, che fusse anche nell'antica Repubblica di Roma, pare che parli Cornelio Tacito nel libro secondo de' suoi Annali etc. e che anche pagassero certa tassa della lor disonestà osserva da Tranquillo."

31. Brackett, "Bureaucracy and Female Marginality," n. 95, pp. 27, 38–39, 41, 22.

32. For the two quotations, see Onestà 3, ff. 27v–28 (Bando of 19 June 1568).

33. Onestà 1, f. 33v (Bando of 12 December 1547). For a later promulgation of the same policy on eviction and relocation, see Onestà 3, ff. 27v–28 (Bando of 19 June 1568).

34. Onestà 1, ff. 38v–39. Duplicated in Onestà 3, ff. 56v–57.

35. Trexler, "La Prostitution," p. 985.

36. The latter two quotations are both from Onestà 1, f. 39. The phrase actually used in regard to leading girls and women astray is "*far capitar male.*"

37. On the aims of the Reform of 1577 in terms of protecting girls, see Onestà 3, f. 18, and Savelli, *Pratica universale,* pp. 239–40. For prostitutes seeking to protect their daughters, see chapter 3, section on Juvenile Residents.

38. Savelli, *Pratica universale,* p. 247, relates what the inheritance law of 1553 actually stipulated. See ASF, Regio Diritto vol. 4896, f. 472 (6 July 1576) for the interpretation by officials: "la legge fatta l'anno 1553 prohibisce che le Convertite non possino ricevere in quel convento se non chi havesse tenuto vita impudica." For the episode of 1647, see Onestà 3, ff. 54–55.

39. Onestà 3, f. 47v. The entire text of this Bando of 15 June 1639 appears in ff. 46–48.

40. Savelli, *Pratica universale,* p. 241. For the magisterial case to which I have alluded, see Acquisti e Doni 292, unpaginated, at the date 1595, description of case heard by the Otto di Guardia involving the participants Fontana Fontani, Bastiano known as Marocco, and Marzia.

41. On marriage as an alternative to prostitution, see Brundage, "Prostitution in Canon Law," pp. 842–44. For the perspectives of institutional administrators, see Bigallo 1691, f. 37v, and Ferrante, "L'onore ritrovato," pp. 513–17. For Agnola of Maremma, a *convertita* who found a husband on her own, see chapter 5, section on New Social Institutions.

42. Onestà 3, f. 27rv (Ordine of Onestà of 8 July 1569), ff. 39v–40 (Ordine of S.A.S. of 12 May 1633); Brackett, "Bureaucracy and Female Marginality," n. 133.

43. Onestà 3, ff. 40v–41 (decree of Magistrato Supremo of 15 January 1635).

44. Savelli, *Pratica universale,* pp. 242–43; Brackett, "Bureaucracy and Female Marginality," n. 133; Onestà 3, f. 61v (decree of Magistrato Supremo of 11 August 1673).

45. Savelli, *Pratica universale,* p. 242.

46. Onestà 3, f. 26rv (Ordine of Pratica Segreta of 5 July 1559), and Savelli, *Pratica universale,* p. 239; Onestà 3, ff. 33v–35v (Ordine of Pratica Segreta of 3 July 1625), and Savelli, *Pratica universale,* pp. 239, 243; Onestà 3, ff. 57v–59 (documents of 1653 and 1665). See also Giovanni Cipriani, "Le 'Zimarrine' e 'l'Offitio dell'Honestà' nella Firenze di Cosimo II de' Medici," *Ricerche storiche* 8 (1978): 801–8; and Ferrante, "Pro mercede," pp. 46–47, for a similar dynamic between civic officials and the convent for *convertite* in Bologna.

47. Onestà 1, ff. 41v–42, 39v–40.

48. Acquisti e Doni 292, unpaginated, at the date 31 August 1614. For restrictions on prostitutes' movements, see Onestà 3, f. 17rv (Riforma of 1577).

49. Onestà 3, ff. 33v–35v. These unregistered suspect women did have to purchase the Onestà's nighttime bulletins and licenses for masking. And they continued, as in the edict of 1559, to be subject to the inheritance law of 1553 governing prostitutes' legacies.

50. On the licenses for riding in carriages, see Onestà 3, ff. 43–45v, 58, 59v–60v, 64. The licenses carried some restrictions regarding destinations, hours, and circumstances of travel. For the earlier history of the edicts on riding in carriages, see Onestà 3, ff. 13v–14, 37rv, 40rv. For sentences for violations, see Onestà 6, ff. 98, 133, 135–36. On Margherita Negri, see CS126:54 Debitori e Creditori (hereafter D&C) (1634–42), f. 95.

51. For privileges and immunities, see CS126:70 Contratti, unpaginated, *entrate* of 1609–14 and undated ones, 18 November 1615 *calculo;* CS126:69 Cartelle, unpaginated, 16 June–October 1663, letters between the convent, the Onestà, and the ducal Scrittoio delle Possessioni; Onestà 3, ff.49v–50 (19–20 January 1564); and Acquisti e Doni 292, unpaginated, at the dates 1614, April 1615, 3 August 1615, citing archiepiscopal records. On Cosimo I's attempted reform of the courts, see Cochrane, *Florence in Forgotten Centuries,* pp. 63–65.

52. The paraphrase of the sixteenth-century legislation is from Savelli, *Pratica universale,* p. 238 (Legge of 29 July 1561). The statement by Machiavelli is from Niccolò Machiavelli, *The Prince,* trans. Luigi Ricci, revised by E. R. P. Vincent (New York: New American Library , 1952), pp. 93–94. The phrase quoted is part of Machiavelli's counsel to statesmen regarding the pious virtues: "I would even be bold to say that to possess them and always to observe them is dangerous, but to appear to possess them is useful. . . . Let a prince therefore aim at conquering and maintaining the state, and the means will always by judged honourable and praised by every one, for the vulgar is always taken by appearances and the issue of the event; and the world consists only of the vulgar."

53. Onestà 3, f. 27rv; Savelli, *Pratica universale,* p. 239. For punishment of a woman who did not live up to her claim of conversion, see Onestà 6, f. 72v.

54. On the staffing of the magistracy, see Brackett, "Bureaucracy and Female Marginality," pp. 13–16, and Onestà 3, ff. 1rv, 4v, 7, 11v. On the complaint of 1649, see Onestà 3, f. 56rv; the quoted phrase is from the earlier complaint of 1642, in Onestà 3, ff. 52–53.

55. This was the response of an early-sixteenth-century magistrate of the Otto di

Guardia, according to his contemporary Giovanni Cambi. It is quoted by Trexler, "La Prostitution," n. 72, and is translated by him in the English version of his article.

56. CS126:69 Cartelle, unpaginated, ca. seventeenth century.

57. The quotation "in order to avoid the worst" appears in Cochrane, *Florence in Forgotten Centuries,* p. 150, and comes from Scipione Ammirato. The moralist's observation is from the same source, p. 205. See also pp. 278 and 351 on the patrician clientele of prostitutes in the seventeenth century.

58. Onestà 3, ff. 59rv (1670), 59v–60v and 64 (1671), 60v–61 (1672). The first tax collection by deputies was a success and won reauthorization, as appears in Onestà 3, ff. 61v–62. For the appointment of aides to work on behalf of the Monastero delle Convertite and the Onestà in 1628, see Onestà 1, f. 44. On incorporation into the Otto di Guardia, see Brackett, "Bureaucracy and Female Marginality," p. 43.

59. Savelli, *Pratica universale,* pp. 244–45. For the subsequent half-hearted moves toward enforcement, see Onestà 3, ff. 64v–69v. For Pietro Leopoldo's action, see Trexler, "La Prostitution," p. 994, and Arnaldo Salvestrini, ed., *Relazioni sul governo della Toscana,* 3 vols. (Florence: Leo S. Olschki, 1969–74), 1:141.

60. Acquisti e Doni 292, unpaginated, at the date 1616, description of case heard by the Otto di Guardia involving Maddalena di Bastiano Gonelli and her daughter Marietta in Certaldo.

61. Onestà 3, ff. 40v–41; Savelli, *Pratica universale,* p. 242. For actual cases of husband-pimps who came before the courts (and were sometimes severely punished), see Brucker, *Society of Renaissance Florence,* pp. 199–201, and Acquisti e Doni 292, unpaginated, passim.

62. Onestà 3, f. 18 (Riforma of 1577); Savelli, *Pratica universale,* p. 239.

63. Onestà 3, f. 54v (20 March 1647).

64. Onestà 3, f. 64v (31 August 1688).

65. For laws concerning prostitutes' relatives, see Onestà 3, ff. 14v–15, and Savelli, *Pratica universale,* pp. 239, 243. The heirs of married prostitutes were, however, entitled to the women's dowries, as in Onestà 3, f. 26v. On Girolamo Stiattesi, see CS126:51 D&C (1616–23), f. 33. For the location of Maddalena Stiattesi's will, see n. 20. On Piera Martini, see CS191:10 Memorie, f. 47rv (31 July 1674).

66. Acquisti e Doni 292, unpaginated, at the date 1603 (case heard by the Otto di Guardia involving Luca sanese coltellinaio e bombardiere di Grosseto and Porzia). On Roman law concerning prostitutes' relatives, see Savelli, *Pratica universale,* p. 244.

67. On the communal statute "Qualiter coniuncti possint facere capi coniunctos malae conditionis, vel vitae" and the request of Salvestro da Uzano, see Lombardi, "L'ospedale dei Mendicanti," pp. 305–6.

68. Savelli, *Pratica universale,* p. 244.

69. An example, in which an early-seventeenth-century Florentine patrician murdered his sister over "honor," appears in Cochrane, *Florence in Forgotten Centuries,* p. 206.

70. Bigallo 1691, f. 36v; also see ff. 33, 37v.

71. Savelli, *Pratica universale,* p. 242. On prostitutes and public ritual life, see Trexler, *Public Life,* p. 4, n. 9, and p. 210.

72. On the law of 1675, see Onestà 3, ff. 62v–63 (28 January–3 February 1675). For the limitations on prostitutes regarding contracts and sales of property, see Onestà 1, ff. 11–12v; Onestà 3, ff. 16–17v. For further differences between prostitutes and other women in Florentine statutes and in juridical law, see Savelli, *Pratica universale,* pp. 131–32, 241–44, and Brundage, "Prostitution in Canon Law," pp. 836–40.

73. On public taunts to prostitutes, see Onestà 1, f. 38, and Trexler, "La Prostitution," pp. 994–95. For neighbors' complaints, see Onestà 3, ff. 25rv, 36v, 53v–54, and Trexler, "La Prostitution," p. 1004. On the Onestà's jurisdictional disputes with other agencies and the threat to prostitutes' persons, see Onestà 1, f. 46v, and Onestà 3, ff. 42v, 48–49v, 57. On prostitutes as victims of rape, see Troiano, "Moralità e confini," p. 255. For sixteenth- and seventeenth-century orders urging greater confidentiality at the Onestà, see Onestà 1, ff. 42v–44, and Onestà 3, ff. 29rv, 38rv.

74. For efforts by officials to protect the economic viability of prostitutes, see Onestà 1, f. 42, and Onestà 3, ff. 18v–19, 24v–25, 32v, 55rv. Onestà 3, f. 17 (Riforma of 1577), alludes to prostitutes' indebtedness.

75. Onestà 3, f. 26v (5 July 1559).

76. Onestà 3, f. 60rv (29 January 1671).

77. Acquisti e Doni 292, unpaginated, at the date January 1564, transcription of case heard by the Otto di Guardia involving the Florentine citizen Niccolò Gianfigliazzi, who arranged for acceptance of a girl of ill repute at the convent of San Paolo. For the comment by the founders of the Casa delle Malmaritate, see Bigallo 1691, f. 1.

78. For the case of a Florentine patrician family bribed to overlook a female relative's liaison, see Cochrane, *Florence in Forgotten Centuries,* p. 205; for possible evidence of neighbors being well disposed toward or perhaps protecting prostitutes, see, in the same source, p. 278. In the account of Angela, translated by Brucker (*Society of Renaissance Florence,* pp. 191–92) and partially quoted in chapter 1, section on Prostitution, the woman's neighbors saw her activity as "dishonest" but they cared sufficiently about her well-being to offer to help feed her if she desisted from prostitution. For the views of the founders of the Casa delle Malmaritate, see Bigallo 1691, ff. 28, 29v.

79. Marilena Mosco, ed., *La Maddalena tra sacro e profano,* exhibition catalog, Palazzo Pitti, May 24–September 7, 1986 (Milan: Arnoldo Mondadori, 1986); Pamela Askew, *Caravaggio's "Death of the Virgin"* (Princeton, N.J.: Princeton University Press, 1990), pp. 86–104; Cochrane, *Florence in Forgotten Centuries,* p. 218, on the casuistical treatise; Giulio Guazzini, *La conversione eroica e cristiana della Maria Lunga detta Carrettina, meretrice famosa in Firenze; la quale essendo stata peccatrice oltre a vent'anni per penitenza de' suoi peccati havendo dato tutto il suo avere ridotto a denari, per l'amor di Dio; si è ritirata a servire alle misere donne oppresse dal contagio nel lazzaretto . . . Palinodia in retrattazione delle lodi già fatte per la Maria Lunga meretrice* (Florence: Zanobi Pignoni, 1633); Acquisti e Doni 292, unpaginated, at the date 19 August 1536 (transcript from Filza Strozziana), letter of Carlo Gualteruzzi, describing entrance of a Roman courtesan into the convent of the *convertite.*

80. Trexler, "La Prostitution," pp. 985–88. Trexler's table on p. 986 indicates that in 1436 non-Italian women constituted 81.5 percent of the population of registered prostitutes in brothels, and Italian women 18.3 percent.

81. Michel de Montaigne, *Montaigne's Travel Journal,* trans. Donald M. Frame (San Francisco: North Point Press, 1983), p. 143.

82. For "il Meschino," see CS191:10 Memorie, f. 27, 1 April 1625. On the lack of children among earlier prostitutes, see Trexler, "La Prostitution," n. 103.

83. Trexler, "La Prostitution," p. 1002, and Pullan, *Rich and Poor,* p. 379, have posed the question of whether refuges for *convertite* served mainly as retirement homes in which longtime prostitutes spent the latter years of their lives. While the scenario fits a small portion of the women at the Tuscan refuges for *convertite,* more than half the residents entered young and thus did not match this description. For the

policy at the Casa delle Malmaritate, see Bigallo 1691, f. 27rv. For the views of a midseventeenth-century administrator at the Monastero delle Convertite, see Acquisti e Doni 230:4 Ricordi, p. 47.

84. Onestà 6, ff. 116, 120–22, 138; CS126:55 D&C (1642–52), ff. 159, 242, 258; CS126:56 D&C (1661–74), ff. XXIII, 109; CS126:70 Contratti, unpaginated, undated (after 1661).

85. CS191:35 Fogli, unpaginated, 1 March 1613, plus another unpaginated, undated sheet of the same time; CS191:10 Memorie, ff. 6v, 8, 9v, 23, 24v, 28v; CS191:36 Fogli, unpaginated, 22 July 1626, 26 May 1637.

86. For the entrance petition, see CS191:35 Fogli, unpaginated, undated (probably mid-to-late seventeenth century). For *mutar' vita,* see CS191:33 Constitutioni, f. 18v.

87. CS126:66 Cause, unpaginated, April 1669.

88. Acquisti e Doni 230:4 Ricordi, ff. 85v–86; CS126:52 D&C (1621–30), f. LXXIV.

89. Onestà 4, f. 143; Onestà 6, f. 71 (11 May 1638); CS126:58 D&C (1687–1725), f. 192.

90. CS114:34 (12) Processo, unpaginated, covering the period 1626–40.

91. On Suor Celeste Costa, see CS126:66 Cause, unpaginated, 9 November 1669–1671, and CS126:56 D&C (1661–74), f. CLXVIIII. On Suor Bartolomea Leonora Corsini, see CS126:66 Cause, unpaginated, 13 March 1669, 20 March 1669, 15 March 1680, 29 March 1689, 22 July 1695.

92. The sources for Margherita Negri's history are CS126:52 D&C (1621–30), f. 43; CS126:54 D&C (1634–42), f. 95; CS126:55 D&C (1642–52), f. LXXXIX; CS126:66 Cause, unpaginated, 6 December 1655.

93. Onestà 1, f. 44v.

Chapter 3

1. Douglas, *Purity and Danger,* pp. 37–40, 94–104. R. W. Southern, in describing the early Middle Ages, ventured that an "unmarried woman was an anomaly in secular society" (*Western Society,* p. 309). While this was still largely true in the early modern period, unmarried women were not institutionalized simply on the basis of their unwed status.

2. On the Casa delle Malmaritate, see Bigallo 1691, ff. 32v–33v. The estimate of one eighth to one quarter is my impression after reading through the refuges' records for various periods.

3. Bigallo 1691, ff. 39rv, 42v–43; CS126:62 Ricordi, unpaginated, list dated 1455–1620.

4. On the Florentine Stinche, see Brucker, *Society of Renaissance Florence,* pp. 166–68; Brackett, "Otto di Guardia," pp. 83–99, 201; Marvin E. Wolfgang, "A Florentine Prison: Le Carceri delle Stinche," *Studies in the Renaissance* 7 (1960): 148–66.

5. Guido Pampaloni, *Lo Spedale di Santa Maria Nuova* (Florence: Casa di Risparmio, 1961); Katharine Park, *Doctors and Medicine in Early Renaissance Florence* (Princeton, N.J.: Princeton University Press, 1985), pp. 101–6; Philip Gavitt, *The Ospedale degli Innocenti, 1410–1536* (Ann Arbor: University of Michigan Press, 1990). On the Ospedale del Ceppo, see Herlihy, *Medieval and Renaissance Pistoia,* pp. 246–49.

6. Richard C. Trexler, "A Widows' Asylum of the Renaissance: The Orbatello of

Florence," in *Old Age in Preindustrial Society,* ed. Peter N. Stearns (New York: Holmes & Meier, 1982), pp. 119–49. Lombardi, *Povertà maschile,* presents a detailed history of the poorhouse.

7. Bigallo 1691, ff. 33v, 29v.

8. ASF, Otto di Guardia Repubblicana 79, 4–20 March 1487, ff. 6v, 8v, 9v, 10, 21.

9. Quoted by Kirshner, *Pursuing Honor,* n. 21.

10. Otto di Guardia Repubblicana 127, 29–30 September 1503, ff. 59rv, 62.

11. Otto di Guardia Repubblicana 212, 14 November 1531, ff. 61–62.

12. On the way that magistrates viewed a female's age and status in adjudicating sex crimes, see Ruggiero, *Boundaries of Eros,* p. 102; Troiano, "Moralità e confini," p. 249.

13. Otto di Guardia Repubblicana 164, 5 January 1515, f. 3.

14. For this law, see chapter 2, n. 20.

15. ASF, Regio Diritto vol. 4896, ff. 472–73; emphasis added.

16. ASF, Mediceo del Principato, filza 3479, letter of Antonio Serguidi to Alessandro de' Medici, 25 January 1577.

17. Regio Diritto vol. 4896, f. 46.

18. ASF, Commissariati di Quartiere di Firenze (hereafter Commissariati di Firenze), parte 1, filza 25, no. 179.

19. On the *commessa* Lisabetta di Marco Fantoni, see CS126:63 Ricordi, f. 8. On the servant Benedetta di Bastiano, see CS126:51 D&C (1616–23), ff. LXVIII, 129. On the weaver's daughter Marietta Tamburini, see CS191:10 Memorie, ff. 8, 9rv, 15.

20. For the warning by the founders of the Casa delle Malmaritate, see Bigallo 1691, ff. 36v–37. For similar distrust of families expressed by an administrator of the Mendicanti and other officials, see Lombardi, "L'ospedale dei Mendicanti," pp. 291–93, 297. Liebowitz, "Conversion or Confinement," p. 6, and Ferrante, "L'onore ritrovato," pp. 507 and 516, provide examples of Milanese and Bolognese women in institutions who had suffered threats or maltreatment at the hands of relatives over sexual misdemeanors or other causes. On the case of the Pisan barber Daniello Becozzi, heard by the Otto di Guardia, see Acquisti e Doni 292, unpaginated, at the date 1603.

21. Lombardi, "L'ospedale dei Mendicanti," pp. 302, 309; Ferrante, "L'onore ritrovato," pp. 508, 510.

22. On the Medici rulers and entourage, see Lombardi, "L'ospedale dei Mendicanti," pp. 293–94, 296, 302, 304. Trexler, "Widows' Asylum," p. 140, notes a related pattern of concern and patronage extended by the ruling elite to its servitors. In the midsixteenth century the Florentine government started to help hard-pressed communal employees to place their unmarried daughters in apartments of the Orbatello formerly reserved for widows.

23. The appellation is from Alberti, *The Family,* p. 227. The criticism is translated by Brucker, *Renaissance Florence,* p. 93.

24. Translated by Brucker, *Society of Renaissance Florence,* p. 122.

25. Translated by Brucker, *Society of Renaissance Florence,* pp. 221, 219.

26. Lombardi, "L'ospedale dei Mendicanti," pp. 297–98.

27. Examples of officials using *onore* in reference to plebeian women or prostitutes appear earlier in this chapter, section on Juvenile Residents; in chapter 2, section on The Family; and in chapter 5, section on New Social Institutions. Trexler, "Widows' Asylum," p. 138, suggests that the administrators of the Orbatello used the term "honorable" to describe the plebeian girls there whom they furnished with dowries.

28. On the search by administrators of Santa Maria Maddalena for relatives to care for released residents and the exile of certain residents, see CS191:36 Fogli, unpaginated, 1 September and 15 September 1621. On the 72 women in the Monastero delle Convertite, see Provvisioni Registri 183, vol. for April–March 1492, f. 21. For the Casa delle Malmaritate, see Bigallo 1691, f. 28v. On the loose ties between plebeian families and their female members, see Herlihy and Klapisch-Zuber, *Les Toscans,* p. 331, and Lombardi, "L'ospedale dei Mendicanti," p. 297.

29. ASF, Mediceo Avanti il Principato (hereafter MAP) LXXXV, 683, letter of the Badessa of the Monastero delle Convertite to Ginevra de' Medici, undated. For the daughters of the formerly well-to-do, see CS126:70 Contratti, unpaginated, 10 January 1512.

30. Mediceo del Principato, filza 3479, letter of Antonio Serguidi to Alessandro de' Medici, 25 January 1577; CS126:57 D&C (1674–87), ff. 183, 233.

31. CS126:55 D&C (1642–52), ff. LXXXXVIII, CLVIII; Acquisti e Doni 230:4 Ricordi, f. 8.

32. For sisters sharing rooms at the Monastero delle Convertite, see CS126:58 D&C (1687–1725), f. 103; CS126:57 D&C (1674–87), f. 147. For the *spoglie*-sharing pact, see CS126:58 D&C (1687–1725), f. 101.

33. For the Casa delle Malmaritate, see Bigallo 1691, ff. 34, 45–46. For Santa Maria Maddalena, see CS191:10 Memorie, f. 3v.

34. An example of the kind of aid these residents extended to one another can be found in CS126:52 D&C (1621–30), f. V, which records the payment of 30 scudi jointly made by two members of the Monastero delle Convertite, Suor Maddalenangiola Fabiani and Suor Smeralda Felice, for the dowry of a third woman, the *convertita* Margarita di Giovanni dal Borgo a Buggiano. Regarding Santa Maria Maddalena, it is noted in CS191:10 Memorie, f. 36, that the burial expenses for Suor Maria Felice were paid by her daughter, Suor Maria Jacinta, a *convertita*. On actual families and surrogate families at other institutions for women, see Trexler, "Widows' Asylum," pp. 134–37, and Ferrante, "L'onore ritrovato," p. 504.

35. MAP LXX, 34, letter of Raphael Johannis to Francesco Fortunato, 10 June 1494.

36. For the pregnant young woman, see MAP LX, 572, letter of Jacopo de Comitibus to the Otto di Pratica, 20 June 1493. On Carlo de' Medici, see Acquisti e Doni 292, unpaginated, at the date 4 January 1527. On the Casa delle Malmaritate, see Lastri, *L'osservatore fiorentino,* 3:125. For bigamy in canon and statutory law, see Savelli, *Pratica universale,* p. 133, and *Leges pistoriensium,* p. 182.

37. For the case of Michele di San Mommi, the Pistoian husband who beat his wife, see Acquisti e Doni 292, unpaginated, at the date 1584 (transcriptions from the Suppliche della Pratica per Pistoia). On unsuccessful marriages and the possibilities of escaping them, see Nino Tamassia, *La Famiglia italiana nei secoli decimoquinto e decimosesto* (Rome: Multigrafica, 1971), pp. 196–217. For examples of spousal support ordered by civil authorities, see chapter 1, end of section on Marriage.

38. On Lisabetta, see Otto di Guardia Repubblicana 80, 8 July 1488, f. 10v. On Antonia, see Otto di Guardia Repubblicana 169, 24 December 1517, f. 92. On the woman whom the officials threatened, see Otto di Guardia Repubblicana 128, 2 March 1503, f. 152v. For cases of unruly or abused wives at Bologna's Soccorso and at Florence's Mendicanti, see Ferrante, "L'onore ritrovato," pp. 505, 507–8, 512–13; Lombardi, "L'ospedale dei Mendicanti," pp. 294–96, n. 13.

39. On the Orbatello, see Trexler, "Widows' Asylum," pp. 128–29. On Lucretia

Ferrini, see CS126:57 D&C (1674–87), f. 183; CS126:58 D&C (1687–1725), f. 49; CS126:66 Cause, unpaginated, 16 September 1684.

40. CS126:55 D&C (1642–52), f. 240.

41. For Lucrezia Bozi (Suor Caterina), see CS191:10 Memorie, ff. 10, 19–21. See chapter 5, section on New Social Institutions, for a different perspective on her story. On Caterina Lanzini, see Ferrante, "L'onore ritrovato," p. 513.

42. In Herlihy and Klapisch-Zuber, Les Toscans, see pp. 405–7 on remarriage, and pp. 322–23 and 348 on the mobility of poor widows. Litchfield, "Demographic Characteristics," p. 199, also provides relevant information from his analysis of 2,427 individuals in twenty-one Florentine patrician families of the sixteenth through eighteenth centuries. Although this was an era in which patrician families permitted only one son to marry, those gentlemen who did marry and were widowed seemed inclined to remarry. Litchfield found that 14 percent of all the husbands in his study married for a second or third time. On the influx of widows during disastrous times, see Trexler, "Widows' Asylum," pp. 139, 141, and Lombardi, "Poveri a Firenze," pp. 170–73, 178, 181.

43. Translated in O'Faolain and Martines, Not in God's Image, pp. 169–70.

44. For a sixteenth-century law helping widows to secure their property, see Provvisioni Registri 205, 22–27 August 1520, f. 18rv; Trexler, "Widows' Asylum," especially pp. 121, 130–31, 139–43.

45. On Florentine widows joining Third Orders or becoming commesse, see Trexler, "Le Célibat," p. 1347, and Richard C. Trexler, "Une table florentine d'espérance de vie," Annales 26 (January–February 1971): 138. For Lucrezia, see CS126:63 Ricordi, ff. 5, 22rv.

46. On Mona Vettoria, see Acquisti e Doni 292, unpaginated, at the date 11 January 1527. For the proceedings of the Otto di Guardia against the innkeeper Biagio in Arezzo and his wife Diamante, see the same source, at the date 1630. Also see the cases discussed by Troiano, "Moralità e confini," pp. 249, 253–55.

47. On Suor Felice Angiola, see CS126:66 Cause, unpaginated, 7 (?) May 1642; Acquisti e Doni 230:4 Ricordi, f. 46v. Onestà 3, f. 27rv, records the ordinance of 1569 pertaining to reformed prostitutes. On seeking evaluations of women's reputations, see Lombardi, "L'ospedale dei Mendicanti," p. 303.

48. CS126:57 D&C (1674–87), f. 115; CS126:69 Cartelle, unpaginated, 12 September 1663.

49. CS126:56 D&C (1661–74), f. 50; CS126:57 D&C (1674–87), f. 83; CS126:66 Cause, unpaginated, 2–3 June 1699.

50. CS126:52 D&C (1621–30), ff. 63, 1, 20.

51. CS191:36 Fogli, unpaginated, 9 August 1646, 14 December 1637, 2 January 1638.

52. On Catholicism and the family, see Natalie Zemon Davis, "Ghosts, Kin, and Progeny: Some Features of Family Life in Early Modern France," Daedalus 106 (Spring 1977): 92–96, 99–104, 106–8. For a somewhat different view, see John Bossy, "The Counter-Reformation and the People of Catholic Europe," Past and Present 47 (May 1970): 56–57, 68–70.

53. For Paolo da Certaldo and for the Tuscan woman's complaint, see Herlihy and Klapisch-Zuber, Les Toscans, pp. 601–2, n. 102. On Bernardino of Siena, see Origo, World of San Bernardino, pp. 49, 55–56. In the latter pages, Origo quotes Bernardino protesting against excessive violence toward wives and urging that "a wise man should never beat his wife, whatever fault she may commit." But in other sermons, as Origo

indicates, Bernardino had suggested, "Were I your husband, I would give you such a mark with hands and feet that you would remember it for a long time!"

54. Translated in O'Faolain and Martines, *Not in God's Image,* p. 177.

55. Brackett, "Otto di Guardia," pp. 193–94. Commissariati di Firenze, parte 1, filza 6, no. 294, 4 November 1783, records the incarceration of a man who "excessively" beat his pregnant wife. For authorities' disapproval of another man who beat his spouse, also see the case of Maria Antonia Assunta Gherardini, discussed later in this section of the chapter.

56. Bigallo 1691, ff. 32v–33v, 36v.

57. Acquisti e Doni 292, unpaginated, at the date 1615.

58. For Violante Guidetti, see Commissariati di Firenze, parte 1, filza 14, no. 313. For the unnamed woman, see ASF, Camera e Auditore Fiscale (hereafter Camera Fiscale), filza 2857, no. 514.

59. On Carmina Pucetti and Giovine Seracini, see Camera Fiscale, filza 2857, nos. 442 and 545 respectively. On Bastiana Grilli, see Commissariati di Firenze, parte 1, filza 6, no. 98.

60. For Jacopo Mazzetti, see Camera Fiscale, filza 2857, no. 546. For Maria Falcini Lotti, see ASF, Commissariato del Quartiere Santa Maria Novella (hereafter Commissariato S. M. Novella) 1, no. 35.

61. Commissariati di Firenze, parte 1, filza 6, no. 74, 24 February 1783. On Vittoria, see also Commissariato S. M. Novella 1, no. 350, and Commissariati di Firenze, parte 1, filza 14, no. 14.

62. Commissariati di Firenze, parte 1, filza 6, no. 222.

63. On the Casa Pia (1563), see Askew, *Caravaggio's "Death of the Virgin,"* pp. 87–92. On the establishments for *malmaritate* in Mantua and Bologna and on other institutions that received such women, see Lucia Ferrante, " 'Malmaritate' tra assistenza e punizione (Bologna secc. XVI–XVII)," in *Forme e soggetti dell'intervento assistenziale in una città di antico regime* (Bologna: Istituto per la Storia di Bologna, 1986), pp. 68–71, 84–92. It should be noted, however, that not all the institutions for *malmaritate* aimed to help women perceived as victimized. Some, like the prototypical refuge of Santa Marta founded by Ignatius Loyola in Rome in 1543, sought at the outset to reform sinful married women engaged in prostitution or adultery; later it accepted victimized women. See chapter 1, n. 20, and Vincenzo Monachino, *La carità cristiana in Roma* (Bologna: Cappelli, 1968), pp. 256–57.

64. Davis, "Ghosts," pp. 101–3, 107; Jean Gaudemet, "Il legame matrimoniale nel XVII secolo. Legislazione canonica e tendenze laiche," in *Le funzioni sociali del matrimonio. Modelli e regole della scelta del coniuge dal XIV al XX secolo,* ed. Milly Buonanno (Milan: Edizioni di Comunità, 1980), pp. 66–67. Although the Protestants ceased to include marriage among the sacraments, the Council of Trent reaffirmed the sacramental nature of marriage and clarified the definition of legitimate marriage. It slightly narrowed the scope of the prohibited degrees of consanguinity, and put an end to the centuries-old tradition of informal, clandestine marriages by declaring that, in order to have a valid marriage, couples had to take their vows publicly in the presence of a priest.

65. Acquisti e Doni 291, unpaginated, at the date 1537 (case heard by the Otto di Guardia involving Betta di Michele and Mona Dianora delli Albizzi). For the two sisters, see Otto di Guardia Repubblicana 157, 1 December 1513, ff. 81, 91, and Acquisti e Doni 292, unpaginated, at the date 1 December 1513.

66. Scull, *Decarceration,* pp. 105, 128. See also Goffman, *Asylums,* pp. 74, 354.

67. On the sodomized girl, see n. 10. For the husband-killer and two kidnap victims, see Acquisti e Doni 292, unpaginated, at the dates October and December 1583 (case heard by the Otto di Guardia that mentions the convent San Matteo di Prato); 1598 (case heard by the Otto di Guardia involving Ser Giovanfrancesco Ramazzotti, Ser Pompeo Fioretti, and Isabella); and 1627 (case heard by the Otto di Guardia involving Andrea Parissi and Maddalena Migliorini). For evidence about the relative harshness of sentences to the Monastero delle Convertite and the Stinche, see the first source cited in n. 68. For a related discussion of how women were confined to different institutions, see Lombardi, *Povertà maschile,* pp. 151, 201–2.

68. For the Monastero delle Convertite, see Otto di Guardia Granducale 66, 13 February 1553 and subsequent dates, ff. 67rv, 74, 78v, 79, 89, 95rv; Otto di Guardia Repubblicana 146, 17 January and 24 January 1509, ff. 35v, 49v. For the two quotations, see *Sommario de capitoli della venerabile compagnia di santa Maria Maddalena sopra le mal maritate* (Florence: Bartholomeo Sermartelli, 1583), pp. 13, 30.

Chapter 4

1. On the history of the Monastero delle Convertite, see n. 121 in chapter 1. At least by 1622 this refuge did have written constitutions, which have not survived. For a record of payment for obtaining a copy of the constitutions from the archiepiscopal chancellery, see CS126:52 D&C (1621–30), f. 15.

2. Bigallo 1691, ff. 34v, 13v, 46v–47, 37v.

3. See ibid., ff. 27v–28, for the phrase *per usurpare la elemosina,* 39v–40; Lombardi, *Povertà maschile,* p. 151, n. 28.

4. Ibid., f. 34.

5. Ibid., ff. 28v–30.

6. Ibid., ff. 34–35v, 15v–16, 29v.

7. Ibid., ff. 46v–47 and Dechiaratione to Capitolo 2 of Capitoli delle Gentildonne (unpaginated folio at end of ms.), 40rv, 41v.

8. Ibid., ff. 36v–37.

9. Ibid., ff. 39v–40, 37v, 17v.

10. Ibid., ff. 34v–35v, 37v–38.

11. CS191:35 Fogli, unpaginated, 10 April 1604.

12. Ibid.; CS191:10 Memorie, f. 8.

13. See CS191:10 Memorie, ff. 1–27v, on the years 1604–26; CS191:33 Constitutioni, f. 10v.

14. CS191:33 Constitutioni, f. 7.

15. Ibid., f. 16. See also ff. 4v, 6rv, 23v–24.

16. Ibid., ff. 18v, 16, 6v, 17rv.

17. Ibid., ff. 3v–4.

18. Ibid., ff. 4–6.

19. Ibid., ff. 6v–7, 11–12v, 23rv.

20. Ibid., ff. 5v–6, 15rv.

21. Ibid., ff. 3v, 8v. On the Capuchins, see H. O. Evennett, "The New Orders," in *The New Cambridge Modern History,* vol. 2, *The Reformation, 1520–1559,* ed. G. R. Elton (Cambridge: Cambridge University Press, 1958), pp. 278–85. For the Ignatian conceptions of calling and vocation, see Ignatius Loyola, *The Spiritual Exercises of St. Ignatius,* trans. Anthony Mottola (Garden City, N.Y.: Doubleday, 1964), pp. 82–87.

22. Bigallo 1691, f. 51v; CS191:33 Constitutioni, ff. 19v, 9.

23. See CS191:33 Constitutioni, ff. 3, 5, 9, 12rv, 14rv, 23, 25v, 26v–28, for references to Church policy, and on the tailored Franciscan rule, ff. 3rv, 10v.

24. For the expanding opportunities in employment open to women in late-sixteenth-century Florence, see Brown and Goodman, "Women and Industry," pp. 78–80. For the more restricted employment available in Pistoia, see Emanuele Repetti, *Dizionario geografico fisico storico della Toscana,* 5 vols. (Florence: Presso l'autore, 1833–43), 4:440–42. Further details about the Pistoian ecclesiastical establishment's close involvement with Santa Maria Maddalena will be provided later in this chapter and in chapter 5. On Alessandro de' Medici's tenure as the often-absentee archbishop of Florence, see Cochrane, *Florence in Forgotten Centuries,* pp. 132–33.

25. On the Casa delle Malmaritate, see Bigallo 1691, f. 40v, Dechiaratione to Capitolo 4 (end of ms.). On Santa Maria Maddalena, see CS191:33 Constitutioni, ff. 10v–11; in addition, CS191:25 Giornale (1605–21), f. 8v, mentions a "camicinola per l'umiltà," which I take to be a hairshirt. For prostitutes' possession of male apparel, see Trexler, "La Prostitution," pp. 995–96.

26. On the Monastero delle Convertite, see CS126:68 Locatieni passim. On Santa Maria Maddalena, see CS191:33 Constitutioni, ff. 14, 21, 16v, 12v. For the Casa delle Malmaritate, see Bigallo 1691, ff. 34, 51–52, 14v; CS143:1 Stati di Consistenza; Lastri, *L'osservatore fiorentino,* 3:126–27.

27. On offices at the Casa delle Malmaritate, see Bigallo 1691, f. 40. For the installation of an officer at the Monastero delle Convertite, see CS126:63 Ricordi (1616–26), f. 26, in the first sequence of pagination. For offices and installations at Santa Maria Maddalena, see CS191:33 Constitutioni, ff. 9v–10v, 20–22v; CS191:10 Memorie, ff. 15v, 18v, 20rv, 24, 26, 27; CS191:32 Entrata e Uscita (1626–51), ff. 36v, 42v, 76v.

28. For prescriptions about visitors to the Casa delle Malmaritate, see Bigallo 1691, ff. 13v–14, 17–18, 25rv, 43v, 44v–45v, 50rv, Dechiaratione to Capitolo 4 (end of ms.). For Santa Maria Maddalena, see CS191:33 Constitutioni, ff. 21v–22, 25v. Actual visitors to the refuges are mentioned throughout this study.

29. Acquisti e Doni 292, unpaginated, at the date October 1583. The same source, at the dates 31 August 1515 and August 1577, describes abductions of nuns from the Monastero delle Convertite and, at the date June 1561, reveals that the Otto di Guardia sought to stop noisemakers who engaged in mockery outside that refuge while the nuns recited their prayers. For a case of abduction from the Casa delle Malmaritate, see chapter 5, n. 48.

30. CS126:66 Cause, unpaginated, documents dated 1661 (headed "Vannucci e Convertite"), 19 and 22 June 1670, and 6 November 1684.

31. Bigallo 1691, f. 31v. Also see n. 76.

32. Trexler, "La Prostitution," p. 1002, errs in saying that the Monastero delle Convertite had no servants.

33. For dowries at mainstream convents (the early-seventeenth-century average was about 200 scudi), see chapter 1, section on Monasticism. As related in Acquisti e Doni 230:4 Ricordi, f. 87v, the archbishop codified and increased the dowries at the Monastero delle Convertite on 1 April 1628. He raised the regular dowry for *velata* from 140 to 160 scudi, and that for *servigiale* from 60 to 70 scudi. Dowries at the Monastero delle Convertite had also risen over time. In CS126:62 Ricordi (1435–1620), unpaginated, notation beginning "Apparisce a un libro segnato B. Debitori e Creditori . . . cominciato l'anno 1564 . . .," we find that in 1566 the dowry for a

servigiale was 40 scudi, almost half the price it would be sixty-two years later. For the Monastero delle Convertite, dowries are recorded in Acquisti e Doni 230:4 Ricordi and in CS126:51–58, the volumes of Debitori e Creditori for the seventeenth century. For Santa Maria Maddalena, dowries can be found in CS191:10 Memorie; CS191:35 Fogli; and CS191:36 Fogli. See the typical accounts there of Suor Maria Francesca (200 scudi for the status of *monacha* [*velata*] in 1637) in CS191:10 Memorie, f. 35, and of Suor Maria Angiola (100 scudi for *monaca servigiale*) in CS191:36 Fogli, unpaginated, 20 March 1638.

34. See CS126:54 D&C (1634–42), f. 95, for the account of Margherita Negri, who purchased such an immunity in 1639.

35. This policy is articulated for Santa Maria Maddalena in CS191:33 Constitutioni, f. 13rv. Based on my examination of the sources already described in n. 33, it is clear that the same practice prevailed also at the Monastero delle Convertite.

36. See the adjustments made to dowries at the Monastero delle Convertite recorded in CS126:52 D&C (1621–30), f. 78, and in CS126:68 Locatieni, nos. 283–85 in the second system of numbering.

37. CS126:70 Contratti, unpaginated, 20 October 1569. For entrants to Santa Maria Maddalena paying their dowries partly in goods, see CS191:36 Fogli, unpaginated, 4 April 1629 and 30 August 1637, regarding Madalena Bolognini and Madalena Marchetti respectively.

38. See for instance the case of the widow Caterina Fabbri, who became Suor Giulia Francesca at the Monastero delle Convertite, in Acquisti e Doni 230:4 Ricordi, ff. 85, 7v; CS126:52 D&C (1621–30), ff. 38, 67, 91, 121; CS126:53 D&C (1630–42), ff. 1, 30, 31, 42, 59; CS126:54 D&C (1634–42), ff. 47, 50, 178.

39. CS126:52 D&C (1621–30), ff. 77, 103, 105, 121; CS126:1 Giornale (1622–30), f. 20; Acquisti e Doni 230:4 Ricordi, ff. 88, 9.

40. For the *povera puttanuccia* Margherita Giardinieri, see CS114:34 (12) Processo, unpaginated, covering the period 1626–40; Acquisti e Doni 230:4 Ricordi, ff. 86v, 8, 55v; CS126:57 D&C (1674–87), ff. 115, 194.

41. CS191:33 Constitutioni, f. 26v.

42. Ibid., ff. 27–28, 11, 14. Chapter 4 of the constitutions said that professions were to be made after at least a year had passed, and chapter 10 said within the first year of the novitiate. For evidence of the pattern at the Monastero delle Convertite, see Acquisti e Doni 230:4 Ricordi, f. 76, where Suor Maria Antonia's obituary explains that at her death "she was not a professed nun, having been a [novice] nun only ten months." For the professions of the three novices who started the controversy, see CS191:10 Memorie, f. 35v.

43. For investiture at the Monastero delle Convertite, see Acquisti e Doni 230:4 Ricordi, ff. 2–11. For Santa Maria Maddalena, see CS191:10 Memorie, ff. 9v–10, 19, 20, 35; CS191:33 Constitutioni, f. 14.

44. See Acquisti e Doni 230:4 Ricordi, f. 7, for an example of particular attention accorded to a woman entering the Monastero delle Convertite on the day of the Lenten sermon. For the policy and ceremonies concerning such entrants to the Casa delle Malmaritate, see Bigallo 1691, f. 32rv, Dechiaratione to Capitolo 30 (beginning of ms. and continued at end of ms.). For the customary rites of welcome for entrants to Santa Maria Maddalena, see CS191:33 Constitutioni, f. 13v.

45. On profession at the Monastero delle Convertite, see Acquisti e Doni 230:4 Ricordi, ff. 54–57. For Santa Maria Maddalena, see CS191:33 Constitutioni, f. 14rv. For Suor Maddalena Costante, see CS126:51 D&C (1616–23), ff. 16, 18; CS126:52

D&C (1621–30), ff. 35, 37–38, 56, 121; CS126:53 D&C (1630–42), ff. 31, 40; Acquisti e Doni 230:4 Ricordi, ff. 6, 76.

46. For expectations about prayer and devotions at the Casa delle Malmaritate, see Bigallo 1691, ff. 40, 38, 17; for Santa Maria Maddalena, see CS191:33 Constitutioni, ff. 11–12v. For sacral obligations that were accepted and carried out at the Monastero delle Convertite and for the participation of the nuns in sacred rites, see CS126:63 Ricordi (1616–26), ff. 6–7 in the first sequence of pagination (copy of a contract of 1495 for offices of the dead); CS126:70 Contratti, unpaginated, 5 June 1585 (also for offices of the dead); CS126:62 Ricordi (1435–1620), unpaginated, seventeenth-century list of sacral obligations; CS126:69 Cartelle, unpaginated, "Ricordo di obblighi che si fanno nella chiesa delle Convertite di Firenze"; Acquisti e Doni 230:4 Ricordi, ff. 55–56. For the same at Santa Maria Maddalena, see CS191:35 Fogli, unpaginated, 18 July 1653; CS191:36 Fogli, unpaginated, 22 July 1626.

47. CS126:62 Ricordi (1435–1620), unpaginated, 3 January 1620.

48. Archivio Segreto Vaticano, Archivio sacra congregazione del concilio, Visite Apostoliche 37 (Florence, 1575), f. 50. For *sagrestane* at Santa Maria Maddalena, see CS191:33 Constitutioni, f. 20, and CS191:10 Memorie, ff. 18v, 20v, 24, 27.

49. See CS191:10 Memorie, f. 10, for the incident of 1607, and CS191:33 Constitutioni, f. 14, for the prohibition.

50. CS126:70 Contratti, unpaginated, undated (probably midsixteenth century).

51. Commissariati di Firenze, parte 1, filza 6, no. 74, 24 February 1783.

52. For reading or visual images at Santa Maria Maddalena, see CS191:33 Constitutioni, ff. 19rv, 23v. For the Monastero delle Convertite, see CS126:61 D&C (1765–1807), f. 181; CS126:62 Ricordi (1435–1620), unpaginated, 14 July 1621 inventory of the convent's books. For the Casa delle Malmaritate, see Bigallo 1691, Dechiaratione to Capitolo 4 (end of ms.).

53. For Botticelli's altarpiece entitled "Pala delle Convertite," see Ronald Lightbown, *Sandro Botticelli,* 2 vols. (Berkeley: University of California Press, 1978), 1:109–12, 2:75–78. The altarpiece remained in the convent's church until the early nineteenth century and is now in the Courtauld Gallery in London. Four predella panels that originally hung beneath it are now at the Philadelphia Museum of Art. For the "tree of all the saints of Saint Augustine," given by Father Girolamo Bii, an Augustinian and the nuns' confessor, see CS126:62 Ricordi (1435–1620), unpaginated, 1 March 1620.

54. CS126:66 Cause, unpaginated, 26 January 1695, and undated list.

55. For the oral survey, see CS126:63 Ricordi (1616–26), f. 27rv in the second sequence of pagination. For the chapel founded in 1661 by Suor Caterina Felice Salvetti, see chapter 2, section on The Women. For the chapel that nuns founded in honor of "Santa Maria Maddalena Penitente," see CS126:61 D&C (1765–1807), ff. 80, 349.

56. CS126:62 Ricordi (1435–1620), unpaginated, 8 May 1621.

57. Bigallo 1691, ff. 40, 52, 38v.

58. On the size of the households, for the Monastero delle Convertite see CS126:70 Contratti, unpaginated, 27 June 1459 (contract listing 17 professed nuns); Visite Apostoliche 37, f. 50 (visitation of 1575 enumerating 83 professed nuns, 10 novices, and 42 servant nuns for a total of 135); CS126:63 Ricordi (1616–26), Father Benedetto di Albizo's inventory of the convent's possessions, compiled in 1620 (noting 204 nuns). For Santa Maria Maddalena, see CS191:36 Fogli, unpaginated, 27 May 1637 (contract listing 18 professed nuns); CS191:10 Memorie, f. 53v (contract of 1687 listing 15 professed nuns). For the Casa delle Malmaritate, see Lombardi, *Povertà*

maschile, p. 202 (citing census of 1632 that listed 5 women there); Camera Fiscale, filza 2857, no. 457, 23 August 1777 (report noting that the refuge could accommodate up to 30 residents). My assertions about the numbers of annual entrants are based on information concerning mainstream convents that was discussed above in chapter 1, section on Monasticism, and on my assessments of the records of the refuges.

59. CS126:66 Cause, unpaginated, undated "Ricordi da presentarsi all' . . . Fra Ipolito Borromei per alcune monache convertite"; CS126:56 D&C (1661–74), f. XXIII. For a legacy another nun gave to "her *conversa,*" see CS126:68 Locatieni, ff. 119v–120 in the first system of numbering.

60. For nursing duties at the Casa delle Malmaritate, see *Sommario de capitoli,* p. 17. For Santa Maria Maddalena, see CS191:33 Constitutioni, f. 21rv; CS191:10 Memorie, ff. 18v, 20v, 24, 27. On the frequency of illness in the refuges, see for example CS126:66 Cause, unpaginated, undated (midseventeenth century) "Ricordi da presentarsi all' . . . Fra Ipolito Borromei per alcune monache convertite," referring to a *servigiale* at the Monastero delle Convertite, Suor Maria Cammilla Ciucci, who was "continually aggravated by illness." Also see the records of illnesses and deaths at that refuge in Acquisti e Doni 230:4 Ricordi, ff. 75v, 77–79.

61. For Suor Bartolomea Leonora Corsini's bequest, see CS126:66 Cause, unpaginated, 22 July 1695. For the rooms bequeathed by Suor Felice Angiola Bracciolini, see CS126:69 Cartelle, unpaginated, 12 September 1663.

62. From Cohn, *Laboring Classes,* p. 9, we learn that thirteenth- and early-fourteenth-century Florentine guildsmen used the term *discepoli* to refer to apprentices. Viviani della Robbia, *Nei monasteri fiorentini,* pp. 101–2, describes *discepole* at the Florentine convent of Montedomini in 1600. On Suor Margherita Argentina, see CS126:52 D&C (1621–30), ff. 91, 104; Acquisti e Doni 230:4 Ricordi, ff. 86v, 9v. On Suor Andrea Angelica, see CS126:55 D&C (1642–52), f. 193.

63. On the Casa delle Malmaritate, see Bigallo 1691, f. 52; on Santa Maria Maddalena, see CS191:33 Constitutioni, ff. 18–19. Liebowitz, "Voices from Convents," p. 7, mentions that the practice of selling rooms prevailed at poor convents as a way to raise money. Sales of rooms were the norm at the Monastero delle Convertite; in the second half of the seventeenth century, they were recorded in a volume devoted to rooming arrangements, CS126:68 Locatieni. At that convent the women's living quarters might range from the comfortable apartment consisting of a "main-floor chamber, kitchen, another room, cellar, garden, and four statues" to a tiny alcove tucked at the foot of a staircase. For these two examples, respectively, see CS126:55 D&C (1642–52), f. 258, and CS126:58 D&C (1687–1725), f. CV. The former cost 200 scudi and the latter, which after the death of one occupant was shared by two sisters, 15 scudi. At the Monastero delle Convertite, the nuns' quarters were usually called *stanze,* or rooms. But in CS126:54 D&C (1634–42), f. 98, the single chamber belonging to a nun was referred to as "her cell." For an apartment containing a room that had "its *oratorio,*" or place for prayer, see CS126:55 D&C (1642–52), f. 115.

64. See CS126:68 Locatieni, ff. 101v–102 in the first system of numbering, a case from 1678 in which administrators sold a set of rooms to the veiled nun Suor Maria Ottavia Lucretia (formerly Contessa Neri) and her sister, Margherita Neri. They stipulated that unless Margherita too became a veiled nun, she would be excluded from the rights guaranteed by the contract, such as the rights to possess and resell the rooms.

65. In "Conversion or Confinement," p. 9, Liebowitz reports that many residents at Milan's refuge for *convertite* paired up, for emotional and sometimes sexual sustenance. One resident there counted thirty couples, a figure that represented just under

half the inhabitants of the refuge. On such behavior at mainstream convents, see Judith C. Brown, *Immodest Acts: The Life of a Lesbian Nun in Renaissance Italy* (New York: Oxford University Press, 1986), p. 8. Regarding sleeping arrangements at the Monastero delle Convertite, see Visite Apostoliche 37, f. 50v. For the Casa delle Malmaritate, see Bigallo 1691, ff. 30v, 52. For Santa Maria Maddalena, see CS191:25 Giornale (1605–21), f. 20v, and CS191:33 Constitutioni, ff. 18v–19, in which is noted the singular exception that it might be permissible for blood sisters to share one bed.

66. For sessions preceding communion in which nuns were supposed to recite their faults at Santa Maria Maddalena, see CS191:33 Constitutioni, ff. 17v–18. See also on f. 17rv the similar provision that anyone who evades undergoing penitential discipline will have to beg pardon from all her fellow nuns for having offered a bad example. For notions of negative and positive role models at the Casa delle Malmaritate, see Bigallo 1691, ff. 25, 38.

67. For the roll call of "holy memory" at the Monastero delle Convertite, see CS126:62 Ricordi (1435–1620), unpaginated, list dated 1455–1620 enumerating the house's gentleborn nuns, notations at the year 1539. On Suor Lucretia Felice and Suor Feliciana Diez, respectively, see Acquisti e Doni 230:4 Ricordi, ff. 77v, 45v. This source indicates that Cosimo II's widow had arranged to have Feliciana Diez enter the Monastero delle Convertite. Feliciana appears in Troiano, "Moralità e confini," p. 250, as the victim of a rape that took place in a church some months before she entered the convent. The Otto di Guardia condemned Feliciana, as well as the rapists, for polluting a holy place. But it is not apparent whether the convent served as a site of punishment or as a place of refuge for her.

68. For examples of deceased nuns' rooms at the Monastero delle Convertite being purchased by entrants, see CS126:68 Locatieni, f. 86v in the first system of numbering, and no. 178 in the second system of numbering. See also that convent's account book, CS126:58 D&C (1687–1725), f. 99, for a notation that one nun's intestate assets were put to use for the benefit of a new entrant. For Domenica Milocchi, see CS191:10 Memorie, f. 38. She was given the bed, clothing, sheets, and other belongings of a nun who had died about two weeks earlier.

69. For Suor Maria Antonia, deceased in February 1626, and an entrant naming herself Suor Maria Antonia three months later, see Acquisti e Doni 230:4 Ricordi, ff. 76, 7. For the similar circumstances under which Suor Baptista Felice and Suor Maria Oretta took their names, see for them respectively in the same source, ff. 76, 8, and ff. 75v, 6v.

70. On death and burial at the Monastero delle Convertite, see Acquisti e Doni 230:4 Ricordi, ff. 75–79; for Santa Maria Maddalena, see CS191:10 Memorie, f. 21.

71. For the votes on new entrants to Santa Maria Maddalena, see CS191:33 Constitutioni, f. 13, and CS191:36 Fogli, unpaginated, passim in the supplications for acceptance.

72. On punishments at Santa Maria Maddalena, see CS191:33 Constitutioni, ff. 24–25, 17v–18, 19v. For the Casa delle Malmaritate, see Bigallo 1691, ff. 38v–39, 50. I am grateful to Sara Matthews Grieco, who in a personal communication of 21 June 1981 identified the image of the virtuous woman with a stick in her mouth as a common figure in sixteenth-century books of emblems.

73. CS191:33 Constitutioni, f. 24v.

74. Commissariati di Firenze, parte 1, filza 6, no. 74, 11 March 1783.

75. For the fears of administrators at Santa Maria Maddalena, see CS191:33 Constitutioni, f. 24v. For the incident at the Casa delle Malmaritate, see Commissariati di Firenze, parte 1, filza 14, no. 14, 10–11 January 1788.

76. On the ideal of egalitarianism at Santa Maria Maddalena, see CS191:33 Constitutioni, f. 23; for the Casa delle Malmaritate, see Bigallo 1691, ff. 40rv, 51v–52.

77. CS126:62 Ricordi (1435–1620), unpaginated, 19 December 1619.

78. CS126:62 Ricordi (1435–1620), unpaginated, 19 January 1619. The amusing passage that I have translated begins "poi che ogni volta che si havevano a risquotere le dette tasse si faceva sempre una comedia, perche. . . ."

79. On Tuscans and tax evasion in the fifteenth century, see Herlihy and Klapisch-Zuber, *Les Toscans,* pp. 71–72, 61.

80. Bigallo 1691, Dechiaratione to Capitolo 26 (beginning of ms.).

81. CS126:70 Contratti, unpaginated, 1585, document beginning "Non e giocosa . . ."

82. For contracts containing the assent of nuns of the Monastero delle Convertite and of Santa Maria Maddalena respectively, see CS126:70 Contratti, unpaginated, 26 January 1559, and CS191:10 Memorie, ff. 45v–47, 54–56. For the nuns' management of the intake of piecework at Santa Maria Maddalena, see CS191:33 Constitutioni, ff. 21, 23.

83. For nuns writing signatures on behalf of ministeresses who did not know how to write, see CS191:36 Fogli, unpaginated, 26 May 1637, 30 August 1637, 6 September 1642, and 7 June 1655. For the female officers' duties requiring literacy, see CS191:33 Constitutioni, ff. 9v–10v, 13, 22rv, 23v, 20rv. Or for the same at the Casa delle Malmaritate, see Bigallo 1691, f. 51rv.

84. CS126:70 Contratti, unpaginated, 1 May 1618.

85. See n. 37.

86. Bigallo 1691, f. 34.

87. CS191:10 Memorie, ff. 6–8; CS191:35 Fogli, unpaginated, 1 March 1613.

88. See Visite Apostoliche 37, ff. 1rv, for the instructions, and 49v–51 for the visitor's report. The visitor did require that some ornamental frames be removed from a nun's room, but his order may have as easily reflected disapproval of the style of the frames, as objection to her possession of them.

89. In the examples that follow to illustrate this point, I cannot demonstrate that every nun was professed. The documents referred to some as both *professa* and *velata,* and to others only as *velata* or *monacha,* as I will indicate. However, the latter two terms cannot be taken as indicating that a nun was not professed, since nuns I know to be professed were sometimes designated by these terms alone.

90. On Suor (Maria) Lavinia Barbigi, professed *velata,* see CS126:54 D&C (1634–42), ff. 52, LII, 64, LXIIII; CS126:69 Cartelle, unpaginated, 1 October 1640, and an undated list of properties formerly owned by the nuns of the convent; Acquisti e Doni 230:4 Ricordi, f. 55.

91. For Suor Maria Silvestra Gozzini, *velata,* serving as guarantor for an entering *convertita* and offering her room as security, see CS126:56 D&C (1661–74), f. 257. For Suor Maria Prudenza Soldani, professed *velata,* see CS126:55 D&C (1642–52), ff. CXIIII, CLVIII.

92. On 31 August 1702 a branch of the Church's hierarchy in Rome issued a decree officially giving nuns a greater measure of freedom in the testamentary disposition of their property. The decree is mentioned in CS126:58 D&C (1687–1725), f. 180, but unfortunately this source offers no further details about the decree's content or significance.

93. See for example CS126:68 Locatieni, f. 77v in the first system of numbering, in which a nun bequeathed her room to another nun, and the room was to revert to the convent's fiscal administrators in the ducal bureaucracy after the death of the legatee.

94. See CS191:33 Constitutioni, ff. 5v, 15v, 23v, for the proscription of private property. For personal *robbe,* or items, left behind when nuns died, see CS191:10 Memorie, f. 36, entries for 21 November 1640 and 12 October 1641.

95. CS191:33 Constitutioni, f. 24v.

96. See chapter 2, section on The State.

97. On Suor Maria Gratia Alberighi, presumably a professed *velata* since she was abbess, see CS126:53 D&C (1630–42), ff. V, 31, 46. For Suor Maria Arcangiola Giorgi, *velata,* see CS126:57 D&C (1674–87), ff. 69, LXIX, 150. All the seventeenth-century account books (Debitori e Creditori) of the Monastero delle Convertite, CS126:51–58, contain entries listing the dividends to be distributed to nuns from the various *monti.* These entries are indexed under "M" or under the names of the *monti.* We can see in CS126:54 D&C (1634–42), f. 135, that over the course of the year 1640 Suor Maria Benigna received paltry dividends of less than a scudo every four months from the Monte delle Graticole.

98. For Suor Caterina Felice Salvetti, professed *velata,* see CS126:69 Cartelle, unpaginated, 22 May 1662; CS126:55 D&C (1642–52), f. 242; CS126:56 D&C (1661–74), f. XXIII; CS126:70 Contratti, unpaginated, (after 1661); and above, n. 55. Despite the unpaid debts, Suor Caterina died a woman of property. Beyond her bequests of a legacy to her *servigiale* and the funding for a new chapel in the convent, she left behind assets of 155 scudi. For the loan from one professed *velata* to another, which was probably for the purchase of a new room, see CS126:66 Cause, unpaginated, 1 July 1695, and CS126:58 D&C (1687–1725), f. (IL).

99. For Suor Bartolomea Leonora Corsini, professed *velata,* see CS126:66 Cause, unpaginated, 12 June 1679. See in the same source a thick file for the years 1697–99 on Suor Francesca Zenobia Strozzi, *monacha.*

100. On Suor Laura Francesca, *velata,* see CS126:56 D&C (1661–74), ff. 83, LXXXIII, 169, 235; CS126:57 D&C (1674–87), f. 80; CS126:58 D&C (1687–1725), ff. 72, 101, 105; CS126:66 Cause, unpaginated, undated "Ricordi da presentarsi all' . . . Fra Ipolito Borromei per alcune monache convertite."

101. CS126:66 Cause, unpaginated, 2–3 June 1699. The entreaty to the magistrate took place when the woman in question was a professed *velata.*

102. For a pharmacist (*speziale*) and a vendor of veils (*velettaio*) as benefactors to women at the Monastero delle Convertite, see CS126:53 D&C (1630–42), ff. 14, 44. For Suor Maria Lorenza Giordani, see CS126:66 Cause, 10 November 1659, 3 and 19 September 1669.

103. For a record of the 343 scudi spent by the Monastero delle Convertite for litigation in one year, 1616–17, see CS126:51 D&C (1616–23), ff. 52, LII. For an example of a nun's repayment, see CS126:52 D&C (1621–30), f. 32, and CS126:56 D&C (1661–74), ff. 84, 90, 93. In this instance Suor Maria Cosima Medici gave the Monastero delle Convertite a little over 2 scudi to reimburse the convent for what it had expended on her suit against Signor Cosimo Medici at the archiepiscopal curia in the 1620s.

104. Acquisti e Doni 230:4 Ricordi, f. 9; CS126:66 Cause, unpaginated, undated "Ricordi da presentarsi all' . . . Fra Ipolito Borromei per alcune monache convertite."

105. CS126:66 Cause, unpaginated, 7 May 1642, 17 January 1679, 16 September 1679, and an undated letter addressed to "Signor Cancelliere"; CS126:69 Cartelle, unpaginated, April 1661–October 1662; CS126:56 D&C (1661–74), f. LXXXXII.

106. CS126:69 Cartelle, unpaginated, 1639.

Chapter 5

1. CS191:10 Memorie, f. 1v.

2. CS191:10 Memorie, ff. 1–5. For the translation of the bull of 1520, see Pullan, *Rich and Poor,* p. 377.

3. For the co-owned property, see CS126:70 Contratti, unpaginated, 24 November 1617. On Gregorio Dezzi, see Onestà 3, f. 59, and CS126:66 Cause, unpaginated, 22 July 1695. On Girolamo Salvatichi, see CS191:33 Constitutioni, f. 25v. For further examples of such interinstitutional links, see Sherrill Cohen, "The Convertite and the Malmaritate: Women's Institutions, Prostitution, and the Family in Counter-Reformation Florence" (Ph.D. diss., Princeton University, 1985), pp. 299–300.

4. Acquisti e Doni 230:4 Ricordi, f. 56. On the Madonna dell'Amore, see Viviani della Robbia, *Nei monasteri fiorentini,* p. 48. In addition, in the fifteenth century Florence's chief magistrate (*podestà*) celebrated the annual feast day of Saint Mary Magdalen by sponsoring a footrace for adolescents. On the footrace, see Acquisti e Doni 292, unpaginated, at the date 15 July 1451 (transcription of letter from Jacopo di Simone di Giovanni del Cerva de' Trefuci to Giovanni di Cosimo de' Medici, in the collection MAP VI); Trexler, *Public Life,* p. 394, n. 138.

5. CS126:62 Ricordi (1435–1620), unpaginated, 5 January 1620.

6. Michele Poccianti, *Vite de sette beati fiorentini fondatori del sacro ordine de' Servi. Con uno epilogo di tutte le chiese, monasteri, luoghi pii, e compagnie della città di Firenze* (Florence: Giorgio Marescotti, 1589), p. 188.

7. On relocating in Pistoia, see CS191:10 Memorie, ff. 14v–15, 5–6. On visitors at ceremonies, see in the same source f. 10 and CS191:25 Giornale (1605–21), ff. 41v, 45v.

8. For scholarship relating to the subjects discussed in this and the next two paragraphs, see chapter 1, nn. 21, 22.

9. Bigallo 1691, f. 28.

10. For the contrasting attitudes on the part of the founders of the Casa delle Malmaritate toward women who had been "abandoned," see Bigallo 1691, ff. 1, 26v, 28v, 31, 35. For an acknowledgment by governmental officials that the 70 women at the Monastero delle Convertite "were increasing every day and deserved to be supported by the public purse," see Provvisioni Registri 183, vol. for April–March 1492, f. 6v.

11. CS126:66 Cause, unpaginated, 12 November 1693. On another Giovanni Nardi, who was the convent's physician in 1617, see CS126:51 D&C (1616–23), f. 55. For Jacopo Nardi, the convent's factor in the late seventeenth century, see CS126:58 D&C (1687–1725), f. 12. For Dottore Ipolito Nardi, who in 1670 paid 40 scudi to buy a room for Vittoria Pistilli upon her second entrance into the convent and was presumably the brother of the letter writer, see CS126:56 D&C (1661–74), f. 73.

12. For donations given by *persone segrete,* see CS126:51 D&C (1616–23), passim.

13. Bigallo 1691, f. 1.

14. On the Casa delle Malmaritate, see Bigallo 1691, f. 39, Capitolo 39; *Sommario de capitoli,* unpaginated prefatory pages citing grand duke's *bando* of 1580; Poccianti, *Vite de sette beati,* p. 191; Lombardi, *Povertà maschile,* p. 150, n. 26; Lastri, *L'osservatore fiorentino,* 3:125–28. On Santa Maria Maddalena, see CS191:10 Memorie, ff. 3v, 6–8. See Lombardi *Povertà maschile,* pp. 181, 188–91, for monastic connotations associated with the Mendicanti and Innocenti institutions.

15. CS191:10 Memorie, ff. 6, 8v–9, 10rv.

16. On the Casa delle Malmaritate, see Bigallo 1691, ff. 36, 42rv. For "three good

women" who accompanied a *convertita* when she made a day-trip between Santa Maria Maddalena and Bologna during the refuge's early years, see CS191:25 Giornale (1605–21), f. 47rv.

17. Acquisti e Doni 292, unpaginated, at the date October 1580 (case heard by the Otto di Guardia).

18. Bigallo 1691, ff. 28v–29, 34v–35v, 47, 37v–38v.

19. Bigallo 1691, f. 37, Dechiaratione to Capitolo 26 (at beginning of ms.), ff. 38–39.

20. Ferrante, "Malmaritate tra assistenza," pp. 77–80, found that three quarters of the women at Bologna's Casa delle Malmaritate in the early seventeenth and eighteenth centuries had short sojourns in the institution, generally staying from one to six months.

21. Evidence survives for a few cases in which the Monastero delle Convertite tracked down escaped nuns. Suor Candida Rosa Celeste was called a *madre,* no doubt short for *madre del titolo,* an appellation often given to professed nuns. Suor Candida Rosa Celeste fled in 1694 after living in the convent as a servant nun for more than eight years alongside three of her siblings. She evaded capture for several months and reached Rome before the archbishopric and police located her and returned her to the convent. She had to sell her room to repay the convent for the expenses incurred in returning her, 59 scudi. For her history, see CS126:57 D&C (1674–87), two folios numbered "183" and f. 233; CS126:58 D&C (1687–1725), two folios numbered "103." Administrators of the convent also enlisted the help of peacekeeping officers to recapture nuns who may or may not have been professed. See the case of Suor Serafina, as recorded in CS126:52 D&C (1621–30), f. 15, and the case of two other servant nuns, Suor Maria Cecilia and Suor Pietra Maria Grois, as recorded in CS126:58 D&C (1687–1725), f. 190. The latter two women, who ran off together in 1702, were arrested and reinstalled in the convent.

22. Information about departures from the Monastero delle Convertite can be found in Acquisti e Doni 230:4 Ricordi, ff. 44–47, and scattered throughout the convent's account books (Debitori e Creditori), CS126:51–58. The most important factor determining whether the dowry of a departing resident was refunded or forfeited seems to have been the woman's status. Generally—but not always—women who had not been invested could obtain refunds, whereas invested *suore* who departed forfeited their dowries to the convent. For examples of forfeits and refunds, see the cases described in nn. 23 and 24.

23. For Suor Maria Anna Scarlatti, who transferred to the monastery for *convertite* in Pisa, see CS126:52 D&C (1621–30), f. 16. For the invested Suor Felitiana Diez, who left after four years to go to her relatives and forfeited the 97 scudi she had paid toward a dowry, see CS126:52 D&C (1621–30), ff. LXXVII, 110; CS126:53 D&C (1630–42), ff. 31, 47; Acquisti e Doni 230:4 Ricordi, f. 45v; and chapter 4, section on Responses to the Institutional Community.

24. On Gostanza Albertini, see Acquisti e Doni 230:4 Ricordi, ff. 86, 44, 6v, 54v; CS126:52 D&C (1621–30), ff. LXXIV, 77. A little over a year after leaving the convent, she received a partial refund, 30 scudi out of the 100 scudi she had paid to enter. In 1634 the administrators of the convent sent 12 scudi to the former *convertita* Maddalena Nini, to put an end to her demands for a refund. She had quit the convent (in her second departure from the Monastero delle Convertite), having "rediscovered her husband, whom she thought dead." On her, see Acquisti e Doni 230:4 Ricordi, ff. 86v, 44v; CS126:54 D&C (1634–42), f. 3.

25. Acquisti e Doni 230:4 Ricordi, f. 46. In 1636 the administrators also released Francesca Conti, who had spent about two years in the convent and departed from it wishing to marry. On her, see CS126:54 D&C (1634–42), ff. 16, XVI; Acquisti e Doni 230:4 Ricordi, f. 46rv.

26. Acquisti e Doni 230:4 Ricordi, f. 46.

27. Acquisti e Doni 230:4 Ricordi, f. 47; CS126:54 D&C (1634–42), ff. CXXIII, 70; CS126:55 D&C (1642–52), f. 95.

28. This was said of Suor Teresia Caterina, who had undergone investiture as a *conversa* in 1627 and then bade farewell to the convent after less than a year. See Acquisti e Doni 230:4 Ricordi, ff. 87, 8v, 44v–45.

29. Acquisti e Doni 230:4 Ricordi, ff. 9, 45rv. As recorded in the same source, ff. 10, 45, and in CS126:54 D&C (1634–42), f. 2, there was also the similar case of the *convertita* Suor Maria Gostanza Guidacci. After undergoing investiture for *velata* and paying a dowry of 140 scudi in 1629, she decided to leave the house within four months. Although Suor Maria Gostanza obtained license to go by telling conventual officials that she did not like the religious life, she may have reentered the institution at a later date.

30. For the initial and revised policies on departures and residents' property, see CS191:10 Memorie, ff. 6–7v.

31. For details on Santa Maria Maddalena's first fifteen entrants and the departures of six of them, see CS191:10 Memorie, ff. 6v, 8rv, 10. Departures from Santa Maria Maddalena are also recorded throughout CS191:35 Fogli and CS191:36 Fogli. Only in one instance in these early years did the Pistoian administrators deal harshly with a woman who departed. In 1605 or 1606, when a former resident of Santa Maria Maddalena, the *convertita* Verginia da Larciano, fled from the husband to whom she had been relinquished, the *operai* did not trust her to be on her own and had the woman incarcerated in Pistoia's civil prison.

32. CS191:10 Memorie, f. 8.

33. On Maria of Statigliana and Sabatina of Bologna, see CS191:10 Memorie, ff. 5v, 8–8v, 10. One woman is designated at entrance as "Maria da Pistoia" and at her exit as "Maria da Statigliana." Maria and Sabatina forfeited their payments, and they may have left the premises together, as did the two residents of the Monastero delle Convertite described in n. 21.

34. On the two *suore,* see CS191:10 Memorie, ff. 10, 15, 19–21. For more about Lucretia Bozi of Cireglio, who became Suor Caterina, see chapter 3, section on Dilemmas of Betrothal, Marriage, and Widowhood.

35. CS191:10 Memorie, ff. 10, 15, 18v, 21.

36. CS191:35 Fogli, unpaginated, undated (probably 1613); CS191:10 Memorie, ff. 19, 20v, 21v–23v, 24v–25, 27, 28v, 30, 31v, 47; CS191:36 Fogli, unpaginated, 20 and 22 July 1626. The quoted phrase is from the second source, f. 24v.

37. CS191:36 Fogli, unpaginated, 1 and 15 September 1621; CS191:10 Memorie, f. 24. The evidence suggests that one of the five evictees was the same Suor Maria Angela described earlier who had been released to her father in January 1621. She may have reentered the convent and then decided to leave again. For data on the two women who seem to have been the same person, regarding Suor Maria Angela (formerly Dianora of Pistoia) see n. 35, and regarding Suor Maria Angela Masetti (formerly Dianora Masetti), see CS191:10 Memorie, ff. 23–24.

38. CS191:10 Memorie, ff. 21v–24, 25–26; CS191:36 Fogli, unpaginated, 16–17 December 1621.

39. CS191:10 Memorie, ff. 25–26.

40. Ibid., ff. 23, 24v, 26v.

41. For Cammilla Tamburini, see CS191:10 Memorie, ff. 21v–25. Another married *convertita* who probably departed before mid-1626 was Lisabetta Magnani. She entered in April 1625 with her husband's and the bishop's permission for her to take vows, but she did not participate in the group profession. For her entrance, see CS191:10 Memorie, f. 27. On the second authorization of claustration and the group profession, see CS191:10 Memorie, f. 27v; CS191:36 Fogli, unpaginated, 9 May 1625, 20–22 July 1626.

42. Bigallo 1691, ff. 39v–41, 2v, 15v, 35rv, 43v.

43. For Caterina Giani, who became Suor Giovanna Batista, see Acquisti e Doni 230:4 Ricordi, f. 46v; CS126:54 D&C (1634–40), ff. III, 104, CIIII; CS126:55 D&C (1642–52), ff. 42, XXXXII. For Luisa Donnini, see CS126:69 Cartelle, unpaginated, 7 April 1661.

44. See the case of the *convertita* Caterina Salvetti, who reentered the Monastero delle Convertite for the second time in 1650, documented in CS126:55 D&C (1642–52), ff. 159, 242. In 1648, at her first entrance, she had paid the usual dowry for the status of *velata,* 160 scudi, and then forfeited that sum when she left. When Caterina wanted to return to the convent in 1650, the state granted that she could gain readmission by paying only an additional 40 scudi.

45. CS191:33 Constitutioni, f. 12v; CS191:35 Fogli, unpaginated, undated subscription pledge and document of 1 March 1613; CS191:36 Fogli, unpaginated, 20–22 July 1626 and 26 May 1637; CS191:10 Memorie, ff. 21v–23v, 24v, 28v, 30, 31v. On Margherita (Pistorozzi) of Sambuca, see also chapter 2, section on The Women.

46. For Suor Annalena Landi (formerly Felice of Arezzo), see CS191:10 Memorie, ff. 6v, 9–10, 14v, 21v–24, 31v; CS191:36 Fogli, unpaginated, 1 and 15 September 1621.

47. See n. 40 and CS191:36 Fogli, unpaginated, 6 September 1642.

48. In Bigallo 1691, f. 3, the founders of the Casa delle Malmaritate voiced suspicions regarding men who might want to be in proximity to the *convertite* for improper reasons. Santa Maria Maddalena's ecclesiastical supervisors expressed similar fears, in CS191:33 Constitutioni, f. 16, that contact with male visitors could tempt the *convertite*. And men did indeed entice or kidnap women from the institutions. See Otto di Guardia Granducale 91, ff. 178v–179, 188, May 1562, for a case of a man suspected of having lured women out of the Monastero delle Convertite. See Brackett, "Otto di Guardia," p. 227, on a case of 1603 in which a citizen abducted three women from the Casa delle Malmaritate.

49. Acquisti e Doni 292, unpaginated, at the date 1603. For another seventeenth-century case in which a resident, Suor Maria Clarice Agostina, left "of her own volition," see Acquisti e Doni 230:4 Ricordi, f. 44v.

50. For such a stipulation concerning an entrant to the Monastero delle Convertite, see CS126:66 Cause, unpaginated, 5 January 1663.

51. See Vasaio-Zambonini, "Miserable Virgins," pp. 3–5, on Rome's Vergini Miserabili and Zitelle Disperse; Pullan, *Rich and Poor,* pp. 379, 391, 389, 393, on the *convertite* in Verona, Rome's Santa Marta, and Venice's Zitelle and Soccorso; Liebowitz, "Prison, Workshop and Convent," pp. 2–3, on Milan's Deposito and Soccorso; idem, "Conversion or Confinement," p. 8, on Siena's Convertite; Ferrante, "L'onore ritrovato," pp. 500, 517, 512–13, on Bologna's Soccorso.

52. Lombardi, "L'ospedale dei Mendicanti," p. 299.

53. See Ferrante, "L'onore ritrovato," p. 500, on Bologna's Convento for *con-*

vertite; Pullan, *Rich and Poor,* pp. 383, 377–78, on the tightening of discipline at institutions for *convertite* in Vicenza and Venice; Liebowitz, "Prison, Workshop and Convent," pp. 4–5, on claustration at Milan's refuge for *convertite,* Santa Valeria; Viviani della Robbia, *Nei monasteri fiorentini,* p. 49, on Florence's Monastero delle Stabilite; Vasaio-Zambonini, "Miserable Virgins," p. 5, on increasing restrictions at Rome's Zitelle Disperse.

54. Pullan, *Rich and Poor,* p. 394; Liebowitz, "Virgins in the Service," p. 143. On the related distrust of Mary Ward's followers and of other uncloistered communities of pious women, see the latter article, pp. 139–43.

55. See D'Addario, *Aspetti della Controriforma,* pp. 296–97, on Annalena. See also Liebowitz, "Voices from Convents," pp. 9–12; idem, "Conversion or Confinement," pp. 9–10.

56. Translated by Liebowitz, "Conversion or Confinement," p. 8, n. 31. In "Voices from Convents," p. 7, Liebowitz also observes that the uncomfortable material conditions at many institutions could cause unhappiness among residents.

57. On Tarabotti, see Ginevra Conti Odorisio, *Donna e società nel Seicento: Lucrezia Marinelli e Arcangela Tarabotti* (Rome: Bulzoni Editore, 1979), p. 205; Viviani della Robbia, *Nei monasteri fiorentini,* p. 74. Liebowitz, "Conversion or Confinement," p. 8, reports that in a conversation with the apostolic visitor, a Milanese *convertita* cursed those she blamed for her presence in the house. For an interesting early-eighteenth-century case of a Milanese woman who fled from a convent and won release from her forced monastic vows, see the translated excerpts in O'Faolain and Martines, *Not in God's Image,* pp. 270–75.

58. See chapter 1, section on Monasticism.

59. Some of the refuges for *convertite* and custodial institutions did seek to have only voluntary entrants. See Ferrante, "L'onore ritrovato," p. 503; Liebowitz, "Prison, Workshop and Convent," p. 6. But such policies did not stop the establishments from retaining some women who wished to depart, or from admitting the females sentenced to compulsory confinements there.

60. On the Zitelle Disperse, see Vasaio-Zambonini, "Miserable Virgins," pp. 5–6. On Santa Valeria, see Liebowitz, "Prison, Workshop and Convent," p. 7.

61. Bigallo 1691, ff. 36v–38, 35rv, 39rv, 16, 18. For similar views on the part of other institutional administrators, see Vasaio-Zambonini, "Miserable Virgins," p. 4, on Rome's Vergini Miserabili; Pullan, *Rich and Poor,* p. 390, on Venice's Zitelle; Ferrante, "L'onore ritrovato," p. 511, on Bologna's Soccorso.

62. Ferrante, "L'onore ritrovato," n. 6.

63. Raimondo Creytens, "La Riforma dei monasteri femminili dopo i Decreti Tridentini," in *Il Concilio di Trento e la Riforma Tridentina,* 2 vols. (Rome: Herder, 1965), 1:45–84.

64. Pullan, *Rich and Poor,* p. 388, relates that the Venetian Zitelle wanted to accept not simply poor or orphaned females, but beautiful, healthy girls in clear danger of losing their virtue.

65. On the Soccorso in Cremona and the conservatory of Saint Francis de Sales, see Lombardi, "L'ospedale dei Mendicanti," n. 39, p. 311. On the Casa delle Malmaritate, see chapter 3, section on The Institution as Warehouse.

66. See Lombardi, "L'ospedale dei Mendicanti," p. 303, on the differentiation of institutions. See also Daniela Maldini, "Donne sole, 'figlie raminghe,' 'convertite' e 'forzate.' Aspetti assistenziali nella Torino di fine Settecento," *Il Risorgimento* 33 (June 1980): 115, 134.

67. Ilaria Porciani, ed., *Le donne a scuola: L'educazione femminile nell'Italia dell'Ottocento. Mostra documentaria e iconografica* (Siena: Università degli Studi di Siena, 1987), p. 150. For the quotation, which is from the Motuproprio of 21 March 1785, Art. 12, see Bargiacchi, *Storia degli istituti,* 3:238–39, and generally pp. 234–42, 223. See also Viviani della Robbia, *Nei monasteri fiorentini,* p. 226. For the statistics, see Ottavio Andreucci, *Nuove osservazioni sui conservatori femminili delle provincie Toscane* (Florence: Civelli, 1872), pp. 47–49, and the same author's *Delle scuole femminili popolane e cittadine e delli instituti ospitalieri* (Florence: Federigo Bencini, 1865), p. 20, n. 1.

68. For the history of the Casa delle Malmaritate after the publication of the second edition of the statutes in 1583, see Lastri, *L'osservatore fiorentino,* 3:127–28. On the Leopoldine reforms in criminal justice, see R. Burr Litchfield, *Emergence of a Bureaucracy: The Florentine Patricians, 1530–1790* (Princeton, N.J.: Princeton University Press, 1986), pp. 305–11; Carlo Mangio, *La polizia toscana: Organizzazione e criteri d'intervento (1765–1808)* (Milan: Giuffrè, 1988).

69. Camera Fiscale, filza 2857, no. 457, 31 July 1777.

70. Commissariato S. M. Novella 1, no. 350, 27 August 1778.

71. For occasional prostitutes threatened with incarceration in the Casa di Correzione, see Commissariati di Firenze, parte 1, filza 6, no. 244, 10 September 1783. On the substitution of the Casa delle Malmaritate, see Mario Simondi, "Classi povere e strategie del controllo sociale nel granducato di Toscana (1765–1790)" (Dipartimento statistico, Università degli studi di Firenze, 1983, photocopy), pp. 74–75.

72. On the Casa delle Malmaritate, see Bigallo 1691, ff. 26v, 28. The remark of the Venetian prioress is translated by Pullan, *Rich and Poor,* pp. 378–79. On Bologna's Soccorso, see Ferrante, "L'onore ritrovato," pp. 504, 510. On the Mendicanti, see Lombardi, "L'ospedale dei Mendicanti," pp. 301–3, 311.

73. Ferrante, "L'onore ritrovato," pp. 510, 500.

74. On the Venetian Zitelle, see Pullan, *Rich and Poor,* p. 389. For similar policies at other institutions, see in the same source p. 393, and Ferrante, "L'onore ritrovato," pp. 501–2.

75. Liebowitz, "Prison, Workshop and Convent," p. 11. For the Tridentine policy, see chapter 1, section on Monasticism.

76. On the Zitelle Disperse, see Vasaio-Zambonini, "Miserable Virgins," p. 5. On Santa Valeria and on the value of the charity collected in the streets, see Liebowitz, "Prison, Workshop and Convent," pp. 10–11. See also Lombardi, *Povertà maschile,* p. 182, on Grand Duke Cosimo III's prohibition of begging by the girls at two Florentine conservatories in 1682 and his contribution of funds to compensate.

77. Liebowitz, "Prison, Workshop and Convent," p. 10, and for a broad interpretation of these issues, pp. 9–11.

78. See chapter 1, end of section on Monasticism, for a quotation from Pope Gregory XIII that epitomizes this outlook. What the Church intended did not uniformly result. Liebowitz notes that, although Santa Valeria in the 1570s was becoming more conventual in form, economic exigencies would not permit a slackening of labor ("Prison, Workshop and Convent," pp. 11–12). Arduous labor became "dominant in the life of the community" there. Santa Valeria, however, was a particularly harsh and grim institution.

79. Ivy Pinchbeck, *Women Workers and the Industrial Revolution, 1750–1850* (London: George Routledge & Sons, 1930), pp. 196–201; Margaret Hewitt, *Wives and Mothers in Victorian Industry* (London: Rockliff, 1958), pp. 48–61; Louise A. Tilly

and Joan W. Scott, *Women, Work, and Family* (New York: Holt, Rinehart & Winston, 1978), pp. 116–23.

80. For example, Piera de Levaldini in chapter 2 and Agnola of Maremma in this chapter. Ferrante believes that the lower classes did have a strong sense of their sexual honor and that they articulated grievances in this language ("Malmaritate tra assistenza," p. 99).

81. Savelli, *Pratica universale*, p. 241.

82. Ferrante, "L'onore ritrovato," p. 514; Ciammitti, "Quanto costa essere normali," pp. 471, 481–82, 486, n. 7.

83. For a somewhat different view of the laicization of civic institutions, see Lombardi, "L'ospedale dei Mendicanti," p. 309.

84. Translated by Brucker, *Society of Renaissance Florence*, p. 192. For more on this woman, see chapter 1, section on Prostitution.

85. Lastri, *L'osservatore fiorentino*, 3:126.

86. On the first three women mentioned, see Serafino Biffi, *Sui riformatori pei giovani* (Milan: Giuseppe Bernardoni, 1870), pp. 90–91, 93. On the first two women, see Pullan, *Rich and Poor*, pp. 382–83. On Lodovica Torelli, see Porciani, *Le donne a scuola*, p. 98. On Rosa Govone, see Sandra Cavallo, "Assistenza femminile e tutela dell'onore nella Torino del XVIII secolo," *Annali della Fondazione Luigi Einaudi* 14 (1980): 151–54. On this subject generally, see Kathleen McCarthy, ed., *Lady Bountiful Revisited: Women, Philanthropy, and Power* (New Brunswick, N.J.: Rutgers University Press, 1990).

87. CS191:10 Memorie, f. 36v.

88. On the *beguines* setting up their communities by buying and selling properties, see Southern, *Western Society*, pp. 323–24. For Madonna Bice, see CS191:10 Memorie, f. 4rv. For women's patronage at the Tuscan refuges, see Cohen, "Convertite and Malmaritate," pp. 200–202. For the same at Venice's Soccorso and Zitelle, see Pullan, *Rich and Poor*, pp. 393, 390. On an eighteenth-century male and female confraternity connected with Santa Maria Maddalena in Pistoia, see ASP, Patrimonio Ecclesiastico E:345 and 346. For *convertite* who took a very active role in the life of the community, see chapter 4, section on Responses to the Institutional Community.

89. For an analysis of financial and other kinds of support given by civic communities to the Tuscan refuges, see Cohen, "Convertite and Malmaritate," pp. 182–209. On the longevity of Santa Maria del Baraccano, see Ciammitti, "Quanto costa essere normali," nn. 1, 72. See Lombardi, "L'ospedale dei Mendicanti," p. 291, for seventeenth- and eighteenth-century Tuscan usage of the concept of *libertà*.

Chapter 6

1. On social knowledge, see Peter B. Evans, Dietrich Rueschemeyer, and Theda Skocpol, "On the Road Toward a More Adequate Understanding of the State," in *Bringing the State Back In*, ed. Peter B. Evans, Dietrich Rueschemeyer, and Theda Skocpol (Cambridge: Cambridge University Press, 1985), pp. 357–58.

2. In addition to the instances discussed below in the text, see Biffi, *Sui riformatori*, p. 153; Pierre-François Aleil, "Le Refuge de Clermont, 1666–1792," *Bulletin historique et scientifique de l'Auvergne* 86 (1973): 13, 21, 23; *Reports and Realities from the Sketch-Book of a Manager of the Rosine Association* (Philadelphia: John

Duross, 1855), pp. 62–74; Annarita Buttafuoco, *Le Mariuccine: Storia di un'istituzione laica l'Asilo Mariuccia* (Milan: Franco Angeli, 1985), pp. 411, 415, 430.

3. Perry, "Deviant Insiders," p. 154; idem, "Lost Women," pp. 195–214; idem, *Gender and Disorder in Early Modern Seville* (Princeton, N.J.: Princeton University Press, 1990), pp. 137–52; María Dolores Pérez Baltasar, *Mujeres marginadas: Las casas de recogidas en Madrid* (Madrid: Gráficas Lormo, 1984), pp. 54, 66, 89, 104; Marta Jové Campmajó and Helena Kirchner i Granell, "Capitaires Prostitutes i Rodamons: Barcelona, 1600–1640," in *Primer congrés d'història moderna de Catalunya*, 2 vols. (Barcelona: Departament d'Historia Moderna, Facultat de Geografia i Historia, Universitat de Barcelona: Diputacio de Barcelona, 1984), 1:471–78; Nikki Harrison, "Nuns and Prostitutes in Enlightenment Spain," *British Journal for Eighteenth-Century Studies* 9 (Spring 1986): 53–60; Josefina Muriel de la Torre, *Los recogimientos de mujeres: Respuesta a una problemática social novohispana* (Mexico: Universidad Nacional Autónoma de México, Instituto de Investigaciones Históricas, 1974).

4. Pierre Pansier, *L'Oeuvre des repenties à Avignon du XIIIe au XVIIIe siècle* (Paris: Honoré Champion, 1910). Georg'ann Cattelona at Indiana University is studying the Refuge in Marseilles. See also Aleil, "Le Refuge," pp. 13–16; Jean-Pierre Gutton, *La Société et les pauvres: l'exemple de la généralité de Lyon, 1534–1789* (Paris: Société d'Edition "Les Belles Lettres," 1970), pp. 101–4; Olwen Hufton, *The Poor of Eighteenth-Century France, 1750–1789* (Oxford: Oxford University Press, 1974), pp. 309–15; Jones, "Prostitution and the Ruling Class," pp. 9–23; Kathryn Norberg, *Rich and Poor in Grenoble, 1600–1814* (Berkeley: University of California Press, 1985), pp. 21–26. On Notre-Dame de Charité du Refuge, see Henri Gaillac, *Les Maisons de correction, 1830–1945* (Paris: Editions Cujas, 1971), pp. 118–22.

5. Roper, *Holy Household*, pp. 89–131; Susan C. Karant-Nunn, "Continuity and Change: Some Effects of the Reformation on the Women of Zwickau," *Sixteenth Century Journal* 12 (Summer 1982): 23–26. For the view on the similar motivations of Catholics and Protestants, see Nicholas Orme, "The Reformation and the Red Light," *History Today* 37 (March 1987): 37–41.

6. Spierenburg, "Sociogenesis of Confinement," pp. 25–40; Thorsten Sellin, *Pioneering in Penology: The Amsterdam Houses of Correction in the Sixteenth and Seventeenth Centuries* (Philadelphia: University of Pennsylvania Press, 1944), pp. 87–101.

7. Donna T. Andrew, *Philanthropy and Police: London Charity in the Eighteenth Century* (Princeton, N.J.: Princeton University Press, 1989), pp. 54–57, 121–22; Edward J. Bristow, *Vice and Vigilance: Purity Movements in Britain Since 1700* (Dublin: Gill and Macmillan, 1977), pp. 54–55; H. F. B. Compston, *The Magdalen Hospital: The Story of a Great Charity* (London: Society for Promoting Christian Knowledge, 1917), pp. 21–24; "Sunderlandensis," letter in *Gentleman's Magazine* (April 1751). For an earlier proposal that did not come to fruition, see Henry P. Thompson, *Thomas Bray* (London: Society for Promoting Christian Knowledge, 1954), pp. 24–25.

8. *Prostitution Reform: Four Documents* [by Robert Dingley, Saunders Welch, John Fielding, and William Dodd] (New York: Garland Publishing, 1985); Compston, *Magdalen Hospital*, pp. 17, 20, 31–32; Andrew, *Philanthropy and Police*, pp. 59–60; Stanley Nash, "Prostitution and Charity: The Magdalen Hospital, a Case Study," *Journal of Social History* 17 (Summer 1984): 617–28; Samuel B. P. Pearce, *An Ideal in the Working: The Story of the Magdalen Hospital, 1758–1958* (London: n.p., 1958).

9. Jonas Hanway, *Reflections, Essays and Meditations on Life and Religion, with a collection of proverbs in alphabetical order, and twenty-eight letters written occasionally*

on several subjects, 2 vols. (London: John Rivington, 1761), 2:5, 8–9. Here and in subsequent quotations from this source, I have deleted the abundant italics.

10. Ibid., pp. 12–13.

11. Ibid., pp. 13–14.

12. Ibid., p. 17, and on the "free country," pp. 11, 16.

13. See, for example, Carl Bridenbaugh, *Cities in the Wilderness: The First Century of Urban Life in America, 1625–1742* (1938; New York: Knopf, 1964), pp. 72–73.

14. The sentiments of the founders were quoted by Marcia Carlisle, "Prostitutes and Their Reformers in Nineteenth-Century Philadelphia" (Ph.D. diss., Rutgers University, 1982), pp. 152–227, and by Negley K. Teeters, "The Early Days of the Magdalen Society of Philadelphia," *Social Service Review* 30 (June 1956): 158–59. See also Steven Ruggles, "Fallen Women: The Inmates of the Magdalen Society Asylum of Philadelphia, 1836–1908," *Journal of Social History* 16 (Summer 1983): 65–82.

15. Ezra Stiles Ely, *Visits of Mercy; or, The journals of the Rev. Ezra Stiles Ely, D.D., written while he was stated preacher to the hospital and alms-house, in the city of New York,* 2 vols. (Philadelphia: Samuel F. Bradford, 1829), 1:78, 164–66, 210–11; Carlisle, "Prostitutes and Reformers," pp. 61–62.

16. John R. McDowall, *Magdalen Facts* (New York: the author, 1832), pp. 95–96.

17. Carlisle, "Prostitutes and Reformers," pp. 62, 66; Carroll Smith Rosenberg, *Religion and the Rise of the American City: The New York City Mission Movement, 1812–1870* (Ithaca, N.Y.: Cornell University Press, 1971), pp. 98–106.

18. McDowall, *Magdalen Facts,* pp. 98–99, 58–62, 54–55; Smith Rosenberg, *Religion and the Rise,* pp. 101–5; Barbara Hobson, *Uneasy Virtue: The Politics of Prostitution and the American Reform Tradition* (New York: Basic Books, 1987), pp. 110–36, especially pp. 118–23 on the (Boston) Penitent Females' Refuge; Barbara J. Berg, *The Remembered Gate: Origins of American Feminism—The Woman and the City, 1800–1860* (New York: Oxford University Press, 1978), p. 180, quoting a publication issued by the Female Benevolent Society.

19. Compston, *Magdalen Hospital,* p. 198; Linda Mahood, *The Magdalenes: Prostitution in the Nineteenth Century* (London: Routledge, 1990), pp. 75–118 (on Scotland); Jean Lawrence L'Espérance, "Woman's Mission to Woman: Explorations in the Operation of the Double Standard and Female Solidarity in Nineteenth Century England," *Histoire sociale—Social History* 12 (November 1979): 316–38; Bristow, *Vice and Vigilance,* pp. 51–71, 94–99, 154–59, 173; Mary S. Sims, *The Natural History of a Social Institution: The Young Women's Christian Association* (New York: Woman's Press, 1936), p. 13; Jenty Fairbank, *Booth's Boots: Social Service Beginnings in the Salvation Army* (London: International Headquarters of the Salvation Army, 1983), pp. 13, 23; F. K. Prochaska, *Women and Philanthropy in Nineteenth-Century England* (Oxford: Oxford University Press, 1980), pp. 188–221; Henry C. Potter, *Sisterhoods and Deaconesses at Home and Abroad* (New York: E. P. Dutton, 1873), pp. 274, 257, 304; Vicinus, *Independent Women,* pp. 74–81.

20. On Philadelphia's Rosine House, see Carlisle, "Prostitutes and Reformers," pp. 125–35; *Reports and Realities,* pp. 171, 173. For the Italian Rosine, see Cavallo, "Assistenza femminile," pp. 151–54; *Dizionario degli istituti di perfezione,* s.v. "Francesca Maria Govone."

21. *Reports and Realities,* p. 174.

22. Ibid., pp. 174–77. See below, n. 44, for a qualification of this assessment of the founders' goal.

23. Otto Wilson, *Fifty Years' Work with Girls, 1883–1933: A Story of the Florence*

Crittenton Homes (Alexandria, Va.: National Florence Crittenton Mission, 1933), pp. 37–48, 114, 297; Kate Waller Barrett, *Some Practical Suggestions on the Conduct of a Rescue Home* (1903; New York: Arno Press, 1974), p. 95; "Project Shows Hookers a Way Out," *Los Angeles Times,* 16 October 1985, "Orange County" sec. I owe thanks to Helen Garon for sending me this article.

24. On Bon Pasteur institutions, see Gaillac, *Les Maisons,* pp. 123–30; Henri Joly, "Les Maisons du Bon-Pasteur," *La Réforme sociale,* July–December 1901, pp. 287–308; *The New Encyclopaedia Britannica,* 15th ed., s.v. "Good Shepherd Sisters"; Franco Bernocchi, *Prostituzione e rieducazione* (Padua: CEDAM, 1966), p. 134. For Catholic institutions not affiliated with Bon Pasteur, see Gaillac, pp. 137–47; Bernocchi, pp. 132, 134, 141; Giovanni B. Penco, *Donna caduta e donna redenta per l'affermazione di un principio di morale sociale,* 2d ed. (Milan: Instituto di Propaganda Libraria, 1954), pp. 170–72; *New Catholic Encyclopedia,* s.v. "Dominicans—Sisters."

25. See Pérez Baltasar, *Mujeres marginadas,* pp. 107–19, on the order and the founder, who was canonized as Saint Maria Micaela in 1934. On the order today, see "Nuns' Sole Ministry Is Working with Prostitutes," *National Catholic Reporter,* 17 January 1991.

26. Judith Godden, "Sectarianism and Purity Within the Woman's Sphere: Sydney Refuges During the Late Nineteenth Century," *Journal of Religious History* 14 (1987): 296, 300. Protestant and Catholic refuges sometimes cooperated in referring and transferring residents, as happened in the case of the Rosine, Magdalen, and Good Shepherd asylums in nineteenth-century Philadelphia. See Carlisle, "Prostitutes and Reformers," pp. 135, 198, 202, 208, 211, 216–19.

27. Buttafuoco, *Le Mariuccine,* pp. 35–36, 313–14; Bernocchi, *Prostituzione e rieducazione,* pp. 144–46, 184–202.

28. Bristow, *Vice and Vigilance,* p. 66; Mary Gibson, *Prostitution and the State in Italy, 1860–1915* (New Brunswick, N.J.: Rutgers University Press, 1986), pp. 79–81, 229–31; Mary Gibson, "Marginalità convergenti. L'immagine borghese della prostituta, 1850–1915," in *Diritto e rovescio: Studi sulle donne e il controllo sociale,* ed. Tamar Pitch (Naples: Edizioni Scientifiche Italiane, 1987), pp. 231–32; Bernocchi, *Prostituzione e rieducazione,* pp. 147–57, 132. With the passage of a 1946 law closing the tolerated brothels, the French government promised to fund reformatories but did not act on its pledge. On the present-day refuge, see "Once a Brothel, Soon a Refuge for Prostitutes," *New York Times,* 5 January 1991.

29. Bernocchi, *Prostituzione e rieducazione,* p. 135.

30. For instance, see Nash, "Prostitution and Charity," p. 622, and Ruggles, "Fallen Women," p. 68. For discussions of durations of other lengths, see Aleil, "Le Refuge," pp. 49–50; Bernocchi, *Prostituzione e rieducazione,* pp. 140–41.

31. Richard Stites, "Prostitute and Society in Pre-Revolutionary Russia," *Jahrbücher für Geschichte Osteuropas* 31 (1983): 360; Sue Gronewald, "The Door of Hope: A Rescue Mission for Shanghai Prostitutes, 1900–1941" (Ph.D. diss. prospectus, Columbia University, 1991); Enrique Rodríguez Solís, *Historia de la prostitución en España y en América* (Madrid: Biblioteca Nueva, 1921), p. 217.

32. On the Communist antipathy toward prostitution and on the Soviet Union, see Elizabeth A. Wood, "The Prostitution Debates in Soviet Russia: Socialist Responses to a 'Bourgeois' Problem, 1917–1927" (Department of History, University of Michigan, 1986, photocopy), pp. 42–46; Maurice Hindus, *The Great Offensive* (New York: Harrison Smith & Robert Haas, 1933), pp. 205–19; Ella Winter, *Red Virtue: Human Relationships in the New Russia* (New York: Harcourt, Brace, 1933), pp. 182–94; Marion Nelson,

"Two Curious Institutions of Soviet Russia," *Canadian Forum* 14 (April 1934): 260–61; Alice Withrow Field, "Prostitution in the Soviet Union," *Nation,* 25 March 1936, pp. 373–74. On China, see Gail Hershatter, "Regulating Sex in Shanghai: The Reform of Prostitution in 1920 and 1951," in *Shanghai Sojourners,* ed. Frederic Wakeman and Wen-hsin Yeh (Berkeley: Institute of East Asian Studies, University of California, forthcoming). On Cuba, see Oscar Lewis, Ruth M. Lewis, and Susan M. Rigdon, *Four Women. Living the Revolution: An Oral History of Contemporary Cuba* (Urbana: University of Illinois Press, 1977), pp. 279–84; Margaret Randall, *Cuban Women Now: Interviews with Cuban Women* (N.p.: Women's Press, 1974), pp. 237–48. My thanks go to Sue Gronewald, Gail Hershatter, Marifeli Perez-Stable, Elizabeth Wood, Stephen Kotkin, and Laura Engelstein for aiding my research.

33. Bernocchi, *Prostituzione e rieducazione,* pp. 159–60; Giles Playfair, "How Denmark Reforms Prostitutes," *New Society,* 12 November 1964, pp. 18–19; "Many Women Held in Zimbabwe Drive" and "Zimbabwe Says It Freed Women Held in Raids," *New York Times,* 14 and 30 November 1983, sec. A.

34. On numbers of urban prostitutes, for the early modern period see Vern L. Bullough and Bonnie Bullough, *The History of Prostitution* (New Hyde Park, N.Y.: University Books, 1964), p. 131. For the modern era, see Abraham Flexner, *Prostitution in Europe* (New York: Century, 1914), pp. 24–28. For the household size of smaller asylums such as the Refuge at Clermont and Philadelphia's Magdalen Asylum, see Aleil, "Le Refuge," p. 52; Ruggles, "Fallen Women," p. 81, n. 42. For household size at larger asylums such as London's Magdalen House and Milan's Asilo Mariuccia, see Andrew, *Philanthropy and Police,* p. 160; Compston, *Magdalen Hospital,* p. 170; Buttafuoco, *Le Mariuccine,* pp. 53–54.

35. Andrew, *Philanthropy and Police,* p. 160; Godden, "Sectarianism," p. 305; Buttafuoco, *Le Mariuccine,* pp. 444, 449, 192.

36. On the Rosine asylum, see Carlisle, "Prostitutes and Reformers," pp. 129–33. For work and training at other asylums, see below, n. 39; Jones, "Prostitution and the Ruling Class," p. 14; Nash, "Prostitution and Charity," p. 620; Godden, "Sectarianism," p. 301; Buttafuoco, *Le Mariuccine,* pp. 347–73, 300–309. Exceptions to my generalization could be found at the Asilo Mariuccia and Florence Crittenton homes, which helped a few women to train for nursing, teaching, clerking, and administrative positions. See Buttafuoco, *Le Mariuccine,* pp. 367–73, and Wilson, *Fifty Years' Work,* pp. 462, 478.

37. Quoted by Carlisle, "Prostitutes and Reformers," pp. 129–30.

38. Quoted by Buttafuoco, *Le Mariuccine,* p. 352. See also pp. 272, 347–58.

39. Joly, "Les Maisons du Bon-Pasteur," p. 303, and for training in skills at the refuges, pp. 299–305. On the question of reinsertion, see also Gaillac, *Les Maisons,* pp. 116, 127.

40. Gaillac, *Les Maisons,* pp. 115–16; Bristow, *Vice and Vigilance,* p. 69; Buttafuoco, *Le Mariuccine,* p. 261; Wood, "Prostitution Debates in Soviet Russia," pp. 45–46.

41. Aleil, "Le Refuge," p. 54; Ruggles, "Fallen Women," p. 69; Bernocchi, *Prostituzione e rieducazione,* p. 140; Buttafuoco, *Le Mariuccine,* pp. 447–48.

42. Buttafuoco, *Le Mariuccine,* pp. 32, 272.

43. Ibid., p. 313; Ruggles, "Fallen Women," p. 79, n. 17.

44. Carlisle, "Prostitutes and Reformers," p. 135, relates that this change had occurred by 1880 at Philadelphia's Magdalen Asylum, Rosine House, and House of the Good Shepherd. Although the founders of the Rosine House hoped to preside

over an institution with voluntary entrances and departures, even in the house's early years they were willing to receive girls compelled to remain for finite periods by terms of "indenture" or judicial orders. See *Reports and Realities,* pp. 88–89, 101.

45. The escapee from the House of Mercy is quoted in Bristow, *Vice and Vigilance,* p. 68. For prostitutes' negative or ambivalent attitudes toward asylums, see ibid., p. 67; Godden, "Sectarianism," pp. 303–4; Ruth Rosen, *The Lost Sisterhood: Prostitution in America, 1900–1918* (Baltimore: Johns Hopkins University Press, 1982), p. 31; Bernocchi, *Prostituzione e rieducazione,* p. 152.

46. Quoted in Frances Finnegan, *Poverty and Prostitution: A Study of Victorian Prostitutes in York* (Cambridge: Cambridge University Press, 1979), p. 199; see also pp. 210–11.

47. For former prostitutes starting refuges or desiring to start them, see Bellini, "Misure di prevenzione," pp. 1137–38, on the Empress Theodora in sixth-century Byzantium; Pullan, *Rich and Poor,* pp. 391–92; Rosen, *Lost Sisterhood,* pp. 66, 165; Joly, "Les Maisons du Bon-Pasteur," p. 287. The comments by residents of the Asilo Mariuccia were quoted by Buttafuoco, *Le Mariuccine,* pp. 287, 297; on incest, see in the same source pp. 477, 108–22; on requests for readmission, pp. 299, 320, 337. The article cited in n. 23, "Project Shows Hookers a Way Out," relates that 70 to 85 percent of the 49 women who lived at the Mary Magdalene Project in Los Angeles in 1980–85 were victims of incest. For similar evidence about both incest and requests for readmission, see Carlisle, "Prostitutes and Reformers," pp. 196–203.

Chapter 7

1. Biffi, *Sui riformatori,* p. 90.

2. Spierenburg, "Sociogenesis of Confinement," p. 60; Sellin, "Dom Jean Mabillon," p. 601. For a general overview of penal history, see Max Grünhut, *Penal Reform: A Comparative Study* (Oxford: Clarendon Press, 1948).

3. Jones, "Prostitution and the Ruling Class," p. 15; Erica-Marie Benabou, *La Prostitution et la police des mœurs au XVIIIᵉ siècle* (Paris: Librairie Académique Perrin, 1987), pp. 84–85; Otis, *Prostitution in Medieval Society,* p. 197, n. 128; Nash, "Prostitution and Charity," pp. 618, 623–24.

4. *New Catholic Encyclopedia,* s.v. "Penance (in the Bible)" and "Penance, sacramental."

5. See Compston, *Magdalen Hospital,* p. 151, on the institution's public fame, pp. 145–46 on Hanway, and p. 91 on the Church Penitentiary Association; Michael Ignatieff, *A Just Measure of Pain: The Penitentiary in the Industrial Revolution, 1750–1850* (Harmondsworth: Penguin Books, 1978), pp. 54, 93–109; Foucault, *Discipline and Punish,* pp. 122–23, 314, n. 13; Grünhut, *Penal Reform,* pp. 31, 36, quoting Hanway and Howard on solitary confinement and repentance; Jonas Hanway, *Solitude in Imprisonment* (London: J. Bew, 1776), pp. 29, 33, 111–24; Sellin, *Pioneering in Penology,* p. 107; John Howard, *The State of the Prisons in England and Wales, with Preliminary Observations, and an Account of Some Foreign Prisons and Hospitals,* 3d ed. (Warrington: William Eyres, 1784), pp. 114, 172; and L'Espérance, "Woman's Mission," p. 320, on the London Female Penitentiary.

6. Carlisle, "Prostitutes and Reformers," p. 156; Ignatieff, *Just Measure,* p. 64.

7. Léon Faucher, *De la réforme des prisons* (Paris: Angé, 1838), p. 39; emphasis added.

8. Ibid., pp. 129, 5. For the Biblical topos and Catholic refuges, see above, chapters 1 and 5; for a Protestant case, see *Reports and Realities,* p. 160.

9. Faucher, *Réforme des prisons,* pp. 115, 119; Carlo Ilarione Petitti di Roreto, "Della condizione attuale delle carceri e dei mezzi di migliorarla," in *Opere scelte,* ed. Gian Mario Bravo, 2 vols. (Turin: Fondazione Luigi Einaudi, 1969), 1:399, on a women's prison in Baden; Melossi and Pavarini, *Prison and Factory,* p. 87. On Rome's Buon Pastore, see Biffi, *Sui riformatori,* p. 154; Angela Groppi, " 'Un pezzo di mercanzia di cui il mercante fa quel che ne vuole.' Carriera di un'internata tra Buon Pastore e manicomio," *Annali della Fondazione Lelio e Lisli Basso-Issoco* 7 (1985): 189–224.

10. Melossi and Pavarini, *Prison and Factory,* p. 126.

11. On labor in prisons, see Grünhut, *Penal Reform,* pp. 196–228, and Melossi and Pavarini, *Prison and Factory,* pp. 1–95. On solitary confinement, see Ignatieff, *Just Measure,* pp. 49, 53–54.

12. O'Brien, *Promise of Punishment,* pp. 71–72; Russell P. Dobash, R. Emerson Dobash, and Sue Gutteridge, *The Imprisonment of Women* (Oxford: Basil Blackwell, 1986), pp. 63–65; Melossi and Pavarini, *Prison and Factory,* pp. 212–13, n. 54. For a house of correction in Turin in the late 1830s that kept prostitutes in solitary confinement for at least one month, see Claudio Cagliero, Barbara Maffiodo, and Luigi Tavolaccini, "L'organizzazione di alcune istituzioni di assistenza e di controllo," *Rivista di storia contemporanea* 11 (July 1982): 385–86.

13. Nicole Hahn Rafter, "Prisons for Women, 1790–1980," in *Crime and Justice: An Annual Review of Research,* vol. 5, ed. Michael Tonry and Norval Morris (Chicago: University of Chicago Press, 1983), p. 174. Cf. O'Brien, *Promise of Punishment,* pp. 50, 74, who does not perceive significant differences in the treatment of the sexes in French prisons. However, her evidence can support the opposite conclusion. See Rothman, *Discovery of the Asylum,* pp. 102–6, for the lash and lockstep in American penitentiaries.

14. Rafter, "Prisons for Women," p. 174.

15. O'Brien, *Promise of Punishment,* pp. 54–61, 68–71, 213–17; Ignatieff, *Just Measure,* pp. 120–23; Melossi and Pavarini, *Prison and Factory,* pp. 57–59; Sonia Ambroset, *Criminologia femminile: Il controllo sociale* (Milan: Edizioni Unicopli, 1984), p. 60; Estelle B. Freedman, *Their Sisters' Keepers: Women's Prison Reform in America, 1830–1930* (Ann Arbor: University of Michigan Press, 1981), pp. 10–21; Rafter, "Prisons for Women," pp. 134–35, 143; Gibson, "Female Offender," pp. 161–63. On nuns as surveillants, in addition to O'Brien and Ambroset, see Gaillac, *Les Maisons,* pp. 131–36; Angela Groppi, "Una gestione collettiva di equilibri emozionali e materiali. La reclusione delle donne nella Roma dell'Ottocento," in *Ragnatele di rapporti: Patronage e reti di relazione nella storia delle donne,* ed. Lucia Ferrante, Maura Palazzi, and Gianna Pomata (Turin: Rosenberg & Sellier, 1988), pp. 139–40. Monks guarded males in a few European prisons, but this practice was far eclipsed in scale by the widespread presence of nuns as guards in women's prisons. On the monks of Saint Joseph in Lyons, see Petitti di Roreto, "Della condizione," p. 387.

16. Nash, "Prostitution and Charity," p. 622; Buttafuoco, *Le Mariuccine,* pp. 32, 272.

17. O'Brien, *Promise of Punishment,* pp. 213–17, 226–57; Potter, *Sisterhoods and Deaconesses,* p. 304; Gaillac, *Les Maisons,* pp. 125, 144, 131–36; Biffi, *Sui riformatori,* p. 32; Ambroset, *Criminologia femminile,* p. 62. On parole, in addition to O'Brien see Ignatieff, *Just Measure,* pp. 201–5; David J. Rothman, *Conscience and Convenience:*

The Asylum and Its Alternatives in Progressive America (Boston: Little, Brown, 1980), pp. 44, 68–81.

18. Foucault, *Discipline and Punish,* pp. 297–99.

19. Biffi, *Sui riformatori,* pp. 81–82.

20. Spierenburg, "Sociogenesis of Confinement," pp. 45–46; Sellin, *Pioneering in Penology,* pp. 18–19, 80–86; Thorsten Sellin, "Filippo Franci—A Precursor of Modern Penology," *Journal of the American Institute of Criminal Law and Criminology* 17 (1926–27): 104–12.

21. John R. Gillis, *Youth and History: Tradition and Change in European Age Relations, 1770–Present* (New York: Academic Press, 1974), pp. 22–34, 95–183; Anthony M. Platt, *The Child Savers: The Invention of Delinquency,* 2d ed., enl. (Chicago: University of Chicago Press, 1977); Joseph M. Hawes, *Children in Urban Society: Juvenile Delinquency in Nineteenth-Century America* (New York: Oxford University Press, 1971).

22. Lombardi, *Povertà maschile,* p. 206, n. 122; Nash, "Prostitution and Charity," p. 619; Carlisle, "Prostitutes and Reformers," pp. 190–93.

23. Gaillac, *Les Maisons,* pp. 116–17, 143, 171–75; Biffi, *Sui riformatori,* pp. 139–40; Katherine G. Aiken, "The National Florence Crittenton Mission, 1883–1925: A Case Study in Progressive Reform" (Ph.D. diss., Washington State University, 1980), pp. 104–9, 200; Joly, "Les Maisons du Bon-Pasteur," p. 295.

24. Aleil, "Le Refuge," pp. 44, 52, 28.

25. Whether they served as de facto prisons or not, women's asylums were sometimes likened to prisons or jails. Reformers in nineteenth-century Philadelphia noted that the prostitutes they attempted to rescue regarded "all asylums as prisons," and their later counterparts in Milan likewise found that some of the residents termed the Asilo Mariuccia a "jail." See Miriam King, " 'They Regard All Missionaries as Enemies and All Asylums as Prisons': Prostitutes' Response to Reform in Nineteenth-Century Philadelphia," paper presented at "Feminism and Its Transitions" conference, Princeton, N.J., March 1987; Buttafuoco, *Le Mariuccine,* pp. 307 (*galera*) and 314 (*gabbia*).

26. Mary Elizabeth Perry, "With Brave Vigilance and a Hundred Eyes: The Making of Women's Prisons in Counter-Reformation Spain," *Women & Criminal Justice* 2 (Fall 1990): 3–17, and personal communication of 21 April 1990; O'Brien, *Promise of Punishment,* p. 62, n. 14; Adolphe Guillot, *Les Prisons de Paris et les prisonniers* (Paris: E. Dentu, 1890), pp. 73–75; Jill Harsin, *Policing Prostitution in Nineteenth-Century Paris* (Princeton, N.J.: Princeton University Press, 1985), pp. 12, 215.

27. Harsin, *Policing Prostitution,* p. 215. On lock hospitals, infirmary-prisons, and police-wards, see Walkowitz, *Prostitution and Victorian Society,* pp. 214–32; F. Montanyà, "L'Hospital de la Magdalena" (1931), as excerpted in Mary Nash, *Mujer, familia y trabajo en España (1875–1936)* (Barcelona: Anthropos, 1983), pp. 263–66; Alain Corbin, *Les Filles de noce: misère sexuelle et prostitution (19e et 20e siècles)* (Paris: Aubier Montaigne, 1978), pp. 131–52; Gibson, *Prostitution and the State,* pp. 191–99; Elizabeth Meyer-Renschhausen, "The Bremen Morality Scandal," in *When Biology Became Destiny: Women in Weimar and Nazi Germany,* ed. Renate Bridenthal, Atina Grossman, and Marion Kaplan (New York: Monthly Review Press, 1984), pp. 87–108.

28. Wilson, *Fifty Years' Work,* pp. 58–59, 245; Mark Thomas Connelly, *The Response to Prostitution in the Progressive Era* (Chapel Hill: University of North Carolina Press, 1980), pp. 143–46. See also Freedman, *Sisters' Keepers,* p. 129, on the internments of prostitutes in asylums for wayward females in New York City during the Progressive era.

29. Ignatieff, *Just Measure,* pp. 143–45; Prochaska, *Women and Philanthropy,* p. 169; Freedman, *Sisters' Keepers,* pp. 28–64, 90–95.

30. O'Brien, *Promise of Punishment,* p. 61; Ambroset, *Criminologia femminile,* p. 60; Freedman, *Sisters' Keepers,* pp. 48–52; Groppi, "Un pezzo di mercanzia," p. 205.

31. Hodder is quoted in Rosen, *Lost Sisterhood,* p. 21. For Lowell, see Freedman, *Sisters' Keepers,* pp. 35, 48–49, 56–57; Mrs. Charles Russell Lowell (Josephine Shaw Lowell), "Houses of Refuge for Women: Their Purposes, Management and Possibilities," in *Women in Prison, 1834–1928,* ed. David J. Rothman and Sheila M. Rothman (New York: Garland Publishing, 1987), pp. 245–56.

32. See Nicole Hahn Rafter, *Partial Justice: Women in State Prisons, 1800–1935* (Boston: Northeastern University Press, 1985), p. 25, for the quotation and, generally, pp. 24–28, 35. See also Grünhut, *Penal Reform,* pp. 66–68, 89–94. On the State Industrial School for Girls in Lancaster, see Barbara M. Brenzel, *Daughters of the State: A Social Portrait of the First Reform School for Girls in North America, 1856–1905* (Cambridge, Mass.: MIT Press, 1983).

33. Hawes, *Children in Urban Society,* pp. 146–53; Rothman, *Conscience and Convenience,* p. 44; Grünhut, *Penal Reform,* p. 381.

34. Rafter, *Partial Justice,* pp. 35–38, 182–84; Freedman, *Sisters' Keepers,* p. 148; Clarice Feinman, *Women in the Criminal Justice System,* 2d ed. (New York: Praeger, 1986), pp. 8–10, 45, 60–63.

35. Quoted by Gabriella Parca, *Voci dal carcere femminile* (Rome: Editori Riuniti, 1973), p. 193. See also ibid., pp. 15–17, 23–25; Silvana Bevione, "Le carceri femminili tra passato e futuro," *Argomenti radicali,* no. 7 (1978), pp. 75–80; Franca Faccioli, "Il 'comando' difficile. Considerazioni su donne e controllo nel carcere femminile," in *Diritto e rovescio,* ed. Tamar Pitch, pp. 117–39; Ambroset, *Criminologia femminile,* p. 65.

36. Hobson, *Uneasy Virtue,* pp. 112, 124–36, also makes this argument.

37. Phyllis Stock, *Better Than Rubies: A History of Women's Education* (New York: G. P. Putnam's Sons, 1978), pp. 59–80.

38. Judith Combes Taylor, "From Proselytizing to Social Reform: Three Generations of French Female Teaching Congregations, 1600–1720" (Ph.D. diss., 2 vols., Arizona State University, 1980), 1:2–7, 222–31, 264–72, 295–305, 319–29. See also Elizabeth Rapley, *The Dévotes: Women and Church in Seventeenth-Century France* (Kingston, Ontario: McGill-Queen's University Press, 1990).

39. Aleil, "Le Refuge," pp. 25–30, 32–33.

40. Biffi, *Sui riformatori,* pp. 93–95; *Dizionario degli istituti di perfezione,* s.v. "Buon Samaritano."

41. Antonio Illibato, *La dónna a Napoli nel Settecento: Aspetti della condizione e dell'istruzione femminile* (Naples: M. D'Auria Editore, 1985), pp. 36–38, 55–75; Laura Guidi, "Il manto della Madonna: L'immagine femminile nei conservatori napoletani dell'Ottocento," *Memoria* 11–12 (1984): 65–81; Pelliccia, Introduction to Masetti Zannini, *Motivi storici della educazione,* pp. ix–xiv; Fabio Saccà, "L'assistenza alle ragazze del conservatorio di S. Giovanni in Laterano nel corso del XVIII secolo," *Storia e politica* 21 (1982): 438–79.

42. Fiorenza Gemini and Eugenio Sonnino, "La Condition féminine dans une structure d'assistance à Rome: aspects démographiques et sociaux," *Annales de démographie historique* (1981), pp. 236–38.

43. See Bargiacchi, *Storia degli istituti,* 4:6–181, on the evolution of education for girls in Tuscany; Illibato, *La donna a Napoli,* pp. 80–88.

44. On the conservatory in Prato, see Porciani, *Le donne a scuola,* pp. 151–52, 130–34, and Andreucci, *Nuove osservazioni,* p. 41, n. 2. On the Rosine, see *Dizionario degli istituti di perfezione,* s.v. "Rosine." On the conservatory in Como and other women's asylums that trained residents to be teachers, see Biffi, *Sui riformatori,* pp. 122–23, 132–33.

45. Porciani, *Le donne a scuola,* pp. 81–86; Silvia Franchini, "L'istruzione femminile in Italia dopo l'Unità: Percorsi di una ricerca sugli educandati pubblici di élite," *Passato e presente* 10 (1986): 67, 83–94; Stock, *Better Than Rubies,* pp. 126–94, 213–31. A critique of conservatories for not producing good wives and mothers is quoted by Andreucci, *Nuove osservazioni,* p. 10.

46. Stock, *Better Than Rubies,* pp. 59–74.

47. Jonas Hanway, *Thoughts on the Plan for a Magdalen-House for Repentant Prostitutes,* 2d ed., enl. (London: J. & R. Dodsley, 1759), p. 53; italics deleted. On the Lambeth Asylum, see Andrew, *Philanthropy and Police,* pp. 115–19.

48. Catherine M. Prelinger, *Charity, Challenge, and Change: Religious Dimensions of the Mid-Nineteenth-Century Women's Movement in Germany* (New York: Greenwood Press, 1987), pp. 1–28; Sherrin Marshall, *The Dutch Gentry, 1500–1650: Family, Faith, and Fortune* (New York: Greenwood Press, 1987), p. 89, on communities of "holy virgins"; Roper, *Holy Household,* pp. 244–51, on communities of "soul-women"; Merry E. Wiesner, *Working Women in Renaissance Germany* (New Brunswick, N.J.: Rutgers University Press, 1986), pp. 77–78, 101; Vicinus, *Independent Women,* p. 165.

49. Anna B. Pratt, "An Old Society Rejuvenates Itself," *Better Times,* February 1929, pp. 12–14; Wilson, *Fifty Years' Work,* p. 72; Aiken, "Florence Crittenton," pp. 161–62.

50. On the YMCA and on differing attitudes toward aiding single men and single women, see Joanne J. Meyerowitz, *Women Adrift: Independent Wage Earners in Chicago, 1880–1930* (Chicago: University of Chicago Press, 1988), pp. 53–54, 65. For an analysis of how single male newcomers to cities were served by the creation of nonresidential institutions, see Allan Stanley Horlick, *Country Boys and Merchant Princes: The Social Control of Young Men in New York* (Lewisburg, Pa.: Bucknell University Press, 1975). On social purity movements, in addition to Bristow's *Vice and Vigilance,* see David J. Pivar, *Purity Crusade: Sexual Morality and Social Control, 1868–1900* (Westport, Conn.: Greenwood Press, 1973).

51. *Chicago Whip,* 22 May 1920.

52. The American writer is quoted in Meyerowitz, *Women Adrift,* p. 55; the Toronto YWCA is quoted in Wendy Mitchinson, "The YWCA and Reform in the Nineteenth Century," *Histoire sociale—Social History* 12 (November 1979): 380–81. See also Alice Klein and Wayne Roberts, "Besieged Innocence: The 'Problem' and the Problems of Working Women—Toronto, 1896–1914," in *Women at Work: Ontario, 1850–1930,* ed. Janice Acton, Penny Goldsmith, and Bonnie Shepard (Toronto: Canadian Women's Educational Press, 1974), pp. 233–36.

53. For company housing, see Thomas Dublin, *Women at Work: The Transformation of Work and Community in Lowell, Massachusetts, 1826–1860* (New York: Columbia University Press, 1979), pp. 75–85; Meyerowitz, *Women Adrift,* pp. 78–79; Jacques Donzelot, *The Policing of Families,* trans. Robert Hurley (New York: Pantheon Books, 1979), pp. 37–40 (originally published as *La Police des familles* [Paris: Les Editions de Minuit, 1977]); Buttafuoco, *Le Mariuccine,* pp. 347–58, 370; Derek S. Linton, "Between School and Marriage, Workshop and Household: Young Working

Women as a Social Problem in Late Imperial Germany," *European History Quarterly* 18 (October 1988): 393. On lodgings for female travelers, see Lynn Y. Weiner, *From Working Girl to Working Mother: The Female Labor Force in the United States, 1820–1980* (Chapel Hill: University of North Carolina Press, 1985), pp. 49–52. On dormitories in women's colleges, see Helen Lefkowitz Horowitz, *Alma Mater: Design and Experience in the Women's Colleges from Their Nineteenth-Century Beginnings to the 1930s* (New York: Knopf, 1984), pp. 314–16.

54. Taylor, "From Proselytizing," 2:432–33, 518–59; Smith Rosenberg, *Religion and the Rise*, pp. 206–17; Sheila Jeffreys, " 'Free from All Uninvited Touch of Man': Women's Campaigns Around Sexuality, 1880–1914," *Women's Studies International Forum* 5 (1982): 634; *Reports and Realities*, pp. 41, 108; Joly, "Les Maisons du Bon-Pasteur," pp. 306–7 on the "asile Sainte-Marthe." For a seventeenth-century French group called the Daughters of Saint Martha, see Taylor, "From Proselytizing," 2:520.

55. Prochaska, *Women and Philanthropy*, p. 183; Weiner, *From Working Girl*, pp. 52–60. For a YWCA hotel in Paris, see Karen Sue Mittelman, " 'A Spirit That Touches the Problems of Today': Women and Social Reform in the Philadelphia Young Women's Christian Association, 1920–1945" (Ph.D. diss., University of Pennsylvania, 1987), p. 133. See also Meyer-Renschhausen, "Bremen Scandal," p. 96; Marion Kaplan, "Prostitution, Morality Crusades and Feminism: German-Jewish Feminists and the Campaign Against White Slavery," *Women's Studies International Forum* 5 (1982): 624.

56. The first statement is quoted in Lynn Weiner, " 'Our Sister's Keepers': The Minneapolis Woman's Christian Association and Housing for Working Women," *Minnesota History* 46 (Spring 1979): 193; the second, in Mittelman, "A Spirit," p. 238; the third, in Dolores Hayden, *The Grand Domestic Revolution: A History of Feminist Designs for American Homes, Neighborhoods and Cities* (Cambridge, Mass.: MIT Press, 1981), p. 168. Cf. an African-American journalist's approving description of "the cloistered walls of the Y.W.C.A.," in *Chicago Whip*, 5 August 1922.

57. Buttafuoco, *Le Mariuccine*, p. 56; *Dizionario degli istituti di perfezione*, s.v. "Rosine."

58. Vicinus, *Independent Women*, pp. 295–99; Meyerowitz, *Women Adrift*, pp. 96–98; Hayden, *Domestic Revolution*, pp. 167–71, 254.

59. "Women's Home Ousting Old-Timers," *New York Times*, 8 February 1985, sec. B. The quoted statement was made by Canadian architect Linda Baker, interviewed in Hinda Avery, "Sitka Housing Co-operative: Women House Themselves," *Women and Environments* 11 (Winter 1989): 23. See also in this issue p. 25, Barbara Sanford, "W[omen] I[n] T[oronto] C[reating] H[ousing]."

60. For early modern asylums for unwed mothers and other institutions that sheltered such women, see Ambroset, *Criminologia femminile*, p. 51, on the Casa di Santa Maria del Soccorso in sixteenth-century Ferrara; Sellin, "Filippo Franci," p. 107, and Lombardi, *Povertà maschile*, pp. 199–200, on the Ospedale di San Filippo Neri in seventeenth-century Florence; Joan Sherwood, *Poverty in Eighteenth-Century Spain: The Women and Children of the Inclusa* (Toronto: University of Toronto Press, 1988), p. 107, on the Desamparados in seventeenth-century Madrid; Pérez Baltasar, *Mujeres marginadas*, pp. 81–85, on a *reclusorio* annexed to the Casa de Recogidas in eighteenth-century Madrid; Benabou, *Prostitution et la police*, p. 90, on Sainte-Pélagie in eighteenth-century Paris; Mary Lindemann, "Maternal Politics: The Principles and Practice of Maternity Care in Eighteenth-Century Hamburg," *Journal of Family History* 9 (Spring 1984): 54–61, on the Lying-In Ward; Trexler, "Widows' Asylum," pp.

142–43, on the transformation of the Orbatello into a place of internment for unmarried pregnant women in the eighteenth century.

61. On changing perceptions of female and male sexuality, see Thomas Laqueur, *Making Sex: Body and Gender from the Greeks to Freud* (Cambridge, Mass.: Harvard University Press, 1990), especially pp. 3–4. On rising illegitimacy, see Joan Jacobs Brumberg, " 'Ruined' Girls: Changing Community Responses to Illegitimacy in Upstate New York, 1890–1920," *Journal of Social History* 18 (Winter 1984): 248–51; Louise A. Tilly, Joan W. Scott, and Miriam Cohen, "Women's Work and European Fertility Patterns," *Journal of Interdisciplinary History* 6 (Winter 1976): 463–76.

62. Hobson, *Uneasy Virtue,* pp. 60, 121; Ann Rowell Higginbotham, "The Unmarried Mother and Her Child in Victorian London, 1834–1914" (Ph.D. diss., Indiana University, 1985), p. 101.

63. On the Salvation Army, see Fairbank, *Booth's Boots,* pp. 27–40. For a Salvation Army confinement home in the United States, see Mabel Agnes Elliott, "Correctional Education and the Delinquent Girl," in *Women in Prison,* ed. David J. Rothman and Sheila M. Rothman, p. 36. On Germany, see Kaplan, "Prostitution, Morality Crusades," p. 625; Amy Hackett, "Helene Stöcker: Left-Wing Intellectual and Sex Reformer," in *When Biology Became Destiny,* ed. Renate Bridenthal, Atina Grossman, and Marion Kaplan, p. 113, where the author argues that the feminist maternity homes were meant as alternatives to the "Christian Magdalene homes with their obligatory moralizing." For the YWCA, see Sims, *Natural History: YWCA,* p. 13.

64. Wilson, *Fifty Years' Work,* pp. 59–60, 14–15, 88; Aiken, "Florence Crittenton," pp. 53–54, 74–75, 197–98, 221–24. For other ex-prostitutes' asylums that turned into maternity homes, see Hobson, *Uneasy Virtue,* pp. 123, 129.

65. Henri Joly, *A la recherche de l'éducation correctionnelle à travers l'Europe* (Paris: Librairie Victor Lecoffre, 1902), pp. 252–68; Brumberg, "Ruined Girls," pp. 253, 263; Michael W. Sedlak, "Young Women and the City: Adolescent Deviance and the Transformation of Educational Policy, 1870–1960," *History of Education Quarterly* 23 (1983): 1–28.

66. Ambroset, *Criminologia femminile,* pp. 51–52; Gianna Pomata, "Madri illegittime tra Ottocento e Novecento: Storie cliniche e storie di vita," *Quaderni storici* 44 (August 1980): 497–542; Maricla Boggio, *Ragazza madre: Storie di donne e dei loro bambini* (Venice: Marsilio, 1975), pp. 198–213; Pérez Baltasar, *Mujeres marginadas,* p. 115; Joly, *A la recherche,* pp. 192–93, for the refuge in Montpellier; Brumberg, "Ruined Girls," pp. 250–51; Robert South Barrett, *The Care of the Unmarried Mother* (1929; New York: Garland Publishing, 1987), pp. 55, 160.

67. "Anti-Abortion Revival: Homes for the Unwed," *New York Times,* 23 July 1989, sec. 1; "Abortion Foes' Centers Guiding Lives after Births," *New York Times,* 13 May 1990, sec. 1.

68. The first statement was quoted by Liane V. Davis, "Battered Women: The Transformation of a Social Problem," *Social Work* 32 (July/August 1987): 308; the second statement is her own comment, on p. 311.

69. Ferrante, "Malmaritate tra assistenza," pp. 90–91; Lastri, *L'osservatore fiorentino,* 3:125; Yannick Ripa, *La Ronde des folles: femme, folie et enfermement au XIXᵉ siècle (1838–1870)* (Paris: Aubier, 1986), p. 83 (for "mal mariées").

70. Elizabeth Pleck, *Domestic Tyranny: The Making of American Social Policy Against Family Violence from Colonial Times to the Present* (New York: Oxford University Press, 1987), pp. 63–64, 57, 96.

71. Pleck, *Domestic Tyranny,* pp. 188–92.

72. Del Martin, *Battered Wives*, rev., updated ed. (San Francisco: Volcano Press, 1981), pp. xi, 225–32; Olga J. Zoomer, "Policing Wife Beating in the Netherlands," in *Women, Policing, and Male Violence: International Perspectives,* ed. Jalna Hanmer, Jill Radford, and Elizabeth A. Stanko (London: Routledge, 1989), pp. 125, 131–32; Sarah Haffner, ed., *Frauenhäuser: Gewalt in der Ehe und was Frauen dagegen tun* (Berlin: Verlag Klaus Wagenbach, 1976), pp. 123–58; Marianne Pletscher, *Weggehen ist nicht so einfach: Gewalt gegen Frauen in der Schweiz. Gespräche und Informationen* (Zurich: Limmat Verlag Genossenschaft, 1977), pp. 73–91, 102; Marie-Thérèse Meulders, "La Violence au sein du couple: ébauches de réponses juridiques en droit continental," in *Family Violence: An International and Interdisciplinary Study,* ed. John M. Eekelaar and Sanford N. Katz (Toronto: Butterworths, 1978), p. 166, on Belgium; Maria Amélia Azevedo Goldberg, *Mulheres espancadas: A violência denunciada* (São Paulo: Cortez Editora, 1985), p. 30, on Spain; Tamar Pitch, "Tra diritti sociali e cittadinanza. Il movimento delle donne e la legge sulla violenza sessuale," *Problemi del socialismo* 27/28 (1983): n. 2; Sherry Galey, "Survivors of Violence: Global Organizing," *Women and Environments* 10 (Fall 1987): 9–10, and also on p. 10, "Fighting Violence in the Global Village."

73. See Kathleen J. Tierney, "The Battered Women Movement and the Creation of the Wife Beating Problem," *Social Problems* 29 (1982): 207, on the antialcoholism shelters; Pletscher, *Weggehen ist nicht,* p. 102.

74. See Marlena Studer, "Wife Beating as a Social Problem: The Process of Definition," *International Journal of Women's Studies* 7 (1984): 418, on the differences between "reformist" and "radical" feminists. See also Martin, *Battered Wives,* pp. 219–22; Meulders, "La Violence," p. 166; Pleck, *Domestic Tyranny,* pp. 193–98; Schur, *Labeling Women Deviant,* p. 163.

75. On Fields, see Beverly Jacobson, "Battered Women: The Fight to End Wife-beating," *Civil Rights Digest* 9 (Summer 1977): 11. On the batterers' house, see Joy Melville, "A Note on 'Men's Aid,' " in *Violence and the Family,* ed. J. P. Martin (Chichester: John Wiley & Sons, 1978), pp. 311–13. On treatment of batterers worldwide, see *Violence Against Women in the Family* (New York: United Nations, 1989), p. 79. I am grateful to Richard Shapiro, formerly of the New Jersey Public Advocate, for his useful comments about shelters.

76. Studer, "Wife Beating as a Social Problem," p. 420.

77. Susan B. Murray, "The Unhappy Marriage of Theory and Practice: An Analysis of a Battered Women's Shelter," *NWSA Journal* 1 (1988): 75–92.

78. Roderick Phillips, *Putting Asunder: A History of Divorce in Western Society* (Cambridge: Cambridge University Press, 1988), pp. 40–94, 572–81.

79. On reuses of convents, in addition to the examples in this chapter, see Osanna Fantozzi Micali and Piero Roselli, *Le soppressioni dei conventi a Firenze: Riuso e trasformazioni dal sec. XVIII in poi* (Florence: Libreria Editrice Fiorentina, 1980); Biffi, *Sui riformatori,* pp. 123, 139–40. On the colleges, see Horowitz, *Alma Mater,* p. 4. For an argument similar to mine about the interrelatedness of women's asylums, see Peggy Pascoe, *Relations of Rescue: The Search for Female Moral Authority in the American West, 1874–1939* (New York: Oxford University Press, 1990).

80. On the Montpellier asylum, see Joly, *A la recherche,* p. 191. For the quotation regarding Saint Mary's, see "Women's Home Ousting Old-Timers," *New York Times,* 8 February 1985, sec. B. On the Vancouver cooperative, see Avery, "Sitka Housing Co-operative," p. 21. For the quotation on shelters, see "Partners for Change: An

Agenda for Planners, Designers and Feminist Activists," *Women and Environments* 8 (Spring 1986): 9 (emphasis added).

Conclusion

1. On the tendency to "see prostitutes everywhere," see Harsin, *Policing Prostitution,* pp. xviii, 241, 252; Walkowitz, *Prostitution and Victorian Society,* p. 80.

2. The first phrase was quoted by Faccioli, "Il 'comando' difficile," p. 122; the second by Andreucci, *Nuove osservazioni,* p. 10; the third by Betty Friedan, "Twenty Years After the Feminine Mystique," *New York Times Magazine,* 27 February 1983, p. 42.

3. Zarri, "Monasteri femminili," pp. 362–64; Trexler, "Le Célibat," pp. 1348–49.

4. Margarita Nelken, *La condición social de la mujer en España. Su estado actual: su posible desarrollo* (1919), as excerpted in Nash, *Mujer, familia y trabajo,* pp. 259–60; Perry, "Deviant Insiders," p. 158.

5. Lombardi, *Povertà maschile,* pp. 135–36, 208.

6. O'Brien, *Promise of Punishment,* pp. 119–20; Biffi, *Sui riformatori,* p. 54; Groppi, "Una gestione colletiva," p. 133.

7. Steven Schlossman and Stephanie Wallach, "The Crime of Precocious Sexuality: Female Juvenile Delinquency in the Progressive Era," *Harvard Educational Review* 48 (February 1978): 72–73, 82, 76; Randall G. Shelden, "Sex Discrimination in the Juvenile Justice System: Memphis, Tennessee, 1900–1917," in *Comparing Female and Male Offenders,* ed. Marguerite Q. Warren (Beverly Hills, Calif.: Sage Publications, 1981), pp. 67, 57; Schur, *Labeling Women Deviant,* pp. 223–24; M. A. Bertrand, "Le Caractère discriminatoire et inique de la justice pour mineurs: les filles dites 'délinquants' au Canada," *Déviance et société* 2 (1977): 187–202; Lesley Shacklady Smith, "Sexist Assumptions and Female Delinquency: An Empirical Investigation," in *Women, Sexuality and Social Control,* ed. Carol Smart and Barry Smart (London: Routledge & Kegan Paul, 1978), p. 82; Barbara Hudson, "Justice or Welfare? A Comparison of Recent Developments in the English and French Juvenile Justice Systems," in *Growing Up Good: Policing the Behaviour of Girls in Europe,* ed. Maureen Cain (London: SAGE, 1989), p. 102.

8. "Drug Use in Pregnancy: New Issue for the Courts," *New York Times,* 5 February 1990, sec. A; "Racial Bias Seen on Pregnant Addicts," *New York Times,* 20 July 1990, sec. A.

9. Mrs. O'Reilly is quoted by Donald G. Wetherell, "To Discipline and Train: Adult Rehabilitation Programmes in Ontario Prisons, 1874–1900," *Histoire sociale— Social History* 12 (May 1979): 162. The quotation from Lowell is in Rafter, "Prisons for Women," p. 158.

10. Elaine Showalter, *The Female Malady: Women, Madness, and English Culture, 1830–1980* (1985; New York: Viking Penguin, 1987), pp. 3, 52; Ripa, *La Ronde des folles,* pp. 9, 187, 17–18, 26–28, 68–83.

11. Groppi, "Una gestione collettiva," p. 130. See also Laura Guidi, *L'onore in pericolo. Carità e reclusione femminile nell'Ottocento napoletano* (Naples: Liguori, 1991).

12. Groppi, "Un pezzo di mercanzia," pp. 204, 207.

13. Elizabeth Lunbeck, " 'A New Generation of Women': Progressive Psychia-

trists and the Hypersexual Female," *Feminist Studies* 13 (1987): 513–43; Rafter, *Partial Justice*, pp. 67–74. For the testing of prostitutes, see Rosen, *Lost Sisterhood*, p. 22. The quotation is from Brenzel, *Daughters of the State*, p. 158.

14. Ambroset, *Criminologia femminile*, p. 105; Phyllis Chesler, *Women and Madness* (Garden City, N.Y.: Doubleday, 1972), especially pp. 5–17, 32–57; Showalter, *Female Malady*, p. 3. For the above-mentioned commitments, see Linda Gordon, *Heroes of Their Own Lives: The Politics and History of Family Violence* (New York: Viking Penguin, 1988), p. 277; Diana E. H. Russell, Introduction to Martin, *Battered Wives*, p. xi; Giuliana Morandini, . . . *E allora mi hanno rinchiusa* (Milan: Gruppo Editoriale Fabbri, Bompiani, Sonzogno, Etas, 1977), pp. 34, 38.

15. Franca Ongaro Basaglia, Preface to Morandini, *Mi hanno rinchiusa*, p. v.

16. Katz, "Origins of the Institutional State," p. 9.

17. Joan Wallach Scott, *Gender and the Politics of History* (New York: Columbia University Press, 1988), p. 38, in the essay "Gender: A Useful Category of Historical Analysis" (emphasis added).

18. In formulating my thoughts about women and institutionalization, I have been helped by the following sources: Carol Smart and Barry Smart, "Women and Social Control: An Introduction," in *Women, Sexuality and Social Control*, ed. Carol Smart and Barry Smart, pp. 1–7; Tamar Pitch, " 'There but for fortune . . .': Le donne e il controllo sociale," in *Diritto e rovescio*, ed. Tamar Pitch, pp. 5–36; Ambroset, *Criminologia femminile*, especially pp. 39–68; Groppi, "Una gestione collettiva," pp. 130–43; Lombardi, *Povertà maschile*, pp. 182–209.

19. Lombardi, *Povertà maschile*, p. 146; Harsin, *Policing Prostitution*, p. 201; Wilson, *Fifty Years' Work*, pp. 419–20; Richard J. Gelles, "No Place to Go: The Social Dynamics of Marital Violence," in *Battered Women: A Psychosociological Study of Domestic Violence*, ed. Maria Roy (New York: Van Nostrand Reinhold, 1977), p. 61. These same themes about women and their place, or lack of place, have also been well stated in Carlisle, "Prostitutes and Reformers," pp. 146–47, 193.

20. Buttafuoco, *Le Mariuccine*, pp. 98, 125–28, 336, 69, and p. 75 on administrators' failures to differentiate among residents in differing circumstances; Wilson, *Fifty Years' Work*, pp. 57, 375; quotation from Aiken, "Florence Crittenton," p. 107, and also pp. 106, 38.

21. On the discriminatory treatment of the sexes with regard to prostitution and sexual misconduct, see Gibson, *Prostitution and the State*, p. 51; Harsin, *Policing Prostitution*, pp. xix, 264; Rosen, *Lost Sisterhood*, pp. 53–55, 163, 176; L'Espérance, "Woman's Mission," p. 331.

22. Annie Winsor Allen, "Former Failures and Present Success in the Institutional Training of Delinquent Girls," in *Women in Prison*, ed. David J. Rothman and Sheila M. Rothman, pp. 109–11 (emphasis added).

23. On eugenics, nativism, and the social control of young women, see Brenzel, *Daughters of the State*, pp. 96–102; Schlossman and Wallach, "Precocious Sexuality," pp. 78–81.

24. Ambroset, *Criminologia femminile*, p. 39.

25. Social psychologist Judith Long Laws, 1979, quoted in Schur, *Labeling Women Deviant*, p. 24.

26. Becker's studies are summarized by Schur, *Labeling Women Deviant*, p. 6.

27. Katz, "Origins of the Institutional State," p. 14. See also Ignatieff, "Total Institutions," pp. 167–73, and Edoardo Grendi, Introduction to *Quaderni storici* 53

(August 1983): 388, 385 (special issue on "Sistemi di carità: Esposti e internati nelle società di antico regime").

28. Buttafuoco, *Le Mariuccine,* p. 326.

29. Joly, "Les Maisons du Bon-Pasteur," pp. 299–302; Gaillac, *Les Maisons,* pp. 139–40 on Notre-Dame-de-Compassion; Michelle Perrot, "1848. Révolution et prisons," in *L'Impossible prison,* ed. Michelle Perrot, pp. 294–95.

30. On "women's communities," see the two issues of *Signs* devoted to this theme, volumes 10 (1985) and 14 (1989); Olwen Hufton and Frank Tallett, "Communities of Women, the Religious Life, and Public Service in Eighteenth-Century France," in *Connecting Spheres: Women in the Western World, 1500 to the Present,* ed. Marilyn J. Boxer and Jean H. Quataert (New York: Oxford University Press, 1987), pp. 75–85; Vicinus, *Independent Women.*

31. Murray, "Unhappy Marriage," pp. 90–91; Buttafuoco, *Le Mariuccine,* p. 462, and also p. 435.

32. Goffman, *Asylums,* p. 12; Andreucci, Nuove osservazioni, p. 45. Also see Biffi, *Sui riformatori,* pp. 2, 178.

33. Rothman, *Conscience and Convenience,* pp. 4–9; Ambroset, *Criminologia femminile,* p. 72; Scull, *Decarceration,* pp. 105–31 on nineteenth-century critiques of institutions, and 41–75.

34. "Use of Crack Is Said To Stifle the Instincts of Parenthood," *New York Times,* 17 March 1990, sec. A; "In Detroit, a Drug Recovery Center That Welcomes the Pregnant Addict," *New York Times,* 20 March 1990, sec. A.

SELECTED BIBLIOGRAPHY

Archival Sources

I. Archivio Segreto Vaticano
   Archivio sacra congregazione del Concilio, Visite Apostoliche 37 (1575)

II. Archivio di Stato, Pistoia
   A. Patrimonio Ecclesiastico
      E:345
      E:346
   B. Statuti 5

III. Archivio di Stato, Florence
   A. Acquisti e Doni
      45 Capitoli della compagnia di Santa Maria delle Laudi di Santo Spirito
      230:4 Ricordi (1622–29)
      291
      292
   B. Bigallo 1691 Veneranda compagnia di Santa Maria Maddalena sopra le mal
      maritate
   C. Camera e Auditore Fiscale, filza 2857
   D. Carte Strozziane series III, vol. 233 Memorie di monasteri
   E. Compagnia delle laudi e Santo Spirito, detta del Piccione 78
   F. Commissariati di Quartiere di Firenze, parte 1:
      filza 6
      filza 14
      filza 25
   G. Commissariato del Quartiere Santa Maria Novella 1
   H. Conventi Soppressi 114:34 (12) Processo
   I. Conventi Soppressi 126:
       1 Giornale (1622–30)
      51 Debitori e Creditori (1616–23)
      52 Debitori e Creditori (1621–30)
      53 Debitori e Creditori (1630–42)
      54 Debitori e Creditori (1634–42)
      55 Debitori e Creditori (1642–52)
      56 Debitori e Creditori (1661–74)
      57 Debitori e Creditori (1674–87)
      58 Debitori e Creditori (1687–1725)
      61 Debitori e Creditori (1765–1807)
      62 Ricordi (1435–1620)
      63 Ricordi (1616–26)
      64 Ricordi (1634)
      65 Lettere (1739–84)

235

     66   Cause (1612–99)
     68   Locatieni (1641–98)
     69   Cartelle (1641–98)
     70   Contratti (1349–1579)
     71   Livelli e Censi
     81   Piante Diverse

J.   Conventi Soppressi 143:
      1   Stati di Consistenza, Santa Maria Maddalena sopra le malmaritate

K.   Conventi Soppressi 191:
      1   Debitori e Creditori (1810)
     10   Memorie (1603–1737)
     25   Giornale (1604–21)
     32   Entrata e Uscita (1626–51)
     33   Constitutioni (1626–1723)
     35   Fogli (1605–1773)
     36   Fogli (1621–93)
     37   Stati di Consistenza (1808)

L.   Mediceo Avanti il Principato
     LX, 572
     LXX, 34
     LXXXV, 683
     CXXXVII, 923

M.   Mediceo del Principato 3479 (1577)

N.   Onestà
      1   Statuti (1403–1597)
      2   Condannazioni (1441–1523)
      3   Riforme di statuti (1577–1747)
      4   Condannazioni (1593–1627)
      6   Sentenze (1629–42)

O.   Or San Michele 16 (1387)

P.   Otto di Guardia Granducale
     66 (1553–54)
     85 (1560)
     2709 (1686–1706)

Q.   Otto di Guardia Repubblicana
     79   (1487–88)
     80   (1488)
     93   (1562)
    127   (1503)
    128   (1503–4)
    146   (1509)
    157   (1513)
    164   (1515–16)
    212   (1531)
    230   (1511–19)

R.   Provvisioni Registri
    137   (1446)
    183   (1492)
    195   (1504)

201   (1511)
205   (1520–22)
S.   Regio Diritto 4896 (1562–81)
T.   Tratte 95

Books, Articles, and Unpublished Works

Aiken, Katherine G. "The National Florence Crittenton Mission, 1883–1925: A Case Study in Progressive Reform." Ph.D. diss., Washington State University, 1980.

Alberti, Leon Battista. *The Family in Renaissance Florence: A Translation by Renée Neu Watkins of I Libri della Famiglia by Leon Battista Alberti.* Columbia: University of South Carolina Press, 1969.

Aleil, Pierre-François. "Le Refuge de Clermont, 1666–1792." *Bulletin historique et scientifique de l'Auvergne* 86 (1973): 13–69.

Alighieri, Dante. *The Divine Comedy.* Translated by H. R. Huse. New York: Holt, Rinehart & Winston, 1954.

Ambroset, Sonia. *Criminologia femminile: Il controllo sociale.* Milan: Edizioni Unicopli, 1984.

Andreski, Stanislav. "The Syphlitic Shock: A New Explanation of the 'Great Witch Craze' of the 16th and 17th Centuries in the Light of Medicine and Psychiatry." *Encounter* 58 (May 1982): 7–26.

———. "'The Syphlitic Shock': Puritanism, Capitalism, & a Medical Factor." *Encounter* 55 (October 1980): 76–81.

Andreucci, Ottavio. *Delle scuole femminili popolane e cittadine e delli instituti ospitalieri.* Florence: Federigo Bencini, 1865.

———. *Nuove osservazioni sui conservatori femminili delle provincie toscane.* Florence: Civelli, 1872.

Andrew, Donna T. *Philanthropy and Police: London Charity in the Eighteenth Century.* Princeton, N.J.: Princeton University Press, 1989.

Askew, Pamela. *Caravaggio's "Death of the Virgin."* Princeton, N.J.: Princeton University Press, 1990.

Avery, Hinda. "Sitka Housing Co-operative: Women House Themselves." *Women and Environments* 11 (Winter 1989): 19–23.

Bainton, Roland. *Women of the Reformation in Germany and Italy.* Boston: Beacon Press, 1971.

Bargiacchi, Luigi. *Storia degli istituti di beneficenza, d'istruzione ed educazione in Pistoia e suo circondario dalle respettive origini a tutto l'anno 1880.* 4 vols. Florence: Tipografia della pia casa di patronato pei minorenni, 1883–84.

Barrett, Kate Waller. *Some Practical Suggestions on the Conduct of a Rescue Home.* Washington, D.C.: National Florence Crittenton Mission, 1903. Reprint. New York: Arno Press, 1974.

Barrett, Robert South. *The Care of the Unmarried Mother.* Alexandria, Va.: N.p., 1929. Reprint. New York: Garland Publishing, 1987.

Barzaghi, Antonio. *Donne o cortigiane? La prostituzione a Venezia. Documenti di costume dal XVI al XVIII secolo.* Verona: Bertani, 1980.

Bellini, A. "Misure di prevenzione e di redenzione risguardanti la prostituzione dalle epoche remote ai tempi nostri." *Giornale italiano di dermatologia e sifilologia* 82 (1941): 1115–1202.

Bellomo, Manlio. *La condizione giuridica della donna in Italia.* Turin: Eri, 1970.

———. *Ricerche sui rapporti patrimoniali tra conjugi.* Milan: Giuffrè, 1961.

Benabou, Erica-Marie. *La Prostitution et la police des mœurs au XVIIIᵉ siècle.* Paris: Librairie Académique Perrin, 1987.

Benvenuti Papi, Anna. "Penitenza e santità femminile in ambiente cateriniano e bernardiniano." In *Atti del simposio internazionale Cateriniano-Bernardiniano,* edited by Domenico Maffei and Paolo Nardi, pp. 865–75. Siena: Accademia Senese degli Intronati, 1982.

Berg, Barbara J. *The Remembered Gate: Origins of American Feminism—The Woman and the City, 1800–1860.* New York: Oxford University Press, 1978.

Bernardino da Siena. *Opera omnia.* 9 vols. Florence: Patres Collegii S. Bonaventurae, 1950–[65].

———. *Le prediche volgari.* Edited by Ciro Cannarozzi. Pistoia: Alberto Pacinotti, 1934.

———. *Le prediche volgari* [Sienese sermons, 1427]. Edited by Piero Bargellini. Milan: Rizzoli, [c. 1936].

Bernocchi, Franco. *Prostituzione e rieducazione.* Padua: CEDAM, 1966.

Bertrand, M.A. "Le Caractère discriminatoire et inique de la justice pour mineurs: les filles dites 'délinquants' au Canada." *Déviance et société* 2 (1977): 187–202.

Bevione, Silvana. "Le carceri femminili tra passato e futuro." *Argomenti radicali,* no. 7 (1978), pp. 75–80.

Biffi, Serafino. *Sui riformatori pei giovani.* Milan: Giuseppe Bernardoni, 1870.

Black, Christopher F. *Italian Confraternities in the Sixteenth Century.* Cambridge: Cambridge University Press, 1989.

Blumer, Herbert. "Social Problems as Collective Behavior." *Social Problems* 18 (Winter 1971): 298–306.

Boggio, Maricla. *Ragazza madre: Storie di donne e dei loro bambini.* Venice: Marsilio, 1975.

Bolton, Brenda M. "Mulieres Sanctae." In *Women in Medieval Society,* edited by Susan Mosher Stuard, pp. 141–58. Philadelphia: University of Pennsylvania Press, 1976.

Borsook, Eve. *The Companion Guide to Florence.* London: Collins, 1966.

Bossy, John. "The Counter-Reformation and the People of Catholic Europe." *Past and Present* 47 (May 1970): 51–70.

Brackett, John K. "Bureaucracy and Female Marginality: The Florentine Onestà and the Control of Prostitution, 1403–1680." Department of History, University of Cincinnati, 1991. Photocopy.

———. "The Otto di Guardia e Bulia: Crime and Its Control in Florence, 1537–1609." Ph.D. diss., University of California, 1986.

Brenzel, Barbara M. *Daughters of the State: A Social Portrait of the First Reform School for Girls in North America, 1856–1905.* Cambridge, Mass.: MIT Press, 1983.

Bridenbaugh, Carl. *Cities in the Wilderness: The First Century of Urban Life in America, 1625–1742.* New York: Ronald Press, 1938. Reprint. New York: Knopf, 1964.

Bridenthal, Renate, and Claudia Koonz, eds. *Becoming Visible: Women in European History.* Boston: Houghton Mifflin, 1977.

Bridenthal, Renate, Atina Grossman, and Marion Kaplan, eds. *When Biology Became*

Destiny: Women in Weimar and Nazi Germany. New York: Monthly Review Press, 1984.

Bristow, Edward J. *Vice and Vigilance: Purity Movements in Britain Since 1700.* Dublin: Gill and Macmillan, 1977.

Brown, Judith C. *Immodest Acts: The Life of a Lesbian Nun in Renaissance Italy.* New York: Oxford University Press, 1986.

———. "A Woman's Place Was in the Home: Women's Work in Renaissance Tuscany." In *Rewriting the Renaissance: The Discourses of Sexual Difference in Early Modern Europe,* edited by Margaret W. Ferguson, Maureen Quilligan, and Nancy J. Vickers, pp. 206–24. Chicago: University of Chicago Press, 1986.

Brown, Judith C., and Jordan Goodman. "Women and Industry in Florence." *Journal of Economic History* 40 (March 1980): 73–80.

Brucker, Gene A. *Renaissance Florence.* New York: John Wiley & Sons, 1969.

———, ed. *The Society of Renaissance Florence: A Documentary Study.* New York: Harper & Row, 1971.

Brumberg, Joan Jacobs. " 'Ruined' Girls: Changing Community Responses to Illegitimacy in Upstate New York, 1890–1920." *Journal of Social History* 18 (Winter 1984): 247–72.

Brundage, James A. "Prostitution in the Medieval Canon Law." *Signs* 1 (1976): 825–45.

Bullough, Vern L., and Bonnie Bullough. *The History of Prostitution.* New Hyde Park, N.Y.: University Books, 1964.

Buttafuoco, Annarita. *Le Mariuccine: Storia di un'istituzione laica l'Asilo Mariuccia.* Milan: Franco Angeli, 1985.

Cagliero, Claudio, Barbara Maffiodo, and Luigi Tavolaccini. "L'organizzazione di alcune istituzioni di assistenza e di controllo." *Rivista di storia contemporanea* 11 (July 1982): 360–98.

Campbell, J.K. *Honour, Family and Patronage: A Study of Institutions and Moral Values in a Greek Mountain Community.* Oxford: Oxford University Press, 1964.

Canosa, Romano, and Isabella Colonnello. *Storia della prostituzione in Italia dal Quattrocento alla fine del Settecento.* Rome: Sapere 2000, 1989.

Carlisle, Marcia. "Prostitutes and Their Reformers in Nineteenth-Century Philadelphia." Ph.D. diss., Rutgers University, 1982.

Cavallo, Sandra. "Assistenza femminile e tutela dell'onore nella Torino del XVIII secolo." *Annali della Fondazione Luigi Einaudi* 14 (1980): 127–55.

Cavallo Sandra, and Simona Cerutti. "Onore femminile e controllo sociale della riproduzione in Piemonte tra Sei e Settecento." *Quaderni storici* 44 (August 1980): 346–76.

Chesler, Phyllis. *Women and Madness.* Garden City, N.Y.: Doubleday, 1972.

Ciammitti, Luisa. "Quanto costa essere normali. La dote nel Conservatorio femminile di Santa Maria del Baraccano (1630–1680)." *Quaderni storici* 53 (August 1983): 469–97.

Cipriani, Giovanni. "Le 'Zimarrine' e 'l'Offitio dell'Honestà' nella Firenze di Cosimo II de' Medici." *Ricerche storiche* 8 (1978): 801–8.

Cochrane, Eric. *Florence in the Forgotten Centuries, 1527–1800: A History of Florence and the Florentines in the Age of the Grand Dukes.* Chicago: University of Chicago Press, 1973.

Cohen, Sherrill. "The Convertite and the Malmaritate: Women's Institutions, Prostitution, and the Family in Counter-Reformation Florence." Ph.D. diss., Princeton University, 1985.

Cohn, Samuel Kline, Jr. "Donne in piazza e donne in tribunale a Firenze nel Rinascimento." *Studi storici* 22 (April–June 1981): 515–33.

———. *The Laboring Classes in Renaissance Florence.* New York: Academic Press, 1980.

Collinson, Patrick. "The Role of Women in the English Reformation, Illustrated by the Life and Friendships of Anne Locke." In *Studies in Church History,* edited by G. J. Cuming, 2:258–72. London: Thomas Nelson & Sons, 1965.

Compston, H.F.B. *The Magdalen Hospital: The Story of a Great Charity.* London: Society for Promoting Christian Knowledge, 1917.

Connelly, Mark Thomas. *The Response to Prostitution in the Progressive Era.* Chapel Hill: University of North Carolina Press, 1980.

Conti Odorisio, Ginevra. *Donne e società nel Seicento: Lucrezia Marinelli e Arcangela Tarabotti.* Rome: Bulzoni Editore, 1979.

Corbin, Alain. *Les Filles de noce: misère sexuelle et prostitution (19ᵉ et 20ᵉ siècles).* Paris: Aubier Montaigne, 1978.

Creytens, Raimondo. "La Riforma dei monasteri femminili dopo i Decreti Tridentini." In *Il Concilio di Trento e la Riforma Tridentina,* 2 vols., 1:45–84. Rome: Herder, 1965.

Cutrera, Antonino. *Storia della prostituzione in Sicilia: Monografia storico-giuridica.* Milan: R. Sandron, 1903. Reprint. Palermo: Editori Stampatori Associati, 1971.

D'Addario, Arnaldo. *Aspetti della Controriforma in Firenze.* Rome: Ministero dell'Interno, 1972.

Davis, Liane V. "Battered Women: The Transformation of a Social Problem." *Social Work* 32 (July–August 1987): 306–11.

Davis, Natalie Zemon. "Ghosts, Kin, and Progeny: Some Features of Family Life in Early Modern France." *Daedalus* 106 (Spring 1977): 87–114.

———. *Society and Culture in Early Modern France.* Stanford, Calif.: Stanford University Press, 1975.

Delcorno, Carlo, *La predicazione nell'età comunale.* Florence: Sansoni, 1974.

Delumeau, Jean. *Catholicism Between Luther and Voltaire: A New View of the Counter-Reformation.* Translated by Jeremy Moiser. London: Burns & Oates, 1977. Originally published as *Le Catholicisme entre Luther et Voltaire* (Paris: Presses Universitaires de France, 1971).

De Roover, Raymond. *San Bernardino of Siena and Sant'Antonino of Florence: The Two Great Economic Thinkers of the Middle Ages.* Boston: Baker Library, Harvard Graduate School of Business Administration, 1967.

Dobash, Russell P., R. Emerson Dobash, and Sue Gutteridge. *The Imprisonment of Women.* Oxford: Basil Blackwell, 1986.

Dodd, William. *An Account of the Rise, Progress, and Present State of the Magdalen Hospital, for the Reception of Penitent Prostitutes.* 4th ed. London: W. Faden, 1770.

Dondori, Gioseppe. *Della pietà di Pistoia in grazia della sua patria.* Pistoia: P. A. Fortunati, 1666.

Donzelot, Jacques. *The Policing of Families.* Translated by Robert Hurley. New York: Pantheon Books, 1979. Originally published as *La Police des familles* (Paris: Les Editions de Minuit, 1977).

Douglas, Mary. *Purity and Danger: An Analysis of Concepts of Pollution and Taboo.* New York: Praeger, 1966.

Dublin, Thomas. *Women at Work: The Transformation of Work and Community in Lowell, Massachusetts, 1826–1860.* New York: Columbia University Press, 1979.

Ely, Ezra Stiles. *Visits of Mercy; or, The journals of the Rev. Ezra Stiles Ely, D.D., written while he was stated preacher to the hospital and alms-house, in the city of New York.* 2 vols. Philadelphia: Samuel F. Bradford, 1829.

Evennett, H. Outram. "The New Orders." In *The New Cambridge Modern History,* vol. 2, *The Reformation, 1520–1559,* edited by G. R. Elton, pp. 275–300. Cambridge: Cambridge University Press, 1958.

———. *The Spirit of the Counter-Reformation.* Cambridge: Cambridge University Press, 1968.

Fairbank, Jenty. *Booth's Boots: Social Service Beginnings in the Salvation Army.* London: International Headquarters of the Salvation Army, 1983.

Fantozzi Micali, Osanna, and Piero Roselli. *Le soppressioni dei conventi a Firenze: Riuso e trasformazioni dal sec. XVIII in poi.* Florence: Libreria Editrice Fiorentina, 1980.

Faucher, Léon. *De la réforme des prisons.* Paris: Angé, 1838.

Feinman, Clarice. *Women in the Criminal Justice System.* 2d ed. New York: Praeger, 1986.

Ferrante, Lucia. " 'Malmaritate' tra assistenza e punizione (Bologna secc. XVI–XVII)." In *Forme e soggetti dell'intervento assistenziale in una città di antico regime,* pp. 65–109. Bologna: Istituto per la Storia di Bologna, 1986.

———. "L'onore ritrovato. Donne nella Casa del Soccorso di S. Paolo a Bologna (sec. XVI–XVII)." *Quaderni storici* 53 (August 1983): 499–527.

———. "Pro mercede carnali . . . Il giusto prezzo rivendicato in tribunale." *Memoria* 17 (1986): 42–58. (Special issue on prostitution.)

Field, Alice Withrow. "Prostitution in the Soviet Union." *Nation,* 25 March 1936, pp. 373–74.

Finnegan, Frances. *Poverty and Prostitution: A Study of Victorian Prostitutes in York.* Cambridge: Cambridge University Press, 1979.

Fiume, Giovanna, ed. *Onore e storia nelle società mediterranee.* Palermo: La Luna, 1989.

Flexner, Abraham. *Prostitution in Europe.* New York: Century, 1914.

Foucault, Michel. *Discipline and Punish: The Birth of the Prison.* Translated by Alan Sheridan. New York: Random House, 1979. Originally published as *Surveiller et punir: naissance de la prison* (Paris: Editions Gallimard, 1975).

———. *Madness and Civilization: A History of Insanity in the Age of Reason.* Translated by Richard Howard. New York: Random House, 1965. Originally published as *Histoire de la folie* (Paris: Librairie Plon, 1961).

Franchini, Silvia. "L'istruzione femminile in Italia dopo l'Unità: Percorsi di una ricerca sugli educandati pubblici di élite." *Passato e presente* 10 (1986): 53–94.

Freedman, Estelle B. "Separatism as Strategy: Female Institution Building and American Feminism, 1870–1930." *Feminist Studies* 5 (Fall 1979): 512–29.

———. *Their Sisters' Keepers: Women's Prison Reform in America, 1830–1930.* Ann Arbor: University of Michigan Press, 1981.

Gaillac, Henri. *Les Maisons de correction, 1830–1945.* Paris: Editions Cujas, 1971.

Galey, Sherry. "Survivors of Violence: Global Organizing." *Women and Environments* 10 (Fall 1987): 9–10.

Garland, David. *Punishment and Welfare: A History of Penal Strategies.* Brookfield, Vt.: Gower, 1985.

Gaudemet, Jean. "Il legame matrimoniale nel XVII secolo. Legislazione canonica e tendenze laiche." In *Le funzioni sociali del matrimonio. Modelli e regole della scelta del coniuge dal XIV al XX secolo,* edited by Milly Buonanno, pp. 64–79. Milan: Edizioni di Comunità, 1980.

Gavitt, Philip. *The Ospedale degli Innocenti, 1410–1536.* Ann Arbor: University of Michigan Press, 1990.

Gelles, Richard J. "No Place to Go: The Social Dynamics of Marital Violence." In *Battered Women: A Psychosociological Study of Domestic Violence,* edited by Maria Roy, pp. 46–63. New York: Van Nostrand Reinhold, 1977.

Gemini, Fiorenza, and Eugenio Sonnino. "La Condition féminine dans une structure d'assistance à Rome: aspects démographiques et sociaux." *Annales de démographie historique* (1981), pp. 235–51.

Gibson, Mary. "The 'Female Offender' and the Italian School of Criminal Anthropology." *Journal of European Studies* 12 (1982): 155–65.

———. *Prostitution and the State in Italy, 1860–1915.* New Brunswick, N.J.: Rutgers University Press, 1986.

Gillis, John R. *Youth and History: Tradition and Change in European Age Relations, 1770–Present.* New York: Academic Press, 1974.

Godden, Judith. "Sectarianism and Purity Within the Woman's Sphere: Sydney Refuges During the Late Nineteenth Century." *Journal of Religious History* 14 (1987): 291–306.

Goffman, Erving. *Asylums: Essays on the Social Situation of Mental Patients and Other Inmates.* Garden City, N.Y.: Doubleday, 1961.

Goldberg, Maria Amélia Azevedo. *Mulheres espancadas: A violência denunciada.* São Paulo: Cortez Editora, 1985.

Gordon, Linda. *Heroes of Their Own Lives: The Politics and History of Family Violence.* New York: Viking Penguin, 1988.

Grendi, Edoardo. Introduction to *Quaderni storici* 53 (August 1983): 383–89. (Special issue on "Sistemi di carità: Esposti e internati nelle società di antico regime.")

Grob, Gerald N. *Mental Institutions in America: Social Policy to 1875.* New York: Free Press, 1973.

Gronewald, Sue. "The Door of Hope: A Rescue Mission for Shanghai Prostitutes, 1900–1941." Ph.D. diss. prospectus, Columbia University, 1991.

Groppi, Angela. " 'Un pezzo di mercanzia di cui il mercante fa quel che ne vuole.' Carriera di un'internata tra Buon Pastore e manicomio." *Annali della Fondazione Lelio e Lisli Basso-Issoco* 7 (1985): 189–224.

———. "Una gestione collettiva di equilibri emozionali e materiali. La reclusione delle donne nella Roma dell'Ottocento." In *Ragnatele di rapporti: Patronage e reti di relazione nella storia delle donne,* edited by Lucia Ferrante, Maura Palazzi, and Gianna Pomata, pp. 130–47. Turin: Rosenberg & Sellier, 1988.

Grünhut, Max. *Penal Reform: A Comparative Study.* Oxford: Clarendon Press, 1948.

Guazzini, Giulio. *La conversione eroica e cristiana della Maria Lunga detta Carrettina, meretrice famosa in Firenze; la quale essendo stata peccatrice oltre a vent'anni per penitenza de' suoi peccati havendo dato tutto il suo avere ridotto a denari, per l'amor di Dio; si è ritirata a servire alle misere donne oppresse dal contagio nel lazzaretto . . . Palinodia in retrattazione delle lodi già fatte per la Maria Lunga meretrice.* Florence: Zanobi Pignoni, 1633.

Guidi, Laura. "Il manto della Madonna: L'immagine femminile nei conservatori napoletani dell'Ottocento." *Memoria* 11–12 (1984): 65–81.

———. *L'onore in pericolo. Carità e reclusione femminile nell'Ottocento napoletano.* Naples: Liguori, 1991.

Guillot, Adolphe. *Les Prisons de Paris et les prisonniers.* Paris: E. Dentu, 1890.

Gutton, Jean-Pierre. *La Société et les pauvres: l'exemple de la généralité de Lyon, 1534–1789.* Paris: Société d'Edition "Les Belles Lettres," 1970.

Haffner, Sarah, ed. *Frauenhäuser: Gewalt in der Ehe und was Frauen dagegen tun.* Berlin: Verlag Klaus Wagenbach, 1976.

Hanway, Jonas. *Reflections, Essays and Meditations on Life and Religion, with a collection of proverbs in alphabetical order, and twenty-eight letters written occasionally on several subjects.* 2 vols. London: John Rivington, 1761.

———. *Solitude in Imprisonment.* London: J. Bew, 1776.

———. *Thoughts on the Plan for a Magdalen-House for Repentant Prostitutes.* 2d ed., enl. London: J. & R. Dodsley, 1759.

Harrison, Nikki. "Nuns and Prostitutes in Enlightenment Spain." *British Journal for Eighteenth-Century Studies* 9 (Spring 1986): 53–60.

Harsin, Jill. *Policing Prostitution in Nineteenth-Century Paris.* Princeton, N.J.: Princeton University Press, 1985.

Hawes, Joseph M. *Children in Urban Society: Juvenile Delinquency in Nineteenth-Century America.* New York: Oxford University Press, 1971.

Hayden, Dolores. *The Grand Domestic Revolution: A History of Feminist Designs for American Homes, Neighborhoods and Cities.* Cambridge, Mass.: MIT Press, 1981.

Herlihy, David. *The Family in Renaissance Italy.* St. Charles, Mo.: Forum Press, 1974.

———. "Mapping Households in Medieval Italy." *Catholic Historical Review* 58 (April 1972): 1–24.

———. "Marriage at Pistoia in the Fifteenth Century." *Bullettino storico pistoiese,* 3d series, 7 (1972): 3–21.

———. *Medieval and Renaissance Pistoia: The Social History of an Italian Town, 1200–1430.* New Haven, Conn.: Yale University Press, 1967.

———. "Some Psychological and Social Roots of Violence in the Tuscan Cities." In *Violence and Civil Disorder in Italian Cities, 1200–1500,* edited by Lauro Martines, pp. 129–54. Los Angeles: University of California Press, 1972.

———. *Women in Medieval Society.* Houston, Tex.: University of St. Thomas, 1971.

Herlihy, David, and Christiane Klapisch-Zuber. *Les Toscans et leurs familles: une étude du catasto florentin de 1427.* Paris: Presses de la Fondation Nationale des Sciences Politiques, 1978.

Hershatter, Gail. "Regulating Sex in Shanghai: The Reform of Prostitution in 1920 and 1951." In *Shanghai Sojourners,* edited by Frederic Wakeman and Wen-hsin Yeh. Berkeley: Institute of East Asian Studies, University of California, forthcoming.

Hewitt, Margaret. *Wives and Mothers in Victorian Industry.* London: Rockliff, 1958.

Higginbotham, Ann Rowell. "The Unmarried Mother and Her Child in Victorian London, 1834–1914." Ph.D. diss., Indiana University, 1985.

Hindus, Maurice. *The Great Offensive.* New York: Harrison Smith & Robert Haas, 1933.

Hobson, Barbara. *Uneasy Virtue: The Politics of Prostitution and the American Reform Tradition.* New York: Basic Books, 1987.

Horlick, Allan Stanley. *Country Boys and Merchant Princes: The Social Control of Young Men in New York.* Lewisburg, Pa.: Bucknell University Press, 1975.

Horowitz, Helen Lefkowitz. *Alma Mater: Design and Experience in the Women's Colleges from Their Nineteenth-Century Beginnings to the 1930s.* New York: Knopf, 1984.

Howard, John. *The State of the Prisons in England and Wales, with Preliminary Observations, and an Account of Some Foreign Prisons and Hospitals.* 3d ed. Warrington: William Eyres, 1784.

Hudson, Barbara. "Justice or Welfare? A Comparison of Recent Developments in the English and French Juvenile Justice Systems." In *Growing Up Good: Policing the Behaviour of Girls in Europe,* edited by Maureen Cain, pp. 96–113. London: SAGE, 1989.

Hufton, Olwen. *The Poor of Eighteenth-Century France, 1750–1789.* Oxford: Oxford University Press, 1974.

Hufton, Olwen, and Frank Tallett. "Communities of Women, the Religious Life, and Public Service in Eighteenth-Century France." In *Connecting Spheres: Women in the Western World, 1500 to the Present,* edited by Marilyn J. Boxer and Jean H. Quataert, pp. 75–85. New York: Oxford University Press, 1987.

Hughes, Diane Owen. "Domestic Ideals and Social Behavior: Evidence from Medieval Genoa." In *The Family in History,* edited by Charles E. Rosenberg, pp. 115–43. Philadelphia: University of Pennsylvania Press, 1975.

———. "Kinsmen and Neighbors in Medieval Genoa." In *The Medieval City,* edited by Harry A. Miskimin, David Herlihy, and A. L. Udovitch, pp. 95–111. New Haven, Conn.: Yale University Press, 1977.

"Humanitarianism or Control? A Symposium on Aspects of Nineteenth-Century Social Reform in Britain and America." *Rice University Studies* 67 (Winter 1981): 1–75.

Ignatieff, Michael. *A Just Measure of Pain: The Penitentiary in the Industrial Revolution, 1750–1850.* Harmondsworth: Penguin Books, 1978.

———. "Total Institutions and Working Classes: A Review Essay." *History Workshop Journal* 15 (Spring 1983): 167–73.

Illibato, Antonio. *La donna a Napoli nel Settecento: Aspetti della condizione e dell'istruzione femminile.* Naples: M. D'Auria Editore, 1985.

Jacobson, Beverly. "Battered Women: The Fight to End Wife-beating." *Civil Rights Digest* 9 (Summer 1977): 2–11.

Jeffreys, Sheila. " 'Free from All Uninvited Touch of Man': Women's Campaigns Around Sexuality, 1880–1914." *Women's Studies International Forum* 5 (1982): 629–45.

Joly, Henri. *A la recherche de l'éducation correctionnelle à travers l'Europe.* Paris: Librairie Victor Lecoffre, 1902.

———. "Les Maisons du Bon-Pasteur." *La Réforme sociale,* July–December 1901, pp. 287–308.

Jones, Colin. "Prostitution and the Ruling Class in 18th-Century Montpellier." *History Workshop Journal* 6 (Autumn 1978): 7–28.

Jové Campmajó, Marta, and Helena Kirchner i Granell. "Capitaires Prostitutes i Rodamons: Barcelona, 1600–1640." In *Primer congrés d'història moderna de Catalunya,* 2 vols., 1:471–78. Barcelona: Departament d'Historia Moderna, Facultat de Geografia i Historia, Universitat de Barcelona: Diputacio de Barcelona, 1984.

Kaplan, Marion. "Prostitution, Morality Crusades and Feminism: German-Jewish Feminists and the Campaign Against White Slavery." *Women's Studies International Forum* 5 (1982): 619–27.

Karant-Nunn, Susan C. "Continuity and Change: Some Effects of the Reformation on the Women of Zwickau." *Sixteenth Century Journal* 12 (Summer 1982): 17–42.

Karras, Ruth Mazo. "The Regulation of Brothels in Late Medieval England." *Signs* 14 (Winter 1989): 399–433.

Katz, Michael B. "Origins of the Institutional State." *Marxist Perspectives* 1 (Winter 1978): 6–22.

––––––. "The Origins of Public Education: A Reassessment." *History of Education Quarterly* 16 (Winter 1976): 381–407.

Kelly, Joan. "Early Feminist Theory and the *Querelle des Femmes,* 1400–1789." *Signs* 8 (Autumn 1982): 4–28.

Kent, F. William. *Household and Lineage in Renaissance Florence: The Family Life of the Capponi, Ginori, and Rucellai.* Princeton, N.J.: Princeton University Press, 1977.

––––––. "A Proposal by Savonarola for the Self-Reform of Florentine Women (March 1496)." *Memorie domenicane,* n.s., 14 (1983): 335–41.

King, Margaret L. "Personal, Domestic, and Republican Values in the Moral Philosophy of Giovanni Caldiera." *Renaissance Quarterly* 28 (Winter 1975): 535–74.

––––––. "Thwarted Ambitions: Six Learned Women of the Italian Renaissance." *Soundings: An Interdisciplinary Journal* 59 (1976): 280–304.

Kirshner, Julius. *Pursuing Honor While Avoiding Sin: The Monte delle Doti of Florence.* Milan: A. Giuffrè, 1978.

Kirshner, Julius, and Anthony Molho. "The Dowry Fund and the Marriage Market in Early *Quattrocento* Florence." *Journal of Modern History* 50 (September 1978): 403–38.

Klapisch, Christiane. "Household and Family in Tuscany in 1427." In *Household and Family in Past Time,* edited by Peter Laslett, pp. 267–81. Cambridge: Cambridge University Press, 1972.

Klapisch-Zuber, Christiane. *Women, Family, and Ritual in Renaissance Italy.* Translated by Lydia Cochrane. Chicago: University of Chicago Press, 1985.

––––––. "Women Servants in Florence During the Fourteenth and Fifteenth Centuries." In *Women and Work in Preindustrial Europe,* edited by Barbara A. Hanawalt, pp. 56–80. Bloomington: Indiana University Press, 1986.

Klein, Alice, and Wayne Roberts. "Besieged Innocence: The 'Problem' and the Problems of Working Women—Toronto, 1896–1914." In *Women at Work: Ontario, 1850–1930,* edited by Janice Acton, Penny Goldsmith, and Bonnie Shepard, pp. 211–60. Toronto: Canadian Women's Educational Press, 1974.

Korn, Richard R., and Lloyd W. McCorkle. *Criminology and Penology.* New York: Holt, Rinehart & Winston, 1959.

Kristeller, Paul Oskar. "Learned Women of Early Modern Italy: Humanists and University Scholars." In *Beyond Their Sex: Learned Women of the European Past,* edited by Patricia A. Labalme, pp. 91–116. New York: New York University Press, 1980.

Kuehn, Thomas. " 'Cum Consensu Mundualdi': Legal Guardianship of Women in Quattrocento Florence." *Viator* 13 (1982): 309–33.

——. *Emancipation in Late Medieval Florence.* New Brunswick, N.J.: Rutgers University Press, 1982.

——. "Honor and Conflict in a Fifteenth-Century Florentine Family." *Ricerche storiche* 10 (May–August 1980): 287–305.

——. "Women, Marriage, and *Patria Potestas* in Late Medieval Florence." *Tijdschrift voor Rechtsgeschiedenis* 49 (1981): 127–47.

Landucci, Luca. *A Florentine Diary from 1450 to 1516.* Translated by Alice de Rosen Jervis: New York: Arno Press, 1969.

Laqueur, Thomas. *Making Sex: Body and Gender from the Greeks to Freud.* Cambridge, Mass.: Harvard University Press, 1990.

Lasch, Christopher. *The World of Nations: Reflections on American History, Politics, and Culture.* New York: Knopf, 1973.

Lastri, Marco. *L'osservatore fiorentino sugli edifizi della sua patria.* 3d ed. 8 vols. Florence: G. Ricci, 1821. Originally published in 1776.

Leges municipales pistoriensium, nuper mandante Serenissimo Ferdinando II, Magno Duce Etruriae V, Reformate & Approbate Anno MDCXLVII. Florence: Ex Typographia Serenissimi Magni Ducis, 1647.

L'Espérance, Jean Lawrence. "Woman's Mission to Woman: Explorations in the Operation of the Double Standard and Female Solidarity in Nineteenth Century England." *Histoire sociale–Social History* 12 (November 1979): 316–38.

Lewis, Oscar, Ruth M. Lewis, and Susan M. Rigdon. *Four Women. Living the Revolution: An Oral History of Contemporary Cuba.* Urbana: University of Illinois Press, 1977.

Liebowitz, Ruth P. "Conversion or Confinement? Houses for Repentant Prostitutes in Late Renaissance Italy." Paper presented at the Sixteenth Century Studies Conference, St. Louis, Mo., 25 October 1980.

——. "Prison, Workshop and Convent: A House of Convertite in Counter-Reformation Milan." Paper presented at the 6th Berkshire Conference on the History of Women, Northampton, Mass., 1 June 1984.

——. "Virgins in the Service of Christ: The Dispute over an Active Apostolate for Women During the Counter-Reformation." In *Women of Spirit: Female Leadership in the Jewish and Christian Traditions,* edited by Rosemary Ruether and Eleanor McLaughlin, pp. 131–52. New York: Simon & Schuster, 1979.

——. "Voices from Convents: Nuns and Repentant Prostitutes in Late Renaissance Italy." Paper presented at the 4th Berkshire Conference on the History of Women, South Hadley, Mass., 23 August 1978.

Lightbown, Ronald. *Sandro Botticelli.* 2 vols. Berkeley: University of California Press, 1978.

Limburger, Walther. *Die Gebäude von Florenz.* Leipzig: F. A. Brockhaus, 1910.

Lindemann, Mary. "Maternal Politics: The Principles and Practice of Maternity Care in Eighteenth-Century Hamburg." *Journal of Family History* 9 (Spring 1984): 44–63.

Linton, Derek S. "Between School and Marriage, Workshop and Household: Young Working Women as a Social Problem in Late Imperial Germany." *European History Quarterly* 18 (October 1988): 387–408.

Litchfield, R. Burr. "Demographic Characteristics of Florentine Patrician Families, Sixteenth to Nineteenth Centuries." *Journal of Economic History* 29 (June 1969): 191–205.

————. *Emergence of a Bureaucracy: The Florentine Patricians, 1530–1790.* Princeton, N.J.: Princeton University Press, 1986.

Lombardi, Daniela. "L'ospedale dei Mendicanti nella Firenze del seicento. 'Da inutile serraglio dei mendici a conservatorio e casa di forza per le donne.' " *Società e storia* 24 (1984): 289–311.

————. "Poveri a Firenze. Programmi e realizzazioni della politica assistenziale dei Medici tra cinque e seicento." In *Timore e carità: I poveri nell'Italia moderna,* edited by Giorgio Politi, Mario Rosa, and Franco della Peruta, pp. 165–84. Cremona: Libreria del Convegno, 1982.

————. *Povertà maschile, povertà femminile. L'ospedale dei Mendicanti nella Firenze dei Medici.* Bologna: Il Mulino, 1988.

Loyola, Ignatius. *The Spiritual Exercises of St. Ignatius.* Translated by Anthony Mottola. Garden City, N.Y.: Doubleday, 1964.

Lunbeck, Elizabeth. " 'A New Generation of Women': Progressive Psychiatrists and the Hypersexual Female." *Feminist Studies* 13 (1987): 513–43.

McCarthy, Kathleen, ed. *Lady Bountiful Revisited: Women, Philanthropy, and Power.* New Brunswick, N.J.: Rutgers University Press, 1990.

McDonnell, E.W. *The Beguines and Beghards in Medieval Culture.* New Brunswick, N.J.: Rutgers University Press, 1954.

McDowall, John R. *Magdalen Facts.* New York: the author, 1832.

Machiavelli, Niccolò. *The Prince.* Translated by Luigi Ricci; revised by E. R. P. Vincent. New York: New American Library, 1952.

Maclean, Ian. *The Renaissance Notion of Woman: A Study in the Fortunes of Scholasticism and Medical Science in European Intellectual Life.* Cambridge: Cambridge University Press, 1980.

Mahood, Linda. *The Magdalenes: Prostitution in the Nineteenth Century.* London: Routledge, 1990.

Maldini, Daniela. "Donne sole, 'figlie raminghe,' 'convertite' e 'forzate.' Aspetti assistenziali nella Torino di fine Settecento." *Il Risorgimento* 33 (June 1980): 115–38.

Mangio, Carlo. *La polizia toscana: Organizzazione e criteri d'intervento (1765–1808).* Milan: Giuffrè, 1988.

Marcolini, Giuliana, and Giulio Marcon. "Prostituzione e assistenza a Venezia nel secolo XVIII: Il pio loco delle povere peccatrici penitenti di S. Iob." *Studi veneziani* 10 (1985): 99–136.

Marshall, Sherrin. *The Dutch Gentry, 1500–1650: Family, Faith, and Fortune.* New York: Greenwood Press, 1987.

Martin, Del. *Battered Wives.* Rev., updated ed. San Francisco: Volcano Press, 1981.

Martin, Gregory. *Roma Sancta.* Edited by George Bruner Parks. Rome: Edizioni di Storia e Letteratura, 1969.

Martines, Lauro. "A Way of Looking at Women in Renaissance Florence." *Journal of Medieval and Renaissance Studies* 4 (1974): 15–28.

Masetti Zannini, Gian Ludovico. *Motivi storici dell'educazione femminile (1500–1650).* Bari: Editoriale Bari, 1980.

Mazzi, Maria Serena. "Il mondo della prostituzione nella Firenze tardo medievale." *Ricerche storiche* 14 (May–December 1984): 337–63.

Melossi, Dario, and Massimo Pavarini. *The Prison and the Factory: Origins of the*

Penitentiary System. Translated by Glynis Cousin. London: Macmillan Press, 1981. Originally published as *Carcere e fabbrica* (Bologna: Il Mulino, 1977).

Melville, Joy. "A Note on 'Men's Aid.' " In *Violence and the Family,* edited by J. P. Martin, pp. 311–13. Chichester: John Wiley & Sons, 1978.

Meulders, Marie-Thérèse. "La Violence au sein du couple: ébauches de réponses juridiques en droit continental." In *Family Violence: An International and Interdisciplinary Study,* edited by John M. Eekelaar and Sanford N. Katz, pp. 141–87. Toronto: Butterworths, 1978.

Meyerowitz, Joanne J. *Women Adrift: Independent Wage Earners in Chicago, 1880–1930.* Chicago: University of Chicago Press, 1988.

Mitchinson, Wendy. "The YWCA and Reform in the Nineteenth Century. " *Histoire sociale–Social History* 12 (November 1979): 368–84.

Mittelman, Karen Sue. " 'A Spirit That Touches the Problems of Today': Women and Social Reform in the Philadelphia Young Women's Christian Association, 1920–1945." Ph.D. diss., University of Pennsylvania, 1987.

Mollat, Michel, ed. *Etudes sur l'histoire de la pauvreté (moyen âge–XVIᵉ siècle).* 2 vols. Paris: Publications de la Sorbonne, 1974.

Monachino, Vincenzo. *La carità cristiana in Roma.* Bologna: Cappelli, 1968.

Monica, Sister M. *Angela Merici and Her Teaching Idea, 1474–1540.* New York: Longmans, Green, 1927.

Montaigne, Michel de. *Montaigne's Travel Journal.* Translated by Donald M. Frame. San Francisco: North Point Press, 1983.

Morandini, Guiliana. . . . *E allora mi hanno rinchiusa.* Milan: Gruppo Editoriale Fabbri, Bompiani, Sonzogno, Etas, 1977.

Mosco, Marilena, ed. *La Maddalena tra sacro e profano.* Exhibition catalog, Palazzo Pitti, May 24–September 7, 1986. Milan: Arnoldo Mondadori, 1986.

Muriel de la Torre, Josefina. *Los recogimientos de mujeres: Respuesta a una problemática social novohispana.* Mexico: Universidad Nacional Autónoma de México, Instituto de Investigaciones Históricas, 1974.

Murray, Susan B. "The Unhappy Marriage of Theory and Practice: An Analysis of a Battered Women's Shelter." *NWSA Journal* 1 (1988): 75–92.

Nash, Mary. *Mujer, familia y trabajo en España (1875–1936).* Barcelona: Anthropos, 1983.

Nash, Stanley. "Prostitution and Charity: The Magdalen Hospital, a Case Study." *Journal of Social History* 17 (Summer 1984): 617–28.

Nelson, Marion. "Two Curious Institutions of Soviet Russia." *Canadian Forum* 14 (April 1934): 260–61.

Norberg, Kathryn. *Rich and Poor in Grenoble, 1600–1814.* Berkeley: University of California Press, 1985.

O'Brien, Patricia. *The Promise of Punishment: Prisons in Nineteenth-Century France.* Princeton, N.J.: Princeton University Press, 1982.

O'Faolain, Julia, and Lauro Martines, eds. *Not in God's Image: Women in History from the Greeks to the Victorians.* New York: Harper & Row, 1973.

Origo, Iris. *The World of San Bernardino.* London: Jonathan Cape, 1963.

Orme, Nicholas. "The Reformation and the Red Light." *History Today* 37 (March 1987): 36–41.

Otis, Leah Lydia. *Prostitution in Medieval Society: The History of an Urban Institution in Languedoc.* Chicago: University of Chicago Press, 1985.

Pampaloni, Guido. *Lo spedale di S. M. Nuova.* Florence: Cassa di Risparmio, 1961.

Pansier, Pierre. *L'Oeuvre des repenties à Avignon du XIIIᵉ au XVIIIᵉ siècle.* Paris: Honoré Champion, 1910.

Parca, Gabriella. *Voci dal carcere femminile.* Rome: Editori Riuniti, 1973.

Park, Katharine. *Doctors and Medicine in Early Renaissance Florence.* Princeton, N.J.: Princeton University Press, 1985.

Paschini, Pio. *Tre ricerche sulla storia della chiesa nel Cinquecento.* Rome: Edizioni Liturgiche, 1945.

Pascoe, Peggy. *Relations of Rescue: The Search for Female Moral Authority in the American West, 1874–1939.* New York: Oxford University Press, 1990.

Passerini, Luigi. *Storia degli stabilimenti di beneficenza e d'istruzione elementare gratuita della città di Firenze.* Florence: Le Monnier, 1853.

Pavan, Elisabeth. "Police des mœurs, société et politique à Venise à la fin du moyen âge." *Revue historique,* no. 264 (1980), pp. 241–88.

Pearce, Samuel B.P. *An Ideal in the Working: The Story of the Magdalen Hospital, 1758–1958.* London: n.p., 1958.

Penco, Giovanni B. *Donna caduta e donna redenta per l'affermazione di un principio di morale sociale.* 2d ed. Milan: Instituto di Propaganda Libraria, 1954.

Pérez Baltasar, María Dolores. *Mujeres marginadas: Las casas de recogidas en Madrid.* Madrid: Gráficas Lormo, 1984.

Peristiany, J.G. *Honour and Shame: The Values of Mediterranean Society.* London: Weidenfeld, 1965.

Perrot, Michelle, ed. *L'Impossible prison: recherches sur le système pénitentiaire au XIXᵉ siècle.* Paris: Editions du Seuil, 1980.

Perry, Mary Elizabeth. "Deviant Insiders: Legalized Prostitutes and a Consciousness of Women in Early Modern Seville." *Comparative Studies in Society and History* 27 (January 1985): 138–58.

———. *Gender and Disorder in Early Modern Seville.* Princeton, N.J.: Princeton University Press, 1990.

———. " 'Lost Women' in Early Modern Seville: The Politics of Prostitution." *Feminist Studies* 4 (February 1978): 195–214.

———. "With Brave Vigilance and a Hundred Eyes: The Making of Women's Prisons in Counter-Reformation Spain." *Women & Criminal Justice* 2 (Fall 1990): 3–17.

Petitti di Roreto, Carlo Ilarione. "Della condizione attuale delle carceri e dei mezzi di migliorarla." In *Opere scelte,* edited by Gian Mario Bravo, 2 vols., 1:321–587. Turin: Fondazione Luigi Einaudi, 1969.

Phillips, Roderick. *Putting Asunder: A History of Divorce in Western Society.* Cambridge: Cambridge University Press, 1988.

Pinchbeck, Ivy. *Women Workers and the Industrial Revolution, 1750–1850.* London: George Routledge & Sons, 1930.

Pitch, Tamar, "Tra diritti sociali e cittadinanza. Il movimento delle donne e la legge sulla violenza sessuale." *Problemi del socialismo* 27/28 (1983): 192–214.

———, ed. *Diritto e rovescio: Studi sulle donne e il controllo sociale.* Naples: Edizioni Scientifiche Italiane, 1987.

Pivar, David J. *Purity Crusade: Sexual Morality and Social Control, 1868–1900.* Westport, Conn.: Greenwood Press, 1973.

Platt, Anthony M. *The Child Savers: The Invention of Delinquency.* 2d ed., enl. Chicago: University of Chicago Press, 1977.

Playfair, Giles. "How Denmark Reforms Prostitutes." *New Society,* 12 November 1964, pp. 18–19.

Pleck, Elizabeth. *Domestic Tyranny: The Making of American Social Policy Against Family Violence from Colonial Times to the Present.* New York: Oxford University Press, 1987.

Pletscher, Marianne. *Weggehen ist nicht so einfach: Gewalt gegen Frauen in der Schweiz. Gespräche und Informationen.* Zurich: Limmat Verlag Genossenschaft, 1977.

Poccianti, Michele. *Vite de sette beati fiorentini fondatori del sacro ordine de' Servi. Con uno epilogo di tutte le chiese, monasteri, luoghi pii, e compagnie della città di Firenze.* Florence: Giorgio Marescotti, 1589.

Pomata, Gianna. "Madri illegittime tra Ottocento e Novecento: Storie cliniche e storie di vita." *Quaderni storici* 44 (August 1980): 497–542.

Porciani, Ilaria, ed. *Le donne a scuola: L'educazione femminile nell'Italia dell'Ottocento. Mostra documentaria e iconografica.* Siena: Università degli Studi di Siena, 1987.

Potter, Henry C. *Sisterhoods and Deaconesses at Home and Abroad.* New York: E. P. Dutton, 1873.

Pratt, Anna B. "An Old Society Rejuvenates Itself." *Better Times,* February 1929, pp. 12–14.

Prelinger, Catherine M. *Charity, Challenge, and Change: Religious Dimensions of the Mid-Nineteenth-Century Women's Movement in Germany.* New York: Greenwood Press, 1987.

Prochaska, F.K. *Women and Philanthropy in Nineteenth-Century England.* Oxford: Oxford University Press, 1980.

Prostitution Reform: Four Documents [by Robert Dingley, Saunders Welch, John Fielding, and William Dodd]. New York: Garland Publishing, 1985.

Pullan, Brian. *Rich and Poor in Renaissance Venice: The Social Institutions of a Catholic State, to 1620.* Cambridge, Mass.: Harvard University Press, 1971.

———. "Support and Redeem: Charity and Poor Relief in Italian Cities from the Fourteenth to the Seventeenth Century." *Continuity and Change* 3 (1988): 177–208.

Rafter, Nicole Hahn. *Partial Justice: Women in State Prisons, 1800–1935.* Boston: Northeastern University Press, 1985.

———. "Prisons for Women, 1790–1980." In *Crime and Justice: An Annual Review of Research,* edited by Michael Tonry and Norval Morris, 5:129–81. Chicago: University of Chicago Press, 1983.

Randall, Margaret. *Cuban Women Now: Interviews with Cuban Women.* N.p.: Women's Press, 1974.

Rapley, Elizabeth. *The Dévotes: Women and Church in Seventeenth-Century France.* Kingston, Ontario: McGill-Queen's University Press, 1990.

Reports and Realities from the Sketch-Book of a Manager of the Rosine Association. Philadelphia: John Duross, 1855.

Riis, Thomas, ed. *Aspects of Poverty in Early Modern Europe.* Florence: Europäisches Hochschulinstitut, 1981.

Ripa, Yannick. *La Ronde des folles: femme, folie et enfermement au XIXe siècle (1838–1870).* Paris: Aubier, 1986.

Rocke, Michael J. "Il controllo dell'omossesualità a Firenze nel XV secolo: Gli 'Ufficiali di Notte.' " *Quaderni storici* 66 (December 1987): 701–23.

Rodocanachi, Emmanuel. *Courtisanes et bouffons: étude de mœurs romaines au XVIᵉ siècle.* Paris: Ernest Flammarion, 1894.

Rodríguez Solís, Enrique. *Historia de la prostitución en España y en América.* Madrid: Biblioteca Nueva, 1921.

Roelker, Nancy L. "The Appeal of Calvinism to French Noblewomen in the Sixteenth Century." *Journal of Interdisciplinary History* 2 (Spring 1972): 391–413.

Roper, Lyndal. *The Holy Household: Women and Morals in Reformation Augsburg.* Oxford: Clarendon Press, 1989.

Rosen, Ruth. *The Lost Sisterhood: Prostitution in America, 1900–1918.* Baltimore: Johns Hopkins University Press, 1982.

Rosenthal, Margaret F. "Veronica Franco's *Terze Rime:* The Venetian Courtesan's Defense." *Renaissance Quarterly* 42 (Summer 1989): 227–57.

Rossiaud, Jacques. *La prostituzione nel Medioevo.* Rome: Laterza, 1984.

Roth, Cecil. *The Last Florentine Republic.* New York: Russell & Russell, 1925.

Rothman, David J. *Conscience and Convenience: The Asylum and Its Alternatives in Progressive America.* Boston: Little, Brown, 1980.

———. *The Discovery of the Asylum: Social Order and Disorder in the New Republic.* Boston: Little, Brown, 1971.

Rothman, David J., and Sheila M. Rothman, eds. *Women in Prison, 1834–1928.* New York: Garland Publishing, 1987.

Rubin, Gayle. "The Traffic in Women: Notes on the 'Political Economy' of Sex." In *Toward an Anthropology of Women,* edited by Rayna R. Reiter, pp. 157–210. New York: Monthly Review Press, 1975.

Ruether, Rosemary Radford, ed. *Religion and Sexism: Images of Woman in the Jewish and Christian Traditions.* New York: Simon & Schuster, 1974.

Ruggiero, Guido. *The Boundaries of Eros: Sex Crime and Sexuality in Renaissance Venice.* New York: Oxford University Press, 1985.

Ruggles, Steven. "Fallen Women: The Inmates of the Magdalen Society Asylum of Philadelphia, 1836–1908." *Journal of Social History* 16 (Summer 1983): 65–82.

Saccà, Fabio. "L'assistenza alle ragazze del conservatorio di S. Giovanni in Laterano nel corso del XVIII secolo." *Storia e politica* 21 (1982): 438–79.

Salvestrini, A., ed. *Relazioni sul governo della Toscana.* 3 vols. Florence: Leo S. Olschki, 1969–74.

Savelli, Marc'Antonio. *Pratica universale: Estratta in compendio per alfabeto dalle principali leggi, bandi, statuti, ordini, e consuetudini, massime criminali, e miste, che vegliano nelli stati del serenissimo Gran Duca di Toscana.* Florence: Vincenzo Vangelisti, 1681.

Schlossman, Steven, and Stephanie Wallach. "The Crime of Precocious Sexuality: Female Juvenile Delinquency in the Progressive Era." *Harvard Educational Review* 48 (February 1978): 65–94.

Schneider, Jane. "Of Vigilance and Virgins: Honor and Shame and Access to Resources in Mediterranean Societies." *Ethnology* 10 (1971): 1–23.

Schur, Edwin M. *Labeling Women Deviant: Gender, Stigma, and Social Control.* New York: Random House, 1984.

Schutte, Anne Jacobson. " 'Trionfo delle donne': Tematiche di rovesciamento dei ruoli nella Firenze rinascimentale." *Quaderni storici* 44 (August 1980): 474–96.

Schwartz, Robert M. *Policing the Poor in Eighteenth-Century France.* Chapel Hill: University of North Carolina Press, 1988.

Scott, Joan Wallach. *Gender and the Politics of History.* New York: Columbia University Press, 1988.

Scull, Andrew T. *Decarceration: Community Treatment and the Deviant—a Radical View.* 2d ed., enl. New Brunswick, N.J.: Rutgers University Press, 1984.

Sedlak, Michael W. "Young Women and the City: Adolescent Deviance and the Transformation of Educational Policy, 1870–1960." *History of Education Quarterly* 23 (1983): 1–28.

Sellin, Thorsten. "Dom Jean Mabillon —A Prison Reformer of the Seventeenth Century." *Journal of the American Institute of Criminal Law and Criminology* 17 (1926–27): 581–602.

———. "Filippo Franci—A Precursor of Modern Penology." *Journal of the American Institute of Criminal Law and Criminology* 17 (1926–27): 104–12.

———. *Pioneering in Penology: The Amsterdam Houses of Correction in the Sixteenth and Seventeenth Centuries.* Philadelphia: University of Pennsylvania Press, 1944.

Shelden, Randall G. "Sex Discrimination in the Juvenile Justice System: Memphis, Tennessee, 1900–1917." In *Comparing Female and Male Offenders,* edited by Marguerite Q. Warren, pp. 55–72. Beverly Hills, Calif.: Sage Publications, 1981.

Sherwood, Joan. *Poverty in Eighteenth-Century Spain: The Women and Children of the Inclusa.* Toronto: University of Toronto Press, 1988.

Showalter, Elaine. *The Female Malady: Women, Madness, and English Culture, 1830–1980.* New York: Pantheon Books, 1985. Reprint. New York: Viking Penguin, 1987.

Simondi, Mario. "Classi povere e strategie del controllo sociale nel granducato di Toscana (1765–1790)." Dipartimento statistico, Università degli studi di Firenze, 1983. Photocopy.

Sims, Mary S. *The Natural History of a Social Institution: The Young Women's Christian Association.* New York: Woman's Press, 1936.

Smart, Carol, and Barry Smart, eds. *Women, Sexuality and Social Control.* London: Routledge & Kegan Paul, 1978.

Smith Rosenberg, Carroll. *Religion and the Rise of the American City: The New York City Mission Movement, 1812–1870.* Ithaca, N.Y.: Cornell University Press, 1971.

Sommario de capitoli della venerabile compagnia di santa Maria Maddalena sopra le mal maritate. Florence: Bartholomeo Sermartelli, 1583.

Southern, R.W. *Western Society and the Church in the Middle Ages.* Harmondsworth: Penguin Books, 1970.

Spierenburg, Pieter, ed. *The Emergence of Carceral Institutions: Prisons, Galleys and Lunatic Asylums, 1550–1900.* Rotterdam: Erasmus Universiteit, 1984.

Stiefelmeier, Dora R. "Sacro e profano: Note sulla prostituzione nella Germania medievale." *NuovaDWF: donnawomanfemme,* no. 3 (April–June 1977), pp. 34–50.

Stites, Richard. "Prostitute and Society in Pre-Revolutionary Russia." *Jahrbücher für Geschichte Osteuropas* 31 (1983): 348–64.

Stock, Phyllis. *Better Than Rubies: A History of Women's Education.* New York: G. P. Putnam's Sons, 1978.

Stone, Lawrence. "An Exchange with Michel Foucault." *New York Review of Books* 30 (31 March 1983): 42–44.

———. "Madness." *New York Review of Books* 29 (16 December 1982): 28–36.

Studer, Marlena. "Wife Beating as a Social Problem: The Process of Definition." *International Journal of Women's Studies* 7 (1984): 412–22.

Tacchi Venturi, Pietro. *Storia della compagnia di Gesù in Italia.* 3 vols. Rome: Edizioni "La civiltà Cattolica," 1950–51.

Tamassia, Nino. *La famiglia italiana nei secoli decimoquinto e decimosesto.* Rome: Multigrafica, 1971.

Taylor, Judith Combes. "From Proselytizing to Social Reform: Three Generations of French Female Teaching Congregations, 1600–1720." Ph.D. diss., 2 vols., Arizona State University, 1980.

Teeters, Negley K. "The Early Days of the Magdalen Society of Philadelphia." *Social Service Review* 30 (June 1956): 158–67.

Temkin, Owsei. "Therapeutic Trends and the Treatment of Syphilis Before 1900." *Bulletin of the History of Medicine* 29 (1955): 309–16.

Thomas, Keith. "The Double Standard." *Journal of the History of Ideas* 20 (1959): 195–216.

Thompson, Henry P. *Thomas Bray.* London: Society for Promoting Christian Knowledge, 1954.

Tierney, Kathleen J. "The Battered Women Movement and the Creation of the Wife Beating Problem." *Social Problems* 29 (1982): 207–20.

Tilly, Louise A., Joan W. Scott, and Miriam Cohen. "Women's Work and European Fertility Patterns." *Journal of Interdisciplinary History* 6 (Winter 1976): 447–76.

Tilly, Louise A., and Joan W. Scott. *Women, Work, and Family.* New York: Holt, Rinehart & Winston, 1978.

Trexler, Richard C. "Le Célibat à la fin du Moyen Age: les religieuses de Florence." *Annales* 27 (November–December 1972): 1329–50.

———. "Charity and the Defense of Urban Elites in the Italian Communes." In *The Rich, the Wellborn and the Powerful: Elites and Upper Classes in History,* edited by F. C. Jaher, pp. 64–109. Urbana: University of Illinois Press, 1973.

———. "La Prostitution florentine au XVe siècle: patronages et clientèles." *Annales* 36 (November–December 1981): 983–1015.

———. *Public Life in Renaissance Florence.* New York: Academic Press, 1980.

———. "Une table florentine d'espérance de vie." *Annales* 26 (January–February 1971): 137–39.

———. "A Widows' Asylum of the Renaissance: The Orbatello of Florence." In *Old Age in Preindustrial Society,* edited by Peter N. Stearns, pp. 119–49. New York: Holmes & Meier, 1982.

Troiano, Lucrezia. "Moralità e confini dell'eros nel seicento Toscano." *Ricerche storiche* 17 (May–December 1987): 237–59.

Vasaio, Maria Elena. "Il tessuto della virtù. Le zitelle di S. Eufemia e di S. Caterina dei Funari nella Controriforma." *Memoria* 11–12 (1984): 53–64.

Vasaio-Zambonini, Maria. "Miserable Virgins and Abandoned Maidens in Tridentine Rome: A Social History of Two Charitable Institutions in the Mid-Sixteenth and Early Seventeenth Centuries." Ph.D. diss. prospectus, New York University, 1984.

Vicinus, Martha. *Independent Women: Work and Community for Single Women, 1850–1920.* Chicago: University of Chicago Press, 1985.

Violence Against Women in the Family. New York: United Nations, 1989.

Viviani della Robbia, Enrica. *Nei monasteri fiorentini.* Florence: Sansoni, 1946.

Walkowitz, Judith R. *Prostitution and Victorian Society: Women, Class, and the State.* Cambridge: Cambridge University Press, 1980.

Weiner, Lynn Y. *From Working Girl to Working Mother: The Female Labor Force in the United States, 1820–1980.* Chapel Hill: University of North Carolina Press, 1985.

————. " 'Our Sister's Keepers': The Minneapolis Woman's Christian Association and Housing for Working Women." *Minnesota History* 46 (Spring 1979): 189–200.

Weissman, Ronald F.E. *Ritual Brotherhood in Renaissance Florence.* New York: Academic Press, 1982.

Wetherell, Donald G. "To Discipline and Train: Adult Rehabilitation Programmes in Ontario Prisons, 1874–1900." *Histoire sociale—Social History* 12 (May 1979): 144–65.

Wiesner, Merry E. *Working Women in Renaissance Germany.* New Brunswick, N.J.: Rutgers University Press, 1986.

Wilson, Otto. *Fifty Years' Work with Girls, 1883–1933: A Story of the Florence Crittenton Homes.* Alexandria, Va.: National Florence Crittenton Mission, 1933.

Winter, Ella. *Red Virtue: Human Relationships in the New Russia.* New York: Harcourt, Brace, 1933.

Wolfgang, Marvin E. "A Florentine Prison: Le Carceri delle Stinche." *Studies in the Renaissance* 7 (1960): 148–66.

Wood, Elizabeth A. "The Prostitution Debates in Soviet Russia: Socialist Responses to a 'Bourgeois' Problem, 1917–1927." Department of History, University of Michigan, 1986. Photocopy.

Zarri, Gabriella. "Monasteri femminili e città (secoli XV–XVIII)." *Storia di Italia: Annali* 9 (1986): 359–429.

Zoomer, Olga J. "Policing Wife Beating in the Netherlands." In *Women, Policing, and Male Violence: International Perspectives,* edited by Jalna Hanmer, Jill Radford, and Elizabeth A. Stanko, pp. 125–54. London: Routledge, 1989.

INDEX

Individuals who are not historical figures are listed only if they appear more than once in the book